MORE THAN BELIEF

MORE THAN BELIEF

A Materialist Theory of Religion

MANUEL A. VÁSQUEZ

OXFORD
UNIVERSITY PRESS
2011

OXFORD

UNIVERSITY PRESS

Oxford University Press, Inc., publishes works that further
Oxford University's objective of excellence
in research, scholarship, and education.

Oxford New York
Auckland   Cape Town   Dar es Salaam   Hong Kong   Karachi
Kuala Lumpur   Madrid   Melbourne   Mexico City   Nairobi
New Delhi   Shanghai   Taipei   Toronto

With offices in
Argentina   Austria   Brazil   Chile   Czech Republic   France   Greece
Guatemala   Hungary   Italy   Japan   Poland   Portugal   Singapore
South Korea   Switzerland   Thailand   Turkey   Ukraine   Vietnam

Published by Oxford University Press, Inc.
198 Madison Avenue, New York, NY 10016

www.oup.com

Oxford is a registered trademark of Oxford University Press

Library of Congress Cataloging-in-Publication Data
Vásquez, Manuel A.
More than belief : a materialist theory of religion / Manuel A. Vásquez.
p.   cm.
Includes bibliographical references and index.
ISBN 978-0-19-518854-7 (pbk.) — ISBN 978-0-19-518853-0 (hardback)
1. Religion—Philosophy. 2. Religion and sociology.
3. Sociology. I. Title.
BL51.V38   2010
200.1′1—dc22   2010001273

1 3 5 7 9 8 6 4 2

Printed in the United States of America
on acid-free paper

Portions of chapter 11 originally appeared in *Method & Theory in the Study
of Religion* 20/2 (2008): 151–84, *African Studies* 68/2 (2009): 273–86,
and the *Journal of the American Academy of Religion* 77/2 (2009): 434–45.

For Anna, Gabriel, Eva, and Rafael, who have taught me the joys, creative power, and challenges of embodiment

Contents

MORE THAN BELIEF

Introduction

To theorize is not to leave the material world behind and enter the domain of pure ideas where the lofty space of the mind makes objective reflection possible. Theorizing . . . is a material practice.

—*Karen Barad (2008: 55)*

Why write yet another theory book, especially at a time when Terry Eagleton, a prominent exponent of the genre, has declared that "the golden age of cultural theory is long past" (2003: 1)? Eagleton quickly qualifies his claim, stating that "[i]f theory means a reasonably systematic reflection on our guiding assumptions, it remains as indispensable as ever." Further, because cultural theory has tended to ignore or dismiss religion, he argues that theorists must reflect systematically on its global visibility.

In my case, theorizing comes out of a practical need. This book grows out of my frustration in the classroom. Trying to engage students about the religious creativity, cross-fertilization, and fluidity that accompany globalization, particularly about the ways in which transnational immigrants transform both their countries of origin and settlement by generating hybrid identities, practices, and spaces, I have found that the dominant "canon" in religious studies is for the most part unhelpful. Emerging from Protestant Biblical hermeneutics, religious studies has tended to focus on the great sacred texts, or the theologies of the Niebuhrs, Barths, and Tillichs of the world, or the symbolic systems of various self-contained, territorialized cultures. Up until very recently, our discipline has taken for granted the view that religion is primarily "private and interior, not shamelessly public; mystical, not ritualistic; intellectually consistent and reasonable, not ambivalent and contradictory." It is "transcendent, not present in things. Religion is concerned, tautologically, with religious matters, not with what Sartre has called the 'equivocal givenness of experience'" (Orsi 1997: 6). This understanding of religion offers few resources to explore the constant movement, contestation, and hybridity involved in what has been called popular religion—religion as it is lived in the streets, workplaces, and schools, for example, by poor Latino immigrants as they settle in small towns in North Carolina or Nebraska.

For these immigrants, what matters religiously is not high doctrine, but everyday existential problems that they often tackle through the practices, narratives, and material culture that they bring with them or that they encounter in their new homes in the United States. How can the heavily textual approaches that are still dominant in religious studies explore the full force of glossolalia, exorcism, and divine healing among Latino(a) Pentecostals and Charismatic Catholics? Or of *rasa*, the emotional flavor of dance or theatrical performances through which first-generation Hindu immigrants inculcate Hindu identity and culture to their children? Or the incorporation of the ancestor spirits among practitioners of African-based religions such as Santería or Candomblé, a phenomenon that blends sonic, tactile, olfactory, gustatory, and kinetic dimensions ranging from drumming and dancing to preparing and sharing a communal meal? Is it fruitful to understand the intense devotion involved in the cult of the saints or Mary among Catholics, with its elaborate home altars, replete with icons brought from the homeland, and its pilgrimages to sacred sites, as nothing more than the enactment of a cultural text? What about what Elaine Peña (forthcoming: 37) calls "devotional labor," the "moments of pain and discomfort—walking on blistering feet, proceeding on injured knees and cramped legs, with growling stomach and salty saliva, with too much light and too little sleep," which *devotos* of the Virgin of Guadalupe endure every December as they embark on a long pilgrimage to visit the site of her apparition at Tepeyac? All these bodily investments and disciplines are crucial for the effectiveness, authenticity, and purifying power of the pilgrimage. Moreover, these investments and disciplines are not only interwoven with the production of sacred space but also with the dynamics of "class stratification among participants [in the pilgrimage], the institutional history of this particular tradition, and the ubiquitous commercial aspects of the ritual" (e.g., the vendors who sell food to the pilgrims along the way and those who provide lodging). And if the journey requires crossing the U.S. border, Latino(a) pilgrims will have to confront the power of a state that has deployed an array of devices and strategies to deter, render visible, capture, and manage "illegal" bodies. Even in this precarious situation, pilgrims will resist, praying to Juan Soldado to intercede and make them invisible to the border patrol.[1] Can an approach that focuses solely on representation and communication take into account of the diverse manifestations of this panoptical power and of the practices to resist it?

Taking note of the strongly embodied and pragmatic character of religion among immigrants, I wrote a piece arguing that post-1965 immigration, which has brought increasing numbers of Latin Americans, Asians, and Africans to the United States, challenge us to de-provincialize the study of religion, to historicize and materialize it. Rather than simply approaching religion as private belief, imperfectly represented by "external" manifestations such as symbols, rituals, and institutions—an approach heavily shaped by the Protestant origins of the *Religionswissenschaft*—I called attention to the need to develop new perspectives that explored the transnational production, circulation, and consumption of religious goods, the fashioning and control of religious bodies, the constrained creativity involved in the emergence of hybrid religious identities, the relations of domination and resistance that mediate the formation of orthodoxy and heterodoxy, the practices that make possible the creation of spaces of livelihood, which often dovetail with sacred landscapes, the ways in which religion enters physical and virtual flows and networks, including the global mass media and the Internet, and the close interplay between popular culture, popular religion, and consumer capitalism. Here I was simply echoing my colleague Vasudha Narayanan's call to "decolonize" our methodologies and challenge "the privileging of the written text and beliefs by dominant, hegemonic cultures [that] has led to a marginalization of other ways of knowing, other sources of knowledge" (2003: 516). Such a decolonization will allow us to take seriously "dances, temples, cities, alternative medical therapies, and so on and appreciate the embodied ways in which knowledge was transmitted in precolonial cultures and still continues to be transmitted in many diasporic realms."

My students were very sympathetic to my proposal. However, they kept asking me how the study of religion in the face of contemporary globalization is related to the literature they studied with me in "Method and Theory I," which covers the "founding fathers" and other classics. What does Eliade's notion of the sacred have to do with the study of the historical interplay between religion, power, and material life? Is this a case of incommensurable epistemologies? What, in any case, is the epistemology behind the call to historicize and materialize the study of religion?

This book is an attempt to answer these questions. It is an effort to explore the sources of a "materialist turn" in religious study that is already underway at the margins of the discipline. Recently, Ivan Strenski has paid tribute to a "relatively small troop of pioneering colleagues [who] have developed the field of the study of the materiality of religious life," a troop that includes the likes of Colleen McDannell, Peter Brown, Caroline Walker Bynum, J. Z. Smith, and Thomas Kselman.[2] To this group of pioneers we may now add a growing number of scholars working on sacred space (Basso 1996; Chidester and Linenthal 1995; Gill 1998; Knott 2008; Lane 2001), architecture (Kieckhefer 2004; Kilde 2004 and 2008; J. Meyer 2001; Waghorne 2004), archaeology (Fogelin

2006; Gilchrist 1994; Insoll 2004), visual culture (Morgan 2005), embodiment (Csordas 1997 and 2004; Klima 2002; Griffith 2004; Laderman 1999), religious experience (S. Harvey 2006; Schmidt 2000; Taves 1999), performance and dance (Daniel 2005; McAlister 2002; Narayanan 2003), popular and material culture (Forbes and Mahan 2005; Chidester 2005; Schmidt 1995), transnational and diasporic religion (Johnson 2007; Tweed 1998; Vásquez and Marquardt 2003), lived religion (Hall 1997 Orsi 2005), and religion and cognitive science (Boyer 2001; Bulkeley 2008; Slingerland 2008a and b; Whitehouse 2004).[3] Together these scholars are giving rise to powerful yet disperse currents spurring a materialist shift in religious studies.

My task in this book is to bring some of these currents into conversation with each other, not with the aim of normalizing diverse and innovative perspectives to religious materiality, but in an attempt to make explicit the implications of these localized efforts for the discipline of religious studies. To facilitate the conversation, I take a genealogical approach, which is simultaneously historical and epistemological. In undertaking this genealogy, I heed Robert Orsi's injunction to avoid falling into a "historiography of sameness that flattens out the contradictions, ironies, fissures, inconsistencies, existential dilemmas, cultural anomalies, and personal circumstances, as well as the religious perplexities, fantasies, fears, and desires, which have characterized the emergence of the study of religion" (Orsi 2008: 136). Thus, I show how there have always been insurgent materialist countercurrents within religious studies and philosophy that have short-circuited the temptation towards idealism, subjectivism, essentialism, and transcendence in religious studies. I then demonstrate how these countercurrents have now been reinvigorated by contemporary work in fields as varied as cultural and ethnic studies, feminist theory, phenomenological anthropology, neuroscience, evolution, ecology, and geography. The result of this revitalization is a flexible, non-reductive materialist framework to study religion.

The framework that I am proposing is not anti-reductive in the Eliadean sense. It is not opposed to reduction in the weak, pragmatic sense. I acknowledge from the outset that our embodiment and emplacement compel us to select, condense, name, break down, and categorize phenomena in order to be able to act effectively in the world. In that sense, no position is innocent, totally anti-reductive, and the best we can do is be self-reflexive, aware of the questions we ask and the localized yet rigorous rules and procedures that we strategically deploy to answer them in fruitful ways. What I oppose is reductionism in the strong, ontological sense, "reduction as nothing buttery" (Davis 2006: 35–52), a theory of knowledge that assumes that all phenomena can be reduced downward to smaller and smaller constitutive components, the behavior of which can be totally determined. In strong reductionism, "the explanatory arrows always point downward," such that "society is to be explained in terms of people, people in terms of organs, organs by cells, cells by biochemistry, biochemistry by chemistry, chemistry by physics. To put it even more crudely, [reductionism] is the view that in the end, all reality is nothing but whatever is 'down there' at the current base of physics: quarks or the famous strings of string theory, plus the interaction among those entities" (Kauffman 2008: 10–11). My framework is non-reductive because it highlights complexity, inter-level connectivity, emergence, situated knowledge, and relative indeterminacy and openness against monocausal, unidirectional, and totalizing explanatory schemes.

I call this framework materialist because it approaches religion as it is lived by human beings, not by angels.[4] As Bruce Lincoln puts it in his now-famous "Theses on Method," to study religion in all its historicity is "to insist on discussing the temporal, contextual, situated, interested, human, and material dimensions of those discourses, practices, and institutions that characteristically represent themselves as eternal, transcendent, spiritual, and divine" (1996: 225). In other words, a well-conceived materialism is not only humbly agnostic about the "supernatural" sources of religion, but it is interested in the conditions that made it possible for these sources to be recognized and felt as supernatural. This does not mean that scholars must disqualify the religious practitioners' appeals to the supernatural as nothing more than delusions, false consciousness, maladaptive habits, pathologies, or even more benignly, social constructs. Thus, biologist Richard Dawkins's positivist call to treat belief in the existence of God as a "scientific hypothesis about the universe," which can be tested against the available evidence, is ultimately fruitless, more the source of polemics than of insights into the complex naturalistic dimensions of religion. As he himself puts it in chapter 4 of *The God Delusion*, it is not possible to rule out the supernatural entirely. Yet, "even if gods do exist, and reveal themselves to humans, the knowledge revealed will become known through ordinary cognitive and communicative processes which can and should be scientifically explained" (Pyysiäinen 2002: 5).

A scholar working within a non-reductive materialist framework, thus, begins with the acknowledgment that the practitioners' appeals to the supernatural, god(s), the sacred, or the holy have powerful material consequences for how they build their identities, narratives, practices, and environments. Thus, it behooves scholars of religion to take seriously the native actor's lived world and to explore the biological, social, and historical conditions that make religious experiences possible as well as the effects these experiences have on self, culture, and nature. Submerging ourselves in history and abandoning the quest for essences and totalizing theories mean that we also have to relativize all approaches to religion, including (and perhaps especially) our own. There will always be a surplus to religion, as for any other realm of human activity, that even our most coherent and astute epistemologies will not capture.

Thus, my call to adopt a materialist framework is not part of a "quest for the holy grail of reductionism" that would make religious studies finally a science, clearly distinctive from theology (Cho and Squier 2008: 434–43). Materialism need not equal reductive physicalism or naive mechanicism. Indeed, I advance a sort of materialism that, while recognizing the material constraints and possibilities entailed by our being-in-the-world through our physical bodies, does not reduce all experiences and cultural productions to the dynamics of the brain, genes, or evolutionary biology. In that sense, the non-reductive materialism that I am proposing should not be confused with anthropologist Marvin Harris's cultural materialism, which posits that society's ideational and symbolic superstructures are unidirectionally determined by infrastructural material forces connected with reproduction or the production and distribution of food (Harris 2001). Harris's paradigmatic thesis that the complex rituals of human sacrifice among the Aztecs were nothing more that post facto rationalization by a priestly elite in response to protein deficiency has been proven to be not only simplistic but factually incorrect (Carrasco 1999; Read 1998).

Against vulgar or mechanistic materialism, I subscribe to a "cultural realism," which assumes that "the emergent world in which our cognizing competence takes form . . . *is quite real*, as real as the physical world from which it 'must' have evolved" (Margolis 2001: 3). Selves and culture are material in their own right. They acquire their distinctive materiality through social practices that mediate how we experience the world and our own embodiment. Because social practices give selves and culture a material density, identities and cultural artifacts also have causal efficacy. That is, they give rise to our life worlds through multilayered relations of reciprocal determination with other physical processes.

The cultural realism I defend certainly bears some resemblances to Durkheim's call to accept the reality of social facts, which are not mere byproducts of the aggregate behavior of unencumbered individuals entering into contractual relations with each other. Cultural realism accepts the notion that, although social facts are the emergent result of the practices of individuals, they precede and transcend specific subjectivities, enabling, shaping, and delimiting the latter's activities. Nevertheless, I wish to go beyond Durkheim's tendency to equate social facts with collective representations, an idealist tendency that has been aggravated by Talcott Parsons's one-sided reading of the Durkheimian legacy. Cultural realism refers not only to shared meanings and values expressed by public systems of symbols, but to spatiotemporal institutions and environments that regulate the behavior of bodies, as well as to embodied dispositions to act in certain ways and to the differential circulation of capital, commodities, and cultural artifacts in social fields laden with power.

Taking the subjective experiences of practitioners and methodological reflexivity and humility as points of departure does not give us license to insulate religion from our analytical tools, treating it as a "timeless nucleus," a self-contained reality with an unchanging core only accessible through a hermeneutics of recovery (Dubuisson 2003). As I said above, my call for a non-reductive perspective has no truck with Mircea Eliade's brand of anti-reductionism, which was heavily imbued with nostalgia for transhistorical origins and a desire for ontological foundations. Rather, the task of the scholar of religion is to study how embodiment and embeddedness in time and place enable and constrain diverse, flexible, yet patterned subjective experiences that come to be understood as religious. So, we begin from the first-person accounts of practitioners on the ground, painstakingly gathering all the claims of individual and collective transformation. Then we explore the complex interplay of phenomenological, sociocultural, and biological conditions that make these accounts possible and authoritative.

A good example of this careful balance between "emic" and "etic" approaches is the cutting-edge research on neurophenomenology, which takes introspective observations by religious practitioners as a point of departure and then contextualizes these first-person reports with brain imaging and other experimental methods in cognitive neurosciences (Harrinton and Zajonc 2003).[5] Neurophenomenology has also begun to dialogue with anthropology, philosophy, and history to provide nuanced pictures of how coherent narratives of religious experience emerge out of the intricate interaction of biological and cultural dynamics (Laughlin and Throop 2006). These studies suggest that the integration of subjective experience depends upon how the architecture of our brain and our body schemas enable invention within the limits of ecology, culture, and society. Through the dynamics of neuroplasticity, culture, which is produced by embodied practice, shapes our brains and bodies (Bourdieu 1977). More specifically, culture offers embodied, and often pre-reflective, ways of sensing, knowing, moving, and doing (Depraz, Varela, and Vermersch 2003).

Thus, non-reductive materialism follows the injunction of anthropologist Talal Asad (2003: 36) that, as scholars, we

> should shift our preoccupation with definitions of "the sacred" as an object of experience to the wider question of how a heterogeneous landscape of power

(moral, political, economic) is constituted, what disciplines (individual and collective) are necessary to it. This does not mean that "the sacred" must be regarded as a mask of power, but that we should look to what makes certain practices possible, desired, mandatory—including the everyday practices by which the subject's experience is disciplined.

For the scholar operating within materialist framework, the primary task is to study the logics of religious ways of being in the world and to elucidate how these logics are inextricably connected with other (nonreligious) ways of being in the world. The sort of materialism I would like to advance approaches religion as the open-ended product of the discursive and nondiscursive practices of embodied individuals, that is, individuals who exist in particular times and spaces. These individuals are embedded in nature and culture, and drawing from and conditioned by their ecological, biological, psychological, and sociocultural resources, they construct multiple identities and practices, some of which come to be designated, often through contestation, as religious at particular junctures. In other words, a materialist approach is interested in the processes behind the naming and articulation of religion as relatively stable and patterned reality recognized by both insiders and outsiders.

In that sense, non-reductive materialism bears some affinities with perspectives that stress the fact that religion is a constructed category. For instance, I endorse Russell McCutcheon's critique of the discourse on sui generis religion, a critique that demonstrates how religion was manufactured by scholars as an autonomous reality, independent of the historical, social, and biological processes. In particular, I agree with McCutcheon's challenge to the "private affair tradition" in religious studies: religion understood subjective reality of a certain kind, "conceived as interior, personal, and utterly unique states and dispositions" (2003: 55) that cannot be properly analyzed through the tools of the social and natural sciences. Having its roots in Cartesian subjectivism, the private affair tradition has gone hand-in-hand with idealism and foundationalism, the search for unchanging essences, the "Platonic forms of religious life," behind the shifting world of history and external appearances. The result has been a dismissal or even a denigration of the materiality of religion, particularly of the entwinement between religion, the body, and society. Even a thinker of the caliber of Williams James, who had a materialist and pragmatist outlook, conducting seminal work on the relation between religion and neurology, ultimately fell prey to this subjectivism. He privileged the original personal experiences of the "pattern-setters," the founders and great mystics, as religion's true essence. While in James's eyes these experiences are authentic and ineffable in their intensity, directness, and spontaneity, theology (dogma) and religious institutions are pale "second-hand" reifications, the extrinsic aspects of religion that are susceptible to rational treatment (James 1961: 42).

McCutcheon's interest in challenging scholarship on sui generis religion, however, is more metatheoretical. The primary data for his analyses is the academic discourses on religion. He presents "a political theory of 'religion,'" that is, a genealogy of the strategies that religion scholars have used to construct religion as an independent and legitimate object of study, advancing their own institutional interests and other nationalist and imperialist agendas without appearing to do so. Instead, I do theory for a more "therapeutic" purpose: to disentangle some of the epistemological knots that have characterized the discipline of religion as way to provide fallible yet effective tools to explore the rich and diverse everyday activities of situated actors who have come to identify what they do as religious.

Here I follow Wittgenstein's view of philosophy not as the maiden of apodictic knowledge but as a cluster of language games that make possible the collaborative construction of viable and meaningful life-worlds. Along the same lines, like the so-called ordinary language philosophers (John Searle 1969 and J. L. Austin 1971), I am more interested in the ways in which common sense and public performance enable the production of our categories of knowledge, including the concept of religion. Thus, while I readily recognize that the concept of religion is a construct deeply implicated with colonialism and capitalism,[6] I agree with Gustavo Benavides (2003) that "there is data for religion." This data is the relatively stabilized and binding discourses, practices, and institutions co-created by religious practitioners, the scholars who study them, and the cultural producers at large. "The determination of what counts as religion is not the sole preserve of academics. The very term *religion* is contested and at stake in the discourses of popular culture" (Chidester 2005: 50). These discourses now circulate transnationally, so that "if religion was ever simply a homunculus alchemically concocted to our specifications within the scholar's study, it has since escaped that room to hang out with people linked by a global system of communication, finance . . ." (Bell 2008: 122).

As I have suggested above, I call my framework non-reductive not because it assumes that religion has an irreducible, unchangeable essence that makes it an autonomous and distinct reality. Quite the contrary, non-reductive materialism explicitly avoids the temptations of foundationalism, the notion that it is possible and desirable to have a god's-eye view of religion, to find its universal essence once and for all and, thus, to be able to reduce all religious manifestations across cultures and history to unchanging truths. The task is not to produce a fully naturalistic account of religion, as if this were possible. Instead, we must recognize that our knowledge is "situated," emerging from our "location, embodiment, and partial perspective" (Haraway 1991: 191). Moreover, our models of religion are always partial and fallible, since, as is the case for any other form of activity, religious practice is shaped by the complex interplay of social, biological, and psychological factors. Because these factors tend not to interact in linear and mechanical fashion, but rather enter into reciprocal relations of determination that may give rise to emergent effects, it is unwise to assume that we can arrive at totalizing understanding of what religion is. The shifting boundaries of what we call religion will continue to defy our most astute efforts to fix them once and for all. Yet, this "transcendence" does not have to rely on theological categories like the sacred, the holy, or the supernatural. It is rather anchored in the relative indeterminacy of our embodied existential condition (Csordas 1999 and 2004).

Such an indeterminacy does not mean that anything goes in the study of religion or that all approaches are equally fruitful (or ineffectual). A scholar of religion operating within a non-reductive materialist framework will try to craft the most robust, context-sensitive, nuanced, and self-reflexive account of particular religious practices. This account will in all likelihood be one among others, with which it will alternatively compete, cross-fertilize, or simply coexist. Perhaps time will tell whether one account can become dominant, showing that it can lead to ever-new insights and elaborations, while the other alternatives remain static in their explanatory power.[7] Perhaps such evolutionary hope may not yield a clear "winner." More than likely, certain accounts will be effective in explaining and doing certain things, while others will exhibit different ranges of utility.[8]

To explore the materialist turn in religious study, I originally proposed to Oxford University Press a broad survey of current literature focusing on embodied and emplaced religion, ranging from practice-centered approaches influenced by the work of Pierre Bourdieu and Michel Foucault, to those dealing with religious space and place, postcolonialism, virtual religion, commodity fetishism, and material and popular culture. The goal was to offer graduate students an accessible map of the evolving field. Nevertheless, I soon discovered that although a survey of this kind would be very useful to teach students about cutting-edge research in religious studies, it really would not answer the epistemological question posed by my students. In fact, work on material religion has hitherto tended to be very descriptive, showing how various religious spaces, performance, and objects have been used or function today (Arweck and Keenan 2006). Providing a detailed inventory of religious materiality is very important, given the longstanding neglect it has suffered. Nevertheless, it is time to begin to explore the larger implications of this multifaceted materialist phenomenology for the discipline of religion. How are the insights generated by the materialist turn transforming the ways in which we view religion? Are we witnessing the emergence of a post-idealist, post-foundationalist, and post-subjectivist paradigm in the study of religion? What are the epistemological bases of this paradigm?

Moreover, my experience in the classroom told me that many graduate students today are afflicted by a bad case of "presentism." They very often have come across in one form or another thinkers like Michel Foucault or Judith Butler. Perhaps they have read a description of the panopticon in *Discipline and Punish* or maybe a couple of chapters of *Bodies that Matter* and assume that they then have a grasp of contemporary critical theory. These students, however, are far less conversant with the intellectual background in which current thinkers operate. As my esteemed colleague Shaya Isenberg once remarked: "they are driving without a rearview mirror." This problem is to a great extent our fault. As educators, we have too easily accepted the rhetoric of discontinuity and rupture, which is closely implicated with commercialization of academy, whereby we are driven to create the latest intellectual fad. It is one thing, however, to critique and avoid teleological readings of history and quite another to decontextualize the production of theory.

In light of this situation, I decided that a better strategy in the writing this book would be to focus on three key sites where some of the most innovative and potentially influential non-reductive materialist work in religion is taking place. This would allow me to map out in a fuller way the legacy of generalized neglect of all things material in the study of religion.

Arguably, the single most important site of contestation in the materialist turn is the body. "As material site, malleable substance, and shifting field of relations, the body is situated at the center of the production and consumption of religion and popular culture" (Chidester 2005: 25). This realization has generated increasing interest on embodiment among religion scholars. "Displacing earlier concerns with religious beliefs and doctrines, with inner experience and spirituality, this interest . . . signals a new engagement with materiality—perhaps a new materialism—in the study of religion and popular culture" (26).

The centrality of the body in a rematerialization of the study of religion is not surprising, given that it has long been at the heart of ongoing debates about the relation between spirit and matter. In telling the story of these debates, I recognize from the outset that there is no such thing as "The Body," an immutable universal and unitary substance under the shifting bustle of discourses about it. As Shildrick and Price (1999: 8) rightly argue: "there are only multiple bodies, marked not simply by sex, but by an infinite array of differences—race, class, sexuality, age, mobility status are those most commonly invoked—none of which is solely determinate." The polyvalence of embodiment is also evident in religion. Barbara Holdrege (2008: 20), for example, refers to a "multilevel hierarchy of structurally correlated bodies corresponding to different orders of reality" in Hinduism. Thus, in Hindu traditions there are divine, cosmic, social, and physical bodies mediated by networked interactions through "processual bodies," include ritual, ascetic, purity, devotional, and Tantric bodies.

However, the multiplicity of concrete embodiments does not mean that there have not been hegemonic discourses and practices that have materialized the body in the West in powerfully normative ways. The story I want to tell is of these normative conceptions and their consequences for the study of religion. Thus, the first section of the book traces the ways in which modern religious studies reproduces the mind-body dualism and the denigration of the body that has been dominant in Western thought since Platonic idealism. I also show how despite this hegemonic flight from the body and aspects associated with it, such as history, practice, materiality, and situatedness, there were countertrends that sought to recover embodiment. Finally, I discuss three contemporary approaches that take embodiment seriously: materialist phenomenology, constructionist critical theory, and evolution and the cognitive sciences. I argue that, although these currents are often in conflict with one another, they offer crucial elements for the articulation of a flexible non-reductive materialist framework to study religion.

I begin by discussing phenomenology, since it is arguably the approach that has inherited and struggled against the contradictions of Cartesian dualism and subjectivism in the most explicit manner. Phenomenology has also been central in the development of the discipline of religious studies through the works of towering figures ranging from Rudolf Otto to Gerardus van der Leeuw and Mircea Eliade. As we shall see, the flight from the body and its situated practices in religious studies results from the appropriation of an idealist, subjectivist, and transcendentalist version of phenomenology that has failed to take seriously our embeddedness in the life-world, in the social and natural worlds as they are mediated through our historical practices. The contradictions of this idealist appropriation of phenomenology have been aggravated by modern hermeneutics (especially from Schleiermacher on), which, despite giving us indispensable insights into the situatedness of the process of interpretation and the materiality of texts, has tended to reduce all human activity to the production and transmission of meaning. The result has been a suffocating textualism that approaches religions as essentially systems of symbols, beliefs, narratives, and cosmologies, ignoring other important material dimensions of religious life. Thus, the task of these early chapters is to recover an alternative (thoroughly historicized, socialized, and naturalized) version of phenomenology and to hold textualism and its cousin discursive social constructionism in check.

In chapter 5, I offer a panoramic sketch of the evolution and claims of social constructionism, an approach that in the wake of the three masters of suspicion—Nietzsche, Marx, and Freud—has become hegemonic in cultural studies, the social sciences, and the humanities. In its focus on the material effects of discursive and nondiscursive practices, particular in the production of the sovereign subject, social constructionism has had a positive rematerializing effect on the study of religion. However, in the quest to indict all attempts at generalizing beyond localized perspectives as domineering metanarratives or essentialist thought, some postmodernist strands of social constructionism have engaged in an excessive semiotic reductionism. This reductionism—of the sort that claims that "there is nothing outside the text"—threatens to turn social constructionism into another version of idealism that glibly dismisses the embodied, sensorimotoric dimensions of religion.

Chapter 6 deals with recent works in "material feminism" that bring into productive dialogue social constructionist critiques of gender and sex with a renewed focus on the lived bodies of women and with efforts to build a robust feminist science studies. What emerges from this conversation is a dynamic, non-dualistic epistemology that views reality as the deployment of semiotic-material, natural-cultural practices. This epistemology breaks sharply with the notion of human uniqueness, which is at the heart of radical social constructionism, recognizing that being embodied means above all being embedded in, dependent on, and interconnected with the nonhuman world. This recognition, in turn, opens the way to bring into the study of religion debates in the natural sciences, particularly in evolution and the neurosciences.

I must confess that, given my background as a sociologist of religion, writing chapter 7 on religion, evolution, cognitive psychology, and the neurosciences was especially challenging. As a religion scholar trained in the social sciences, I have no trouble defending the material density of cultural practices and their role, for example, in constituting religious bodies as social artifacts. Rather, the problem lies in acknowledging the limits of social constructionism, asking with Ian Hacking (1999) about the kind of social constructionism that is best suited to deal with the complexity of religious life. In contrast, arguing for the need to take biology seriously in the study of religion, I always felt that I was about to succumb to essentialism and determinism. Yet, I believe that if we are really serious about materiality, social constructionism must confront "the stubbornness of the materiality of things" (Appadurai 2006: 21), including our bodies in their environments. Remaining ensconced safely in the anthropocentric cocoon of social constructionism and failing to confront the natural sciences in a truly cross-disciplinary dialogue only leaves the door open for simplistic and totalizing forms of reductionism.

At the end of chapter 7, I distinguish my non-reductive materialist episte-mological framework from the recent thoughtful attempt by Edward Slinger-land (2008a and b) to approach the humanities through the lens of cognitive science. According to him, humans "appear to be robots, all the way down, whether we like that idea or not" (Slingerland 2008a: 392). More specifically, he claims that religious experience and practices can be explained as complex emergent effects of lower-level neurobiological processes. As an alternative to this position, I argue that religious phenomena are not merely derivative; just like any sociocultural and phenomenological reality, they are also supervenient materialities, which exert downward determination. I fully accept the claim that the evolution of our brain has set broad limits for the fitness of religious categories. It helps explain why some of these categories (such as the notion of supernatural agents) are consistently found across ages and cultures. Neverthe-less, within the dynamic parameters set by the evolution and the relative plas-ticity of neural networks, religious practices and beliefs exhibit great local and global variability and creativity, as a result of intricate, often non-teleological relations of codetermination among social, cultural, neurophysiological, and ecological dynamics. In turn, the outcomes of these relations of mutual deter-mination set the conditions for the performance of new embodied religious experiences and practices. Put in other words, my appeal to cultural realism goes hand in hand with what cognitive scholars George Lakoff and Mark John-son (1999: 89–117) call a non-dualist "embodied realism." In contrast to "metaphysical realism," which assumes that there is an independent world out-side of our understanding that our minds can copy or mirror through concepts when we adopt the right philosophical method, embodied realism sees reality as emerging from our ongoing physical-cultural interactions with the environ-ment. Our bodies and the environment in which we act "afford" each other, they make each other available. Our bodies, which have been shaped by the surrounding environment, which includes cultural artifacts of various kinds, allow us to perceive, transform, and accommodate to the environment.

The world, then, is not just language, the endless reference of texts to other texts, as some radical version of social constructionism would have it. Rather, "[w]hat we understand the world to be like is determined by many things: our sensory organs, our ability to move and manipulate objects, the detailed struc-ture of our brain, our culture, and our interactions in our environment, at the very least. What we take to be true in a situation depends on our embodied understanding of the situation, which in turn is shaped by all these factors" (Lakoff and Johnson 1999: 102).

The second site I address is practice, with all the attendant tensions between agency and structure, and between domination and resistance. As with my rejection of "The Body" as a universal category, I readily acknowledge that "there is no unified practice approach" in the social sciences and humanities (Schatzki, Knorr Cetina, and von Savigny 2001: 11). Again, my aim is not to offer a comprehensive account of the practice turn in contemporary theory. Instead, I am more interested tracing how and why the notion of practice has been consistently excluded from religious studies. Further, I would like to offer examples of approaches that have fruitfully brought practice back into the study of religion.

I begin in chapter 8 by tackling head on the textualism that has dominated the discipline of religion. By textualism, I do not just mean the focus on the great sacred texts produced by religious elites, but a kind of natural attitude, as phenomenologist Edmund Husserl would term it, a taken-for-granted approach to religious practices as if they were only texts, symbolic systems that scholars of religion must understand empathetically, decode through thick description, or endlessly postpone interpretively (as in the case of those influenced by deconstruction). As I state above, the "linguistic" and "hermeneutic" turns in the social sciences have been immensely fruitful, allowing us to critique reductive and simplistic positivisms and other forms of correspondence theories of truth, whereby we can access the world once and for all. However, this turn has itself become another form of theoretical totalization that does not allow us to explore practice in its multiple forms and expressions.

Anthropologist Thomas Csordas puts our predicament well when he declares that textualism in the humanities

> has become, if you will, a hungry metaphor, swallowing all of culture to the point where it became possible and even convincing to hear the deconstructionist motto that there is nothing outside the text. It has come to the point where the text metaphor has virtually (indeed, in the sense of virtual reality) gobbled up the body itself—certainly we have all heard phrases like the "body as a text," "the inscription of culture on the body," "reading the body." I would go so far as to assert that for many contemporary scholars the text metaphor has ceased to be a metaphor at all and is taken quite literally. (1999: 146)

Thus, turning the tables on the hungry metaphor of textualism, I argue for an approach to texts as relatively stable "objectifications" of historical, social, and biophysically emplaced activity.

The final fault line that I examine is "emplacement," a rather inelegant term I use to examine the interplay between culture and nature in the diverse ways in which individuals and groups draw from religion to negotiate spaces and build places. As critical geographers such as Edward Soja, David Harvey, and

Doreen Massey tell us, space has been traditionally understood as an inert context, a bare stage where historical individuals act. They also tell us that this understanding fails to see how space is "agentic," how it is inextricably connected with time and how it enables and constraints our activities. Therefore, this section also contains a chapter on mobility, which draws from the concept of networks to make explicit how, particularly at a time when a great deal of the world is in motion, place-making is related to processes such as migration, diaspora, trade, pilgrimage, tourism, and mission. The notion of networks, which has been useful in connectionist and enactive approaches to cognition, allows me to return to the body. Here, the trope of networks allows me to bring in ecology to enrich our understanding of how our bodies are emplaced in "nature."

In the conclusion, I return to the notion of non-reductive materialism to discuss more fully the implications of this framework for the study of religion. I also show what remains to be done: a detailed exploration of how the materialist turn around the sites of embodiment, practice, and emplacement is connected with the interplay of religion, global capitalism, popular culture, mass media, virtuality, and the postcolonial condition. I hope to be able to address these topics in a second volume in the near future.

Although focusing on three key nodes in the materialist turn allows a more in-depth treatment, I caution readers that this is not a straightforward textbook covering the great figures who have defined the field or are now transforming it. I cannot, for example, claim that I offer exhaustive accounts of St. Augustine, Descartes, Spinoza, Nietzsche, Heidegger, Merleau-Ponty, Foucault, Deleuze, or Bourdieu. Rather, I foreground aspects of their thinking that help us illuminate debates around the body, practice, and space/place/mobility. Although my aim was not to write a textbook, I have kept graduate students at the University of Florida very much in mind as I drafted the various chapters. Thus, I tried to give enough signposts for them to draw their own conclusions about the contours and stakes of the materialist turn in religious studies. With them in mind, I have also tried to bring abstract debates down to earth by providing examples in the various sections of how scholars are studying religion in new ways.

This book would not have been possible without the support of a myriad of dear friends and colleagues. First and foremost is my beloved wife, Anna Peterson, who not only read the manuscript in its various iterations and commented extensively, but also provided great inspiration through her groundbreaking work on the intersection between religion and nature. I also would like to thank Joe Margolis, who planted the seed of non-reductive materialism during my graduate years at Temple University. Theo Calderara at Oxford University

Press deserves special thanks for sticking with this book project despite repeated metamorphoses and delays. Katherine Ulrich did an excellent job copyediting the manuscript, and Joellyn Ausanka ably managed production. My gratitude also goes to those who have kindly read the manuscript, either partly or in its entirety: Connie Buchanan, David Chidester, James Cochrane, Sheila Davaney, Mark Gornik, Karen King, Peggy Levitt, Russell McCutcheon, Robert Orsi, Heidi Ravven, Chad Seales, David Smilde, Samuel Snyder, Thomas Tweed, and Robin Wright. Finally, I would like to thank my colleagues at the religion department at the University of Florida, particularly David Hackett and Vasudha Narayanan, for providing such a supportive environment. My students in the graduate seminar on material religion—Natalie Broadnax, Rose Caraway, Rocio de la Fuente, Shreena Gandhi, Sean O'Neil, Leah Sarat, and Jimi Wilson—were wonderful intellectual partners as I sought to order, clarify, and refine my thoughts. I have written this book as a partial answer to their probing and provocative questions.

PART I
Embodiment

1

The Rise of Foundational Dualism
and the Eclipse of the Body

"We need to *exorcize* the Cartesian Anxiety and liberate ourselves from its seductive appeal."

—*Richard J. Bernstein (1983: 19)*

The recent recentering of the body in religious studies is but an installment of age-old epistemological debates in Western thought. In the next two chapters, I highlight some of the important arguments and figures that have shaped the ways in which religion scholars have traditionally ignored the body. I also explore the countertrends that have facilitated the recovery of the body, along with dimensions like practice, performance, power, emplacement, historicity, and mobility. Given the breadth of the survey, the various accounts of complex thinkers will necessarily be far from exhaustive. My intension is modest: to highlight key ideas, arguments, and methods at stake in order to frame current approaches to the body.

In addition, I would like to acknowledge from the outset the limits of an approach that relies heavily on the origin and development of ideas. As Karen King (2003: 221) has shown in reference to early Christianity, "literary works, let alone 'intellectual influences,' can 'belong' to and move among heterogeneous social groups (as did Scripture and Platonic writings among Jews, Christians, and Greek philosophers)," who transform them in the process of appropriation, cross-fertilizing them with other influences. Thus, just as there is no "Gnosticism" as a unitary, all-encompassing essence that we can set against orthodoxy, there is also no generic body in Christianity. In fact, there is no monolithic and static Christianity, Platonism, or Cartesianism that we can simplistically turn into the archenemy of embodiment. "Essentializing categories tend to reify the complex, overlapping, and multifarious clusters of material that constitute the continually shifting interacting forms of early Christian meaning-making and social belonging into homogeneous, stable, well-bounded theological and sociological formations" (King 2008: 71). Thus, it may be best to approach early Christianity and its variegated Greco-Roman milieu as relatively stabilized but always contested and cross-fertilizing clusters of narratives, practices, institutions, and landscapes connected with activities as diverse as sacrifice, martyrdom, marriage, child-rearing, celibacy, healing, and fasting.

Ideally, in order to understand the evolution of the body in the West, we would need to construct overlapping yet often disjunctive genealogies of the dominant ideas and discourses about the body as well as of everyday bodily practices. Obviously, such a wide-ranging survey is beyond the scope of this chapter, or even this book. But even if we had the space to undertake a reconstruction of this sort, the notion of the "classical body" might be too unstable to produce a definitive account. In fact, some scholars go as far as claiming that "there is a tenuous and possibly insoluble relationship between the received and ideal classical body and the 'real' bodies of ancient Greece and Rome" (J. Potter 1999: 1).

The fact that we confront great local diversity and tensions among fluid discursive and nondiscursive practices or that we cannot recover the "pure essence" of philosophical traditions by referring back to their original sources in Jesus Christ, Plato, or Descartes (often the strategy of those who wish to turn a particular reading of the tradition into orthodoxy) does not mean that we cannot reconstruct hegemonic readings that have buttressed our understandings of modernity and religion. We can excavate the salient lines of force that constituted a relatively stable somatophobic "regime of knowledge" (Foucault 1980), which hardened with the Cartesian entry to modernity.

SOURCES OF THE MODERN MIND-BODY DUALISM: THE HELLENISTIC BACKGROUND

Postmodernists, poststructuralists, and feminist philosophers commonly trace the contradictions of modernity to Descartes. In particular, his search for firm foundations gave rise to a host of unsolvable dualisms, such as those between mind and body, matter and spirit, and the self and his/her social and natural environment, that echo throughout the centuries all the way to the Holocaust and the generalized violence of the twentieth century. For example, Bordo (1987: 75–118) sees Cartesianism as "nothing if not a passion for separation, purification, and demarcation" which leads to a "masculinization of thought," where the masculine is equated with detached objectivity and a domineering ego that relates to others and the outside world through a purely instrumentalist ethic.

Such an assessment is certainly on target. And since religion as a concept and a discipline is a modern construct, it would make sense to begin my account with Descartes. However, we must acknowledge that the dualities he codifies into a foundational epistemology were already part of the matrix of philosophical and religious discourses since Plato and early Christianity. Plato's famous allegory of the cave offers a dramatic example of the quest to find Truth above the contingencies of history and the phenomenal world.[1] If the world as it appears to us is nothing but the shadows, the distorted images of supra-historical forms that contain the essence of reality itself, then the task of philosophy is to free us from the constraints of bodily existence, which force us to have only partial viewpoints. The task of philosophy is to train gradually our eyes so that we can finally look directly into the sun of knowledge, the source of light that makes possible the world of shadows and vision itself. Philosophy, thus, must engage in what Donna Haraway (1991: 189) calls the "god-trick," the "gaze from nowhere," the search an Archimedean point, a fixed pivot from where we can have a totalizing view of the universe, from where we can move the universe without moving ourselves. As we shall see later on in Foucault's work, Platonic visual metaphors are part of a domineering rationality that seeks to control reality, self, society and nature by rendering them fully transparent, by establishing a one-to-one relationship between a disembodied mind and the external world.

In the Platonic self, the soul, which, like the forms, is invariable and immortal, is "fastened" or "riveted" to a mortal and corruptible body that imprisons it. In *Phaedo*, Plato has Socrates declaring: "For the body is a source of endless trouble to us by reason of the mere requirement of food; and also is liable to diseases which overtake and impede us in the search after truth; and by filling us as full of loves, and lusts, and fears, and fancies, and idols, and every sort of folly, prevents us ever having, as people say, so much as a thought."[2] When the soul uses the body to perceive things, it is "dragged down" "into the region of the changeable . . . [where it] wanders and is confused; the world spins round her [the soul], and she is like a drunkard when under [the] influence [of the senses]."[3]

To liberate itself from the "turmoil," "confusion," and "lust" associated with physical existence, the soul "must be quit of the body" and return to itself, recollecting the eternal, unchangeable, and pure forms of Beauty, Justice, Truth, and Goodness that are part of its own essence. The soul "is like the eye: when resting upon that on which truth and being shine, the soul perceives and understands and is radiant with intelligence; but when turned towards the twilight of becoming and perishing, then she has opinion only, and goes blinking about. . . ."[4] To turn the eye of the soul toward truth entails a "journey upwards . . . into the intellectual world," away from the purely visible, away from the natural world, including our bodies. Through this ascent, the soul will be able to behold its true essence. Plato has Socrates tell his student Glaucon to see the soul "as she really is, not as we now behold her, marred by communion with the body and other miseries, you must contemplate her with the eye of reason, in her original purity; and then her beauty will be revealed, and justice and injustice and all the things which we have described will be manifested more clearly."[5]

While somatophobic idealism dominates Plato's philosophy, there is a significant undercurrent that runs counter to his outright rejection of the body. This alternative voice, which focuses on the "disciplining and refining of the body, to make it a worthy, or at least noninjurious receptacle of the soul" (Dillon 1995: 80), is most evident in *Timaeus*, where he presents a vision of a harmonious universe, with every part, including the body, the product of the activities of a rational, purposive, and benevolent demiurge. This craftsman-god "was good, and nothing good is ever characterized by mean-spiritedness over anything; being free of jealousy, he wanted everything to be as similar to himself as possible."[6] Therefore, finding everything in "a state of turmoil," the creator "led it from chaos to order, which he regarded as in all ways better." In the process, "he constructed the universe by endowing soul with intelligence and body with soul, so that it was in the very nature of the universe to surpass all other products in beauty and perfection."[7]

The holistic cosmology of *Timaeus* mitigates considerably Plato's dualistic tendencies. Since "anything created . . . is bound to be corporeal—visible and tangible"[8] and since every part is necessary to make the universe beautiful and perfect, the body cannot be rejected. Still, Plato insists on separating the soul from the body and giving it preeminence as "the supreme creation of the supreme intelligible and eternally existing being." The creator made the soul "prior and senior, in terms of both birth and excellence, since it was to be the mistress—the ruler, with the body as its subject."[9] Error and injustice emerge when the soul's preeminence over the body is overturned by the latter's desires, needs, flawed perceptions, and mortality. Thus, in *Timaeus*, Plato "is still emphatic that our true kingdom is not of this world, but the difference is now that our presence in this world is not a mistake or a disaster (though it is a challenge), and salvation lies not in rejecting the body, but rather in refining it, to make it a suitable vehicle for the soul" (Dillon 1995: 85). As Timaeus declares to Socrates's approval: "at the beginning, a soul lacks intelligence when it is first bound into a mortal body." As time passes, however, the erratic soul recovers from the shock of its encounter with the body and regains its "tranquility." And "if proper nurture is supported by education, a person will become perfectly whole and healthy, once he has recovered from this most serious of illnesses; but if he cares nothing for education, he will limp his way through life and return to Hades unfulfilled and stupid."[10]

It is important not only to recognize Plato's ambivalence toward the body, but also to avoid assuming that somatophobic idealism is paradigmatic of all Greek philosophy. The more "life-affirming" tenor of *Timaeus* prefigures Aristotle's notion of hylomorphism, which states that form (*morphe*) and matter (*hule*) are not two separate entities, but complementary and inextricably connected aspects of all beings. More specifically, in order for life to exist, the soul and the body are intermingled in a necessary, natural, and mutually beneficial way. The soul provides the body not only its *élan vital*, but its essential entelechy, its shape, organization, and purpose, the basis for its ultimate fulfillment. In this sense, the soul is like the artist who, in molding clay into a beautiful sculpture, realizes matter's potentiality. As Aristotle writes: the soul is "the first grade actuality of a natural body having life potentially in it."[11] It is "the definitive formula of a thing's essence. That means that it is 'the essential whatness' of a body." Or even more clearly: "The soul is the cause or source of the living body. It is (a) the source or origin of movement, it is (b) the end, it is (c) the essence of the whole living body."[12] The body, in turn, allows the soul to operate in space and time, to move, perceive, and feel. Thus, "we can wholly dismiss as unnecessary the question whether the soul and the body are one: it is as meaningless as to ask whether the wax and the shape given to it by the stamp are one, or generally the matter of a thing and that of which it is the matter."[13]

As a rematerialization of Platonic dualistic idealism, Aristotelian hylomorphism represents a salutary recovery of the body and nature, one that sets the basis for the emergence of the natural sciences. If the forms are always embodied, and universals cannot exist by themselves but only in particular entities, empirical knowledge of the physical world is legitimate and valuable. This is the reason why Aristotle did not hesitate to plunge into the worlds of physics, biology, and psychology. After all, in the Aristotelian worldview, all of nature is endowed with necessity, with a telos that determines its normal functions and optimal goals. The scientist can grasp this telos rationally and systematically. At a deeper level, Aristotelian hylomorphism gives rises to various forms of organicism and vitalism that will see the universe as a complex, evolving, interconnected organism in which humans are deeply enmeshed. We will see that when conceptualized strategically, organicism provides a valuable trope to construct a non-reductive materialism, one that approaches religion at the intersection of cultural practices and natural processes, including psycho-cognitive ones.

Despite these important contributions, Aristotle, in the end, remained a metaphysician like Plato, pursuing transcendental and foundational truths.

The intermingling of body and soul does not seem to apply to the intellect (*nous*). "While the faculty of sensation is dependent upon the body, mind is separable from it."[14] It is "able to think itself." Moreover, the mind "is separable, impassible, unmixed, since it is in its essential nature activity (for always the active is superior to the passive factor, the originating force to the matter which it forms)."[15] Therefore, since the mind is "the form of forms," when it is "set free from its present conditions it appears as just what it is and nothing more: this alone is immortal and eternal. . . ."[16]

Despite his materialist turn, Aristotle reinscribes the Platonic hierarchy that places the disembodied mind (being) above nature (becoming), a strategy that Descartes will replay but now under the corrosive power of the doubting self. In Descartes, the decontextualized mind becomes the point of departure and bedrock for a new philosophy, rather than being the most perfect manifestation of an evolutionary scale of animated beings that includes plants and animals, as in Aristotle. In spite of this shortcoming, Aristotelian materialism will prove influential in later attempts in the Greco-Roman world to recover the body and nature from dualistic idealism. For instance, the so-called Hellenistic philosophers and physicians, including Epicurus, Galen, and the Stoics, tended to eschew polarities such as matter versus form and mortality versus immortality. For all their diversity, these thinkers shared a cluster of beliefs that were more in line with Aristotle than Plato: "that all psyche is soma but not all soma is psyche; that only what is spatially extended, three-dimensional, and capable of acting or being acted upon exists; that the soul meets these criteria of existence; that this corporeal psyche, like the rest of the body, is mortal and transient; that the psyche is generated with the body; that it neither exists before the body nor exists eternally after its separation from the body—that is, the soul does not exist independently of the body in which it exists" (von Staden 2000: 79). Moreover, Aristotelian teleology will make its way into Thomistic Catholicism, particularly in the notions of divine providence and natural law. As we shall see below, Catholicism has traditionally made the body central to its doctrine, ritual practices, and organization.

Platonic attitudes toward the body, however, subsisted and were further elaborated in the Greco-Roman tradition by Neoplatonists such as Plotinus. He proposed a monistic philosophy in which all things are "ensouled," as a single supreme and absolutely free and good nonmaterial source that emanates and extends itself to lower and less perfect levels of being. In this sense, Plotinus is closer to Aristotelian hylomorphist metaphysics than Platonic dualism. However, Plotinus stressed that the telos of the soul (*psykhe*), which is ultimately a projection of the mind (*nous*), is to liberate itself from the body and to ascend and achieve unity with the One. A liberation of this kind is necessary because the body and the visible world represent only imperfect and weakened copies of the originative source. "Life here, with the things of earth, is a sinking, a defeat, a failing of the wing."[17] *Nous* must then turn inward and contemplate itself to grasp its true source. As Plotinus writes:

> Withdraw into yourself and look. And if you do not find yourself beautiful yet, act as does the creator of a statue that is to be made beautiful: he cuts away here, he smoothes there, he makes this line lighter, this other purer, until a lovely face has grown upon his work. So do you also: cut away all that is excessive, straighten all that is crooked, bring light to all that is overcast, labour to make all one glow of beauty and never cease chiseling your statue, until there shall shine out on you from it the godlike splendor of virtue, until you shall see the perfect goodness surely established in the stainless shrine.[18]

In his quest for immortality through unity with a transcendental and true reality, a quest that is centered around the soul, particularly the mind, Plotinus echoes Platonic idealism. As we will see later, Plotinus's Neoplatonism will provide many tropes for Augustine's and Descartes's conceptions of the body and the self.

This very brief account demonstrates that there were diverse ways of understanding the tension between spirit and matter and between mind and body among Greek thinkers. These attitudes ranged from outright hostility and ambivalence toward the body to its full recognition as a crucial component of the self. These variegated positions were also evident "on the ground" in classical antiquity. David Potter, for example, shows how odor was central to the ways in which Romans controlled their bodies and marked social distinction and political power.

> No member of the ruling classes could soil their bodies with the performance of banausic tasks: the ruling classes were those that oversaw the bodily labors of others. They also sought to ensure that their bodies did not smell like lower-class bodies, and they were concerned to control the smell of their physical environment. The capacity to improve one's overall olfactory environment was an important sign of one's superiority over the ordinary run of mortals. The connection between smell and power was so basic that it was projected upon the gods. (D. Potter 1999: 171)

Note here the simultaneous intense concern for the body and its physiology and for the capacity to hold this physiology at arm's length, the "capacity to neutralize ordinary urgencies and bracket off practical ends" (Bourdieu 1984: 54), so as to become god-like. This complex ambivalence toward the body in the ancient Greco-Roman world interacted with Christian views of the body, setting the stage for Cartesian dualism as the entry point to modernity.

SOURCES OF THE MODERN MIND-BODY DUALISM: THE CHRISTIAN BACKGROUND

Early Christianity, if we can use the term heuristically to characterize very diverse discourses, practices, institutions, and communities, also had its ambivalences about history, the natural world, and the body. This is not surprising given its incarnational theology in which the "Word was made flesh." On the one hand, following the non-dualism of its Jewish sources that stress a God acting in history to bring a this-worldly redemption, Christianity sacralizes the body by making Jesus Christ, who is both fully divine and fully human, the protagonist in an intra-historical salvific project. As Paul asks in 1 Corinthians 6:19, "Do you know not that your body is a temple of the Holy Spirit within you, which you have from God?"[19] On the other hand, in order to release humanity from the bondage created by Adam's sin of disobedience and pride, the savior must be obedient onto death, humbly submitting his body to punishment and martyrdom. As the writings of Church Fathers such as Tertullian and Origen show, under persecution, early Christian communities made the body of the crucified savior the model for authentic faith: in order to have life in abundance, the believer must ultimately lose him/herself, literally die to the world.

Indeed, the theological notion of *imitatio Christi* is a poignant example of Christianity's paradoxical view of the body and the material world. This notion served early Christian communities not only to differentiate the elect from unbelievers, but also informed a widespread cult of the martyrs and the veneration of their relics. Note here that while early Christians saw sharing Jesus Christ's physical suffering as a privilege, they did not reject the body and the world. Quite the contrary: the bodies of the martyrs are affirmed as earthly vessels of sacred power, capable of healing and performing other miracles. Furthermore, life in abundance did not mean a disembodied union with an ethereal divinity, as was the case for Neoplatonists. Rather, it meant a full restoration of the body. This paradoxical view of the body leads Porterfield (2005: 4) to argue that "the real genius of Christianity has been to embrace pain and disability and death and not to limit the meaning of health and healing to their expulsion. Thus, many Christians have accepted the onset and persistence of suffering as part of religious life, while also celebrating relief from suffering as a sign of the power and meaning of their faith."

Christianity also subscribes to a tensile "already-and-not-yet" eschatology (Cullman 1962), in which the reign of God is already in our midst, in the deeds of Jesus Christ and his disciples as they gather a new community that transcends the rules and social divisions of the time. These deeds include powerful material expressions of charisma, glossolalia, prophecy, healing, and physically expelling demons. However, the material expressions of charisma in the early Christian community are seen as mere signs, a foretaste of an altogether new reality that overcomes the limitations of the flesh. Mortal life, then, is more like a testing ground to prepare us for things to come. Pauline Christianity, in particular, initiated a movement toward the "private affair tradition" in religious studies, which understands religion not as public material practices, but as "interior, personal, and utterly unique states and dispositions" (McCutcheon 2003: 55). As Paul writes in Romans: "he is not a real Jew who is one outwardly, nor is true circumcision something external and physical. He is a Jew who is one inwardly, and real circumcision is a matter of the heart, spiritual not literal. His praise is not from men but from God" (3:28–29). This denigration of the law, "external" works, and the ritual marking of the physical body and the elevation of inner faith and spirituality as signs of authentic selfhood will interact with Greco-Romans anti-materialist tendencies, feeding into Western thought via Augustine, who, in turn, inspired Descartes's less ambivalent mind-versus-body and spirit-versus-matter dualisms. It will also be magnified by Protestant thinkers such as Martin Luther and Friedrich Schleiermacher, influencing phenomenological and hermeneutic approaches to religion. Nevertheless, in using the stark image of a circumcision of the heart, Paul is dramatizing the holistic power of a conversion to Jesus Christ: it is literally a radically transformative process of inscribing the law into the believer's body, generating a new Christian habitus, to draw from sociologist Pierre Bourdieu. So, while Paul privatizes Christianity, his anthropology still maintains a strongly materialist undercurrent.[20] This paradox, which runs through early Christianity, is best summarized by Paul's affirmation that Christians are "in this world but not of this world."[21]

Maintaining a productive tension between immanence and transcendence, between the denial and affirmation of life, has not been easy for Christians, particularly for the generations following the powerful originative experiences of the early community. Different Christian communities emphasized different aspects of these tensions, producing significant variations in terms of theology and practice. Moreover, as Weber puts it, all religions go through a routinization of charisma, as they seek to establish themselves, generating doctrinal and ethical systems, as well as a cadre of specialists to produce, interpret and manage them. The advantage of this process is that it allows the religion to become portable because it is systematized and, thus, rendered potentially universal. However, in the process some of the dynamism of the religion is lost: a relatively stable core emerges around canonical texts, doctrines, and practices, but at the cost of turning dissent into heresy and producing schisms. In Christianity, the body was consistently at the center of the struggles to draw the line between orthodoxy and heterodoxy, as illustrated in the controversies surrounding Docetism, Manicheanism, Monophysitism and other "heresies," including perspectives that apologists and modern scholars have grouped under the constructed category of Gnosticism.[22] Indeed, the danger of Christianity's creative tensions becoming reified into dualisms runs through the whole tradition, certainly from Paul's views about sexuality and women and to the disciplines of monastic life and the celebration of the life, miracles, and martyrdom of saints in medieval Catholicism.[23] Peter Brown (1981: 2), for example, states that while religion in the late-antique Mediterranean "may not have become markedly more 'otherworldly,' it was most emphatically 'upperworldly.'" In particular, the cult of relics, the belongings and parts of the bodies, of saints became a very powerful way to localize and transport the holy. "[T]he Christian cult of the saints rapidly came to involve the digging up, the moving, the dismemberment—quite apart from much avid touching and kissing—of the bones of the dead, and frequently, the placing of these in areas from which the dead had once been excluded" (4). These traveling relics served as the basis for a creative and unruly grassroots Catholicism, in which communities and individuals far from the centers of clerical power could establish an intimate, corporeal relation with the sacred.

The materiality of medieval Catholicism was also expressed in rituals. As Philip Mellor and Chris Schilling rightly argue, in placing the sacraments, and particularly communion understood as transubstantiation, at the center of ecclesial life, medieval Catholicism fashioned itself as an "embodied community," more specifically a "sacred eating community." Drawing from Durkheim, they claim that "the medieval Church was . . . a collective Subject: God was incorporated into the world through the Incarnation of Christ, while the world was incorporated into God through the Body of Christ, the Church. By organizing activities through sacred and symbolically sacrificial rituals, by defining itself as the Body of Christ, and by having as its main cultic act the Eucharist, the Church was able to engage thoroughly with its constituents' fleshy sensuality, reactions and impulses" (Mellor and Schilling 1997: 68).

The centrality of public rituals in late-antique Christianity also meant that the senses were key loci where humans encountered the sacred. Dovetailing with David Potter's work on odor during the Roman empire, Susan Ashbrook Harvey documents the development of "a lavishly olfactory piety" in post-Constantinian Christianity: "incense, almost uniformly condemned in Christian writings prior to the late fourth century, now drenched every form of Christian ceremonial, both private and public; scented oils gained sacramental usage; perfumed unctions were liberally applied in paraliturgical rites" (Harvey 2006: 2). Harvey links the rise of this olfactory piety to the legalization of Christianity and its eventual close association with the Roman Empire. This change in political status gave Christianity a decidedly this-worldly orientation. "As Christianity laid increasing claim to social and political power, the church also showed increasing emphasis on claiming the physical world as a realm of positive spiritual encounter through the engagement of physical experience. In this changed situation, the sensory qualities of Christian piety bloomed. The Christian's religious experience in ritual, art, and devotional piety, previously austere in their sensory aspects, became in the post-Constantinian era a feast for the physical senses" (57–58).

This sensory plenitude carried on through the Middle Ages. Historian Caroline Walker Bynum finds a remarkable continuity in the medieval church's concern for the resurrection of the body, which was consistently represented through tropes of organic growth, of fertility and decay: a seed that to bear fruit must be destroyed, "the flowering of a dry tree after winter . . . the hatching of an egg . . . the growth of the fetus from a drop of semen . . . the vomiting up of bits of shipwrecked bodies by fishes that have consumed them" (Bynum 1995: 6). In Bynum's eyes, such concern points to a materialistic eschatology built not around "body-soul dualism but rather a sense of self as a psychosomatic unity. The idea of person, bequeathed by the Middle Ages to the modern world, was not a concept of soul escaping body or soul using body; it was a concept of self in which physicality was integrally bound to sensation, emotion, reasoning, identity—and therefore finally to whatever one means by salvation. Despite its suspicion of flesh and lust, Western Christianity did not hate or discount the body" (11).

While Bynum might be overstating her case for Christian non-dualism, it is safe to say in medieval Catholicism made the body a central focus of theological and eschatological concern. This focus was eventually challenged by the Protestant Reformation and its emphasis on individual conscience and the primacy of justification by faith through a reinterpretation of Pauline theology. In their attempts to undermine the priest's monopoly of ritual power, the power to perform the sacraments legitimately, Protestant reformers not only advocated the priesthood of all believers, but disenchanted the world, rejecting the materialized expressions of sacred that emerge amidst the effervescence of collective life in the Catholic Church. Protestantism, particularly in Reformed churches, meant "word without sacrament" (Tillich 1948: 94–112). As historian Colleen McDannell notes, in stressing God's absolute sovereignty and humanity's utter brokenness, theologians like John Calvin and Ulrich Zwingli exacerbated Christianity's ambivalence toward the body and the material world. "Divinity, the wholly other and sacred, should not be brought into the profane world of bodies and art" (McDannell 1995a: 6). To do so would run the risk of falling into idolatry and magical superstition, which had corrupted the Catholic Church. McDannell sees this mistrust of materiality clearly reflected in traditional, Puritan-centric readings of U.S. religious history. These Puritan models have prevented us "from seeing that the demonstrations of supernatural intervention were (and are) essential to the religious lives of Americans. While the Puritans may have seen the divine everywhere, the Puritan model preferred Christianity separated from home life, sexuality, economic exchange, and fashion" (6).[24]

While the Reformation was a diverse movement, its overall effect was the increasing "excarnation, the transfer of religious life out of bodily forms of ritual, worship, practice, so that it becomes more and more to reside 'in the head'" (C. Taylor 2007: 613). Rather than religious images, which could easily lead to idolatry and manipulation by the Catholic hierarchy, the "truth of Christianity was to be conveyed through the Word of God, contained in the words of the scripture, preached from the pulpit, or read from the Bible" (McDannell 1995a: 13). Moreover, the Reformation reinforced a view of ritual as superstitious, mindlessly repetitive behavior, discounting its efficacy and performative creativity. Ritual then became a pejorative term "to describe the disreputable practices of somebody else: what I do is ordained by God and is 'true religion': what you do is 'mere ritual,' at best useless, at worst profoundly evil" (Muir 1997: 7). I will argue in chapter 4 that Protestant excarnation combined with German Idealism and phenomenological subjectivism to give rise to a somatophobic *Religionswissenschaft* whose seductive power still holds sway today.

We should, however, be careful not to cast Protestantism as the villain in modern Christianity's denigration of the body and the external world. McDannell recognizes that Protestant logocentric orthodoxy has not determined every aspect of lived religion in America. "Once we shift our attention from church and seminary to the workplace, home, cemetery, and Sunday school, another side of Protestantism appears. In the nineteenth century, Methodists displayed statues of Wesley and Protestants in Philadelphia placed sculptures of angels at the graves of their loved ones. . . . Mormons may give prints of temples as wedding gifts and wear Angel Moroni tie-clasps" (McDannell 1995a: 273).

Moreover, there have been powerful reactions to excarnation within Protestantism, as Methodism, Pietism, the Holiness movement, and more recently Pentecostalism show. Yet, religious embodiment for these rebellious traditions is understood not sacramentally, as collective materializations of the encounter with the sacred, but as primarily personal experiences. This sort of incarnate religious subjectivism, which leads directly to William James's materialist psychology of religion, still represents an incomplete recovery of the body, particularly of its embeddedness in society and nature.

Even in the wake of the Reformation's excarnational tendencies, Protestant Christianity continued to be ambivalent toward the body. For example, it is true that Luther dematerialized the sacred and individualized salvation by undermining the efficacy of good works and making authentic faith an inward matter. As he writes in *The Freedom of a Christian*, "no good work can profit an unbeliever to justification and salvation; and, on the other hand, no evil work makes him an evil and condemned person, but that unbelief, which makes the person and the tree bad, makes his works evil and condemned. Therefore, when any man is made good or bad, this does not arise from his works, but from his faith or unbelief . . ." (Luther 2008: 192–93). However, in Luther's view, Christians justified by faith through grace cannot but voluntarily perform good works and glorify God through their vocations, fulfilling the requirements of life station to the best of their abilities, without the need to renounce the world. Thus, as Weber (1958) has demonstrated, Luther's idea of calling strengthened Christianity's this-worldly orientation, even if the doctrine of *sola fides* disenchanted the world.

Beyond the Reformation, there were elements within medieval Christianity as a whole that contributed to a flight from the body. Peter Brown (1988), for example, has shown that while sexual renunciation was a polysemic and contested aspect of life for early Christian communities, by the fourth century influential thinkers such as Tertullian, Origen, and the Desert Fathers had succeed in turning perpetual chastity, the cult of the virgin, and clerical celibacy into dominant ideologies that buttressed a new spiritual hierarchy within Christianity. As the vestal virgins of Rome demonstrate, "pagans" also considered continence a religious "technology of the self" (Foucault 1999). However, Christianity gradually changed the valence of sexual renunciation, transforming in the process public morality and domestic life. Vestal virgins and Greek virgin prophetesses, "[t]hough eminent and admired . . . were not thought to stand for human nature at its peak. Their virginity did not speak to the community as a whole of a long-lost perfection. It did not represent the primal state of humankind, that could, and should, be recaptured by men quite as much as by women. Chastity did not announce the dawning light of the end of time,

after millennia of misplaced skirmishing with death through married inter-
course. . . ." (Brown 1988: 8).

Asceticism and the renunciation of the body had been a privileged way of
engaging the sacred, long before the Reformation disenchanted the Catholic
world of miraculous saints and relics. Asceticism associated sin, hell, and the
devil with the needs and limitations of the flesh. This association extended to
sexuality and women, whose bodies were considered particularly dangerous
and impure unless modeled on Mary's virginal and immaculate body. Eve, the
original temptress, was counterposed to Mary to construct a dichotomous view
of femininity. As the daughter of Eve, "woman is the other from whom one
must protect oneself. And if she too must be protected, and against herself, this
will most often be by imprisoning her. Here again it is because of its dangerous
proximity to the soul that the body particularly the feminine body—is
curbed, imprisoned and despised" (Nadeau 2002: 63).

Thus, in medieval Christianity, the body is a powerful trope, on the one
hand, for the redeemed religious community and, on the other, for our utter
fallenness and the dangers of damnation and hell. Arguably, no one has
expressed this ambivalence toward the body more passionately than Augustine, who is claimed as a seminal thinker by Catholics and Protestants alike. In
contrast to Platonists and Manicheans, both of whom influenced his thinking,
Augustine unequivocally affirmed the goodness of all creation, including the
natural world. For him, sin and corruption are the deprivation of good rather
than the result of the actions of an evil demigod that rules over matter. "*God
made all things very good*. To You [God], then, there is no such a thing at all as
evil. And the same is true not only of you but of your whole creation, since
there is nothing outside it to break in and corrupt the order which you have
imposed on it. But in some of the parts there are some things which are considered evil because they do not harmonize with other parts; yet with still other
parts they do harmonize and are good and they are good in themselves" (Augustine 2001: 141). So, the body, along with earthly things, is not to be condemned
as evil and thus renounced. However, Augustine, like Paul and the Neoplatonists, is concerned that concupiscence, "the muddy cravings of the flesh,"
would get in way of the self having an intimate relationship with the divine. As
he writes in *The Confessions*:

> Worldly honor also has its own grace and the power to command and prevail
> over others (from which comes too the eagerness to assert one's own rights); yet
> in following all these things, we must not depart from you, Lord, or transgress
> your law. The life too, which we live here, has its own enchantment because of a
> certain measure in its own grace and a correspondence with all these beautiful

things of this world. Yet for all these things and all things of this sort sin is committed. For there are goods of the lowest order, and we sin if, while following them with too great an affection, we neglect those goods which are better and higher—you, our Lord God, your truth and your law. Certainly these lower things have their delights, but not like my God, who made all things, for *in Him doth the righteous delight, and He is the joy of the upright in heart.* (Augustine 2001: 31)

In order to focus on the higher good Christians must renounce mundane desires that lead the believer away from God. Going back to Pauline anthropology, Augustine reaffirms the fact that we are "embodied souls," that there is no possibility of rejecting the body. However, the body must serve the soul.[25] The body must be the soul's obedient and disciplined instrument in the latter's quest for God. As Paul tells the Romans: "yield your bodies to God as implements for doing right . . . you once yielded your bodies to the service of impurity and lawlessness, making for moral anarchy, so now you must yield them to the service of righteousness, making for a holy life" (Rom. 6:14, 19). Christians must go about the world, "not in rioting and drunkenness, not in chambering and wantonness, not in strife and envying: but put ye on the Lord Jesus Christ, and make not provision for the flesh in concupiscence" (Rom. 13:14). The body, however, will not yield easily; it will seek to reassert its appetitive, animal drives. Only with the resurrection will there be harmony in the self, as the body becomes one with the soul's designs. With the resurrection, the soul "will have the perfect measure of its being, obeying and commanding, vivified and vivifying with such a wonderful ease that what was once [its] burden will be its glory."[26]

To find God, Augustine, like Plato and Plotinus, turns inward, beholding his own soul in the search for God. While the soul is not identical with God, it was created by God in his image so that we may have a glimpse of his greatness, perfection, and immortality. In a passage which echoes Plato's doctrine of recollection, Augustine writes, "For the Light is God Himself, whereas the soul is a creature; yet since it is rational and intellectual it is made in His image. And when it tries to behold the Light, it trembles in its weakness and finds itself unable to do so. Yet from this source comes all understanding it is able to attain. When, therefore, it is thus carried off and, after being withdrawn from the senses of the body, is made present to this vision in a more perfect manner . . . it also sees above itself that Light in whose illumination it is enabled to see all the objects it sees and understands in itself" (Augustine 1974: 97). As we shall see later on, Augustine's inward turn and his quest to render subjectivity transparent through self-reflection are at the root of what Michel Foucault calls "pastoral power." With Augustine, "self- examination takes the form of self-deciphering. The *mode d'assujettissement* [mode of subjection] is now divine law" (Foucault 1984: 358). This subjectivizing pastoral power will be a precursor of modern forms of disciplinary power over the body's most intimate desires. The stress on self-deciphering will also strongly shape the ways in which the founders of *Religionswissenschaft* appropriated phenomenology and hermeneutics.

Augustine, then, stands at the crossroads of the evolving views of the body in the Greco-Roman and Christian traditions. His thought shows that Christian anthropology, in intense cross-fertilization with the Greco-Roman world, served as a salutary albeit contradictory counterbalance to dualistic idealism. The body in Christianity, while always problematic and often denigrated and renounced as the source of sin, was an essential aspect of doctrine and practice, serving also as the locus of potential redemption. Descartes's legacy is the destruction of this precarious and tense balance. He polarized the mind-body tension, grounding this sharp dichotomy on a scientific rationality that depends on the total subordination of nature and the body to the soul, since God created the latter in his image, free to act according to its own principles. Descartes grounded modern Western thought on a dichotomous self constituted by an autonomous mind, the essence and raison d'être of which is immortality, truth, and justice, and a body subject to the laws of nature. While the mind can only be approached through a contemplation of the ideas it contains, the body is nothing but a sentient machine that can be studied through reductive materialism. I argued in the introduction that, in its search for the essence of religion in beliefs, doctrines, or texts, or in contemplation and the inner life of the soul, the discipline of religious studies reproduces and reinforces this dichotomy.

DESCARTES'S DUALISM

Descartes picked up where Augustine left off. In fact, Arnauld, a distinguished contemporary of the French thinker, characterized Cartesianism as Augustinianism in "philosophical matters." Such a characterization is a bit extreme. Nevertheless, we must recognize that "in France there was no rival to Augustine's prestige. He was an ineffaceable part of the intellectual background against which thinkers of the seventeenth century defined themselves" (Menn 1998: 6). In Augustine, Descartes found a model for his first philosophy.[27] While Augustine's introspection was an attempt to heal the rift between the human and the divine produced by sin, Descartes retreated inward in search of unshakable foundations for natural reason, but without abandoning the notion of an immortal soul that sets humans above all other entities. In the process, he legitimized the development of mathematics and the natural sciences, while preserving the foundational role of metaphysics.

Seeking to reconstruct knowledge in the face of challenges posed to scholasticism by the work of scientists such as Galileo, Copernicus, Kepler, and Newton, Descartes turned the tables on theology. He did not start from God's speech or by deducing the order of things from his essence, as Thomistic philosophy would, but with the cogito. It is no longer a question of "faith seeking understanding." Descartes inaugurates modernity when he "reverses the traditional order from God to the soul. All ideas—including the idea of God—have their formal basis in the mind, which envisions all beings as *cogitata*. God has to be proven, and to be proven on the basis of the prior certainty of the self" (Dupré 1993: 117–18).

> I decided to pretend that nothing that ever entered my mind was any more true than the illusions of my dreams. But I noticed, immediately afterwards, that while I thus wished to think that everything was false, it was necessarily the case that I, who was thinking this, was something. When I noticed that this truth "I think, therefore I am" was so firm and certain that all the most extravagant assumptions of the skeptics were unable to shake it, I judged that I could accept it without scruple as the first principle of the philosophy for which I was searching. (Descartes 1999: 24–25)

What is this self that Descartes recovers as the irreducible foundation of knowledge? Having applied the corrosive power of doubt to the external world and his body, which can be illusions created by an "omnipotent deceiver," what is left is *res cogitans*, a "thing that thinks." In a famous passage in *Meditations on First Philosophy*, Descartes asks:

> Can I not affirm that I possess at least a small measure of all those traits which I already have said pertain to the nature of the body? I pay attention, I think, I deliberate—but nothing happens. . . . How about eating or walking? These are surely nothing but illusions, because I do not have a body. How about sensing? Again, this also does not happen without a body, and I judge that I really did not sense those many things I seemed to have sensed in my dreams. How about thinking? Here I discover that thought is an attribute that really does belong to me. This alone cannot be detached from me. I am; I exist; this is certain. But for how long? For as long as I think. . . . I am therefore precisely only a thing that

thinks; that is, a mind, or soul, or intellect, or reason—words the meaning of which I was ignorant before. Now, I am a true thing, and truly existing; but what kind of thing? I have said it already: a thing that thinks. (1979: 19)

While Descartes celebrates having found his Archimedean point in the cogito, he acknowledges throughout his meditations that the "thinking thing" is constantly besieged by threat of madness and the possibility of being deceived or falling into a dream world. This is what philosopher Richard Bernstein calls the "Cartesian anxiety." Whereas Christian and Greco-Roman thinkers hold ambivalent positions toward the body, Descartes sets a radical either/or that still haunts Western thought: "either there is some support for our being, a fixed foundation for our knowledge, or we cannot escape the forces of darkness that envelop us with madness, with intellectual and moral chaos" (Bernstein 1983: 18). This anxiety compels Descartes to abandon history and the body and ultimately to appeal to theology, to an unchanging God to ground the beleaguered cogito. Not unlike Augustine's *Confessions*, "*The Meditations* portray a journey of the soul, a meditative reflection on human finitude through which we gradually deepen our understanding of what it really means to be limited, finite creatures who are completely dependent on an all-powerful, beneficent, perfect, and infinite God." The treacherous and terrifying journey within fortunately culminates "in the calm reassurance that although we are eminently fallible and subject to all sorts of contingencies, we can rest secure in the deepened self-knowledge that we are creatures of a beneficent God who has created us in his image" (Bernstein 1983: 17). Thus, in Descartes, subjectivism is inextricably tied to theological ontology. We will see in the coming chapters the same appeal to theology, to transcendental grounds for legitimation, in religious studies' appropriation of phenomenology. Thinkers like Rudolf Otto, Gerardus van der Leeuw, and Mircea Eliade will appeal to onto-theological terms like the Holy, the Power, and the Sacred to escape the Cartesian anxiety of contingency, fallibility, and finitude and to ground their internalist and anti-materialist approaches to religion.

What are the ontological implications of hitting rock bottom in the cogito? That the thinking thing is not only different from the extra-world and the body, but that it is autonomous, that it does not need material reality to exist. "I knew from this that I was a substance, the whole essence or nature of which was to think and which, in order to exist, has no need of any place and does not depend on anything material. Thus this self—that is, the soul by which I am what I am—is completely distinct from the body and is even easier to know than it, and even if the body did not exist the soul would still be everything that is" (Descartes 1999: 25). Notice here also how Descartes argues that the soul is more accessible than the material world. Pragmatist philosopher Richard Rorty (1979) has called this argument the "glassy essence" thesis, which claims that with the right method or attitude the mind can be self-transparent. And once we clearly behold ourselves in the mirror, all the mysteries of the universe are revealed, since all ideas about the universe are in the mind. This thesis has been the basis for the hermeneutics of interiority and authenticity that has dominated the study of religion in the West. Once we grasp the phenomenology of *homo religiosus*, we have found the true essence of religion.

But if *res cogitans* is "a thing that doubts, understands, affirms, denies, refuses, and also imagines and senses," what is the extra-mental world? To say that it is a mere illusion would hardly provide a firm foundation for Newtonian physics. After undergoing some arduous mental gymnastics that retrieve innate ideas of goodness and perfection instilled in our soul by a benevolent God, Descartes recovers the extra-mental world as a *res extensa*, a substance that is characterized by attributes like divisibility, motion, and shape, the attribute of occupying space. By body, Descartes understands "all that is suitable for being bounded by some shape, for being enclosed in some place, and thus filling up space, so that it excludes every other body from that space; for being perceived by touch, sight, hearing, taste or smell; for being moved in several ways, not by itself, but by whatever else that touches it" (Descartes 1979: 18).

Although Descartes recognizes that nature and the body move and change, he does not give them agency. Rather, they are characterized by their givenness, by lawful mechanics imposed on them by God. Lawful behavior, in turn, makes it possible for *res cogitans* to order reality according to universal principles à la Newton. In Descartes's eyes, nature functions more like "automata" and "clockworks." In particular, nonhuman animals are complex "sentient machines," which teach us about the operations of our own bodies. Animals have "no intelligence at all . . . it is nature which acts in them in accordance with the dispositions of their organs, just as we see that a clock, which is made only of wheels and springs, can count the hours and measure time more accurately that we can with all of our efforts" (Descartes 1999: 42). It is not that animals do not feel (just as our bodies do) or that animals are not valuable. After all, complex machines were regarded with awe in Descartes's time; they were the highest expression of scientific progress. Rather, Descartes wishes to explain animal sentience as simply the outcome of purely physical, mechanical operations. What Descartes wants to do is to disenchant the Aristotelian world, in which the movements of nature were informed by a hidden telos. The structures and dynamics of nature are not the products of some mysterious process along the lines of transubstantiation; they can be solely captured in mathematical terms. Such scientific disenchantment makes possible the instrumentalism toward nonhuman animals and our bodies that critics see as the hallmark of a destructive modernity. Environmental historian Carolyn Merchant (1983: 193) puts the matter in stark terms: "the removal of animistic, organic assumptions about the cosmos constituted the death of nature—the most far-reaching effect of the Scientific Revolution. Because nature was now viewed as a system of dead, inert particles moved by external, rather than inherent, forces, the mechanical framework itself could legitimate the manipulation of nature. Moreover, as a conceptual framework, the mechanical order had associated with it a framework of values based on power, fully compatible with the directions taken by commercial capitalism."

The bottom line for Descartes is that while nature may be composed of multiple self-moving flows of energy, it does not have the spontaneity and flexibility to generate or even contribute to faculties he attributes only to humans, such as consciousness, intentionality, and the production of language. The rational soul cannot be derived from matter. Descartes authorizes a crude form of materialism directed at nature and the body that will haunt Western thinkers from La Mettrie to Feuerbach, failing to hold in check more highly developed philosophical idealisms dealing with the mind/soul. In that sense, what is at stake epistemologically in the recovery of embodiment, practice, and emplacement in cultural theory and religious studies is the possibility of constructing historicized, contextualized, and more holistic forms of materialism.

"Descartes's error," then, is not just to have argued that the mind and the body are two distinct substances, but to have defined their attributes is absolutist terms. It is "the abyssal separation between body and mind, between the sizable, dimensioned, mechanically operated, infinitely divisible body stuff, on the one hand, and the unsizable, undimensioned, un-pushpullable, non-divisible mind stuff; the suggestion that reasoning, and moral judgment . . . might exist separately from the body. Specifically: the separation of the most refined operations of the mind from the structure and operation of a biological organism" (Damasio 1994: 249–50). We must add to this error, the Cartesian mind's alienation from the social and historical world that is produced by the human praxis that, as Marx tells us, serves as the precondition for meaningful and creative action. I shall have more to say about praxis in chapters 8 and 9. For now, I just want to call attention to this Cartesian notion of an autonomous, disembodied and decontextualized rational mind at the center of the philosophical enterprise. This idealism will dominate philosophy from Enlightenment notions of sovereignty to Kant's phenomenological turn. Even Hegel, who, as phenomenologist Maurice Merleau-Ponty (2002: 398) would put it, adds "temporal thickness" to the cogito by portraying the Spirit as having to enter history in order to become aware of itself, represents extra-mental reality as nothing more than the gallery of externalizations in the *Geist*'s self-propelling march toward full rationality.

Having separated the mind from the body and established its transcendence, Descartes is then faced with the problem defining the proper relation between these two distinct substances. He needs to reconcile common sense, what he experiences in everyday life, with his intellectualist exercise of methodical doubt. To explain the human self as we encounter it, as we are "taught by nature," it is not enough to claim that the rational soul was "lodged in the human body as a pilot in their ship, but that it has to be joined and united more closely with the body in order to have, in addition, sensations and appetites like ours and thus constitute a real human being" (Descartes 1999: 42). Here we have a "return of the repressed" of sorts. To deal with this problem, Descartes sets up an interactive system in which the rational soul has the power to move the body in intentional and voluntary ways and the body can act on the soul as it gathers sense-perceptions. Descartes hypothesizes that the interaction took place in "one small part of the brain—namely, [in] that part in which the 'common sense' is said to be found."[28] Superfine particles accumulate in this part and convey to the mind how the body is affected by external stimuli. This move is, however, problematic to say the least. For how can two utterly heterogeneous substances act on one another and genuinely "intermingle"? How can a thing that is immortal, incorporeal, and indivisible be affected by another that is perishable, corporeal, and divisible? If there is a point of contact, would that not mean that the mind is also *res extensa*, that it exists in space and time like our bodies and nature?[29] We are back, then, to the tension inherent in the Christian doctrine of incarnation, which Kierkegaard considered to be a paradox, a scandal that no amount of dialectical thinking could bridge.[30]

The aporias of Descartes's dualism very quickly led to attempts to revise and go beyond his foundational philosophy. In the process, philosophical countercurrents emerged that are crucial to the genealogy of rematerialized religion. I now turn to two seminal figures in the recovery of the embodied and emplaced self.

2

"Body Am I Entirely, and Nothing Else"

Non-Reductive Materialism and the Struggle against Dualism

Henceforth, my dear philosophers, let us be on guard against the dangerous old conceptual fiction that posited a "pure, will-less, painless, timeless knowing subject."

—*Friedrich Nietzsche (1969: 119)*

In the previous chapter, we saw how diverse and ambivalent approaches to the body fed into Cartesian dualism, which provided one of Western modernity's central pillars: the autonomous, rational, disembodied, unified, and self-transparent cogito. This cogito not only served as the Archimedean point for Newtonian science, but also allowed religion to withstand the pressures of rising modern skepticism. After all, it was an all-perfect, universal, and benevolent God who made it possible for the cogito to escape solipsism, to defeat the evil demons of madness. *Res cogitans*, in fact, was the mirror image of God, the ultimate sovereign and all-seeing subject that vouched for the innate ideas of goodness and truth. Beset by Cartesian anxiety, the study of religion became "the study of human beings as if they simply were believing, disembodied minds." This move allowed scholars of religion to avoid "confronting the relations between material, cultural productions . . . and the concrete political and economic conflicts and inequalities of the people under study" (McCutcheon 1997: 13).

While there was a broad post-Cartesian materialist reaction that included Hobbes, Malebranche, and Leibniz, in this chapter I have chosen to focus primarily on Benedictus de Spinoza, given the continuity of his work with that of modern and postmodern materialists such as Nietzsche, Marx, and Deleuze. Arguably, Spinoza's materialism is not as radical as Hobbes's. The latter, for example, saw mental events, such as dreams, memories, and imagination, as purely epiphenomenal of physical processes, that is, reducible to processes within the body as it resists and reacts to the motions of adjacent objects. Thus, he defined sense as "a phantasm, made by the reaction and endeavour outwards in the organ of sense, caused by an endeavour inwards from the object, remaining for some time more or less" (Hobbes 1999: 215). Nevertheless, Hobbes's radical materialism and empiricism is too impoverished to make sense of complex processes of cultural (and religious) production. For one thing, Hobbes proposed an atomistic worldview that resonated with the Cartesian focus on autonomy in its emphasis on irreducible individualities. Spinoza's holism, in contrast, provides a more fruitful source for a networked materialism that does not equal physical reductionism.

I close the chapter with a discussion of Friedrich Nietzsche, who has been seminal for several strands of social constructionism, ranging from post-structuralism and postmodernism to pragmatism. These strands of social constructionism, in turn, have until recently been the dominant ways in which the body has been theorized. We shall see that, while various versions of social constructionism have been extremely valuable in historicizing and contextualizing the Cartesian subject, they are still infected by a fear of the biological body. Nietzsche's uncompromising naturalism and his relentless challenge to Cartesian disembodied rationalism provide a much needed antidote to this fear, opening the way for a fully somatocentric non-reductive materialism. This materialism will be crucial in later chapters, as I articulate contemporary alternatives to internalist, textualist, and transcendentalist biases that have dominated the study of religion.

SPINOZA'S "MONISM": AN EARLY FORM
NON-REDUCTIVE MATERIALISM

Spinoza's philosophy was constructed in motion. His diasporic experiences as a Sephardic Jew in Holland, where his religious community excommunicated him, gave Spinoza a destabilizing cosmopolitanism that enabled him to challenge the rigidity of Cartesian dualism. Rather than treating mind and body as distinct substances, which need to be brought into interaction to make sense of the human self, Spinoza saw them as two of the multiple attributes of a single substance—God—who informs the entire universe. Here, Spinoza draws from the non-dualism dominant in medieval Jewish philosophy, particularly from Maimonides, Hasdai Crescas, Gersonides, and Kabbalah.[1]

Rather than starting from a solitary, inward-looking, and insecure subject searching for firm foundations, Spinoza departs from God. This is paradoxical for someone who was accused of being a blasphemous atheist. However, the paradox is only apparent, for Spinoza bases his philosophy on an immanent God who transcends the Cartesian gaps between creator and creature, between spirit and matter, and between mind and body. In *Ethics*, one of his most important works, Spinoza defines God as "an absolutely infinite being, that is, substance consisting of infinite attributes, each of which expresses eternal and infinite essence."[2] Since God is absolutely infinite and indivisible, "there can be, or be conceived, no other substance but God."[3] Therefore, "all things emanate necessarily from God's nature and . . . the universe is God."[4] And "that eternal and infinite being, which we call God, that is, nature [*Deus, sive Natura*]" is self-moving.[5] He "acts solely from the laws of his own nature, constrained by none."[6]

Against Cartesian dualism and the privileging of the rational mind over the body, "Spinoza posits the equality of all forms of being, and the univocity of reality which follows from this equality. The philosophy of immanence appears from all viewpoints as the theory of unity Being, equal Being, common and univocal Being. It seeks the conditions of a genuine affirmation, condemning all approaches that take away from Being its full positivity, that is, its formal community" (Deleuze 1990: 167).

As we saw in the previous chapter, Descartes had proposed to explain *res extensa*, nature and the body, through an account of its physical mechanisms. Nonetheless, this materialism was thoroughly schematic. He understood the workings of nature as regularities reducible to abstract laws, foundational representations that the mind could hold as true. "Descartes dominated the first half of the seventeenth century by succeeding in the venture of a mathematical mechanical science, whose first effect was to devaluate Nature by taking away from it any virtuality or potentiality, any immanent power, any inherent being. Cartesian metaphysics completes the venture, because it seeks Being outside of Nature, in a subject which thinks it and a God who creates it" (Deleuze 1990: 227). In contrast, the "anticartesian reaction," which Deleuze sees Spinoza and Leibniz leading, reestablishes "the claims of a Nature endowed with forces or power" (228). If nature is indeed fully active and creative, we need a new materialism that can follow its infinite permutations.

While Spinoza's naturalism strives for unity and totality, it should not be confused with a reductive monism. The divine substance expresses itself in various modes that are in creative and constant interaction. God is both a thinking thing and an extended thing. Thus, mind and body are distinguishable modes of expression of the same reality. There is no possibility of separating mind and body as radically heterogeneous substances; they are *eadem res*, "one and the same thing." What we have here, then, is "aspect dualism" rather than the Cartesian "substantive dualism." Aspect dualism allows Spinoza to claim that "the order and connection of ideas is the same as the order and connection of things." What does the fact that spirit and matter interact in the same system mean for the recovery of the body? In a line that Marx would echo centuries later when he turned Hegelian idealism upside down, Spinoza states that "that which constitutes the actual being of the human mind is basically nothing else but the idea of an individual actually existing thing."[7] The Cartesian autonomous, supra-historical mind is nothing more than the idea of the historical and embodied Descartes. The Cartesian mind cannot but be embedded in the natural and social world.

Embeddedness is perhaps too mild a way of putting things. Spinoza proposes a truly incarnate self. This self is not characterized by sharp duality but parallelism and unity: "The idea of the mind is united to the mind in the same way as the mind is united to the body."[8] This means, then, that, in contrast to the Cartesian attitude, it is not possible to doubt the body and privilege the mind and inward reflection as the locus and method to access true knowledge. However, within this unity, Spinoza, as a good materialist, tends to stress the unheralded role of the body. "The object of the idea constituting the human mind is the body—i.e., a definite mode of extension actually existing, and nothing else."[9] Further, "the mind does not know itself except insofar as it perceives ideas of affections of the body."[10] The body, in turn, is directly affected by its relations with the world in which it finds itself, including its relation with other human bodies. "The idea of any mode wherein the human body is affected by external bodies must involve the nature of the human body together with the nature of the external body."[11] Thus, foreshadowing Merleau-Ponty's notion of the "tacit cogito," which I will discuss later, Spinoza claims that body is consciousness's unrecognized, unspoken primordial source. It affords us the possibility of being in and with the world.

To foreground the creative power of the body and nature, Spinoza introduces the concept of *conatus*, which characterizes the inherent tendency in all things toward activity to assure self-preservation. In Spinoza's words: "Each thing, insofar as it is itself, endeavors to persist in its own being." In humans, the *conatus* describes the body's basic urge toward self-preservation and enhancement of its well-being in the shifting balance between pleasure and pain as it negotiates the environment in which it is embedded. *Conatus* shapes our thinking in powerful ways: "the mind, as far as it can, endeavors to think of those things that increase or assist the body's power of activity." In truth, *conatus* represents the most fundamental way in which organisms express their organic integrity and desires, "projecting an identity beyond the empiric given and making demands on the environment in a way that both defines an emergent character and demands its recognition" (Goodman 2002: 39). Here, Spinoza, in presenting the *conatus* as self-affirming and identity-constructing striving, foreshadows Nietzsche's even more radical notion of the will to power.

It follows from Spinoza's dynamic monism that individual expressions of the *conatus* are always in interaction with each other, thus making ethics necessarily social. Although *conatus* expresses itself individually, it is essentially mimetic: we understand our emotions by empathizing and imitating others, by drawing from a common pool of metaphors and symbols to make sense of our own affects. Spinoza's *conatus*, thus, lays the foundation for a naturalized holism that stresses interconnectivity without erasing particularity and makes room for sociocultural mediation of embodied affective processes. In that sense, Spinoza's materialism builds upon and goes beyond Aristotelian hylomorphism. Spinoza offers "not a neutral universe of mechanical causation but a universe in which purpose is made immanent in the form of the conatus. [T]he conatus is goal directed. It simply not directed toward (or by) a single, externally assigned end that beckons from a telic never-never land. Rather it pursues goals that are, in varied degrees, even in some measure, self-defined" (Goodman 2002: 72–73).

With this understanding of the body and nature, Spinoza breaks the primacy of representation in Cartesianism. Knowledge does not entail recovering correct images from the mind. Rather, the task is to explain how mind and ideas are constituted by a confluence of material—biological and sociocultural—processes. As Macherey (1998: 123) puts it, "[f]or Spinoza knowledge is not 'representation' of the thing to the mind through the mediation of a mental image itself capable of being relayed through a system of signs; rather, knowledge is expression, that is, production and constitution of the thing itself in the mind. 'It is now the object that expresses itself, the thing itself that explicates itself.'" Studying religion, thus, does not mean retrieving from the believer's taken-for-granted psyche or mind some archetype that represents the sacred, the ground of all being, but exploring how specific experiences deemed religious came to be constituted through activities on and by the body, along with particular ways of being a subject.

Do these moves not lead to a reductive materialism? Is Spinoza's stress on the body not simply reversing the terms of Cartesian dualism, rather than overcoming it altogether? For Spinoza, the mind is not a mere reflex of bodily processes. "The human mind perceives not only the affections of the body but also the ideas of these affections."[12] The mind is capable of self-reflection and, in the process, of producing second-order ideas, ideas about ideas, that can then make sense of and orient the actions of the body. Thus, by presenting a dialectical understanding of consciousness—the result of the complex interplay of body and mind—Spinoza goes beyond post-Cartesian schematic materialism.

Spinoza offers an early version of non-reductive materialism, in which "the mind and the body are parallel and mutually correlated processes, mimicking each other at every crossroad, as two faces of the same thing" (Damasio 2003: 217).[13] As we shall see in the following chapters, this materialist framework is very helpful for cross-fertilizing the sociocultural materialism of constructionist theories of the body—such as those of Michel Foucault and Judith Butler—with cognitive psychology, the neurosciences, and ecology.

To be sure, as a man of his time, Spinoza is, like Descartes, also interested in the processes and mechanisms that order the universe. This search for systematicity and totality leads him into serious contradictions. These are nowhere more apparent than in his rejection of free will. "In the mind there is no absolute, or free, will. The mind is determined to this or that volition by a cause, which is likewise determined by another cause, and this again by another, and so ad infinitum."[14] Having demonstrated that God is the absolute infinite and the cause of all things, Spinoza must logically reject the idea that there is free will. God cannot be conditioned by anything to make him create the world in a certain way since there is nothing outside of him. If God informs all things, all things, including human beings, must obey the eternal laws of his own nature. "[F]rom God's supreme power or infinite nature an infinity of things in infinite ways—that is, everything—has necessarily flowed or is always following from that same necessity, just as from the nature of a triangle it follows from eternity to eternity that its three angles are equal to two right angles."[15] God's direction entails "the fixed and immutable order of Nature, or the chain of natural events . . . the universal laws of Nature according to which all things happen and are determined are nothing but God's eternal decrees, which always involve eternal truths and necessity."[16]

Such a cosmology has two major consequences. On the positive side, it erases that untenable distinction between humans and nature, particularly nonhuman animals, which Cartesian dualism had erected. Just as we can explain the behavior of animals and stars by discovering the diverse ways in which the attributes of the divine substance interact, so too can we derive a naturalistic ethics that reflects and guides human activity. In fact, Spinoza notes that "[m]ost of those who have written about the emotions [effectibus] and the human conduct seem to be dealing not with natural phenomena that follows the common laws of Nature but with phenomena outside of Nature. They appear to go so far as to conceive man [sic] in nature as a kingdom within a kingdom. They believe that he disturbs rather than follows Nature's order, and has absolute power over his actions, and is determined by no other source than himself."[17] To challenge this anthropocentric prejudice, Spinoza declares in his Political Treatise, which was written a couple of years before his death: "I have taken care not to deride, bewail, or execrate human actions, but to understand them. So I have regarded human emotions such as love, hatred, anger, envy, pride, pity, and other agitations of the mind not as vices of human nature but as properties pertaining to it in the same way as heat, cold, storm, thunder, and such pertain to the nature of the atmosphere. These things, though troublesome, are inevitable, and have definite cause through which we try to understand their nature."[18]

By trying to understand human nature in this manner, Spinoza is prefiguring contemporary work on the evolutionary, cognitive, and environmental dimensions of emotion (Ravven 2003). He certainly offers an alternative way to explore religious feelings, not as part of some sort of private, transcendent aesthetic experience that can only be approached through empathy, as traditional hermeneutics tells us, but as an embodied response to phenomena that are materially mediated, through social, psychological, and biological dynamics. In anthropologist Talal Asad's words, "the possibility is opened up of inquiring into the ways in which embodied practices (including language use) form a precondition for varieties of religious experiences. [For example,] the inability to enter into communication with God becomes a function of untaught bodies. 'Consciousness' becomes a dependent concept" (Asad 1993: 77).

On the negative side, Spinoza overplays necessity and determination over contingency and chance, valuing harmony, homeostasis, and submission over struggle, rupture, and resistance. The proper ethical stance for Spinoza is one of learning to adjust rationally to the internal dynamics of the totalizing system constructs. Since we are part of nature, we cannot avoid or deny our appetites. However, to the extent that we pursue a rational life, we can learn to educate and regulate them so as not experience any excessive "disturbance of spirit" and, thus, possess "true spiritual contentment."[19] The most important ethical goal is "to perfect the intellect, or reason, as far as we can, and the highest happiness or blessedness for mankind [sic] consists in this alone. For blessedness is nothing other than self-contentment that arises from the intuitive knowledge of God. Now to perfect the intellect is also nothing other than to understand God and the attributes and actions of God that follow from the necessity of his nature."[20]

Spinoza's dynamic non-reductive materialism is invaluable in disentangling "the mind from the illusion of transcendent or transcendental subjectivity as a guarantee or foundation of every meaning or every experience of possible truth" (Althusser 1997: 5). However, he engages in another god-trick, embedding himself in totalizing monism that gives him access to immortality and infinity. Spinoza's materialism, therefore, needs to be decentered, stripped from onto-theological assumptions. If it is problematic to elevate the mind and the self as the epistemological Archimedean pivot, so too it is to divinize nature as an all-encompassing essence, operating with full necessity (and paradoxically full freedom, since it is not constrained by anything outside of it).

Spinoza's totalizing "necessitarianism" was recognized as a problem right away by his fellow materialist Leibniz. The latter tried to overcome it by proposing a universe made by a multitude of monads—eternal, discrete, and simple soul-like substances endowed with their own perceptions and appetites, which aggregate in harmonious ways preestablished by God to give rise to composites. Leibniz's concept of monads was a way to enhance free will, pluralism, particularity, spontaneity, and chance. Leibniz understood monads as self-legislating units, each of which contains the totality of the universe. This leads Deleuze to associate monadology with "the fold." Leibniz "borrows [the monad] from the Neoplatonists who used it to designate a state of One, a unity that envelops a multiplicity, this multiplicity developing the One in the manner of a 'series'" (Deleuze 1992: 23). However, despite the tight "One-Multiple" relation, Leibniz runs into problems of his own by conceiving each monad as only being governed by its own intrinsic properties, by its preceding states, and not subject to intersubstantial causal relations (among monads). Monadology, thus, loses Spinoza's interactive, organicist holism, becoming a (complex) version of atomism.[21]

Finally, there is the problem of Spinoza's quest for a totalizing rationality (which may not be possible but remains as a horizon). Spinoza's rationalism is starkly different from Descartes,' but it is rationalism as a god-trick nonetheless. A more flexible, radical, yet more humble type of materialism is needed, one that gives ample room for paradox, tension, particularity, and indeterminacy, but without surrendering Spinoza's holism, as in the case of Leibniz's monadology. We need a materialism that is even more somatocentric. The opening for this materialism was provided by Friedrich Nietzsche, who stands at the crossroads of all contemporary constructionist attempts to recover the body.

NIETZSCHE: THE BODY AND POWER

As Deleuze is fond of quoting, Spinoza once stated that "nobody as yet has determined the limits of the body's capabilities: that is, nobody as yet has learned from experience what the body can and cannot do, without being determined by the mind, solely from the laws of its nature insofar as it is considered as corporeal."[22] Nietzsche makes this insight a centerpiece of his philosophy.

When Zarathustra, Nietzsche's prophet, attempts to teach his doctrine of over-coming, he challenges the "despisers of the body."

> "Body am I, and soul"—thus speaks the child. And why should one not speak like children?
>
> But the awakened and knowing say: "Body am I entirely, and nothing else; and soul is only a word for something about the body."
>
> The body is a great reason, a plurality with one sense, a war and a peace, a herd and a shepherd. An instrument of your body is also your little reason, my brother, which you call "spirit"—a little instrument and a toy of your great reason.
>
> "I," you say, and are proud of the word. But greater is that in which you do not wish to have faith—your body and its great reason: that does not say "I," but does "I."
>
> Instruments and toys are sense and spirit: behind them still lies the self. The self also seeks with the eyes of the senses; it also listens with the ears of the spirit. Always the self listens and seeks: it compares, overpowers, conquers, destroys. It controls, and it is in control of the ego too.
>
> Behind your thoughts and feelings, my brother, there stands a mighty ruler, an unknown sage—whose name is self. In your body he dwells; he is your body."
> (1954: 146)

Besides the thoroughly embodied notion of the self (e.g., the self is the body and rationality is merely a derivative part of the activities of the body), Nietzsche also claims that the modus operandi of the body is not signification but practice—it "does not say I but does I." Like Spinoza, Nietzsche wishes to move beyond Cartesian representational epistemology, based on the glassy-essence thesis, toward a praxis-oriented philosophy. Nietzsche's conception of the body as a "mighty ruler" follows directly from his own version of monism. Under the influence of Arthur Schopenhauer and Richard Wagner, the early Nietzsche adopted a dualistic worldview, seeing history and civilization as expressions of the struggle between, on the one hand, the Apollonian principle of order, rationality, and contemplation, and, on the other hand, the Dionysian principle of transformation, creative destruction and viscerality.[23] Later on, Nietzsche came to the conclusion that Apollonian rationality and aesthetic contemplation are but aspects of Dionysian change and tension. The Diony-sian is nothing more than what Nietzsche calls the "will to power." Moving away from the Platonic conception that reality is informed by independent universal essences and from the Aristotelian notion of hylomorphism (that forms actualize themselves in matter), Nietzsche "de-ontologizes" the will to power. For Nietzsche, the death of God meant the death of all foundational contrivances. Thus, will to power is not a pure substance, an immutable essence, a transcendental ego, or even a single dynamic principle that dwells in and orders everything according to a telos. It is not Spinoza's *conatus*, a divinely grounded drive toward self-preservation or organic balance. Rather, the will to power is an ever-shifting concatenation of forces, a protean field made of differential, temporary quanta of energy that constitute the incessant unfolding of organic and inorganic processes. The will to power is "an abyss (*Abgrund*), the groundless chaos beneath all the grounds, all the foundations, and it leaves the whole order of essences groundless" (Lingis 1985: 38). The will to power is "Being" as pure becoming.

In contrast to Spinoza, Nietzsche envisions the universe produced by the will to power not as an ordered, rational system, but as a vast and unruly sea of ever-changing forces, always in tension, assembling and disassembling values, ideas, identities, environments, and practices. As he writes in *The Will to Power*,

> And do you know what "the world" is to me? Shall I show it to you in my mirror? This world: a monster of energy, without beginning, without end; a firm, iron magnitude of forces that does not grow bigger or smaller, that does not expend itself but only transforms itself . . . set in a definite space as a definite force, and not a space that might be "empty" here or there, but rather as force throughout, as a play of forces and waves of forces, at the same time one and many, increasing here and at the same time decreasing there; a sea of forces flowing and rushing together, eternally changing, eternally flooding back, with tremendous years of recurrence, with an ebb and a flood of it forms . . . this, my Dionysian world of eternally self-creating, eternally self-destroying, this mystery world . . . my "beyond good and evil," without goal, unless the joy of the circle is itself a goal . . . do you want a name for this world? . . . This world is the will to power—and nothing besides! And you yourselves are also this will to power—and nothing besides! (Nietzsche 1967: 549–50)

Nietzsche thus shares Spinoza's monism and materialism, but he rejects the appeals to necessity, rationality, and order. "Let us here dismiss the two popular concepts 'necessity' and 'law': the former introduces a false constraint into the world, the latter a false freedom. 'Things' do not behave regularly, according to a rule: there are no things (—they are fictions invented by us); they behave just as little under the constraint of necessity. There is no obedience here: for that something is as it is, as strong or as weak, is not the consequence of an obedience or a rule or a compulsion—The degree of resistance and the degree of superior power—this is the question in every event" (Nietzsche 1967: 337).

According to Nietzsche, the body, as sheer will to power, as the will to overcome, master, and affirm itself in relation to others and the natural world, is a particularly important field of contestation. The body carries the historical and social manifestations of the will to power as individuals act upon themselves and each other. The stable, authentic selves and egos that we think we are, the cogitos that we hold as foundational and sovereign, are nothing more than the transitory constructions of the body's will to power seeking to assert itself in a particular space and at a particular moment in time. The body and the self are positioned artifacts, the products of specific struggles, desires, and interests. Thus, the knowledge that the body and the self produce is always perspectival. It is not an absolute truth that transcends the contingencies of history and nature, but a situated truth inflected by power.

> Henceforth, my dear philosophers, let us be on guard against the dangerous old conceptual fiction that posited a "pure, will-less, painless, timeless knowing subject"; let us guard against the snares of such contradictory concepts as "pure reason," "absolute spirituality," "knowledge in itself": these always demand that we should think of an eye that is completely unthinkable, an eye turned in no particular direction, in which active and interpreting forces, through which alone seeing becomes seeing *something*, are supposed to be lacking; these always demand of the eye an absurdity and a nonsense. There is *only* a perspective seeing, *only* a perspective "knowing." . . . But to eliminate the will altogether, to suspend each and every affect, supposing we were capable of this—what would that mean but to *castrate* the intellect? (Nietzsche 1969: 119)

For Nietzsche, the body is "the inscribed surface of events (traced by language and dissolved by ideas), the locus of a dissociated Self (adopting the illusion of a substantial unity), and a volume in perpetual disintegration. Genealogy, as an analysis of descent, is thus situated within the articulation of the body and history. Its task is to expose a body totally imprinted by history and the process of history's destruction of the body. Genealogy . . . seeks to reestablish the various systems of subjection: not the anticipatory power of meaning but the hazardous play of domination" (Foucault 1977a: 148). As such, Nietzsche's concepts of embodied will to power and genealogy entail a more radical notion of sociocultural mediation than Spinoza's mimetic *conatus*. The construction of the self is not simply an exercise of imitation, identification, and empathy, but a product of the application, on both self and the other, of practices of "subjectivation," which articulate a competent body, a body with certain skills, dispositions, tastes, and internalized boundaries. I will have more to say about this in the chapters on practice.

Nietzsche's conception of the body as a contested field of forces, as an artifact marked by power relations, is a major turning point in the recovery of a materialist theory of body and its practices, including religious ones. This conception offers a method to understand why we moderns have lost the body. If the body is the mighty lord of the self, how come Western philosophy and civilization have been so intent on rejecting it? According to Nietzsche, the modern body has a genealogy, a history of its disciplining that has a lot to do with religion. The attempt to flee the body by controlling it, by denying its will to power, has to do with humanity's failure to embrace contingency and the endlessly changing character of nature. Instead of facing life with all its contradictions, pains, sorrows, and joys, we become despisers of the body. We seek a stable refuge in social conventions (the herd), an other-worldly God, a sovereign ahistorical self, or Truth for all times and places. This drive toward unshakable foundations is itself an expression of the body's will to power: not having the courage to affirm itself as pure becoming, it turns against itself, fleeing from itself into the world of disembodied rationality and essences. We then become god-like, as with the Cartesian cogito, but only at the cost of sacrificing the core of the self, the body in all its unruly creativity, suffering, and joy.

Nietzsche traces the rise of what he calls modernity's "reactive nihilism"—a nihilism that, rather than affirming sheer becoming, turns into the outright denial of life—to Christianity.[24]

> The Christian conception of God—God as god of the sick, God as a spider, God as spirit—is one the most corrupt conceptions of the divine ever attained on earth. It may even represent the lower-water mark in the descending development of divine types. God degenerated into the *contradiction* of life, instead of being its transfiguration and eternal Yes! God as the declaration of war against life, against nature, against the will to live! God—the formula for every slander against "this world," for every lie about the "beyond"! God—the deification of nothingness, the will to nothingness pronounced holy! (1954: 585–86)

More specifically, Nietzsche saw in Christianity a "slave religion" of the masses. Failing to assert directly its will to power over the Roman masters, the Christian mob surreptitiously turned everything that is good, life-enhancing, into evil. Thus, the will to control, to satisfy the body's natural needs and desires, is deemed shameful and sinful. Further, the body is subjected to the harsh discipline of an other-worldly asceticism, and it is martyred and crucified in the quest for immortality.

We can no longer conceal from ourselves what is expressed by all that willing which has taken its direction from the ascetic ideal: this hatred of the human, and even more of the animal, and more still of the material, this horror of the senses, of reason itself, this fear of happiness and beauty, this longing to get away from all appearance, change, becoming, death, wishing, from longing itself—all this means—let us dare to grasp it—a will to nothingness, an aversion to life, a rebellion against the most fundamental presuppositions of life; but it is and remains a will ... And to repeat ... man [sic] would rather will nothingness than not will. (1967: 162–63)

In the end, it came to pass that the meek inherited the earth, as Christianity conquered Rome, by rendering the noble warriors into tame, guilty, and wretched creatures afraid of damnation in hell. The victory, however, was pyrrhic, for Western Christian civilization was then built on a truly pathological self. In an analysis that would influence Freud, Nietzsche sees the modern self at war with itself. The will to power, as its inherent nature demands it, still wants to affirm itself. However, having internalized Christianity's morality, it is impotent to do so. The will to power can only will itself by emasculating itself. When the will to power finally expresses itself openly, it does so only in twisted ways as, for examples, in the graphic dreams of retribution in the book of the Apocalypse or in the self-destructive resentment and aggression that characterized the Nazi regime. In the latter, the self, rather than deploying the will to power in affirmative ways, as the drive to create new partial and temporary yet valuable truths that enhance life, surrenders to dictates of the state, which Nietzsche called the "new idol."

Nietzsche's reading of Christianity and its role in the rise of modernity is too simplistic. In fact, as I showed at the beginning of this chapter, there are many Christianities, with diverse and often conflicting understandings of the body and nature. Nevertheless, Nietzsche's key point remains: the values and truths that we consider universal have a history and that history involves the exercise of power by and over the body. If this is the case, the task of the critical philosopher is not to search for universal values and truths in a kind of "hermeneutics of recovery," but to apply a "hermeneutics of suspicion" that seeks to map out the situated conditions under which certain values and truths come to be considered normative. This is why Nietzsche advises us to "philosophize with a hammer," not just to shatter obvious idols outright, but to "sound out" the "eternal idols," the foundations of our knowledge to diagnose those parts that may be hollow or rotten to the core, that may not be useful anymore. This diagnosis, in turn, becomes the basis for "a transvaluation of all values," an exercise in which the will to power overturns received wisdom and creates new ways to enhance and affirm life.

Let us articulate this new demand: we need a critique of moral values, the value of these values themselves must first be called into question—and for that there is needed a knowledge of the conditions and circumstances in which they grew, under which they evolved and changed (morality as consequence, as symptom, as mask, as tartufferie, as illness, as misunderstanding; poison), a knowledge of a kind that has never yet existed or even been desired. (Nietzsche 1969: 20)

The wisdom to be overturned includes not only other-worldly religions but science, the rationality that was so dear to Descartes, Spinoza, and their contemporaries. For the scientist, in the quest to find a truth for all times and places, is also an ascetic, a despiser of the body. "No! Don't come to me with science when I ask for the natural antagonist of the ascetic ideal." According to Nietzsche (1969: 153), science challenges "not the ideal itself but only its exterior, its guise and masquerade, its temporary dogmatic hardening and stiffening, and by denying what is exoteric in this idea, it liberates what life is in it. This pair, science and the ascetic ideal, both rest on the same foundation—I have already indicated it: on the same overestimation of truth (more exactly: on the same belief that truth is inestimable and cannot be criticized)." Against this life-denying will to truth, Nietzsche counterposes a new notion of truth:

A mobile army of metaphors, metonyms, and anthropomorphisms—in shot, a sum of human relations, which have been enhanced, transposed, and embellished poetically and rhetorically, and which after long use seem firm, canonical, and obligatory to a people: truths are illusions about which one has forgotten that this is what they are; metaphors which were worn out and without sensuous power; coins which have lost their pictures and now matter only as metal, no longer coins. (1954: 46–47)

What would it mean to take Nietzsche seriously in religious studies? What are the values, metaphors, illusions, and puffed-up idols that we want to sound out and contextualize as a way to open spaces for new perspectives on religion? How did the trope of the sacred, as a Platonic transcendental reality, come to be constituted as the unchangeable essence of religion, the thing for which both believers and scholars must strive? Why is it that private, inward feelings and beliefs are seen as the authoritative and authentic dimensions of religion? Is this a replay of Augustinian and Cartesian aporias? Why is it that souls/minds, texts, and doctrines considered to be more central to religious life than bodies, material culture, and practices? Is religious studies not involved in its own version of life-denying asceticism, one that, as Asad (1993) claims, shares a lot with Christian ascetic practices of extracting truth and constituting "authentic" religious subjects? Is religious studies, despite the claim to be different from theology, not another onto-theological enterprise, based on the quest for foundations? Nietzsche's materialism, perspectivism, and genealogy make it possible for us to interrogate religious studies in this way.

The notion of the will to power, just like any trope, has its limitations. In the next chapter, we shall see that Heidegger considered the idea of the will to power as the culmination of Cartesian metaphysics and instrumentalism. With Nietzsche, the ego becomes so unmoored that it not only controls and destroys others and nature, but turns against itself, dismembering itself, just as Dionysus was torn to pieces.[25] Despite these limitations, it is impossible to overstate the importance of Nietzsche in the emergence of the broad currents of non-reductive materialism in cultural and religious studies today. Nietzsche's concern for the present and his desire to affirm embodied life proved tremendously influential to a phenomenological and existentialist strand of materialism, represented by Heidegger, Sartre, and Merleau-Ponty. His theories of the self and the will served as the bases for psychoanalytical theories of the body, from Freud to Lacan and Žižek. Moreover, his historicist hermeneutics of suspicion inspired the work of constructionist materialists such Foucault, Deleuze, Butler, Bordo, and Braidotti. His perspectivism, which is a precursor of what Donna Haraway (1988: 581) calls "feminist objectivity . . . mean[ing] quite simply situated knowledge," also opened the way to begin to talk about specific bodies rather than the abstract category of "The Body." Finally, Nietzsche's critique of science and truth sets the difficult task of attempting to reconcile a historicist reading of religion—religion as simply the product of situated and power-inflected practices—with emerging perspectives on the cognitive and evolutionary dimensions of religious experience. Nietzsche forces us to ask the difficult question: can non-foundational, perspectival materialism be reconciled with forms of materialism that presuppose some biological and ecological foundations? Perhaps the key lies in proposing historicized, localized, open-ended "foundations" that involve multiple and interacting levels of mediation and determination. In the next chapters, I shall attempt to characterize the currents that Nietzsche unleashed, as well as their contributions to the recovery of the body and a non-reductive rematerialization of religion.

3

Toward a Materialist Phenomenology
of Religion

Merleau-Ponty, and also Heidegger, opened the way for a non-intellectualist, non-mechanistic analysis of the relations between agent and world.

—Pierre Bourdieu (1990a: 10)

In the previous two chapters, I outlined the sources of the spirit-matter split and the denigration of body in the Christian and Greco-Roman strands that came together in Descartes's philosophy to usher in Western modernity. Further, I discussed attempts by Spinoza and Nietzsche to overcome Cartesian dualism and to construct a somatocentric non-reductive materialism. This chapter focuses on the development of phenomenology, which as the "philosophy of the subject," inherits many of the contradictions of Cartesian thinking, as well as the struggles to move beyond them. Moreover, along with the history of religions, phenomenology has been central in the rise of the contemporary discipline of religion. Prominent religion scholars from Pierre Daniel Chantepie de la Saussaye and Gerardus van der Leeuw to Mircea Eliade, Ninian Smart, and Wilfred Cantwell Smith have made one version of phenomenology or another a key ingredient in their work. Thus, an examination of the various ways in which phenomenology has been appropriated in the study of religion can offer important insights on how this study has reproduced the Cartesian flight from the body, history, and practice.

My aim is to recover alternative materialist currents within phenomenology which challenge somatophobic internalism and idealism. These alternative phenomenological currents stress historicity, facticity, enfleshment, and embeddedness in everyday life as the inescapable conditions for construction of selfhood. Armed with the theoretical and methodological tools of a materialist phenomenology of embodiment, I will, in the next chapter, critique and rethink traditional phenomenological approaches in religious studies, which have privileged the internal life of *homo religiosus* not only as an autonomous sphere of inquiry but as the royal road to the "essence" of religion. This privileging has, in turn, made it difficult to foreground the "external manifestations" of religion—embodied, emplaced, and performative aspects that are deemed as mere reflections of subjective dynamics.

EDMUND HUSSERL, THE RETURN OF CARTESIAN ANXIETY, AND THE TEMPTATION OF TRANSCENDENCE

According to Ryba (2006: 93), phenomenology "is scientific or analytic discourse about anything that appears subjectively and objectively to consciousness as pointing to something else; as such, it is about the very nature of those appearances but especially as they refer to or reveal an underlying, invariant structure or essence." Conceptualized this way, the roots of phenomenology may be traced as far back as Plato's distinction between the forms and the world as it appears to the senses. However, Kant arguably provided the basis for the modern use of the term, when, in response to the dualities set by Descartes, he ushered in a "Copernican turn" in philosophy by delimiting the horizons of the knowable only to what appears to the human mind (phenomena) rather than to the things-in-themselves (noumena).[1] Our knowledge of phenomena is made possible by a priori structures of reason, a grid of categories, which organize sensory data, allowing us to apprehend reality in systematic and meaningful ways. For Kant, these synthetic a priori structures of cognition and ethical and aesthetic judgment are transcendental in the sense that they are supra-historical, universal, and constitutive of the self. As such, these structures serve as our epistemological foundations. The task of philosophy, then, is to reconstruct these structures and to use them to critique various forms knowledge and experience.

Besides merely displacing the Cartesian spirit-matter split to the phenomena-noumena antinomy,[2] Kant failed to explain satisfactorily the origin of a priori structures of apperception. To go beyond the staticity of Kantian epistemology, Hegel historicized the phenomenological enterprise. In Hegel's hands, phenomenology becomes the "science of the experience of consciousness," that is, the systematic reflection on the gallery of historical experiences the human spirit (*Geist*) undergoes as it seeks to educate itself, to achieve identity with itself. Hegelian phenomenology is the self-consciousness of the teleological process through which the mind comes to realize that it is the source of reality itself. There is no noumena, no outside of rationality. "What is rational is real; and what is real is rational" (Hegel 2008: xix).

Kant and Hegel gave rise to two distinctive, albeit often interacting, versions of phenomenology.[3] The Kantian transcendental version leads directly to Edmund Husserl, while the Hegelian historicist reading influences Wilhelm Dilthey, as well as phenomenologists of religion such C. P. Tiele and Brede Kristensen, whom I will discuss in the following chapter. Despite their differences, these two currents within phenomenology share an emphasis on the primacy of inner subjective life, understood not as embodied, material process but rather as workings of a mind/spirit unconditioned (or at best superficially conditioned) by historical, environmental, or somatic processes. Even in the Hegelian version of phenomenology where the Spirit must "fall into history" and externalize itself in particular historical events and phases in order to come back dialectically to itself, what matters is the underlying movement of Absolute Reason, not its specific material manifestations. The latter are steps in the unfolding of humanity's collective rationality.

Most scholars trace the rise of phenomenology as a discernible philosophical movement to the work of Edmund Husserl, particularly to the publication of his *Logical Investigations* in 1900–1. Coming from the field of mathematics, Husserl was concerned with the relativism that was beginning to enter the intellectual scene at the turn of the twentieth century. More specifically, Husserl challenged what he called psychologism, the belief associated with his teacher Franz Brentano that the truths of logic could be explained by elucidating psychological laws, the operations of consciousness, through purely empirical, descriptive approaches.[4] Husserl felt that psychologism reduced universals to the idiosyncrasies of private psychic phenomena. In doing so, psychologism not only replayed the Cartesian *res cogitans–res extensa* split, but denigrated the "objective" pole of knowledge. In response, Husserl called for a return to the "things themselves" (*Zu den Sachen*), distinguishing between the objects of consciousness and psychic processes. However, he borrowed from Brentano the notion of intentionality, or object-directedness: things present themselves as things to us and for this "presencing" to take place there are structures that direct the mind toward its intended object. Intentionality is what binds the self and the world in a single, meaningful noetic act. All experiences are inherently intentional: we are always conscious *of* something, striving *for* something, and deciding *on* something.

In order to discover the structures that make cognition possible, Husserl argues that description of multiple mental acts is necessary but insufficient. We must go beyond this diversity to apprehend the common structures that underlie mental acts. Thus, Husserlian phenomenology departs from "the natural attitude," in which "the world is for us the self-evidently existing universe of realities which are continuously before us in unquestioned givenness." This world is "always there as an actuality," as a taken for granted, "on-hand" world that serves as the background for consciousness. It is "the general field of our practical and theoretical activities" (Husserl 1999: 328, 60–63). Unlike Descartes, who, in his attempt to apply a universal doubt, ends up with an unbridgeable gap between mind and body, between subject and object, Husserl accepts the world "as it presents itself to [us] as factually existing." In that sense, the motto "back to the things themselves" injects a useful bit of realism, since it means that our starting point should be the world as we ordinarily experience it.[5]

Nevertheless, Husserl finds in Descartes's doubt a useful "methodic expedient for picking out certain points which, as included in its essence, can be brought to light and made evident by means of it" (Husserl 1999: 63). Cartesian doubt is a tool that can break through the givenness of the world as it presents itself to the natural attitude and introduce a "theoretical" or "reflexive" attitude, allowing us examine the conditions that have made this world possible. This strategic rupture from the naïveté of the natural attitude is what Husserl calls the *epoché*, the bracketing, "putting into parenthesis," "suspension," or "withholding" of the objects as given, external realities that impinge on our perceptual apparatus. This bracketing allows us to focus on the objects as phenomenological data, as data present to us. *Epoché*, thus, should not be confused with sophist skepticism and relativism: "I am *not negating* this 'world' as though I were a sophist; I am *not doubting its factual being* as though I were a skeptic" (Husserl 1999: 65, italics in the original). Rather, the *epoché* is an attempt to see reality as it really is for us, as being for us in certain ways. In effect, the *epoché* shifts the focus of analysis of the noetic act to the subject's meaning-producing activities and processes. Once this shift has taken place, the phenomenologist engages in a series of "reductions," careful experimental operations that progressively identify the various components that constitute a given phenomenon, as well as the multiple variations to which these components and their relations may give rise. Here the phenomenologist calls on memories, fantasies, and changes in perspective to identify possible permutations. As the phenomenologist goes through these variations, s/he begins to elucidate the features of the phenomenon without which it would no longer be meaningful as the phenomenon that it is. This is what Husserl called the eidetic reduction (eidetic, coming from the Greek *eidos*, meaning ideas or forms), the distillation of the invariant elements, the essences or "pure generalities," that inform phenomenal reality.

In a Cartesian-Kantian move, Husserl argues that these unchangeable elements are ultimately synthetic structures of the intentionality of a "transcendental subjectivity," which, as Descartes had shown through the *cogito ergo sum* formula, cannot be bracketed or subjected to further reduction. This transcendental subjectivity is the ground not only for the unity of science but for all apperception. "All objective being and all truth has in transcendental subjectivity the ground for its being. . . . Something objective is nothing other than the synthetic unity of actual and potential intentionality, a unity belonging to the proper essence of transcendental subjectivity. . . ." (Husserl quoted in Smith 2003: 188).

Transcendental subjectivity provides the unbreachable line of defense against all forms of relativism, including psychologism and historicism. For example, without transcendental subjectivity, phenomenology would dissolve into the Nietzschean perspectivism that we encountered last chapter, where the value of a particular standpoint is dependent on its capacity to enhance the will to power at a given juncture. This is why Husserl concludes in his *Cartesian Mediations* (1973: 156–57) that

> the path leading to knowledge absolutely grounded in the highest sense, or (this being the same thing) a philosophical knowledge, is necessarily the path of universal self-knowledge—first of all monadic, and then intermonadic. We can say also that a radical and universal continuation of Cartesian meditations, or (equivalently) a / universal self-cognition, is philosophy itself and encompasses all self-accountable science.
>
> The Delphic motto, "Know thyself!" has gained a new signification. Positive science is a science lost in the world. I must lose the world by epoché in order to regain it by a universal self-examination. "*Noli foras ire*," says Augustine, "*in te redi in interiore homine habitat veritas*."[6]

There are several startling aspects to this passage. First, there is a clear reiteration of the Cartesian anxiety in the fear and loathing of getting "lost" in the world. As we saw in the last chapter, Nietzsche associated this fear and negation of life with self-destructive deployments of the will to power, including Christian morality and science. Second, in order to allay this fear and disgust, we must lose the world in all its chaos in order to gain it, to redeem it as a systematized and totalized reality. From a Nietzschean, constructivist perspective, a phenomenology of this type, despite its claims to scientific rigor, appears suspiciously like a secular reworking of Christian theology and eschatology, nothing more than another version of the Western god-trick. Third, losing the world to regain it requires turning inward and engaging in an "all-embracing self-investigation." Only this investigation of the truth in the "monad," the analytics of the ego in its "transcendental ownness," can lead us to an understanding of its contexts (the "intermonadic"). This truth is certainly not a personal relationship with a God that we encounter when we look into ourselves, as is the case for Augustine. Yet, it is the truth of a self-transparent and foundational subject beholding itself.

The privileging of the glassy, pure, and transcendental subjectivity has been one of the problematic elements that the modern discipline of religion has borrowed from phenomenology to legitimize and buttress its own brand of subjectivism and internalism. In religious studies, the pure subjectivity of the believer—whether expressed in the raw power of his/her inner states, or through his/her "ultimate concerns," or in the search for meaning—provides the ultimate, authentic, and irreducible foundation to avoid getting lost amid the diverse and ever-changing world of discourses, practices, and institutions. The result of this "jargon of authenticity" (McCutcheon 2003: 173) has been consistently the same: the denigration of "external" religious phenomena, often tied to the body, as mere manifestations of a deeper inner and supra-historical reality.

Husserl is keenly aware that his transcendental move threatens to undermine phenomenology's call to go back to the things themselves, since it sets up a radical form idealism that abstracts a pure foundational ego disembedded from its materiality, its thrownness in time and space and amidst social relations. Like Cartesian radical doubt, *epoché* and other phenomenological reductions raise the specter of solipsism, of a disembodied mind trapped in its private mental life. "When I, the meditating I, reduce myself to my absolute transcendental ego by phenomenological *epoché* do I not become *solus ipse*; do I not remain that, as long as I carry on a consistent self-explication under the name phenomenology? Should not a phenomenology that proposed to solve the problems of Objective being, and to present itself actually as philosophy, be branded therefore as transcendental solipsism?" (Husserl 1999: 135).

To neutralize this threat, Husserl posits, particularly in his later writings (from *Ideas II* to *Cartesian Meditations* and *Crisis of European Sciences*), that intersubjectivity, embeddedness in the "life-world" (*Lebenswelt*), and embodiment are constitutive of transcendental subjectivity. "[W]ithin myself, within the limits of my transcendentally reduced pure conscious life, I experience the world (including others)—and, according to its experiential sense, not as (so to speak) my private synthetic formation but as other than mine alone [*mir fremde*], as an intersubjective world, actually there for everyone, accessible in respect of its Objects to everyone" (Husserl 1999: 136). Although each monad constitutes the world as his/her own phenomenon, this world is intersubjectively transcendent, that is, it has a "thereness-for-everyone" by virtue of being a co-intended reality. This reality serves as a shared "world-horizon" that grounds all pre-theoretical and theoretical praxis. "The intrinsically first being, the being that precedes and bears every worldly Objectivity, is transcendental intersubjectivity: the universe of monads, which effects its communion in various forms" (Husserl 1973: 156). Husserl goes as far as to state that transcendental subjectivity's "synthetic unity is relative to the universal community of the transcendental egos communicating with me and with one another. That is to say, it is a synthetic unity of the intentionalities belonging to this community as part of its own essence."

The "first thing constituted in the form of community, and the foundation for all other intersubjectively common things, is the commonness of Nature, along with that of the Other's organism and his psychophysical Ego, as paired with my own psychophysical Ego" (Husserl 1973: 120). Thus, the body is essential in Husserlian phenomenology. Husserl distinguishes between the "capital B" Body, which he uses to refer to the lived body (*Leib*), as characterized not just by material and spatiotemporal attributes but also by intentionality and self-awareness, and the physical body (*Körper*), a natural object, purely defined in terms of space, time, and causality. Although different from each other, the physical body and the lived body are mutually implicative. The human being is a "psychophysical" being, "who knows himself [*sic*] to be in the world with living body and soul, who moves in space and works with his hands, as a manual worker, or in some other way with his living body, who, in battle, also fights with his living body, [and] is naturally always conscious of his living body, acting through it upon his external world or experiencing through it a touch, a push, a wound" (Husserl 1970: 322).

It is clear, thus, that Husserl has a much more nuanced conception of the body and a more holistic understanding of the self than Descartes's precariously embodied cogito. For Husserl, the "Body is, in the first place, the medium of all perception; it is the organ of perception and is necessarily involved in all perception," such that all that is "thingly-real in the surrounding world of the Ego has its relation to the Body" (Husserl 1999: 163, 164). Moreover, the lived body is the "bearer of the zero point of orientation, the bearer of the here and the now, out of which the pure Ego intuits space and the whole world of the senses" (164). The body is the "zero point of orientation" because it marks in the most poignant way the boundaries of subjectivity, of self-identity, vis-à-vis other objects in the world. Husserl is even more specific in his materialism: the body is "a localization field for sensations and for stirring of feelings" (183), with tactility and kinesis as the most originative activities, since the ego becomes my ego when it literally rubs against the world. The body, in its "spatial thinghood" and mobility, is central in the constitution of the synthetic categories of space and time. The body also plays a crucial role in intersubjectivity since "all objects are apprehended 'objectively' as things in the one Objective time and one Objective space of the one Objective world" (Husserl 1999: 170–71). Without corporality, each monad would not be able to experience the shared life-world, the things that populate the world that is always there for us, including other embodied consciousnesses. Corporality is a necessary precondition for a relation of empathy among monads.

For Husserl, the concept of empathy (*Einfühlung*) plays an important role in guarding against the threat of solipsism. Although the "I" encounters others always within its "primordial ownness," within the horizons of its self-experience, it does so analogically, seeing others "as if I were there." Thus, I do not experience the other as a directly accessible and transparent mind, but as another living body like myself. I become conscious of another person by the associative pairing of my consciousness of my own lived body with the consciousness of the other person's sentient body. While "I am here somatically" and the other is there, we coexist as embodied and intentional consciousnesses. Through his/her own apperceptions, the other reciprocates recognition. This co-intentionality is what makes intersubjective communication and the construction of a shared life-world possible. In turn, this life-world serves as the basis for self-experience.[7]

In his affirmation of "the real givenness of the soul and Ego," through embodiment and intersubjectivity, Husserl is certainly no Descartes. For Husserl's notion of subjectivity is much richer and contextualized than the Cartesian "thinking thing." Husserl, in fact, deals with themes that the more materialist and historicist phenomenologies of Heidegger and Merleau-Ponty will later elaborate. For example, Husserl's notion of intentionality entails not a detached and sovereign consciousness, but one that, in being always directed toward its object, is deeply engaged in and concerned about its life-world. As we shall see later on, Heidegger elaborates this understanding of consciousness through the angle of praxis with his notion of care (*Sorge*). Furthermore, Husserl's analysis of the body as the "zero point of orientation" and "a localization field for sensations and for stirring of feelings" opens the way for Merleau-Ponty's fuller recovery of the body.

Still, has Husserl really overcome all the contradictions of Cartesian subjectivism? Despite the centrality of the life-world for Husserl, he fails to specify its rich and ever-changing structures. While Husserl recognizes "the relativity of the surrounding life-worlds of particular human beings, peoples, and periods," he insists, in his transcendental move, that the search for the "universal framework," the "general ground of the validity" of all life-worlds is the end of phenomenology (Husserl 1970: 146–47). Going beyond Dilthey's historicism, which seeks to capture the structures of a particular *Zeitgeist* by empathically standing in the flux of history, Husserl wants ultimate grounds (*Gründe*) for Objectivity, that is, for a "world that is identical for everyone." This quest for foundations blunts the historicist and realist thrust of the call to return to the things themselves. Bracketing the natural attitude and investigating the conditions that make it possible are fruitful strategies. However, reducing all these conditions to the universal structures of transcendental subjectivity and inter-subjectivity severely limits our capacity to understand empirically the complex relations of determination among sociocultural, psycho-cognitive, and ecological factors that enable the construction of life-worlds, of the world as it becomes accessible to us in diverse albeit remarkably consistent ways. In other words, the turn toward transcendental idealism prematurely truncates the possibility for a rich, non-reductive analytics of the material conditions of being-in-the-world. Even if there are "invariant" or relatively stable aspects of experience, they can only be found in the dynamics interactions between individuals and their contexts.

In the next chapter, I will show how the Cartesian anxiety and the temptation of transcendence in Husserl interact with the quest in religious studies to establish a comparative science of religion centered around the archetypal and irreducible experiences of the believer. To the extent that religion scholars borrow from Husserlian phenomenology, it is to operationalize and legitimate scientifically the search for religious essences that inform the historical and embodied practices of believers. Once again, the body is dismissed as an obstacle in this search for deep essences.

Even though Husserl refers to the need to undertake a "genetic phenomenology," a "phenomenology of phenomenological reduction" (Mohanty 1995: 68), challenging, for example, the assumption that *epoché* immediately breaks from the pre-given world and yields transcendental experience, he fails to bracket his natural attitude toward the subject, as a reality always there for us. As Heidegger (1984: 134) puts it, "we must . . . make intentionality itself into a problem," since "it does not primordially constitute [the] relating-to [beings themselves] but is founded in a being-amidst beings. This being-amidst is, in its intrinsic possibility, in turn grounded on existence."

In spite of his discussions of the body and the life-world, Husserl's philosophy remains internalist "because it is committed to the idea that one can understand experience in a manner that is methodologically solipsistic. One can understand experience in a manner that abstracts from the existence of other persons and of the external world in general" (Keller 1999: 8–9).

Husserl thinks that we can and must "reconstruct the existence of other minds and the external world from the vantage-point of how the existence of the external world modifies individual experience" (Keller 1999: 9). As Nietzsche showed, individual experience and the subject, like Truth, are the product of multiple situated practices and power relations that have shaped the body into an illusion of a unified, sovereign self. While the Husserlian monad is always embedded in an intersubjective world, this intersubjective world is understood primarily as the collection of the objectifications of the intentionalities of a "community of monads." Husserl's reliance on methodological individualism leads him directly into the problem of solipsism and a thin characterization of sociality (as dyadic exchanges between an ego and the Other) and history.

This phenomenological subject-centeredness, with its attendant appeal to transcendental categories, spills into religious studies with deleterious consequences. In particular, the search for the essence of religion in the believer's inner mental and affective life, characterized by universal phenomenological structures, contributes to the widespread failure to historicize and contextualize religious experiences. By making the believer's intimate experiences of the sacred its main focus, religious studies' appropriation of phenomenological subjectivism contributes to the intractable dichotomy between insider and outsider. How can scholars of religion penetrate the inner life of the religious monad? They can only do so by "bracketing" and moving beyond the surface contingencies that characterize the monad as a historically situated individual to recover empathetically the underlying experiential stratum that makes us all *homo religiosus*.

The problem of solipsism and the appeal to empathy to enable communication among two irreducible subjectivities would not arise if we were to start from the notion of praxis, from situated, sociocultural, and biologically grounded practices that produce both subjectivity and objectivity. As we shall see in the chapters dealing with practice, praxis necessarily demands a dialectical interplay between structure and agency, between the individual and the social, between culture and nature, and between the body as construction and constructor, which avoids the contradictions posed by transcendental phenomenology. Thus, if the discipline of religious studies is to move beyond the contradictions of Cartesian foundationalism, dualism, and subjectivism, it must enter into conversation with a phenomenology that makes practices and embodiment its primary loci.

The task of working out Husserl's innovative insights on the body and his call for an "ontology of the life-world" in a more materialist and historicist fashion was left to his students Martin Heidegger and Maurice Merleau-Ponty.

I turn to them now as a prelude to my exploration of how the modern discipline of religion has appropriated phenomenology.

HEIDEGGER'S *DASEIN*: A HISTORICIZED AND EMPLACED SELF

Heidegger's contribution to the historization and materialization of phenomenology comes from his turn toward ontology.[8] Concerned that the question of Being has been "forgotten" or "covered up" by modernity's instrumentalist focus on producing and controlling things, Heidegger asks how the world is possible in the first place. To answer this question, he turns to the being for whom the meaning of Being is constitutive of its existence. "Thus to work out the question of Being adequately, we must make an entity—the enquirer—transparent in his own Being. The very asking of this question is an entity's mode of *Being*; and as such it gets its essential character from what is inquired about—namely, Being. This entity which each of is himself [*sic*] and which includes inquiring as one of the possibilities of its Being, we shall denote by the term '*Dasein*'" (1962: 27).

Heidegger uses the term *Dasein* (Being-there) to offer an embodied and emplaced notion of selfhood that overcomes the contradictions of Descartes's dualistic, decontextualized, and static concept of subjectivity. Heidegger believes that Husserl has not been able to break from Cartesian subjectivity. However, despite this crucial flaw, Heidegger does not reject Husserlian phenomenology. He simply uses it as a tool to ask a new set of questions. Rather than using phenomenology to search for epistemological foundations, Heidegger applies it to illuminate in a rigorous way how the question of Being emerges for *Dasein*. "Phenomenology," he writes, "is our way of access to what is to be the theme of ontology, and it is our way of giving it demonstrative precision" (1962: 60). Phenomenology, then, becomes an analytics of existence, of the structures of *Dasein*'s Being, that is, the conditions that make it possible for us, as historical beings, embedded in a world of beings, to have a relation with Being. As Heidegger puts it: "Philosophy is universal phenomenological ontology, and takes its departure from the hermeneutic of *Dasein*, which, as an analytic of *existence*, has made fast the guiding-line for all philosophical inquiry at the point where it arises and to which it returns" (Heidegger 1962: 62).

Notice here that Heidegger introduces the concept of hermeneutics to signal that phenomenology is not a scientific endeavor charged with finding universal laws and unchangeable foundations. Instead, it is an interpretive method seeking to understand how *Dasein* creates meaning as it discloses Being to itself within historical horizons. This creation involves the use of language and other forms of cultural mediation, which is why the analytics of *Dasein* necessarily involve hermeneutics. Heidegger's appeal to hermeneutics is, then, key in introducing the notions of positionality, practice, and historicity to Husserlian phenomenology. Hermeneutics challenges Husserl's methodological individualism, showing how the self is inextricably embedded in preexisting and public webs of signification, immersed within interpretive historical horizons that make it possible to articulate subjectivity in a meaningful way. However, Heidegger's hermeneutic turn ultimately reinforces the internalism of phenomenology by overstressing meaning-making and signification among *Dasein*'s diverse practices. This overemphasis leads to a hermeneutical textualism that claims the primacy of texts and practices of representation in the analysis of social and cultural phenomena, religion included. Because the texts to be interpreted are the product of *Dasein*'s being-in-the-world, hermeneutics ultimately dovetails with phenomenology's privileging of the believer's inner states, thus undermining the exploration of the multiple roles of nondiscursive practices in the production of religion. A certain deployment of hermeneutics and phenomenology leads to internalist idealism, a "linguistification" of experience that ignores material dimensions of religion that are not fully accountable in terms of meaning-making. I will have more to say about the relation between hermeneutics and phenomenology in the study of religion in the next chapter.

Heidegger's notion of *Dasein*, however, can be read in a materialist key as the cornerstone of a phenomenological anthropology that makes embodiment, time, and space central categories. The Being-thereness of *Dasein* is above all a "Being-in-the-world," that is, existence within a pre-given reality constituted by other things and *Dasein*s. Because of its "facticity," its "thrownness" among other entities, *Dasein* does not have the option of suspending the world in a transcendental move à la Husserl. "The concept of 'facticity' implies that an entity 'within-the-world' has Being-in-the-world in such a way that it can understand itself bound up in its 'destiny' with the Being of those entities which it encounters within its own world" (Heidegger 1962: 82). *Dasein* "has been delivered over to beings which it needs in order to be able to be as it is" (462). Heidegger uses notion of destiny here to undermine the subject-centeredness of Husserlian phenomenology: it is not the world that belongs to the subject but the subject to the world. Thus, the hermeneutics of *Dasein* cannot start in the Husserlian mode from "an inner space in which it has been proximally encapsulated." Rather, "its primary kind of Being is such that it is always 'outside' alongside entities which it encounters and which belong to world already discovered" (Heidegger 1962: 89).

Even though *Dasein*'s fate is to be alongside other entities, it is not a thing like any other. *Dasein* stands out in the midst of things because it has a particular form of temporality; it has what Heidegger calls historicality (*Geschichtlichkeit*). Its existence is always a project oriented to the future. In Nietzschean terms, *Dasein* is Being as becoming, but, for Heidegger, a becoming that is made possible by a past and a present that provide the horizon for unrealized possibilities. Since *Dasein* is a project, it cannot have a disinterested attitude toward other beings. Rather, *Dasein* acts with concern and care (*Sorge*) for these beings, which it must transform into its life-world, into the meaningful world in which it dwells. Here Heidegger is elaborating and criticizing Husserl's notion of object-directedness. Whereas Husserl saw the self's involvement with the world in primarily intellectual terms, as the constitution of meaningful phenomena, Heidegger understands this engagement as praxis.

For Heidegger, praxis is constitutive of *Dasein*. For instance, *Dasein* does not recognize a hammer "theoretically," by abstracting it from everyday life and finding the essence of "hammerness" through phenomenological reductions, but in our "dealings" with it, in the process of putting the hammer to use. Practical behavior discloses the life-world to us, as a world that is "ready-to-hand." Knowing is "a comportment toward beings." As a historical being, *Dasein* "is stretched along and stretches itself along" (Heidegger 1962: 427), making choices and acting to create his/her life-world. However, *Dasein*'s choices and activities are enabled and constrained, although never totally determined, by the life-world in which it is embedded. This life-world is itself the product of *Dasein*'s "co-historicizing" with others, of the decisions and actions that *Dasein* takes every day as it fulfills its destiny of creatively disclosing and foreclosing of Being. Put in other worlds, the historicality of *Dasein* is "the power of finite freedom" (436).

The consequences of this turn to everyday practices for the study of religion are momentous. Instead of approaching religion as an intellectual or contemplative experience, or even as the inner affective life of a transcendental subjectivity, a Heideggerian perspective would focus on the historical practices that make inhabiting the world in a religious way possible. Religion, thus, would not be some special realm of experience above history and nature, a "sacred" that is experienced by an abstract *homo religious* in archetypal, irreducible ways, but it would be sets of practices among other everyday practices through which concrete individuals are in the world. As we shall see later in the book, constructionists like Foucault and Bourdieu radicalize Heidegger's phenomenological anthropology, seeing these practices as contingent and the product of endless contestation and variation.

Besides presenting a view of the self in which situated practices are essential, Heidegger, expanding on Husserl, also stresses *Dasein*'s spatiality. According to

Heidegger (1962: 82), "*Dasein* itself has a 'Being-in-space of its own,'" which is "a result of his bodily nature (which, at the same time, always get founded upon corporeality)." However, he is more concerned with "*Dasein*'s existential spatiality," for, once again, *Dasein* is not just like any object merely occupying a position in space. Instead, *Dasein* appropriates the objects that are given by its Being-in-the-world, by its embodied nature, "giving space" to and "making room" for them. Objects that would be inert, amorphous, and static realities become "ready-to-hand," transformed into meaningful artifacts by *Dasein*'s involvement. As *Dasein* projects itself to its future and moves around, it also can "move things around and out of the way or 'make room' for them only because making-room—understood as an *existentiale*—belongs to its Being-in-the-world" (Heidegger 1962: 112). Because existence is inescapably spatio-temporal, *Dasein* can construct spatiality by drawing things near, into its field of interest and activity.

By presenting space as both the outcome and the background for *Dasein*'s practical experiences and activities, Heidegger is more successful than Husserl in holding in check the threat of Cartesian disembodied subjectivism. *Dasein* is not an indivisible, autonomous, and universal mind connected in some obscure way to a body occupying space (a *res extensa*) that can be suspended by radical doubt. *Dasein*'s spatiality cannot "be interpreted as an imperfection which adheres to existence by reason of the fatal 'linkage of the spirit to a body.' On the contrary, because *Dasein* is 'spiritual,' and only because of this, it can be spatial in a way which remains essentially impossible for any extended corporeal Thing" (Heidegger 1962: 419). By "spiritual" here, Heidegger means that *Dasein* is creative in the way it discloses itself as spatial: as "a taking up residence," a "dwelling" alongside things (1962: 88–89).

If *Dasein* creates space because it is itself spatial, then there is no Cartesian subject/object split. "Space is not in the subject, nor is the world in space. Space is rather 'in' the world in so far as space has been disclosed by that Being-in-the-world which is constitutive of *Dasein*. Space is not to be found in the subject, nor does the subject observe the world 'as if'' that world were in a space; but the 'subject' (*Dasein*), if well understood ontologically, is spatial" (Heidegger 1962: 112).

Heidegger's conception of the *Dasein*'s existential spatiality has important ramifications for the study of religion. Traditional Eliadean approaches to religious space see it as a by-product of the manifestations (hierophanies) of an ahistorical sacred, which *homo religiosus* simply reenacts through ritual. In contrast, Heidegger would see religious space as the result of the practices of historical, context-bound individuals as they "make room," carve out spaces by manipulating things, establishing boundaries, pathways, and networks that make traveling and dwelling possible. As I will show in chapter 10, this alternative understanding of space dovetails nicely with the work of religion scholars such as J. Z. Smith (1987), Sam Gill (1998), David Chidester and Edward Linenthal (1995), and Thomas Tweed (2006). The Heideggerian notion of existential space also opens the possibility for fruitful dialogue with humanistic and critical geographers, such as Lucien Lefebvre (1991), Yi-Fu Tuan (1974), and Edward Soja (1989), who have challenged the traditional Euclidean notion of space as an inert context that can be plotted mathematically. These geographers have been exploring how our notions of space have been transformed as a result of human-made processes such as urbanization, industrialization, globalization, and transnational migration.

Heidegger's idea that *Dasein*'s existential space is itself grounded in ontological spatiality challenges the Kantian-Cartesian view that only the human subject has the agency to impose order on the world. Some constructionists have given this claim a new twist, arguing that there is no nature or body as such, only our discourses about them. This attitude leads to an instrumentalism toward nature and the body, which are seen as mere historical artifacts of our practices, without recognizing that they are in the first place the enabling and constraining grounds for our activity. Heidegger's understanding of *Dasein*'s complex spatiality resonates with emerging work by ecologists, environmental philosophers, and ethicists on the interplay between religion and nature. This literature can be seen as working out the implications of Heidegger's notion of "finite freedom" when it asks, for example, about the extent to which our embeddedness in a particular physical landscape, a bioregion, is linked with our religious ideas, practices, and institutions. How do religious narratives and practices shape our lived landscapes? Conversely, how do our landscapes shape the religious ethics and the narratives of our place in the world that we tell each other? I will tackle these questions on chapter 11.

Being-in-the-world is not just being-in-space but also "Being-with" (*Mitsein*). "Dasein is essentially Being-with" others (Heidegger 1962: 156), since it is "absorbed" in the everyday world that others have constructed. In fact, for Heidegger, "the Self of everyday Dasein is the *they-self*" (1962: 167), meaning the public identities that *Dasein* adopts as a member of a community. This community coproduces the life-world, the language that makes it possible for *Dasein* to disclose itself to itself. Echoing Ludwig Wittgenstein's claim that there are no private languages, Heidegger argues that it is absurd to posit a "bare subject," a self-contained monad transparently accessible to itself and struggling to build an intersubjective world through empathy with other free-floating egos. "Being-with is an existential characteristic of Dasein even when factically no Other is present-at-hand or perceived. Even Dasein's

Being-alone is Being-with in the world. The Other can *be missing* only *in* and *for* a Being-with. Being-alone is a deficient mode of Being-with; its very possibility is proof of this" (Heidegger 1962: 156–57). Husserlian self-reflection and transcendental reductions, thus, are only possible because *Dasein* is always "for the sake of others." "Knowing oneself [*Sichkennen*] is grounded in Being-with, which understands primordially. It operates proximally in accordance with the kind of Being which is closest to us—Being-in-the-world as Being-with; and it does so by acquaintance with that which Dasein, along with the Others, comes across in its environmental circumspection and concerns itself with . . ." (Heidegger 1962: 161). If this is the case, it follows that empathy does not enable Being-with. Rather, it is the opposite: "only on the basis of Being-with does 'empathy' become possible" (162). Because sociality is the ground on which *Dasein* discloses itself, it "cannot be conceived as a summative result of the occurrence of several 'subjects'" (163).

In seeing *Dasein* as *Mitsein*, Heidegger has given us a richer understanding of the life-world than Husserl's. This life-world is inextricably social: society is not merely the product of the subject's activities; society itself is "agentic." That is, social processes have the power to shape the subject, to articulate his/her identity, to mould his/her body, and render inner experiences meaningful. This insight is key in the development of constructionist approaches. It provides the nexus for an interactive materialism that takes the interplay between embodied self and society/culture seriously.

Despite these undeniable contributions to a materialist phenomenology, Heidegger's hermeneutics of *Dasein* contains some serious lacunae and contradictions. First, his affirmation that *Dasein* is essentially Being-with stands in tension with his claim that "the they," the world of everydayness that "possesses" *Dasein* is "inauthentic." In Heidegger's eyes, *Dasein* literally "falls into," is "ensnared by," or forgets itself in the midst of the world of things. This world that is characterized by "levelling down [*Einebnung*] of all possibility of Being," by its "averageness," in which "everyone is the other, and no one is himself" (Heidegger 1962: 164–65). Here Heidegger is influenced by Søren Kierkegaard's mistrust of the power of the crowd to flatten the originality and creativity of the individual self.[9] To be sure, Heidegger does not use the terms "fallen" (*verfallen*) or "inauthenticity" in a moralistic or religious sense. These terms simply point to the existential reality of *Dasein*, of being always a project but one immersed in a world already constituted by others, and thus essential for the fulfillment of its possibilities. Nevertheless, the terms carry a heavy normative baggage that makes it difficult to understand social construction except as a process of subjection and alienation, which paradoxically robs *Dasein* of the existential agency Heidegger wanted to open with his notion of historicality.

According to Heidegger, *Dasein*, "as everyday Being-with-one-another, stands in *subjection* [*Botmässigkeit*] to Others. It itself *is* not; its Being has been taken away by the Others. *Dasein*'s everyday possibilities of Being are for the Others to dispose of as they please. These Others, moreover, are not *definite* Others. On the contrary, any Other can represent them." Under "the dictatorship of the they," we "take pleasure; we read, see, and judge about literature and art as *they* see and judge; likewise we shrink back from the 'great mass' as *they* shrink back; we find 'shocking' what they find shocking. The 'they,' which is nothing definite, and which all are, though not as the sum, prescribes the kind of Being of everydayness" (1962: 164). Submerged safely in "the they," *Dasein* "disburdens" itself, fails to answer its call to become. Only when *Dasein* confronts its own finitude, a death that is only its own, can it recover and resolutely face its authentic destiny as a historical project. As Heidegger puts it, "Authentic Being-towards-death—that is to say, the finitude of temporality— is the hidden basis of Dasein's historicality" (1962: 438). In all fairness to Heidegger, we should note that the recovery of *Dasein*'s authenticity does not entail detachment from the "they," as if this were existentially possible. Rather, it calls for the "modification of the 'they,'" such that it becomes but a way of being in the world, a way of disclosing truth.

This equation of the "they" with subjection resonates with constructionist efforts to understand how society and culture shape the body. Notions like hegemony (Gramsci), doxa (Bourdieu), and normalization of the body through panoptical practices (Foucault) dovetail with Heideggerian conceptions of sociality. These notions, in turn, provide a way to construct a hermeneutics of suspicion of the mechanisms by which religious discourses, narratives, and institutions articulate the religious self and other. In particular, the postcolonial approaches to religion show the ways in which social and cultural apparatuses use the category of religion to give rise to and control colonial subjects (Chidester 1996). Nevertheless, Heidegger's "they" offers an incomplete, one-sided notion of praxis and of the relation between self and society. It will be left to scholars like Alfred Schutz, Peter Berger, and Thomas Luckmann to develop a more balanced and holistic phenomenology of the social world, which shows how sociality makes possible interpretation and purposive experience and action.[10] According to Schutz and Luckmann (1973: 15), for example, the life-world appears as "something to be mastered according to my particular interests. I project my own plans into the life-world, and it resists the realization of my goals, in terms of which some things become feasible for me and others do not."

Moreover, we cannot ignore the ways in which the individual also resists and transforms society, and particularly the ways in which the body refuses to be rendered docile by dominant discourses and practices. As cultural theorists such as Raymond Williams and Stuart Hall argue, the relationship between the embodied self and society is not simply one of authenticity versus inauthenticity, but a creative interplay between production and re-production, between domination and resistance. I will explore this interplay in more detail, particularly in relation to the tension between "official" and "popular" religion, in the chapters on practice.

Heidegger is also not consistent in his treatment of space. Despite his important contribution in foregrounding the existential dimensions of space, Heidegger tends to overemphasize *Dasein*'s historicality, its capacity to construct existential spatiality, over against *Dasein*'s corporality, its somatic presence among other things in nature (Dreyfus 1991: 128–40). In fact, Heidegger overplays the uniqueness of *Dasein* in relation to the material objects that surround it (which do not have a privileged access to Being), reinscribing a milder version of the classical mind-body, spirit-matter split. As he writes in his famous *Letter on Humanism*:

> Ek-sistence[11] can be said only of the essence of man [*sic*], that is, only of the human way "to be." For as far as our experience shows, only man is admitted to the destiny of ek-sistence. Therefore ek-sistence can also never be thought of as a specific kind of living creature among others—granted that man is destined to think the essence of his Being and not merely to give accounts of the nature and history of his constitution and activities. Thus even what we attribute to man as *animalitas* on the basis of comparison with "beast" is itself grounded in the essence of ek-sistence. The human body is something essentially other than an animal organism. (Heidegger 1977a: 204)

As we shall see in later chapters, evolutionary biology shows that the difference between human and nonhuman animals is a matter of degrees rather than a sharp contrast. By overemphasizing *Dasein*'s ontological uniqueness, Heidegger does not analyze in sufficient depth the spatial implications of our thrownness as embodied beings among other material beings and objects. Heidegger does not explore how our physical immersion in this material world enables and constraints *Dasein*'s capacity to mark difference from other corporal beings. As a corollary of Heidegger's stress on the uniqueness of *Dasein* as a being who stands out among other things and animate beings, he does not make the body a central focus in his philosophy. In fact, he all but brackets the physical body altogether.[12] While Heidegger recognizes that that the physical body is primordial for *Dasein*, he tends to see it as a present-at-hand reality, a givenness, the physiology of which is not explored as part of *Dasein*'s thrownness and historicality. *Dasein* is rather the province of hermeneutics, understood specifically through the production of meaning through symbol.

In his later writings, Heidegger deepens his critique of Cartesian subjectivism, recognizing that his attempt in *Being and Time* to derive time from *Dasein*'s temporality is still contaminated by Cartesianism. Instead, he makes the "temporality of Being" central in the "clearing" (*Lichtung*), the event (*Ereignis*) through which Being opens itself in time and space to *Dasein*: "Man [*sic*] does not decide whether and how beings appear, whether and how God and the gods or history and nature come forward into the lighting of Being, come to presence and depart. The advent of beings lies in the destiny of Being. But for man it is ever a question of finding what is fitting in his essence which corresponds to such destiny: for in accord with this destiny man as ek-sisting has to guard the truth of Being. Man is the shepherd of Being" (1977: 210).

The "turning toward Being" (*Kehre*) has contradictory consequences for a materialist approach to religion. On the one hand, by enjoining us to "let beings be," to listen to Being rather than cover over it with our idle talk and calculative rationality, Heidegger opens the way for a more radical immersion of *Dasein* in time and space, particularly in nature. In fact, as Zimmerman (1997) argues, Heidegger's later work has great affinities with the deep ecology, Mahayana Buddhism, and Daoism. On the other hand, the growing mistrust of human praxis as necessarily "enframing" (*Gestell*), reducing the world to a kind of apparatus, standing in reserve, leads Heidegger further away from an exploration of the sociocultural conditions that make the articulation of selfhood possible.[13]

To recover a phenomenology of the body that recognizes the full creativity behind its materiality, I turn to Merleau-Ponty.

MERLEAU-PONTY'S TACIT COGITO AND THE FLESH

Like Heidegger, Merleau-Ponty seeks to overcome the contradictions of Cartesian dualism in order to be able to fulfill Husserl's call to return to the things themselves. Also like Heidegger, Merleau-Ponty sees in Husserlian phenomenology a helpful method to ask the right questions and recover the conditions that make the Cartesian cogito possible, as one, albeit misguided, way to construct selfhood. However, in contrast to Heidegger, who is more interested in clearing a space to explore how Being is disclosed by *Dasein*, Merleau-Ponty uses phenomenology to affirm the primacy of perception and embodiment.

For Merleau-Ponty, the various phenomenological reductions do not lead to a transcendental ego who makes sense of the world though the synthetic work of its eidetic structures, but to an incarnate "being-in-the-world" (*être au monde*). "When I reflect on the essence of subjectivity, I find it bound up with that of the body and that of the world . . . because my existence as a subjectivity is merely one with my existence as a body and with the existence of the world, and because the subject that I am, when taken concretely, is inseparable from this body and this world" (Merleau-Ponty 2002: 475).

For Merleau-Ponty, phenomenology leads inescapably to the body as the self's primary datum. And contrary to Plato, Descartes, and other idealists, who mistrust the senses and seek to flee into the realm of essences, Merleau-Ponty makes perception, the direct encounter of the body with its world, the unavoidable source of consciousness. Since the "world is not what I think, but what I live through," perception is not primarily "a science of the world, it is not even an act, a deliberate taking up of a position; it is the background from which all acts stand out, and is presupposed by them" (Merleau-Ponty 2002: xviii, xi). Thus, the sort of reflection that Descartes and Husserl conceive as the foundation of mathematics and the natural sciences depends heavily on the body's interface with the material world. But Merleau-Ponty goes further, "[o]ur body, to the extent that it moves itself about, that is, to the extent that it is inseparable from a view of the world and is that view itself brought into existence, is the condition of possibility, not only of the geometrical synthesis, but of all expressive operations and all acquired views which constitutes the cultural world" (Merleau-Ponty 2002: 451). We can no longer set the body in opposition to culture, as part of a nature devoid of agency. Without the body in all its materiality and contingency, there would be no praxis, language, culture or history.

If the foundational role of the body is true, then, "to return to things themselves is to return to that world which precedes knowledge, of which knowledge always speaks, and in relation to which every scientific schematization is an abstract and derivative sign-language, as is geography in relation to the country-side in which we have learnt beforehand what a forest, a prairie or a river is" (Merleau-Ponty 2002: x). Indeed, the focus on the body and perception leads Merleau-Ponty to the paradoxical task of recovering the conditions that make knowledge possible before knowledge has already thematized the world, rendered it abstract, solidified it into the "natural attitude" that makes reality a given for a unified cogito. Merleau-Ponty is interested in the "unreflective experience" of "the real," by which he means the primordial knowledge of the world, before articulation in propositional form. By the "primacy of perception," Merleau-Ponty means that the experience of perception is our presence at the moment when things, truths, values are constituted for us; that perception is a nascent logos; that it teaches us, outside all dogmatism, the true conditions of objectivity itself; that it summons us to the tasks of knowledge and action. It is not a question of reducing human knowledge to sensation, but of assisting at the birth of this knowledge, to make it as sensible as the sensible, to recover the consciousness of rationality. (1964: 25)

The most basic experience of the body is as a unity that is mine, not as simply as an already-dissected sum of separate parts (a *res extensa*). "Whether it is a question of another's body or my own, I have no means of knowing the human body other than that of living it, which means taking up on my own account the drama which is being played out in it, and losing myself in it. I am my body . . . [t]hus experience of one's own body runs counter to the reflective procedure which detaches subject and object from each other, which gives us only the thought about the body, or the body as an idea, and not the experience of the body or the body in reality" (Merleau-Ponty 2002: 231).

According to Merleau-Ponty, before the glassy Cartesian-Kantian-Husserlian ego, "before any speech can begin," the body sustains a "tacit cogito," as it becomes pre-reflectively aware of itself in its interaction with the world. "Behind the spoken cogito, the one which is converted into discourse and into essential truth, there lies a tacit cogito, myself experienced by myself [*une épreuve de moi par moi*]" (Merleau-Ponty 2002: 469). As "pure feeling of the self," this "silent," "unspoken" cogito is "anterior to any philosophy." Merleau-Ponty likens it to the inchoate awareness of a newborn.

> The consciousness which conditions language is merely a comprehensive and inarticulate grasp upon the world, like that of the infant at its first breath, or of the man about to drown and who is impelled towards life, and though it is true that all particular knowledge is founded on this primary view, it is true also that the latter waits to be won back, fixed and made explicit by perceptual exploration and by speech. Silent consciousness grasps itself only as a generalized "I think" in the face of a confused world "to be thought about." (2002: 470)

In his later writings, particularly in *The Visible and the Invisible*, an incomplete work that was only published after his death, Merleau-Ponty radicalizes his position, introducing the notion of "the flesh" (*la chair*), which allows him to move beyond the subject-object split still implicit in the notion of the cogito's lived body. Building on and going beyond Husserl's distinction between *Leib* and *Körper*, which I discussed above, Merleau-Ponty understands the body as a "two-dimensional being," at once a "phenomenal" and "objective," at once sentient and sensible. "We say therefore that our body is a being of two leaves, from one side a thing among things and otherwise what sees and touches them; we say, because it is evident, that it unites these two properties within itself, and its double belongingness to the order of the 'object' and to the order of the 'subject' reveals to us quite unexpected relations between the two orders. It cannot be by incomprehensible accident that the body has this double reference; it teaches us that each calls for the other" (1968: 137).[14]

The integration of the objective and subjective poles into a sole body is possible because the body is made of the same "substance" as the world that surrounds it: "my body is made of the same flesh as the world (it is a perceived), and moreover . . . this flesh of my body is shared by the world, the world reflects it, encroaches upon it and it encroaches upon the world (the felt [*senti*] at the same time the culmination of subjectivity and the culmination of materiality), they are in a relation of transgression or of overlapping" (Merleau-Ponty 1968: 248). Existence is, thus, "flesh applied to a flesh" (1968: 138), and to characterize this tight "intertwining" (*entrelacs*), Merleau-Ponty uses the term "the chiasm" to denote the "reversibility" of the flesh, the doubling back onto itself. Even though there is a gap (*écart*) between our body and the world, the fact that they are both flesh allows for a coiling over (*enroulement*) that makes the body and the world interdependent in the act of perception.

Does the notion of chiasm mean that Merleau-Ponty is a monist who reduces everything to a single material substance? No, for Merleau-Ponty does not want to reduce the phenomenal or lived body to undifferentiated matter. Reworking the apostle Paul's famous dictum, Merleau-Ponty writes that "the presence of the world is precisely the presence of its flesh to my flesh, that I 'am of the world' and that I am not it" (1968: 127). What we have here is another version of non-reductive materialism or non-dualistic divergence: "[T]here is not identity, nor non-identity, or non-coincidence, there is inside and outside turning about one another" (264). The flesh "is not matter. It is the coiling over of the visible upon the seeing body, of the tangible upon the touching body, which is attested in particular when the body sees itself, touches itself seeing and touching the things, such that, simultaneously, as tangible it descends among them" (1968: 146).[15] As we shall see in the next chapter, the dialectic of identity and nonidentity in the flesh, the simultaneous presence and alterity that our body affords us and burdens us with, plays a central role in anthropologist Thomas Csordas's embodied phenomenology of religion.

With the notions of the flesh and the chiasm, Merleau-Ponty has pushed Husserlian phenomenology to its limits.[16] It is no longer tenable to privilege the analytics of the ego, even if embedded in the life-world, as the precondition for rigorous knowledge. For the "inside" is no longer a self-contained space, separated from the "outside" by a barrier. The self is not just in the world but tightly connected to it by the porous and flexible tissue that is our body. This is why Merleau-Ponty writes: "[t]ruth does not 'inhabit' only the 'inner man [sic],' or more accurately, there is no inner man, man is in the world, and only in the world does he know himself" (2002: xii). And if there is no inner person, the meaning of the *epoché* changes: "The most important lesson which the reduction teaches us is the impossibility of a complete reduction. This is why Husserl is constantly re-examining the possibility of the reduction. If we were absolute mind, the reduction would present no problem. But since, on the contrary, we are in the world, since indeed our reflections are carried out in the temporal flux on to the which we are trying to seize . . . there is no thought which embraces all our thought" (Merleau-Ponty 2002: xv).

Merleau-Ponty offers thoroughly historicist and materialist phenomenology that can serve as a powerful counterpoint not just to the most radical versions of postmodern constructionism, which we will encounter later on, but also to the internalist phenomenology that has dominated religious studies. As we shall see in chapter 5, some social constructionists balk at the idea that we can have unmediated access to our bodies, that we can recover the originative source of our experiences outside of the horizons of language and thought. Merleau-Ponty himself realizes the precarious nature of this claim. "What I call the tacit cogito is impossible. To have the idea of 'thinking' (in the sense of the 'thought of seeing and feeling'), to make the 'reduction,' to return to immanence and to the consciousness of . . . it is necessary to have words" (1968: 171). The mere mention of the tacit cogito implies the use of "sedimented significations" that already reify our "direct and primitive contact with the world." Nevertheless, Merleau-Ponty insists that "there is a world of silence, the perceived world, at least, is an order where there are non-language significations— yes, non-language significations, but they are not accordingly *positive*" (1968: 171).

To illustrate the "non-language significations" of carnality, Merleau-Ponty points at how the body operates by incorporating the world, particularly space, through socially constructed "habits" of which we are often not conscious. These embodied habits produce a natural competence that is difficult to render into words, that can be rationalized only post facto. Thus, a practitioner of Umbanda or Candomblé, for example, learns to incorporate his/her head spirit only through practical training under the supervision of a *pai* or *mãe de santo* who already embodies the proper habits to relate to the world of the spirits. Relating to the spirits through the right ritual etiquette is like learning an ethos, a way of locating and carrying oneself in a world constituted by a single vital energy, *axé*, which becomes materialized in different forms, ranging from humans and animals to plants and stones. Becoming a Candomblé initiate is an embodied and performative way of religiously being-in-the-world that cannot be fully captured by a manual or any other "textual" representation. As scholars of religion, we certainly can study a particular sacred-drumming session hermeneutically, breaking down and interpreting its various symbolic meanings. Nevertheless, these meanings are made possible in the first place by the encounter between the embodied ways of being-in-the-world of the practitioners, which serve as the authorized media for the spirits to materialize themselves, and our own embodiments of the proper habits of scholarly research. And however valuable it may be to ask the practitioner to articulate what s/he felt during the incorporation of the spirit, we cannot assume that this account will exhaust the multiple sensorimotor processes associated with the experience. According to Yvonne Daniel (2005: 78),

> The ceremonial structure of Haitian Vodou, Cuban Yoruba, and Bahian Candomblé reveals deep knowledge of the body, emotional states, and social psychology and its functioning. Dance ceremonies are carefully constructed sets of deeply engaging, visual, rhythmic, sensory stimulation that result in specific emotional and physical behaviors. While unfolding religious liturgies and sacred orders of chants, drumming, and dancing, the ceremonies also compound and layer physiological principles that result in ecstatic experiences, both conscious and unconscious. . . . Concentration on specific body parts and also on the whole dancing body implies knowledge about what occurs inside the human body with repetitious, improvisational dance behavior.

For Merleau-Ponty, "the acquisition of habit is a rearrangement and renewal of the corporeal schema" that allows the body to "cultivate" its "power of dilating our being-in-the-world, or [to change] our existence by appropriating instruments" (2002: 164, 166). In chapters 4 and 9, we will see how his idea of corporeal schemas as "neither a form of [explicit] knowledge nor an involuntary action," but as "sediments" or "stable dispositions" left behind by previous performances, as embodied wisdom that allows the body to know its place in the world, parallels Marcel Mauss's concept of "techniques of the body" and Pierre Bourdieu's notion of habitus. We can see, then, that despite the controversial appeal to "origins" in the tacit cogito or in the flesh, Merleau-Ponty's materialist phenomenology contains productive spaces for a conversation with constructionist approaches on the politics of embodiment, on the ways in which the gaze and practices of self and others come to construct particular bodies, such as criminal bodies, sexualized bodies, sick bodies, "mad" bodies, or religious bodies of various types (ascetics, mystics, martyrs, vestal virgins, miracle workers, etc.).

From the perspective of evolutionary biology, cognitive psychology, and neuroscience, Merleau-Ponty's "phenomenological positivism" (2002: xix), his appeal to the "real" body rather than to the "body as an idea," a mere construct of discursive and nondiscursive practices, is not problematic at all. Rather, this appeal serves as a reminder that there are physiological, biochemical, and eco-logical conditions that, operating in conjunction with sociocultural dynamics, make possible the rise of consciousness and language. Merleau-Ponty's phe-nomenology of the flesh is a type of "embodied realism, a form of interaction-ism that is neither purely objective nor purely subjective" (Lakoff and Johnson 1999: 25). Reality is neither "out there," in the "things themselves," nor is it only constructed by our discourses. Instead, it is an embodied being-in-the-world, a joint creation of our bodies in close interface with our environment.[17]

To insist on our carnality is to recognize the limits of anthropocentric dis-cursive reductionism, to ask about the social and biological genesis of our con-dition of being suspended in webs of symbols of our own making. Our grasp of and action upon the world are surely mediated by symbols and concepts. "[T]he world as we know is not pre-given; it is, rather, *enacted* through our history of structural coupling" with that world (Depraz, Varela, and Vermersch 2003: 157). Our lived reality emerges from the reciprocal exchanges between our embodied practices and material apparatuses (art, popular culture, tech-nology, and science) and the environment that is itself summoned and enacted by those practices and apparatuses. In this interplay, our systems of symbols represent malleable pragmatic responses to constraining and enabling bodily and environmental processes, to the "obduracy" and "affordancy" of "the earthly ground of rock and soil that we share with the other animals and the plants" (Abram 1996: 281). By obduracy, I mean "*the characteristic of reality to resist the will and intentionality of the psyche. If we try to walk through a wall without the benefit of a door, we will come up against the obdurate nature of reality*" (Laughlin and Throop 2006: 322, italics in the original). Affordancy, in turn, refers to what the environment "*offers* the animal, what it *provides* or *furnishes*, either for good or ill" (Gibson 1979: 127).

Like the tight coiling of the inside and outside of the flesh, language and the world have ways of "beckoning," "summoning," "invading," and "encroaching upon" each other in a non-dualistic manner. Both our material practices and the material world in which we are embedded are agentic. As Merleau-Ponty puts it: it is "flesh applied to a flesh." We will see in chapter 6, where I offer a more sustained critique of the excesses of social constructionism, that this same point is made by materialist feminists, such as Donna Haraway and Karen

Barad, as well as by science studies scholars like Andrew Pickering and Bruno Latour. Pickering (1995), for instance, talks about the "mangle of practice" to characterize the "dialectic of resistance and accommodation" through which human and nonhuman agencies co-emerge.

The insight that language is not the only form of material agency is crucial in my call for scholars to avoid semiotic reductionism and to engage in a holistic exploration of the diversity of practices that constitute religion as a constructed yet lived category. In this approach, signification, representation, and hermeneutics would be clusters of practices in a shifting interplay with other forms of material activity.

Merleau-Ponty's notions of the tacit cogito and the flesh call us to recognize the creative power of corporality, in the same way that, as we saw in the previous chapter, Spinoza argued that nature is endowed with power and agency. The body is not something we can reject or bracket (as if this were possible) in order to have Truth, be it as the Platonic forms, the Cartesian cogito, or the Husserlian transcendental ego. Rather, the body, with in all its materiality, positionality, finitude, and contingency, is essential to the production of our life-world. Both Husserl and Heidegger took significant steps to overcome the Cartesian dualism and its denigration of the body by embedding the self in the life-world and showing its historicality.[18] However, it is only with Merleau-Ponty that philosophy truly fulfills Nietzsche's call in his *Thus Spoke Zarathustra* to "remain faithful to the earth," not to believe the "despisers of life" who preach fixed suns in the beyond.[19]

In Merleau-Ponty, religion scholars can find the seeds of what Mark Taylor (2001: 204) calls "a radical style of *incarnational* thinking and practice." By placing carnality as the core of our being-in-the-world, Merleau-Ponty allows us to appreciate the full force of religious phenomena such as healing, glossolalia, conversion, trance, and other ecstatic states that may or may not involve the use of psychoactive components, as well as practices such as fasting, penance, dancing, pilgrimage, rites of passage, and funerary rituals. Further, a materialist phenomenology can recover the material dimensions of texts, doctrines, cosmologies, worldviews, narratives, and religious symbols, which have been the traditional concern of modern religious studies and which have been primarily understood through a hermeneutic, mentalist lens, as the ideational creations of the meaning-making religious person. A materialist phenomenology would explore how religious meanings are created and experienced by specific embodied individuals endowed with sensorimotor and cognitive capacities and limits, as they encounter the world praxically, as they shape and are shaped by the natural and social environments, and as they enter into power relations with other individuals with whom they share spaces of livelihood.

In the next chapter, I draw from Merleau-Ponty's non-reductive materi-alism to show how religious studies has confused phenomenology with certain kind of subjectivism linked to a transcendental idealism that posits the sacred as the foundational category for religious studies. This strategy has led to decontextualized analyses of religion that ignore or denigrate the body, prac-tices, and institutions. Using ethnographies that build on Husserl's, Hei-degger's, and Merleau-Ponty's work, I will also show how we can recover a non-reductive materialist phenomenology of religion that places the body and its processes and activities front and center.

4

The Phenomenology of Embodiment and the Study of Religion

Chapter 3 sketched broadly the evolution of phenomenology in order to highlight tendencies that have militated against a full recognition of the body's centrality in human experience. In particular, I showed how, despite the call to return to the things themselves, phenomenology has always been vulnerable to the twin threats of transcendental subjectivism and foundational idealism. Especially in its early Husserlian days, phenomenology relied on a heavily Cartesian-Kantian notion of the self, positing it as a fixed epistemological pivot, as a being engaged in the world primarily through its mental operations, not through its social practices and carnality. However, I also demonstrated that, from the outset, there were significant countercurrents within phenomenology that have affirmed the centrality of embodiment. Deployed strategically, these countercurrents can contribute to a rematerialization of the study of religion.

In this chapter, I show how transcendental subjectivism and foundational idealism in phenomenology as a philosophical movement reinforced anti-materialist and anti-somatic tendencies within the phenomenology of religion and history of religions, the two approaches that have defined the modern discipline of religious studies. Given the limited space, I can only provide a limited treatment of the rich school of phenomenology of religion proper, which runs from Pierre Chantepie de la Saussaye to Gerardus van der Leeuw. Detailed genealogies of this sort have already been produced and they have shown that the phenomenology of religion is a highly contested research programme, encompassing a diversity of perspectives, not all of which make explicit reference to Husserl.[1] In fact, Strenski (2006) makes the plausible case that phenomenology of religion owes more to Protestant theology, which was, in turn, influenced by

Schleiermacher, Fichte, and Hegel, than to Husserl. The need to develop a phe-nomenology of religion arose when Schleiermacher identified religion's essence as "intuition and feeling," the "innermost feelings of piety" that "are self-contained in their own coming and going." A special empathetic methodology was needed to retrieve these inward sentiments, since religion "maintains its own sphere and its own character only by completely removing itself from the sphere and character of speculation as well as from that of praxis" (Schleierm-acher 1988: 23).[2] Here, Schleiermacher was simply echoing the Protestant Ref-ormation's bias against potentially idolatrous images and superstitious public rituals, while also expressing the Romantic reaction against Enlightenment rationalism. Schleiermacher's view of religion is further elaborated by Rudolf Otto in *The Idea of the Holy*, where he identifies heart of religion in the "sudden, strong ebullitions of personal piety," the "stupor" that arises as we encounter "the wholly other," *mysterium tremendum et fascinans*. These ebullitions are only secondarily frozen in "the fixed and ordered solemnities of rites and lit-urgies, and . . . in the atmosphere that clings to old religious monuments and buildings, to temples and to churches" (Otto 1958: 12).

Building on Strenski, I contend that the rise of phenomenology of religion as a core method in the academic study of religion was the result of the conver-gence of German Idealism, Protestant Pietism, and the Husserlian (Cartesian and Kantian) temptation of transcendence and his adherence to the Augustin-ian motto "Do not wish to go out; go back into yourself. Truth dwells in the inner man." Phenomenology of religion operates with the notion that the self has a "glassy essence" (Rorty 1979), that the religious subject is potentially self-transparent, having privileged access to its thoughts, feelings, and emotions, which once retrieved can serve as the foundations for a theory of religion. Prot-estant Pietism and the early Husserl shared a mistrust of the "external" world and situated praxis, the former because it wanted to avoid appealing to media-tion in the relation between the believer and God (arguing against the efficacy of works in Catholicism) and the latter because it saw the contingencies of the external world as an obstacle to the recovery of the transcendental ego.

Certainly, internalism and abstraction in the study of religion cannot, in all fairness, be only attributed to early phenomenological approaches. Max Müller, considered to be the father of the "science of religion," proposed a theory of religion that contained these blind spots. Working also within the German Romantic tradition, he argued that religion originated in the feelings our ancestors experienced as they encountered "the infinite," as manifested the majestic powers of nature (Müller 2002: 167–91). These feelings, in turn, were mediated by language, which as time passed, came to stand for the experiences it meant to name, describe, and control. Müller theorized that language always bears the traces of decay, mutation, and transmigration of words and of the early transformations of nomina into noumena. Nevertheless, he believed that, as civilizations developed, language became more capable of abstract reflection on the universality of the consciousness of the infinite, making possible the rise of great speculative systems like Christianity and Vedantic Hinduism. Hence, in Müller's theory, we see the focus on inner religious experience mediated by symbolic systems, particularly sacred texts. The notion that philological approaches are the golden road to religion's essence, understood as a deep-seated "mental faculty," intuition, or consciousness, has been the mainstay of both traditional phenomenological and hermeneutic approaches. The consequences of Müller's theory of religion in the construction of "Hinduism" as a unified "textualized religion" are well known.[3] He—along with other Orientalists, Transcendentalists, and cosmopolitan indigenous intellectual elites like Swami Vivekananda, who translated India for the metropole—had a profound influence on how Hindu traditions are imagined in the West: "as interior, mystical, and other-worldly." As Diana Eck (1998: 11) points out, "one need only raise the head from the book to the image to see how mistakenly one-sided such a characterization is. The day to day life and ritual of Hindus is based not upon abstract interior truths, but upon the charged, concrete, and particular appearances of the divine in the substance of the material world."

Traditional phenomenology of religion is, therefore, hardly the only current that contributed to the flight from the body and materiality in religious studies. Nevertheless, just like Cartesian rationality hardened the ambivalent dualisms within Christianity and Greco-Roman thought by polarizing them and giving them firm, scientific, and secular foundations, a certain appropriation of phenomenology made internalism the basis for an autonomous scientific discipline of religion. As early phenomenologists of religion sought to set *Religionswissenschaft* apart from theology and speculative philosophy as a rigorous secular science, they borrowed, adapted, and often distorted analytical tools from Husserlian phenomenology. The result was a phenomenology of religion that on the surface renounced Christian exceptionalism but that at its heart was still beholden to the excarnate subjectivism of Protestant Christianity. The history of religions approach then appropriated the tools of phenomenology of religion, adding an ontological dimension (through a rereading of Otto's notion of the Holy) that did not challenge internalism, but rather accentuated their flight from the body.

To avoid getting bogged down on endless debates about the "essence" of the phenomenology of religion and its relation to the history of religions approach, I focus here on an attitude, shared by these two schools, that dominated the discipline of religion in the twentieth century about what is important in approaching religion, namely the believer's affective and cognitive experiences, of which practices, institutions, and material culture are mere external, surface manifestations. Through the strategic analysis of key texts and figures, I trace a widespread tendency in religious studies to treat inner subjective states as autonomous and to see "external" practices, institutions, and objects (including the body as both creative actor and constructed artifact) as derivative manifestations of those states.

I shall also argue that narrative theory and hermeneutics, which Gavin Flood (1999) has proposed as alternatives to the phenomenology's subjectivism and foundationalism, do not provide enough resources to recover the body in religious studies. In fact, in its overriding concern with signification and interpretation, often at the cost of ignoring practices aimed at other goals, hermeneutics shares a great deal with Müller's linguistification of religion. Hermeneutics' tendency toward symbolic reductionism stands in the way of a fuller appreciation of the multiplicity of religious materiality. A more productive solution to phenomenology's contradictions lies in recovering its seminal insights on embodiment, social practice, and emplacement.

I conclude the chapter by pointing to the emergence of phenomenology of the body in the study of religion that takes materiality seriously, developing the work of Heidegger and Merleau-Ponty on embodiment, existence, praxis, and space. This "new" phenomenology of religion will also sets the stage for a conversation in later chapters with other non-reductive forms of materialism, such as constructivism in it various forms as well as neurocognitive and evolutionary approaches, as part of an overall effort to rematerialize the study of religion.

TO CLASSIFY AND COMPARE: THE EARLY DAYS OF PHENOMENOLOGY IN THE STUDY OF RELIGION

The close connection between phenomenology and the study of religion goes back to the early days of the scientific study of religion. Twenty years after Max Müller's famous lectures at Royal Institute in London (1870), in which he advocated for an autonomous *Religionswissenschaft*, Dutch theologian Pierre D. Chantepie de la Saussaye in *Manual of the Science of Religion* defined the task of this science to be "the study religion in its essence and its manifestations" (1891: 7). To carry out this task, Chantepie de la Saussaye divides the science of religion into two branches. The first one is the history of religions, which contains an "ethnographical" approach that "gives us the details of the religions of the savage tribes, the so-called children of nature (*Naturvölker*), or that part of mankind [*sic*][4] that has no history," and a historical approach proper that follows the "development of the religions of the civilized nations." The second branch is the philosophy of religion which "treats religion according to its subjective and objective side, and therefore consists of a psychological and metaphysical part" (Chantepie de la Saussaye 1891: 8). In characterizing the relationship between these two branches of the science of religion, Chantepie de la Saussaye follows Hegel. In *The Phenomenology of the Spirit*, the latter had reconstructed the evolution of human spirit in its various manifestations across history and cultures, as a precondition for the systematic presentation of Absolute Truth. Similarly, Chantepie de la Saussaye (1891: 8) saw "the collecting and grouping of various religious phenomena" as a transitional step toward the philosophy of religion, to the consideration of the more foundational analysis of the psychological and metaphysical dimensions of religion.

The bipartite division of the science of religion leads Chantepie de la Saussaye to argue that the phenomenology of religion is not the mere ethnographic description of religious phenomena, nor is it a simple recounting of historical facts. Rather, "the phenomenology of religion is most closely connected with psychology, in so far as it deals with facts of human consciousness." This focus on the inner life is justified by the fact that "the outward forms of religion can only be explained from inward processes: religious acts, ideas, and sentiments are not distinguished from non-religious acts, ideas, and sentiments by any outward mark, but only by a certain inward relation" (Chantepie de la Saussaye 1891: 67). What defines the essence of religion is the religious person's intentionality as s/he relates the natural and supernatural worlds.

Chantepie de la Saussaye is clear that the study of the essence of religion is beyond phenomenology's purview, being the task of the philosophy of religion, particularly of metaphysics. Nevertheless, religious phenomenology prepares the ground for this metaphysical exploration by systematizing diverse religious phenomena, arranging them according to their essential features. Prima facie, the phenomenologist confronts a multiplicity of religious symbols, practices, and forms of organization. In order to make sense of this variegated reality, s/he must categorize and compare these varying religious manifestations across time and space by tracing the "religious impressions, sentiments, and states" that gave rise to them. Therefore, although "the richest material . . . for the phenomenology of religion is supplied by religious acts, cult, and customs," these practices and embodied habits are only important insofar as they serve as a "mirror that reflects something of [nations' and periods'] religious ideas and sentiments" (Chantepie de la Saussaye 1891: 69). To be sure, for Chantepie de la Saussaye, practices and institutions are central to religion, but this is so because they ensure its reproduction, not because they are the creatively constitute religion as a contingent but binding sociohistorical phenomenon. Practices are mere material vehicles to support and enhance particular types of inner religious life. "Cult is the form in which religion manifests, maintains, and extends itself. Rites are the bond of the unity of religion, by which individuals enter into communion with their brothers in the faith, however distant from them in time and space. Lastly, by means of rites, laymen, half-believers, and children are educated so as to become fit to participate in the benefits of religion" (Chantepie de la Saussaye 1891: 71).

Although Chantepie de la Saussaye wrote before Husserl, when he tells us that "religious states and sentiments are the efficient causes and forces of the external phenomena of religious life" (Chantepie de la Saussaye 1891: 67), his understanding of the phenomenology of religion dovetails nicely with Husserlian internalism, the claim that knowledge of the essential features of the phenomenal world must depart from and refer back to subject's inner dynamics. Moreover, Husserl's methodology of rigorous and gradual phenomenological reductions can offer a helpful tool to undertake Chantepie de la Saussaye's call to construct comparative taxonomies of religious forms. This is indeed what happens as the science of religion evolved into the twentieth century.

Writing just a few years after publication of *The Manual of the Science of Religion*, C. P. Tiele reiterates and builds on many of the arguments made by Chantepie de la Saussaye. For Tiele, the aim of the science of religion is to study "those manifestations of the human mind in words, deeds, customs, and institutions which testify to man's belief in the superhuman, and serve to bring him into relation with it" (Tiele 1979: 4). By claiming that the science of religion does not focus on the supernatural itself, but rather on the psychological and sociocultural implications of the belief in the supernatural throughout history, Tiele is introducing a form of bracketing that phenomenologists of religion will eventually come to associate with Husserl's *epoché*. This association is not unwarranted, for what Tiele is asking religion scholars to bracket or suspend is the natural attitude of the religious believer who takes the supernatural as given. For Tiele, the science of religion is not in the business of adjudicating religious truth claims, a fact that distinguishes it from theology.

Nonetheless, despite the focus on "wholly human phenomena," Tiele still preserves a Christian, more specifically Protestant, metaphysics. Drawing from Hegel, Tiele sees religion as a universal reality that evolves in history from nature cults toward its highest monotheistic and ethical forms. "Religion is certainly rooted in man's nature—that is, it springs from his inmost soul" (Tiele 1979: 15). However, just as adults have "once been helpless children," the notion of development applies to "mental endowments, of artistic skill, of individual character, and generally of civilization, art, science, and humanity. We therefore think that in view of what anthropological-historical investigation of religion has brought to light, we are fully entitled to apply the term to religion also" (Tiele 1979: 29). Religion's development for Tiele is not the "development of religious externals," or even of particular local forms of religious life, but is rather "the evolution of the religious idea in history, or better as the progress of the religious man, or of mankind as religious by nature" (Tiele 1979: 32). In other words, the phenomenology that Tiele is proposing has to do with systematic study of the religious mind. Like Chantepie de la Saussaye's privileging of religious ideas and sentiments over practices and institutions, Tiele's idealism contributes to the denial of the body and materiality in the formative stages of the science of religion.

Confronted with the evolution of religion, Tiele sees the task of scholar of religion as ultimately the retrieval, in a Hegelian fashion, of the deeper meaning, "the laws," behind the multiplicity of historical manifestations. This search for meaning in the "evolution of the religious idea" warrants a turn toward the discursive aspects of religion. Although religion combines belief and practice, ritual and myth, the scholar of religion recognizes that "doctrine, whatever be its form, mythological and poetical, or dogmatical and philosophical . . . [is] the fountainhead of each religion. The chief thing of all in religion is doubtless its spirit, yet it is the doctrine that affords us most light. Through it alone we can learn what man thinks of his God and of his relation to Him. Cult, ritual, and ceremonies teach me nothing when I contemplate them, unless I have some explanation of their meaning" (Tiele 1979: 22–23).

To discern the meaning of religion, the scholar needs to understand that religion is above all "a frame of mind adapted to the relation between man and his God." This is why religious practices "have value for our research only where we know the conception attached to them by the believers and thus learn their significance" (Tiele 1979: 25). This frame of mind is most directly expressed through the "mythology," which shapes and is reflected by rituals and institutions. Without an informing "doctrine" that makes sense of the believer's relation to the supernatural, religious practice would appear as mere mechanical behavior. Here, Tiele has arrived at a phenomenological-hermeneutic understanding of religion that is preoccupied with retrieving the religious subject's inner experiences, which are mediated by a web of discursive forms, ranging from myth to theology, that guide practice. As I shall show throughout this chapter, this understanding will dominate the field of religion, from Eliade's idea of religious rituals as the reenactment of primal narratives to Geertz's notion of religion as a model of and for cultural activity in the face of existential situations like suffering, bafflement, and moral evil.

William Brede Kristensen, one of Tiele's most distinguished students and the eventual holder of the famous Chair of History and Phenomenology of Religion in the theological faculty at the University of Leiden, elaborates on the ideas of the early Dutch phenomenologists of religion. Kristensen sees phenomenology of religion as the "systematic treatment of History of Religion. That is to say, its task is to classify and group the numerous and widely divergent data in such a way that an over-all view can be obtained of their religious content and the values they contain" (1960: 1). Kristensen, thus, equates phenomenology of religion with the comparative study of religion, a study that identifies "the similar facts and phenomena which it encounters in different religions, brings them together, and studies them in groups" (Kristensen 1960: 2). But it is not enough to discover commonalities and to order them in analytical categories. Ultimately, the task of the phenomenology of religion is "to become acquainted with the religious thought, idea or need which underlies the group of corresponding data." So that, for example, a phenomenologist of religion does not just recognize that sacrifice is a widespread religious phenomenon, or even categorize the different forms sacrifice takes across history and religions. Rather s/he is interested in uncovering "the basic idea of sacrifice." The scholar of religion wishes to know more: "what religious need has caused men, in all times and places, to present offerings to the gods?" The answer to this question is "not to be sought in the outward traits which are held in common, in how priests are clad and how rites are divided among them. It is the common meaning of the sacrificial acts that is important, and that we must try to understand" (Kristensen 1960: 3).

For Kristensen, then, phenomenology of religion is "at once systematic History of Religion and applied Philosophy of Religion." It is the rigorous, empirically based, and comparative search for common religious patterns that leads "to a deeper insight into the essence of a whole group of similar phenomena" (1960: 417). In that sense, phenomenology of religion "makes use of comparison only in order to gain a deeper insight into the self-subsistent, not the relative, meaning of each of the historical data. It wishes only to learn to understand the conception of the believers themselves, who always ascribe an absolute value to their faith" (418).

The "self-subsistent . . . meaning[s]" of religion that Kristensen is looking for are not to be found by simply capturing the morphology and evolution of common patterns.[5] The point of view of the believer is crucial.[6] "The scholar must be able to separate the essentially religious from the unessential in all the given historical phenomena which are object of research. In order to reach the right conclusions he must have a feeling for religion, an awareness of what religion is" (Kristensen 1960: 12). The scholar must "investigate what religious value the believers (Greeks, Babylonians, Egyptians, etc.) attached to their faith, what religion meant for them. It is their religion that we want to understand, and not our own" (13).

Just like Husserl is aware of the danger of solipsism behind his quest for the noetic structures of the transcendental ego, Kristensen recognizes the difficulty of understanding the believer's religious life-world. This is why he argues that phenomenology of religion is not about certainties but about approximations. Borrowing from the hermeneutic tradition of Schleiermacher and Dilthey, Kristensen argues that the scholar of religion can approximate the believer's religion through empathy and intuition. "We make use of our own religious experience in order to understand the experience of others. We should never be able to describe the essence of religion if we did not know from our own experience what religion is (not: what the essence of religion is!)." Therefore, "[a]n appeal is made to our feeling for the subjects which we want to understand, a feeling which gives us a sureness of our 'touch.' There is an appeal made to the indefinable sympathy we must have for religious data which sometimes appear so alien to us" (Kristensen 1960: 10).

Empathy and intuition are not, however, exact sciences. Thus, while "we must always try in our study to put ourselves in the position of the believer, because it is there alone that the religious reality is to be found which we wish to understand," we should not expect to be able to become one with the religious practitioner. For "the research of Phenomenology is not the practice of religion. The attempt to understand religious phenomena historically and psychologically is a reflective and intellectual activity, not a religious one. We come to see the absolute character of particular religious data in an approximate way, but never more than approximately" (Kristensen 1960: 423). There is then a "distance" between the scholar of religion and the believer, which mirrors the irresolvable gap in Husserlian phenomenology between two irreducible egos seeking to establish intersubjectivity. The scholar "cannot identify himself with [the religion] as the believer does. We cannot become Mohammedans [sic] when we try to understand Islam, and if we could, our study would be at an end: we should ourselves then directly experience the reality." The scholar of religion can only engage in "imaginative reexperiencing," "since the 'existential' nature of the religious datum is never disclosed by research. That cannot be defined" (Kristensen 1960: 7).

In his insistence that we take each religion seriously on its own terms, rather than reducing it to a stage in the evolution of humanity's religiosity, Kristensen follows Husserl's call to return to the things themselves, or in Merleau-Ponty's words, to "put essences back into existence." He goes beyond Chantepie de la Saussaye and Tiele in differentiating the study of religion not only from other disciplines like theology and philosophy, but also from the actual practice of religion. The scholar of religion can never be an insider when approaching religious phenomena comparatively; nor can s/he be a total outsider. This neither-nor position requires special theoretical and methodological tools, which mark the study of religion as its own discipline.

Kristensen, however, reiterates the Chantepie de Saussaye's and Tiele's language of depth, underlying essences, inwardness, and meaning, exacerbating phenomenology of religion's flight from the body, historical practices, and material reality. Kristensen endorses the idealist essentialism of his predecessors through a focus on meaning and his reduction of meaning to the "basic idea" behind the diversity of religious practices. Moreover, by linking this idea to the inner life of the believer, he engages in the same subjectivism that runs from St. Paul and Augustine through Descartes and Husserl.

Phenomenology of religion arguably reaches its pinnacle with Gerardus van der Leeuw, a student of Kristensen's at Leiden. Van der Leeuw develops the school's epistemological foundations, making explicit references to Dilthey, Husserl, and Weber. According to van der Leeuw, while the natural scientist works by distancing her/himself for the object of study, "the psychologist and historian should, after having started likewise and after having ascertained all effects of the temporal and spatial distance, make another effort and penetrate into the object. This is what is called 'empathy,' transposing oneself into the object or re-experiencing it" (1973: 401). Here van der Leeuw borrows the notion of re-experiencing from Dilthey, who had argued that the historian is capable of grasping a particular *Zeitgeist* by standing in the flow of history, since this flow is nothing more than the unfolding of humanity's creative powers. Experiencing other times, cultures, and religions is possible because we are part of the same meaning-making humanity. Thus, phenomenology is not like behaviorist psychology and other forms of positivism, whose modus operandi is comparable to

someone drawing up the water of a stream in innumerable buckets. All these buckets together will never constitute the stream. Life has been exhausted in the full meaning of the word. He who wants to experience the stream in its living coolness must learn how to swim. But this too is an art. Here the phenomenological analyst makes his appearance. He is the swimmer familiar with the stream. He does not dissect the psychological phenomena like the experimentalist does; he takes them as they present themselves. He tries to contemplate the essence of the phenomena, and not to comprehend their factual existence. He analyzes in an intuitive, not in a rational manner; he is concerned not with empirically comprehensible events, but with events that are directly intelligible in their general being. (van der Leeuw 1973: 402)

Only after the phenomenologist's "spontaneously warm," "living and loving devotion to experience," can phenomenological bracketing take place. The *epoché* seeks to identify the "structural relations" that make a particular experience into a meaningful whole. Van der Leeuw is here reading Husserlian phenomenology through the lens of hermeneutics. The task is not just to isolate in a static manner the essential components of a given religious experience but to understand how the parts originate from and constitute the whole. For van der Leeuw, the *epoché* is a divinatory hermeneutic circle, a skillful simultaneous engagement with parts and wholes, through which the phenomenologist comes to understand the religious experience as a single, dynamic process. The structure that this hermeneutic circle recovers is "an organic whole which cannot be analyzed into its own constituents, but which can from these be comprehended; or, in other terms, a fabric of particulars, not to be compounded by the addition of these, nor the deduction of one from the others, but again only *understood* as a whole" (van der Leeuw 1963: 672).

Phenomenological bracketing, in turn, leads to a deeper level of analysis: ideal types. Drawing from Max Weber, van der Leeuw sees ideal types not as generalizations of structural relations that become overarching theories that predict the lawful behavior of objects, as in the natural sciences. Rather, ideal types are strategic constructs that the phenomenologist creates by highlighting salient structural relations in order to make sense cogently of the plethora of empirical data, the multiplicity of religious beliefs and practices. An ideal type "in itself . . . has no reality; nor is it a photography of reality. Like structure, it is timeless and need not actually occur in history. Nevertheless, it is alive and appears to us" (van der Leeuw 1963: 673). Ideal types represent the manner in which religious phenomena appear to the scholar after s/he has applied various forms of phenomenological bracketing.

Agreeing with Kristensen that the phenomenologist of religion can only approximate the "thing itself," the religious experience in all its immediacy, van der Leeuw stresses that "phenomenology is the systematic discussion of what appears. 'Religion,' however, is an ultimate experience that evades our observation, a revelation which in its very essence is, and remains, concealed" (van der Leeuw 1963: 683).

There are three significant aspects of van der Leeuw's phenomenology of religion worth highlighting for our intents and purposes. The first one relates to the "entry point" of phenomenological analysis, which demands the erasure of the distance between the scholar and the religious practitioner. This erasure does not just call for empathy, "a self-denying devotion" to and immersion in experience, but the elision of the constraining and enabling power of time and space ("all effects of the temporal and spatial distance"). The phenomenologist can enter the stream of religious experience only by bracketing context, by suspending the positionality of the scholar and religious practitioner, their embeddedness in political, social, cultural, and ecological dynamics. To the extent that van der Leeuw considers positionality at all, it is within a spiritualized and unified flow of history. Thus, even though the reexperiencing a religious phenomenon is not a rational but an intuitive phenomenon, it is ultimately a disembodied and dematerialized one.

Second, the critical step that distinguishes phenomenology of religion from theology and from the practice of religion is the *epoché*. The latter is what marks the break between phenomenology as "the systematic discussion of what appears," the study of the structural features of religious experience, and religion as revelation. Phenomenology of religion is not

> theology. For theology shares with philosophy the claim to search for truth, while phenomenology, in this respect, exercises the intellectual suspense of the *epoché*. But the contrast lies deeper even than this. Theology discusses not merely a horizontal line leading, it may be, to God, nor only a vertical, descending from God and ascending to Him. Theology speaks about God Himself. For phenomenology, however, God is neither subject nor object; to be either of these He would have to be a phenomenon—that is, He would have to appear. But He does not appear: at least not so that we can comprehend and speak about Him. (van der Leeuw 1963: 687–88)

Here we see how, despite giving the *epoché* a different reading than that intended by Husserl, the most accomplished version of phenomenology of religion draws from the Husserlian conceptual apparatus to mark its disciplinary boundaries and define its scholarly identity. The trouble is that what is taken from Husserlian phenomenology is precisely that which Heidegger and Merleau-Ponty have shown to be the most problematic: the bracketing of the body and the lifeworld, understood not as spiritualized connection with humanity, but as a world of practices and emplacement. The discipline of religion inherits an internalist phenomenology that is only prevented from utterly falling into the traps of solipsism and transcendental foundationalism by hermeneutics. As we see in the case of van der Leeuw, through hermeneutics, phenomenology of religion emphasizes the fact that empathy is possible because there is a unity of history as the human spirit expresses itself. Hermeneutics also stresses the intuitive dimensions of knowledge, moving away from the search for foundational truths in Husserlian phenomenology. Hermeneutics, however, can do little to hold in check the anti-materialist tendencies behind concepts like empathy and understanding. I shall have more to say about hermeneutics later in the chapter, when I discuss ways to recovering key insights about embodiment in a rematerialized phenomenology of religion.

Thirdly and finally, by making revelation the essence of religion (the thing in itself), van der Leeuw paves the way for the turn toward the sacred as an ontological category in Mircea Eliade's work. In a passage that could have been written by Eliade, van der Leeuw writes:

> . . . religion implies that man does not simply accept the life that is given to him. In life he seeks power; and if he does not find this, or not to the extent that satisfies him, then he attempts to draw the power, in which he believes, into his own life. He tries to elevate life, to enhance its value, to gain for it some deeper and wider meaning. In this way, however, we find ourselves on the horizontal line: religion is the extension of life to its uttermost limits. The religious man desires richer, deeper, wider life: he desires power for himself. In other terms: in and about his own life man seeks something that is superior, whether he wishes merely to make use of this or to worship it. (van der Leeuw 1963: 679)

In this passage, van der Leeuw opens the phenomenology of religion, already beset with a dismissal of context, embodiment, and material, to an even more deleterious form of transcendentalism: the notion that religion has an essence, which is not only autonomous but ultimately determinative of historical expressions. The essence of religion is the sacred, as being-itself, as the ground of all there is. And given the irreducibility of the sacred to the contingencies of the world, we can only study religion indirectly, through its hierophanies, which appear to us in cross-cultural patterns. Thus, phenomenology of religion gives ways to the new Eliadean synthesis in the history of religions school.

MIRCEA ELIADE: PHENOMENOLOGY AT THE SERVICE OF ONTO-THEOLOGY

It is debatable whether Eliade can be considered a phenomenologist of religion at all. In fact, he sees his history of religions approach in creative tension with phenomenology of religion, both complementary ingredients of an integral *Religionswissenschaft* (Eliade 1969: 9). More specifically, Eliade critiques van der Leeuw for not taking "the history of religious structures" seriously. The weakness of van der Leeuw's approach lies in the failure to recognize that "even the most elevated religious expression . . . presents itself through specific structures and cultural expressions which are historically conditioned. As a matter of fact, van der Leeuw never attempted a religious morphology or a genetical phenomenology of religion" (Eliade 1969: 35).

At least on the surface, Eliade presents himself as a historicist and a materialist in tension with phenomenology's search for eidetic structures. As he starkly puts it: "There is no such thing as a 'pure' religious datum, outside of history, for there is no such thing as a human datum that is not at the same time a historical datum. Every religious experience is expressed and transmitted in a particular historical context" (Eliade 1969: 7). Therefore, the task of the historian of religions is to study hierophanies, the manifestations of the sacred in history. "Every hierophany we look at is also an historical fact. Every manifestation of the sacred takes place in some historical situation. Even the most personal and transcendant mystical experiences are affected by the age in which they occur" (Eliade 1996: 2). Moreover, many of these hierophanies take material form—sacred stones, trees, animals, mountains, springs, rivers, planets, kings, and so on. The material nature of hierophanies is the inescapable result of what Eliade calls the "paradox" or the "dialectic of the sacred," whereby the sacred always "expresses itself through something other than itself," through the profane, which it then transforms into the sacred. The process behind the dialectic of the sacred is *coincidentia oppositorum*, the "coexistence of contradictory essences: sacred and profane, spirit and matter, eternal and non-eternal" (Eliade 1996: 29). To be a historian of religions, it would seem, is to be a materialist, a scholar interested in embodied and emplaced religious expressions in history.

Despite the avowed tensions with phenomenology of religion, Eliade, like Kristensen and van der Leeeuw, stresses the need for the religion scholar to take the religious person's point of view. "The ultimate aim of the historian of religions is to understand, and to make understandable to others, religious man's behavior and mental universe" (Eliade 1959a: 162). The key for the modern scholar of religion lies in bracketing the secular skepticism of his/her age, in order to understand the power that the religious person encounters in hierophanies. However, because Eliade believes that modernity has disenchanted reality, dulling our sense for the sacred, the scholar of religion should not be primarily interested in contemporary experiences of the sacred. In fact, in the present age, one is more likely to find the life-world littered by "hybrid forms of black magic and sheer travesty of religion . . . countless 'little religions' that proliferate in all modern cities . . . pseudo-occult, neospiritualistic, or so-called hermetic churches, sects, or schools . . . all these phenomena [which] belong to the sphere of religion, even if they almost always present the aberrant aspects of pseudomorphs" (Eliade 1959a: 206). Thus, to approach the real power of the sacred, of which many present religious expressions are mere "degenerations" or "caricatures," the scholar of religion must turn his/her gaze toward the "primitive man." For

> the man of archaic societies tends to live as much as possible *in* the sacred or in close proximity to consecrated objects. The tendency is perfectly understandable, because, for primitives as for the man of all pre-modern societies, the *sacred* is equivalent to a *power*, and in the last analysis, to *reality*. The sacred is saturated with *being*. Sacred power means reality and at the same time enduringness and efficacy. The polarity sacred-profane is often expressed as an opposition between *real* and *unreal* or pseudoreal. Thus it is easy to understand that religious man deeply desires to be, to participate in reality, to be saturated with power. (Eliade 1959a: 13)

In approaching so-called primitive societies, Eliade is not interested in the particularities of the ethnos. He does not aspire to construct a painstaking "thick description" of the native's local, ever-changing intersubjective world, as an interpretive ethnographer working in Clifford Geertz's mold would. Instead, Eliade is interested in the "primitive man" as the privileged point of entry in the journey toward the origins of religion.[7] Making the same argument that Durkheim leveled in his *Elementary Forms of Religious Life* (1965) against arm-chair anthropologists like E. B. Tylor and James Frazer, Eliade writes that "the historian of religions aims to familiarize himself with the greatest possible number of religions, especially with archaic and primitive religions, where he has a chance to encounter certain religious institutions still in their elementary stages" (1959b: 89).

However, unlike Durkheim, Eliade is not after the simplest forms of religious life out of which more complex religions evolved out of a process of socioeconomic differentiation. Rather, Eliade wants to study early peoples because he thinks they provide an open window to the essence of humanity, which in *illo tempore* was inextricably bound up with the sacred. Eliade constructs his abstraction of "the primitive man" as a special species of the genus *homo religiosus*, whom he conceives as the "total man." In other words, "the history of religions opens the way to a philosophical anthropology. For the sacred is a universal dimension and . . . the beginnings of culture are rooted in religious experiences and beliefs" (Eliade 1996: 9). What the historian of religions is ultimately after is "the original religious matrix" that grounds our *Dasein*, to use a Heideggerian term. S/he seeks to "grasp the permanence of what has been called man's specific existential situation of 'being in the world,' for the experience of the sacred is its correlate. In fact, becoming aware of his own mode of being and assuming his presence in the world together constitute a 'religious experience" (Eliade 1996: 9).

As Murphy (2001) rightly argues, *homo religiosus* functions in the Eliadean conceptual framework as a religious version of Husserl's transcendental subjectivity, whose worldview the scholar of religion must understand in order to retrieve the true power of the sacred. Eliade also borrows from phenomenology the language of depth, universal structures, foundations, irreducibility, and autonomy to illuminate *homo religiosus*'s mental world and to separate it from the "terrors of history," the contingencies that have made secularization possible. It is true that the historian of religion uses "an empirical method" in approaching "religio-historical facts." Yet, s/he "completes his[/her] historical work as phenomenologist or philosopher of religion." S/he applies herself/himself "to deciphering in the temporally and historically concrete the destined course of experiences that arise from an irresistible human desire to transcend time and history. All authentic religious experience implies a desperate effort to disclose the foundation of things, the ultimate reality" (Eliade 1959b: 88).

For Eliade, just as in Husserl's case, phenomenology is a tool to search for foundations. Borrowing from Otto, Eliade sees the recovery of the sacred as an a priori category of existence as the ultimate task of the historian of religions.[8] The goal of history of religions is "to identify the presence of the transcendent in human experience, to isolate, within the vast mass of the 'unconscious,' that which is transconscious . . . 'to unmask' the presence of the transcendent and the suprahistoric in everyday life" (Otto quoted in Eliade 1982: 148). To characterize the sacred as an a priori, Eliade strikes a decidedly Cartesian-Kantian-Husserlian tone, rather that the Hegelian-Diltheyan historicist one taken by some of the Dutch phenomenologists. "The sacred is not a stage in the history of consciousness, it is a structural element *of* that consciousness. Experience of the sacred is inherent in man's mode of being in the world. Without experience of the real—and of what is not real—the human being would be unable to construct himself" (Eliade 1982: 154).

Eliade, in effect, places phenomenology at the service of ontology, of the search for the "spiritual unity subjacent to the history of humanity" (1969: 70). After all, archaic religious symbols, as the most poignant ciphers of the religious man's *Weltanschauung*, carry an "ontology . . . a presystematic ontology, the expression of a judgment about the world and simultaneously about human existence" (1959b: 70). In the previous chapter, we saw how Heidegger also used phenomenology to ask ontological questions. However, in contrast to the early Heidegger, who understood ontology as the world that *Dasein* discloses to itself through its historical and social practices, Eliade seems at times to associate *ontos*, that is, the sacred, with the noumenal, Being-itself, a supra-historical essence that acts in space and time. Taking a Heideggerian view of ontology as the historico-praxical conditions through which Dasein discloses being to itself would imply the sacred as *ontos* would be analyzable through the tools of the interpretive social sciences. But this would run counter to Eliade's wish to treat religion as sui generis, through the autonomous discipline of history of religions. Therefore, Eliade must stress the total irreducibility and alterity of the sacred: the sacred is the *ganz Andare* (wholly other) that founds and drives history through its hierophanies. Human beings tend to experience these hierophanies in archetypal ways, and thus the need for phenomenology and other tools like psychoanalysis, hermeneutics, and structuralism to understand the meaning of these experiences and trace their connection to the "ontic primordium" of the sacred (Smith 1982: 42).

Eliade, as McCutcheon correctly points out, "sets up an implicit distinction between the study of religious aspects of human life and the study of that which is expressed in these varied forms, the study of the sacred conceived as an ahistorical agent that operates outside and through the natural world" (1997: 13). This distinction is a deepening of van der Leeuw's proposal to study "religion in essence and manifestation," where manifestation as the denigrated term in the duality stands for the external, material dimensions of religion. With his pursuit of religious ontology, Eliade has exacerbated the disembodied and anti-materialist tendencies already apparent in the work of Kristensen, van der Leeuw, and other phenomenologists of religion. Despite the claim that the sacred is always manifested in history and in material objects, Eliade's reliance on the *homo religiosus* as a transcendental subjectivity and on the sacred as Being-itself ultimately leads away from history, materiality, and praxis. According to Strenski (2003: 1), "while Eliade was particularly sensitive to religious space, and to the riotous array of concrete sacred objects, such as trees, ropes, rocks and such . . . he never really accepted religious materiality on its own terms, in the religiousness of its material historicity. For Eliade, material things were religious in spite of being material—because they transcended their historicity and materiality in being symbols of divine archetypes." Moreover, Eliade reaffirms Chantepie de la Saussaye's and Tiele's prejudice against rituals. In his view, "symbol and myth will give a clear view of the modalities [of the sacred] that a rite can never do more than suggest. A symbol and a rite . . . are on such different levels that the rite can never reveal what the symbol reveals" (Eliade 1996:9).[9]

Phenomenology, thus, makes its way into the dominant school of religious studies not as the investigation of the cultural, historical, and psychosomatic conditions that make experience possible, but as the quest for *homo religiosus*'s deep mental structures, which are manifested most clearly in myths and symbols (as opposed to embodied and emplaced rituals) and which point to the irreducible reality of the sacred. The history of religion approach appropriates phenomenology as onto-theology.[10]

SCENES FROM THE "POST-ELIADEAN" ERA

The synthesis between history of religions and phenomenology of religion built on the creative tension between surface and depth, appearance and essence, performance and structure, change and continuity, and materiality and worldview became dominant in the study of religion in the United States from the 1950s to 1980s. Raffaele Pettazzoni, who was associated with both the history and phenomenology of religions, put matters well when he writes in an influential essay:

> Religious phenomenology has nothing to do with the historical development of religion. . . . It sets itself above all to separate out the different structures from the multiplicity of religious phenomena. The structure, and it alone, can help us find out the meaning of religious phenomena, independently of their position in time and space and of their attachment to a given cultural environment. Thus the phenomenology of religion reaches a universality which of necessity escapes a history of religion devoted to the study of particular religions, and for that very reason liable to the inevitable splitting up of specialization. (1967: 218)

Phenomenology of religion, however, "depends" of the history of religions for its comparative raw material and to correct mistaken ascriptions of meaning as it is confronted with new data. Phenomenology and history of religions are "in reality simply two interdependent instruments of the same science, two forms of the science of religion, whose composite unity corresponds to that of its subject, that is to say of religion, in its two distinct components, interior experience and exterior manifestation" (218) Note how Pettazzoni equates phenomenology with interiority and essences, while he associates history with externality and particulars. This understanding of phenomenology as the quest for the internal, transcendental structures of experiences, which in the case of religious studies, is precisely the type of anti-materialist phenomenology that I criticized in the previous chapter through Heidegger's and Merleau-Ponty's work. And it is this phenomenology of religion that we must overcome if we are to escape the somatophobic internalism and idealism that has dominated much of the contemporary study of religion.

This internalism and idealism makes its way into the post-Eliadean scene through the persistent stress on religious meaning and worldviews. For example, Jacques Waardenburg, while criticizing classical phenomenologists of religion for a "strongly idealistic bent" that absolutized categories "such as the Holy, the Completely Different (*das ganz Andare*), Power," still makes meaning, intentionality, and *mentalité* the core concerns of phenomenology. To understand a religious expression "implies what this expression means to the person concerned, and that core of this meaning, phenomenologically speaking, is the intention which has given rise to the expression. Now in my opinion the scholar's whole effort to interpret what we have called religious meaning, intention and intended object of the religious expression, implies the reconstitution of a mental universe on his part, a universe which is aligned upon what appears to be the basic problems of the culture or person studied . . ." (Waardenburg 1978: 103).

The phenomenological focus on the "mental universe" of the religious person is explicit in Ninian Smart. He endorses the *epoché*, which allows the religion scholar to distance him/herself from the believer and to describe the latter's beliefs and activities without making value judgments on their content and truth claims. However, phenomenology "needs to be evocative as well as descriptive. . . . Thus the neutralism of phenomenological inquiry aimed at revealing the content of religious pictures is not 'flat' neutralism, that is, it should not engage in those deflationary and wooden descriptions which destroy the evocative" (Smart 1973: 34). The religion scholar must not engage in a "'flat' neutralism" that is merely descriptive of the overt characteristics of religious behavior. Instead, his/her phenomenology entails an "empathetic neutralism" that enters "into the experiences and intentions of religious participants" (Smart 1996: 2). These experiences and intentions form coherent worldviews. Smart is careful to emphasize that worldviews are not "something cerebral." They "should be studied at least as much through their practices as through their beliefs. So when I use 'worldview' I mean incarnated worldview, where the values and beliefs are embedded in practice. That is they are expressed in action, laws, symbols, organizations" (Smart 1996: 2–3). To study these multiple expressions in a dynamic and holistic manner, Smart suggests seven dimensions of the sacred, ranging from "the ritual or practical dimension" and "doctrinal or philosophical dimension" to the "organization and social component."

Notice here that, despite the significant move away from subjectivism, by placing the religious person within shared worldviews and embedding these worldviews in a *Lebenswelt* that includes sociopolitical and material dimensions, it is "values" and "beliefs" that constitute the core of worldviews that get represented in particular practices and religious artifacts. The underlying values and beliefs give coherence and continuity to the diverse expressions that the worldview encompasses. "The study of religions and secular worldviews— what I have termed 'worldview analysis'—tries to depict the history and nature of the beliefs and symbols which form a deep part of the structure of human consciousness and society" (Smart 1983: 2).

Smart's stress on beliefs and symbols and his quest to explore the deep structures of consciousness ends up reinforcing the mind-body, internal-external dualism. Smart assumes a mentalist perspective that gives the symbolic, ideational, and axiological dimensions of religion privileged agency: essentially they function as the underlying "models of and for" practices, institutions, and other material expressions. In contrast, taking a non-reductive materialist approach would entail seeing values and beliefs as the changing and contested products of embodied, integrated practices, which are constantly trying to normalize the boundaries and configurations of the worldviews that traditional religious scholars construct as coherent belief systems.

The tensions and contradictions inherent in the split between surface and depth, practice and symbol, externality and internality are even more dramatic in Wilfred Cantwell Smith. While he challenges the category of religion in ways that anticipate critiques by J. Z. Smith, Willi Braun, and Russell McCutcheon, W. C. Smith replaces the term with the highly problematic faith-tradition binomial.[11] For W. C. Smith, faith is ultimately "something too profound, too personal, and too divine for public exposition"; it lies in "the hearts of men" as they seek transcendence (Smith 1991: 170, 185). Nevertheless, "faith can be expressed—more historically: faith has been expressed, observably—in words, both prose and poetry; in patterns of deeds, both ritual and morality; in art, in institutions, in law, in community . . ." (Smith 1991: 171). This is where tradition comes in: "the cumulative tradition is the mundane result of the faith of men in the past and is the mundane cause of the faith of men in the present" (Smith 1991: 186).

Smith does not deny that tradition is active. In fact, religion is "the dialectical process between the mundane and the transcendent," such that tradition not only expresses personal faith but also informs it by providing the resources to experience transcendence in given ways, ways that can be shared with others. "The tradition, in its tangible actualities, and his fellows, in their comparable participation, nourish [the believer's] faith and give it shape." However, the locus for "dialectical process between the mundane and transcendent" is "the personal faith and the lives of men and women not altogether observable and not to be confined within any intelligible limits" (Smith 1991: 187). There is an irreducible element of religion that cannot be captured by any approach focusing simply on the externals. This irreducible element has to do with the internal life of the religious subject. And yet, we are told that the believer's faith "is new every morning. It is personal; it is no more independent of his mundane environment (including the religious tradition) that is his personal life at large."

Smith, it seems, wants to have it both ways, recognizing the believer's situatedness while preserving a mysterious, irreducible subjective core that points ultimately to supra-historical transcendence, to God, to be more specific. "The ideal towards which I move is not an ideal of my own faith but is God himself, and my neighbour himself. Faith is not part of eternity; it is my present awareness of eternity" (Smith 1991: 192). Once again, phenomenology is subsumed under onto-theology in the effort to avoid reductionism. A non-reductive materialist phenomenology, nevertheless, does not need to rely on this internalism buttressed by an appeal to ontology. We can recognize that consciousness, and particularly religious experience, may not be fully definable, fully reducible either to neural processes or sociohistorical practices, or to a combination of both. Certain aspects of religious experience—or any experience, for that matter—may be emergent effects of the complex and fluid interplay among ecological, neurosomatic, and sociocultural factors. But this non-reductive, nontotalizing phenomenology of embodiment has little in common with the essentialist, subjectivist, and idealist phenomenology that has been appropriated by religious studies.

HERMENEUTICS AND NARRATIVES TO THE RESCUE?

Critiques of the phenomenology of religion are not new, as the references to McCutcheon, Strenski, Wiebe, and Murphy show. In recent years, phenomenology of religion has been most explicitly challenged by Gavin Flood. Many of the arguments he makes in his *Beyond Phenomenology: Rethinking the Study of Religion* resonate with the points I argue. He contends that phenomenology of religion "contains implicit assumptions about an ahistorical subjectivity—it entails a philosophy of consciousness—that is inevitably imported into practice" (Flood 1999: 7). And by "adopting phenomenology, the science of religion carries with it the idea of the detached observer or epistemic subject who understands the presentations to consciousness from a privileged distance" (Flood 1999: 117). This distancing allows the phenomenologist to ignore the body and claim that s/he can retrieve the unchanging essence of religion through successive reduction.

Against phenomenology's reliance on transtemporal subjects and objects, Flood counterposes a "philosophy of the sign," which holds that "the self is a sign-bearing agent embodied within social and historical contexts, within narratives, rather than a disengaged consciousness" (Flood 1999: 14). Borrowing from Hans-Georg Gadamer, Paul Ricoeur, and Mikhail Bakhtin, Flood argues that selfhood is possible in the first place because individuals are "emplotted" in public webs of signification, in shared narratives that provide the horizons of intelligibility. Since for Flood, following Ricoeur, these narratives are stories not only told but also lived, "the shift to the sign deprivileges consciousness, experience and inner states, and places religion squarely within culture and history" (Flood 1999: 118). Thus, "[r]ather than the transcendental ego performing the acts of bracketing, eidetic reduction and empathy, in order to objectively understand the data presented to it, we have the observer within her own narratives engaging in a dialogical process with another narrative" (Flood 1999: 137–38). Rather than looking for deep and timeless typologies and structures, the religion scholar takes "the creation of typologies to be the mapping of intersubjective networks of communication and the relating of diverse networks to each other" (Flood 1999: 98). The shift of emphasis from consciousness to communication and signification leads the scholar of religion to focus on texts as narratives in space and time. "Text, a complex of signs given coherence through narrative, is therefore the primary object of investigation for the study of narrative" (Flood 1999: 121).

There is no question that Flood's appeal to narratives has enormous salutary effects for the discipline of religion. Just like Heidegger bypassed the danger of solipsism in early Husserl by introducing hermeneutics, Flood opens up the possibility of studying the inescapably social and historic nature of religion, expressed materially in shared signs. As he puts it, "[r]ather than the cogito with its stream of cogitations being the methodological basis of inquiry, the center of gravity becomes the intersubjectivity of the social world mediated through language" (Flood 1999: 124). This is precisely the approach that anthropologist Clifford Geertz develops so masterfully in his ethnographies. Nonetheless, the turn to narrative is insufficient to foreground the body and the multiplicity of its material practices. Ricoeur's valuable insight that culture and praxis can be approached as texts has interacted in deleterious ways with the strong tradition in *Religionswissenschaft* which equates religion with the great sacred texts. By claiming that "there is no lived reality external to and unmediated by narrative" (Flood 1999: 118), narrativism has radicalized Max

Müller's assumption that the secrets of a religion lie in language, in its myths and doctrines as enshrined in the canonical literature. Moreover, it is not only that texts take precedence over any other form of religious production but that all religious activities, regardless of their diverse contexts, aims, means, and effects are primarily understood as texts to be read and decoded. As Flood puts it: "religious research needs to develop the anthropological reading of texts, rather than the simply philological, and to recognize the importance of texts in fieldwork" (1999: 236).

The main weakness of narrativism is that it overplays the ontogenic power of language, not just defending its mediating role but often reducing all materiality to discourse and textuality. As we shall see in the next chapter, philosopher Judith Butler falls into a similar trap when she reduces all materiality to the materiality of the signifier, that is, to the power that latter has to form the subject with a "sexed," and "natural" body through iteration. According to Susan Bordo, this "discourse foundationalism," despite its powerful challenge to disembodied universalism, ultimately refuses to acknowledge that "our materiality (which includes history, race, gender, and so forth, but also the biology and evolutionary history of our bodies, and our dependence on the natural environment) impinges on us—shapes, constrains, and empowers us—both as thinkers and knowers, and also as 'practical,' fleshy bodies" (Bordo 1998: 91).

We will see in chapter 7 that ongoing research on cognition and perception indeed shows the central role of language, particularly of metaphors (Lakoff and Johnson 1999). The point, thus, is not to reject the narrativist turn, but to nuance and contextualize it vis-à-vis other approaches that seek to highlight multiple forms of embodiment, practice, and emplacement. We have seen in the previous chapter how Merleau-Ponty offers a radical vision of a materialist phenomenology that recognizes the limits of language and strains to intuit the "unspoken" enfleshed conditions that make consciousness and language possible.

Reference to Merleau-Ponty brings me to a final critique of Flood's attempt to replace phenomenology wholesale with a philosophy of the sign. For all his sophistication and careful argumentation, Flood tends to present a very one-sided view of phenomenology. He reads Husserl's entire philosophical output through the prism of his early Cartesianism-Kantianism. Such a reading ignores Husserl's important insights on embodiment, space, and the life-world. We saw how these insights provided the bases on which Heidegger and Merleau-Ponty built more historicist, praxis-oriented, and somatic phenomenological approaches. Because Flood ignores this whole materialist tradition, he presents a static and simplistic version of phenomenology that can be easily dismissed by his appeal to narratives. In that sense, I agree with Ryba when he writes that "Flood's criticism of Husserlian phenomenology is *meto-nymic*. It damns the whole on the basis of selective criticism of the parts, and it neglects those parts that are open to improvement. It does not imagine the phenomenology that might be" (Ryba 2006: 118). The task is not to reject phenomenology tout court and to substitute it with a narrativism that left to its own devices becomes "a hungry metaphor" (Csordas 1999: 146), devouring everything in its path. Instead, it is to reconstruct a non-reductive materialist phenomenology of embodiment that focuses on the interplay of culture and nature, of neurophysiology, consciousness, practice, and history.

PHENOMENOLOGY OF EMBODIMENT AT WORK: ANTHROPOLOGY

Some of the most exciting work on the phenomenology of embodiment is taking place in anthropology, with scholars such as Paul Stoller, Thomas Csordas, and Michael Jackson among those leading the way.[12] Working on sorcery and spirit position among the Songhay of Mali and Niger, Stoller advocates for a "sensuous scholarship" that can overcome interpretive anthropology's visual bias. He traces this visual bias to the Cartesian disembodied representationalism, whereby we can only have access to the "outside world," including our bodies, through the cogito's mental activity. Stoller sees this attitude in contemporary scholars like Foucault and Butler: "even the most insightful writers consider the body as a text that can be read and analyzed. This analytical tack strips the body of its smells, tastes, textures and pains—its sensuousness. . . . recent writing on the body tends to be articulated in curiously disembodied language" (Stoller 1997: xiv). Such "bloodless language reinforces the very principle they critique—the separation of mind and body, which . . . regulates and subjugates the very bodies they would liberate" (Stoller 1997: xv).

To show how religion involves a materiality that cannot be reduced to discourse, Stoller discusses the body of the Songhay sorcerer. For the Songhay, the path to sorcery literally starts with the body, with the stomach of the would-be sorcerer, who must ingest *kusu*, a cake containing cosmic powers that his master has prepared. This is not surprising since the Songhay "fuse body and being" not through some mentalist or visual exercise, but "through gustatory metaphors. . . . The stomach is considered the site of human personality and agency. Social relations are considered in terms of eating" (Stoller 1997: 7). In the case of the sorcerer, his body is "an arena for learning about Songhay sorcery. Once individuals have eaten the *kusu* of initiation, they are implicated in a system of sorcerous relations, a network of rivalry in which the body eats power and power eats the body" (Stoller 1997: 21–22). Given the physicality of sorcery, it is no wonder that the body of the sorcerer bears the marks of training and performance. The battles that he wages are not only "inscribed" in the sorcerer's consciousness, as a mentalist phenomenologist would argue, or even in his body, as textualist hermeneutics would have it. Rather, "they are worn in and on their (extended) bodies. They walk with a limp. Their arms are impaired. They are blind. Their children die young. Their betrothed die just before their marriages are consummated. In the Songhay world, sorcerous embodiment always exacts a high price" (Stoller 1997: 15).

Embodiment is also key in the ways in which the Songhay deal with the politics of colonialism and postcolonialism. In order to relive the past and negotiate current tensions, they often summon ancestral and European spirits who bring with them habits, gestures, postures, movements, tastes, and embodied memories. By entering the bodies of contemporary Songhay, they come to literally perform history, not as a reenactment of some ahistorical myth of origins as in Eliade's version of phenomenology, but as the contested commemoration of a specific history of power struggles that have shaped the bodies of a people. In other words, through the practices of spirit possession the Songhay spark embodied memories and counter-memories in "sound, odor, and taste,—in the flesh" (Stoller 1997: 63), which can lead to the reproduction of or resistance against entrenched power asymmetries that characterize the relation among the local, the national, and the global.

As we saw in the last chapter, Merleau-Ponty uses the notion of sedimented habits to point to the pre-reflective embodiment, to go beyond mentalism and textualism. For Merleau-Ponty, our body encounters the world in myriad of ways of which we are not consciousness, and thus which cannot be accessed solely through thematized discourse. Later on, we will see how thinkers such as Marcel Mauss and Pierre Bourdieu rework the notion of habit as part of a theory of practice. Similarly, Stoller argues that spirit possession as the performance of embodied memories and counter-memories is "a set of practices that constitutes power-in-the-world" (1997: 55). Habit "is something which does not lend itself to the visual bias that is central to discursive analysis. In their insistence on the discursive, scholars transform the figurative into language and text—into discourse. And yet our memories are never purely personal, purely cognitive, or purely textual" (Stoller 1997: 57). This is the reason why "embodiment is not primarily textual; rather, the sentient body is culturally consumed by a world filled with forces, smells, textures, sights, sounds, and tastes, all of which trigger cultural memories" (Stoller 1997: 54).

The phenomenology of embodiment is also central in anthropologist Michael Jackson's "radical empiricism," which calls us to go beyond the individual subject and his/her mental and interpretive world to focus on lived experience that "is grounded in bodily movement within a social and material environment" (Jackson 1989: 124). Although Jackson borrows heavily from William James and the pragmatist tradition, he argues that the "phenomenological turn prepares the ground for detailed descriptions of how people immediately experience space, time, and the world in which they live" (Jackson 1996: 12). Drawing from Merleau-Ponty, Jackson shows that the body is the locus of this immediate experience through a "practical mimesis," whereby particular ways of inhabiting the world are inculcated.

To illustrate his point, Jackson explores the initiation of girls into adulthood among the Kuranko of northern Sierra Leone. This initiation is part of a public festival that includes nightly dances by the initiates and other performers. The latter often dress in men's clothes and imitate the men's awkward dance moments and their stern facial expressions. In fact, throughout the celebrations, "mimicry of men was a recurring motif. Several young women marched up and down shouldering old rifles, other donned the coarse cloth leggings and tasseled caps of hunters, while others pretended to be the praise-singers of the hunters and plucked the imaginary strings of a piece of stick signifying a harp" (Jackson 1989: 125). As a diligent cultural anthropologist, Jackson wanted to know right away what these dances meant. He wanted to uncover the underlying symbolic code that was being enacted through the performances. His informants, however, told him that the performances were simply "just for entertainment," "for no other reason but to have everyone take part" (132).

These responses lead Jackson to take an approach that foregrounds body praxis, rather than to search for semiotic codes. Rather than assigning priority to the worldview, as a religion scholar working in Ninian Smart's mould would do, Jackson departs from the practices of the life-world (Jackson 1998: 5). "[T]o hold that every act signifies something is an extravagant form of abstraction, so long as this implies that the action stands for something other than itself, beyond the here and now" (Jackson 1989: 127). He realizes that by taking a Cartesian approach, distancing himself from the rituals in order to grasp them intellectually, as part of a structured symbolic system, he is missing the power of the performance, which is all about doing things together through bodily movement and posture. These dances are mimetic performances through which the Kuranko are creating gendered adults by inculcating dispositions, skills, and comportments. The dances are "work done with the body" to produce subjectivity, to ground orientation, cognition, and language in space and time. During initiation festivals, the Kuranko are engaged in "kinaesthetic learning," "based upon bodily awareness of the other in oneself, thus . . . bringing into relief a reciprocity of viewpoints" (Jackson 1989: 130). This is why the dances take place for no other reason than to have "everyone take part." "The Kuranko people are far less exercised by the conceptual question, What is in my neighbor's mind? than by practicing social wisdom (*hankili*) and cultivating copresence—'greeting,' 'sitting together,' 'working together,' and 'moving as one'" (Jackson 1998: 12).

For Jackson, a radical phenomenological empiricism has important implications for the scholar. Participation in the performances "becomes an end in itself rather than a means of gathering closely observed data which will be subject to interpretation elsewhere *after the event*." The scholar's embodied involvement in the event, in turn, serves to break "the habit of seeking truth at the level of disembodied concepts and decontextualized sayings. To recognize the embodiedness of our being-in-the-world is to discover a common ground where self and other are one, for by using one's body in the same way as others in the same environment which may then be interpreted according to one's own custom or bent, yet which remains grounded in a field of practical activity and thereby remains consonant with the experience of those among whom one has lived" (Jackson 1989: 135). Jackson is then advocating for a new, material form of empathy, not based on a transcendental ego, an essence that we all share as *homo religiosus*. It is empathy as "intercorporeity" made possible by the "field of inter-experience, inter-action, and inter-locution" that constitutes everyday life for a certain group (Jackson 1998: 3).[13]

While Stoller and Jackson make references to phenomenology, Thomas Csordas states clearly that he is interested in constructing a cultural phenomenology of embodiment. Like Stoller, Csordas points to the limitations of the use of the metaphor of the text in the humanities and social sciences. He acknowledges that the trope of textuality has opened a "stimulating wave of interdisciplinary thinking," bringing anthropologists and historians into conversation with philosophers, theologians, and literary scholars. Nevertheless, in his view, the text has become "a hungry metaphor" that has swallowed up everything in its path, including culture, nature, the body, and experience.

> Among the radical moves entailed by the text metaphor was the thesis that representation does not denote experience, but constitute it. This move closes the gap between language and experience, and thereby eliminates a dualism, but does so not by transcending the dualism but by reducing experience to language, or discourse, or representation. It allows for a powerful critique of specific representations, but does so by insulating representation as a mode of knowledge from epistemological critique. That is, it makes difficult the posing of questions about

the limits of representation, or whether there is anything beyond or outside representation, implying that to ask "representation of what" is fallaciously essentialist. (Csordas 1999: 183)

In order to challenge the totalizing pretensions of textualism, Csordas borrows from Merleau-Ponty and Heidegger and introduces the notion of embodiment as "being-in-the-world," as the intersubjectively mediated subjective experience of embodied immediacy. "My suggestion is that the phenomenological tradition offers us being-in-the-world as a dialogical partner for representation. In brief, the equation is that semiotics gives us textuality in order to understand representation, phenomenology gives us embodiment in order to understand being-in-the-world." And, as in Merleau-Ponty's chiasm, or reversibility, the body is both a "source of representations" and "a ground of being-in-the-world" (Csordas 1999: 184).

Csordas illustrates what he means by embodiment as the ground of being-in-the-world in his research on healing among Charismatic Catholics and the Navajo. He shows how the cultivation of a particular style of relationship to God among Charismatics leads to a complete transformation of the self, a process of "self-objectification" that touches the whole person, producing a new integrated habitus. This habitus is expressed not just in the gestures, postures, utterances, movements, and uncontrollable emotions of joy and empowerment that accompany practices such as praying, praising, signing, glossolalia, or the laying of hands, but also in everyday preferences and inclinations, in the need to dress modestly or the rejection of the temptations of alcohol, for example. The religious experience "is a template for orientation in the world, and the exercise of spiritual gifts [such as glossolalia and the power to prophesize and heal] is a template for self processes that bring about that orientation" in the flesh (1994a: 18).

Central to the process of self-transformation is the intimate, spontaneous, and embodied encounter with divine alterity. These powerful emotions belong to the "preobjective field of embodiment, that field of immediacy where (among others) the analytical dualities of subject and object, conscious and unconscious are collapsed" (Csordas 1994a: 282), at least momentarily, until they are semiotically disclosed, that is, thematized and conceptually understood as narratives about the encounter with God or the sacred. Csordas argues that the experiences of Charismatic Catholics cannot be reduced to intertextuality, to representations of other representations. Their materiality as modes of embodiment cannot be exhausted by discourse. "There is a real sense in which the 'texts' on which we rely—reports, interviews, narratives, or observations— can be construed as giving access to the experience. Language is not only 'about' itself: it can be the source of a genuine communication in which the existential situation of others is disclosed and recognizable" (1994a: 282).

It is fair to ask whether by making reference to "divine alterity" Csordas is not reintroducing an appeal to theology that recalls the grounding of internalism in ontology in the phenomenological approaches of Otto and van der Leeuw. In fact, Csordas states that he wants to "rehabilitate" the notion of otherness found in these scholars (2004: 176). Moreover, Csordas even makes reference to the problematic category of *homo religiosus* (1997: 41–42). However, what Csordas retrieves from Otto and van der Leeuw are not metaphysical or theological essences but resources to think about the specificity of religion as an existential phenomenon, resources that he does not find in the giants of the anthropology of religion, such as Clifford Geertz and Victor Turner, for whom the study of religion is "often means to an end," that is, means to study culture. More importantly, Csordas finds in Otto and van der Leeuw resources to think about alterity as "the inescapability of our embodied nature and the limitations it imposes [which] contribute to the feeling that our bodies are in a sense 'other' that ourselves" (Csordas 2004: 170). For Csordas, what is pre-objective, and thus "foundational," is not the sacred as an autonomous reality, as noumena, but the embodied, biological-cultural experience of finitude, of simultaneous intercorporality and estrangement from others and from "nature," including our own bodies. Alterity is "an elementary structure of existence" (Csordas 2004: 167) because the thrownness of our bodies implies both identity and non-identity, in much the same way Merleau-Ponty characterized "the flesh" as a chiasm, as a reversible principle that folds onto itself but never coincides fully. Alterity is about the dialectic of presence and absence that is part of our "creatureliness."[14]

Thus, where phenomenologists of religion like Otto and van der Leeuw go wrong is in "reifying alterity—reifying otherness as an object, rendering 'out there' in such a way that we can be 'in its presence'" (Csordas 2004: 167). Despite this serious mistake, phenomenologists of religion offer crucial tools to understand how our embodied condition, with its thrownness among other beings and things, is the source of transcendence and sacrality. Just like Heidegger found in Husserl's phenomenology a useful tool to approach *Dasein*'s existential structures (i.e., its historicity and emplacement among others and in a world of things), Csordas recognizes in Otto and van der Leeuw a way to explore the "origin" of religion in alterity. In Csordas's words,

> [T]he phenomenologists' error was to make a distinction between the object and the subject of religion when the actual object of religion is objectification itself, the rending apart of subject and object that makes us human and in the same

movement bestows on us—or burdens us with—the inevitability of religion. The "object" of religion is not the other; it is the existential aporia of alterity itself. (2004: 167)

For Csordas, then, cultural phenomenology of embodiment is only concerned with how we live our existential condition, which makes the issues of otherness, indeterminacy, situatedness, and surplus unavoidable. Transcendence, thus, "does not outrun its embodied situation" (Csordas 1994a: 12), and "defining the sacred is not a theological but an ethnological task" (Csordas 1997: 265). This assertion is certainly compatible with the materialist anthropology I have been sketching. Where I part ways with Csordas is in his totalizing claim that alterity leads inevitably to religion and, thus, that religion is a universal feature of humanity. Transcendence is something that "deserves attention as potentially widespread if not universal among humans . . . [but] this something need not be conflated with theism or divine beings" (Taves 2009: 14). The alterity that is part of *Dasein*'s destiny, to use Heideggerian language, does open humanity toward transcendence. However, this transcendence is expressed in multiple ways, some of which come to be defined as religious at certain historical junctures. The boundaries of these definitions are relatively fluid and contested. To say that when alterity is elaborated "in and for itself, we are in the domain of religion" is to hold a static conception of religion, to accept naïvely a taken-for-granted notion of religion, failing to recognize the political genealogy of the term. What are the boundaries of this domain we call religion? How did they come to be just so?[15] In other words, I take a more constructionist approach to the "origin" of religion, without denying that there are corporal, psycho-cognitive realities that make it not only possible but widespread.

In his later writings, Csordas appears to have taken an increasingly Kantian-Husserlian line, seeking to ground religious experience as an a priori. This might explain the reference to the category of *homo religiosus*, which he rereads in existential, historicist terms. Indeed, his thesis is "that religion is predicated on and elaborated from a primordial sense of 'otherness' or alterity. Furthermore, because of this the religious sensibility exists sui generis, that is, is not reducible to any other category. . . . Insofar as alterity is part of the structure if being-in-the-world—an elementary structure of existence—religion is inevitable, perhaps even necessary" (Csordas 2004: 162). Again, it is not clear why a phenomenology of embodiment necessarily entails the universalization of religious sensibility as an a priori of pre-reflective experience. If the issue is not to reduce religion to another category, the scholar can recognize the specificity of religion as historical constellations of discourses, practices, and institutions made possible by our bodily being-in-the-world. The fact that religion is a set of embodied practices among other practices does not make it less relevant or an epiphenomenal reflection of something more real. In other words, guarding against reduction does not require a transcendental turn, a turn toward a prioris of religious experience.

I believe that, stripped of the totalizing pretension to explain the universal reality of religion, Csordas's phenomenology does offer a viable way to explore how religion and embodiment are closely entwined. In his work on the Navajos, for example, he discusses the compelling case of Dan, who, suffering from a brain tumor, surgery, chemotherapy, and radiation therapy, struggles with the possibility of regaining speech as a strategy to reconstruct his life. In this struggle, Dan draws from traditional Navajo religion to fashion himself as a medicine man and a peyote spiritualist just like his father. To be a medicine man among the Navajo is to have the power of words. Csordas cites studies showing that patients who have had Dan's critical profile are prone to "hyper-religiosity" and particularly to "mystical" experiences. Nevertheless, according to Csordas, Dan's "search for words is thematized as religious not because religious experience is reducible to a neurological discharge but because it is a strategy of the self in need of a powerful idiom for orientation in the world" (1994b: 287). Nor does Csordas try to reduce Dan's experience of his body to a set of discourses. Dan's attempt to construct a new religious self is a biological-cultural way to deal with his existential condition, to turn an embodied experience of pain, suffering, and disability into a "life plan in conformity with cultural and religious meaning" (Csordas 1994b: 278).

Through this example, Csordas shows how embodiment must not be confused with textuality and how the task of the cultural phenomenologist is not to search for the irreducible essence of religion inside the religious person. Rather, the task is to explore specific modes of embodiment, biological-cultural "modulations of being in the world."

PHENOMENOLOGY OF EMBODIMENT AT WORK: RELIGIOUS STUDIES

As religious studies seeks to recover the body, Stoller's, Jackson's, and Csordas's historicist and materialist phenomenologies can offer fruitful alternatives to subjectivist, idealist, internalist, and metaphysical approaches that have dominated the discipline. In fact, similar phenomenologies of embodiment are already at work in religious studies, producing impressive results. For example,

Ann Taves's exploration of religious experiences in America from the seventeenth to nineteenth centuries focuses on the "lived experiences of persons within traditions of interpretation" (1999: 9). A crucial element of this experience is "its involuntary aspect, that is, the sense that 'I' am not the agent or cause of 'my' experience." More specifically, Taves's historical sources "depict subjects whose usual sense of themselves as embodied agents is altered and discontinuous. Their experiences . . . include the loss of voluntary motor control, unusual sensory perceptions (kinesthetic, visual, auditory, and tactile), and/or discontinuities of consciousness, memory, and identity" (Taves 1999: 9). To study these involuntary experiences, Taves relies on the notion that they are grounded on "bodily knowledges that people acquire in part 'insensibly and unconsciously,' in the way that an apprentice acquires 'the principles of the "art"' and the art of living—including those which are not known to the producer of the practices or work imitated" (Taves 1999: 10). The fits, trances, and visions that Taves documents involve a "practical mimesis" and a cultivated bodily memory, as Jackson and Stoller would put it, that allows for the production of relatively patterned experiences that are then interpreted in diverse ways by the various communities of discourse and practice in which the actors are embedded. The thematization of experiences, their characterization through religious or naturalistic language, is not separated from nor does it precede their embodied production. Narratives about these experiences are anchored in and dependent on the biological-cultural processes of embodiment. Therefore, the task for the scholar is neither to seek empathetically and introspectively for some intangible a priori experience within the subject, nor to merely decode through a careful hermeneutics the conscious narratives that actors and non-actors tell about the experience. Rather, it is to study the genesis and transformation of an embodied practical mastery that makes the at once disciplined and creative performance of fits, trances, and visions a way of inhabiting the world. In Taves's words:

> The mesmeric tradition presumed that a common mental state . . . whether designated as mesmeric, magnetic, somnambulistic, trance, or hypnotic—informed the whole gamut of what I have called involuntary experiences. While mesmeric discourse postulated a common mental state, I want to suggest that mesmeric practice, rather than evoking some common mental state, instead evoked bodily knowledges, including personal and cultural memories, and recast them in new forms that were secular and naturalistic. (1999: 353)

Leigh Schmidt's work on religion and the senses is also informed by a phenomenology of embodiment that resonates with some of the themes I have been discussing in this chapter. However, it also shows how difficult it is for religion scholars to abandon the private-affair tradition entirely and to accept a fully materialist framework. In *Hearing Things: Religion, Illusion, and the American Enlightenment*, Schmidt undertakes "by the way of the ear . . . an excursion into the sensuousness of Christian experience and its denials." In this excursion, he highlights the "new sensory disciplines" introduced by Enlightenment thinkers. According to Schmidt, "the Enlightenment changed the senses," demanding a new "range of performances and embodied regimes" (2000: 3, 6). On the one hand, in its attempt to render the world fully transparent to human reason, the Enlightenment intensified "the sovereign nobility of vision," which, as we have seen, is part of the search for foundations from Plato through Descartes. This "objectifying ocularcentrism" led to a profound mistrust of the hearing, particularly of hearing unseen things. On the other hand, the Enlightenment sharpened hearing as part of an "acoustics of demystification" that sought to disqualify the beckoning sounds of the supernatural amid the secular world of modernity. This accounts for the fact that Schmidt's book is populated not only by Christian mystics but also by debunkers who fashion themselves after the *philosophes*, jostling to define the boundaries of authoritative experience. The tension between tradition and modernity, the "unresolvable struggles of enchantment and disenchantment . . . have been imprinted on a very specific part of the human body, the ear" (Schmidt 2000: 6). Here, Schmidt's approach to the evolution of the religious sensorium dovetails nicely with Stoller's phenomenological notion of embodied memory.

Part of the richness of Schmidt's account lies in the fact that he does not portray religious practitioners as passive victims of "reeducation" of their senses and the inculcation of new legitimate habits of listening by the elites. Instead, Enlightenment reformers and figures in Christian Pietism engage in a complex negotiation of the boundaries between acoustic truth and illusion. As the case of Spiritualism shows, in many instances, religious practitioners use the language of science to defend the validity of their spiritual perceptions.

From the foregoing, it would appear that Schmidt's approach owes more to social constructionism, with its language of spiritual disciplines and regimes of experience, than to phenomenology. To study the senses in religion then requires "moving through a wide expanse of lived experience and everyday objects. . . . The very corporality of hearing needs to be materialized, snatched out of an airy evanescence through the rituals, disciplines, performances, mechanisms, and commodities that make up the sounding body as well as the attentive ear" (Schmidt 2000: 35–36).

Nevertheless, Schmidt turns the tables on approaches that see the senses as mere artifacts of particular historical and cultural processes. Today's hermeneutics of suspicion, which reduces religious experience to naturalistic causes, are part of the same "objectifying ocularcentrism" that characterized the Enlightenment. Citing Feuerbach's claim that "the only fearful, mystical, and pious sense is that of hearing," Schmidt argues that "the development of a philosophical critique of religion was joined to a specific pedagogy of the senses in which the reeducation of the Christian ear was axiomatic. The history of the critical study of religion is also a history of the senses." It is, thus, not surprising that "[t]hose who are most intent on burying the self-assured rationality of the Enlightenment often stay to ventriloquize the ghosts of absence, illusion, and simulation. It requires no theological leap, only historical canniness, to suggest that suspicion be turned on the suspicious" (Schmidt 2000: 251).

Therefore, as a corrective to extreme forms of social constructionism, "religious affirmations of presence, whether in hearing or being heard or in seeing or being seen, need to be taken seriously on their own terms, but, at the same time, the acknowledgement of that intersubjective framing is not intended to free such experiences from the contextual densities of culture and power. A poetics does not exclude a politics and vice versa" (Schmidt 2000: 35).

Schmidt, however, goes beyond critiquing the excesses of social constructionism. "With a respectful patience for the arcane, the historian follows the devout to those bodily thresholds where the senses themselves seem to lose their sensuousness, where the dangers and limitations of the sensual are transfigured" (2000: 36). It is hard to read what Schmidt means here: is it a move beyond the tacit cogito, toward the flesh à la Merleau-Ponty in his later years? Or is it a veiled appeal to transcendental experiences that reinscribes the internalism in Otto's, van der Leeuw's, and Eliade's phenomenologies? Are we not running into the same problem that Csordas confronted when he referred to "divine alterity"? It seems as if Schmidt wants to have it both ways. At times, his appeal to strike a phenomenological attitude seems part of methodological populism that seeks to "recover the voices of common folks . . . to attend to the quotidian and the ordinary without assuming an interpretive model of decline, control, banality, or manipulation" (1995: 307). This is a useful strategic move that subaltern scholars have applied to disclose unseen forms of domination and resistance, elaborating on Antonio Gramsci's notions of hegemony and counter-hegemony.[16] At other times, however, it seems as if the critique of "a view from nowhere when it comes to a topic as freighted as 'spirituality'" gives Schmidt cover to join the "spiritual seekers" (2005: xi–xiii). But here Schmidt seems to misunderstand what is at stake. The issue is not an ocularcentric objectivity or a detachment that practitioners of the hermeneutics of suspicion like David Chidester and Russell McCutcheon, whom he criticizes, would readily recognize as illusory. Rather, the crux of the problem is the extent to which a phenomenological approach not balanced by an incisive-though-chastened social constructionism and a nuanced appeal to neurophysiology, evolution, and ecology turns the scholar into a "caretaker" of the private-affair tradition in religious studies. At issue is the possibility an thoroughly imma-nentist materialism that does not reduce religious experiences to a single vari-able or claim to provide a totalizing view on the basis of a synthesis of multiple factors.

Perhaps this type of materialism is what Schmidt has in mind when he states in his analysis of consumer rites that he tries "to preserve ambivalence and multivocality, to construct a complex and open-ended narrative of shifting perspectives that invites others to join in and redirect the story. There is no closure or finality in such a narrative, only circling dialogue" (Schmidt 1995: 308). I would hasten to add, however, that these shifting perspectives—Schmidt's included—are embedded not in just the everyday situations that the lived-religion approach tries so lovingly to portray, but also in the interaction among psychological, sociocultural, and biological processes operating at mul-tiple scales. Phenomenology is simply one set of practices in "the range of per-formances and embodied regimes" that constitute the religion scholar as a subject.

Schmidt's ambivalences can be reread through Csordas's phenomenological conception of the sacred—the sacred not as self-sustaining essence that must be protected against the reductive gaze of secular modernity, but as bodily and culturally mediated experience of limits and otherness. As Schmidt writes, sum-moning Merleau-Ponty to his aid: "[t]he grounds that I have used for thinking about the [divine] presences in voices are not metaphysical or theological. Instead, this interpretation rests on the historical recognition of perception as commonly entailing an active exchange, a participatory encounter" (Schmidt 2002: 33). This encounter is necessarily embodied and emplaced and, thus, available to a materialist analysis. Yet, as part of a mode of being-in-the-world, it is open-ended and uncertain, allowing for "this-worldly transcendence."

My qualms about Schmidt and Csordas foreground the tensions between phenomenology's quest for foundations (even if properly materialized) and social constructionism. In the next chapter, I focus on social-constructionist approaches to the body in order to see how they can enter into conversation with materialist phenomenologies of religion and later on with perspectives that take evolution and neuroscience as their point of departure.

5

Religious Bodies as Social Artifacts

Social constructionism is an umbrella term that characterizes diverse approaches sharing the epistemological assumption that our experiences and practices are unavoidably shaped by the contexts that we collectively construct. Knowledge does not emerge as the individual, sovereign mind simply mirrors or automatically copies the external world or as a result of direct divine revelation. Rather, knowledge is only possible because we are embedded in sociocultural matrixes that provide us with the categories with which we make sense of reality. Thus, above all, social constructionism entails a rejection of the possibility and desire to attain a God's-eye view of the world, favoring instead a historicized, positioned, embodied theory of knowledge.

Beyond this common assumption, constructionist perspectives come in many forms. Some "softer" versions recognize the existence of a material body and extra-mental reality but affirm that our access to this reality is always mediated by forms of knowledge—narratives, metaphors, disciplinary schemas, rituals—that are produced socially. Alternatively, stronger versions of social constructionism claim that the appeal to the "real body" or the "real world" does not make sense, since the body and nature are from the outset and always social constructs. Some social constructionists choose to emphasize the discursive, the fact that, of all social artifacts, language is the most "foundational," since it makes intelligibility possible in the first place. These versions of constructionism tend to see the body primarily as contested text or a mobile cluster of discourses. In referring to the body, the discourses constitute it as a meaningful and relatively stable category. Other forms of social constructionism will recognize the "nondiscursive" social practices, beyond signification, that go into the articulation of a body as empowered to do certain things and restricted from undertaking others. These approaches may see the body as a tabula rasa, a malleable surface that gets molded by society through the application of various disciplinary techniques, or in a Spinozan and Nietzschean way, as a shifting reservoir of energies that are harnessed and channeled by social means.

My goal in this chapter is to explore some important versions of social constructionism in an effort to build an approach that, while recognizing the inescapable role discursive and nondiscursive social practices play in constituting the lived body and religious experience, does not fall into a self-defeating reductionism. I am after a robust yet fallible and nontotalizing version of social constructionism that can enter into conversation with the materialist phenomenology that I have sketched in the previous chapters and with the evolutionary, ecological, and neurocognitive theories that I will discuss in chapter 7.

THE ORIGINS AND EVOLUTION OF
MODERN SOCIAL CONSTRUCTIONISM

Modern social constructionism originated from the Enlightenment's attempt to establish reason as an autonomous and legitimate ground for knowledge over against the claim that revelation is the ultimate source of truth. Enlightenment thinkers sought to ground knowledge on natural causes, rather than on supernatural sources. By making reason the arbiter of all truths, the Enlightenment opened the door to two broad naturalistic epistemologies. The first one holds that reality is organized by universal principles, which can progressively be apprehended by reason. Thus, in this epistemology, the search for truth involves induction: starting from empirical data accessible to all rational human beings, it seeks to go beyond the contingencies of history to uncover underlying, transcendental laws of nature. Such an epistemology informed the Newtonian revolution and has been at the heart of the natural sciences, spawning various versions of positivism, empiricism, logical positivism, and other foundationalisms.

The second theory of knowledge to emerge from the Enlightenment stresses the active role that human rationality has in constituting the world that we perceive. Since "man is the measure of all things," to know something is to shape it in such a way that it becomes intelligible and useful to us. A subset of this epistemology holds that, since human beings are inherently social, the categories through which we know the world must have their origin in society. Further, since language is an essential dimension of our sociality, this second epistemology argues that we can only know through linguistic mediation. This social constructionism, the idea that the "social must be explained by the social," has been, of course, central to the social sciences, the humanities, and, most recently, cultural studies.

These two epistemologies have been in tension with each other, despite Kant's efforts to reconcile them through his notion of a prioris. Hegel's move to historicize reason, to show its laborious trajectory to absolute knowledge, can be seen as an attempt to re-inject some social constructionism to Kantian foundationalism. Kant recognized the active role of reason in shaping knowledge. As we saw in chapter 3, for him, we can only know the world as it appears to us (phenomena) not the things in themselves (noumena). However, Kant assumed that categories that made it possible for things to appear to us in a given way were transcendental, not the product of cultural or historical variation. I have argued that this transcendental temptation has dominated modern Western thought from Descartes to Husserl, making its way into the discipline of religion.

Hegel's contribution, then, was to challenge the staticity of Kant's epistemology, showing the sociohistorical genesis and evolution of human knowledge. Nevertheless, Hegel did not apply social constructionism consistently. He posited a teleological, albeit conflict-ridden, movement toward absolute knowledge. At the end of the Spirit's journey was a standpoint where all things would come together once and for all. From that sublime summit, we would see that all history makes sense, since it was from the beginning progressing toward this Archimedean point. Contemporary forms of social constructionism can be seeing as radicalizing Hegel's historicist project: there is no Archimedean point upon which we can stand to claim a final synthesis and, since this point does not exist, the claim that history is a progressive movement toward absolute knowledge is indefensible.

Social constructionism takes a definite step forward with Marx, who begins with the premise that "all human history is, of course, the existence of living human beings," not the march of an abstract concept like the *Geist* (Marx 1978a: 149). Moreover, for Marx human beings are always embedded in "a definite form of activity . . . a definite form of expressing their life, a definite *mode of life* on their part. As individuals express their life, so they are. What they are, therefore, coincides with their production, both with *what* they produce and with *how* they produce" (Marx 1978a: 150). Human beings gain their identity by acting in and through a collectively constructed world. Marx characterizes the historicity and positionality of human activity thus: "Men [*sic*][1] make their own history, but they do not make it just as they please; they do not make it under circumstances chosen by themselves, but under circumstances directly found, given and transmitted from the past. The tradition of all the dead generations weighs like a nightmare on the brain of the living" (1978e: 595). Here Marx is anchoring social constructionism around the concept of praxis, which as we shall see in chapters 8 and 9, is also one of the supporting pillars of non-reductive materialism.

> The materialist doctrine that men are products of circumstances and upbringing, and that, therefore, changed men are products of other circumstances and changed upbringing, forgets that it is men who change the circumstances and that it is essential to educate the educator himself. . . . The coincidence of the changing circumstances and of human activity can be conceived and rationally understood only as revolutionising practice. (1978b: 144)

In other words, humans are the artifacts of their own social activity, which becomes objectified as the historical condition in which they find themselves and which makes possible their practices. The quote that "tradition . . . weighs like a nightmare on the brain of the living" seems to imply that social construction operates primarily at the ideological level, influencing the consciousness of current actors. Marx, however, is clear that the capitalist mode of production shapes, or "objectifies" the body of the worker in certain ways, separating it from the bodies of his/her peers and forcing it to engage in repetitive motions in crowded assembly lines. "Owing to the extensive use of machinery and to division of labour, the work of the proletarians has lost all individual character, and consequently, all charm for the workman. He becomes an appendage of the machine, and it is only the most simple, most monotonous, and most easily acquired knack, that is required of him" (1978d: 479).

Marx was not the only one arguing for a materialist social constructionism. As we saw in chapter 2, Nietzsche had advocated a genealogical approach to uncover how those values that Western modernity took for granted and held in highest regard were in fact the product of a twisted will to power expressed as historically and socially constructed asceticism. The Christian ascetic in his/her quest for eternal salvation and the scientist in search of absolute truth were two types constructed out of the social emasculation of the body. And although Freud would give society a limited role in shaping an individual's personality (during the first four years of his/her life), he borrowed from Nietzsche the notion that the self is not a unified entity, but an unstable artifact that is the product of underlying tensions. The body is the material surface on which those conflicts are expressed, as the person evolves from the oral through the anal to the phallic phase.

Added to Marxist and Nietzschean constructionisms was Emile Durkheim's effort to develop sociology as a discipline independent from psychology and biology. For Durkheim, sociology distinguishes itself from related disciplines by focusing on "social facts," collective representations and forms of organization that are not reducible to the aggregate of activities of individuals acting independently. Nor are social facts the mechanical outcome of biological processes. Social facts collectively constructed realities that not only transcend individuals but shape their ideas and behaviors. For example, Durkheim argues that the distinction between sacred and profane is not only central to all religions, but it plays a foundational role in the formation of our categories of cognition.

> For a long time it has been known that the first systems of representation with which men have pictured to themselves the world and themselves were of religious origin. There is no religion that is not cosmology at the same time that it is a speculation upon divine things. If philosophy and the sciences were born of religion, it is because religion began by taking the place of the sciences and philosophy. . . . At the roots of all our judgments there are a certain number of essential ideas which dominate all our intellectual life . . . ideas of time, space, class, number, cause, substance, personality, etc. . . . They are born in religion and of religion; they are a product of religious thought. (Durkheim 1965: 21–22)

In effect, Durkheim claims that humanity's primal engagement in religion, which is "something eminently social," a way to celebrate and reinforce the power of the group to protect and provide for the individual, has enabled the internalization of the cognitive dualities that make experience and perception possible. The opposition between sacred and profane anchors other oppositions such as those between high and low (space), day and night (time), man and woman, culture and nature, raw and cooked, and purity and danger, which are crucial to meaning, knowledge, and action.

Society, thus, is not simply a by-product of sovereign individuals entering into a social contract to facilitate the survival of the species. Instead, society is the womb of civilization and, more importantly, of the modern Western subject. The latter is a recent historical artifact made possible by social differentiation. In primitive societies, which are organized along the lines of extended families or clans, there is no concept of individuality, since everybody performs more or less the same functions. In contrast to these societies that are held together by a "mechanical solidarity," a solidarity of sameness, modern Western societies are marked by social complexity and differentiation. Given this complexity and differentiation, these societies require individuals specialized in various functions. These specialized individuals then enter into relation with each other on the basis of interdependence, what Durkheim called organic solidarity, giving a post facto impression that society is nothing more than a social contract among individuals with different talents and interests.

The distinction between primitive and modern societies has been rightly criticized for providing moral and intellectual justification for colonialism.

Nevertheless, what I would like to highlight here is the fact that Durkheim advanced a strong version of social constructionism, a "social Kantianism" that traces the origin of a priori categories of perception and cognition not to God or the structure of the brain but to society. "[S]ocial time, social space, social classes and causality" are "the basis of the corresponding categories, since it is under their social forms that these different relations were first grasped with a certain clarity by the human intellect" (1965: 492).

Durkheim's social Kantianism, cross-fertilized in varying degrees with Marxism and Max Weber's interpretive sociology, was elaborated later by sociologists such as Karl Mannheim in his *Ideology and Utopia*, Peter Berger and Thomas Luckmann in *The Social Construction of Reality*, and Alfred Schutz and Thomas Luckmann in *The Structures of the Life-World*. All of these thinkers build on the basic Durkheimian insight that our categories of perception and schemes of action emerge from the incorporation and performance of patterns that we collectively stabilize, habitualize, or routinize, as Berger and Luckmann put it. Incorporation and performance, in turn, depend on how we are embedded in society. However, our ideas and practices are not simply the mere reflection of brute material conditions, as a reductive kind of materialism would claim. Rather, incorporation is part of a dialectic process whereby we creatively externalize what we have internalized from society and we internalize the sedimented social reality that our practices have produced. As Mannheim (1936: 3), echoing Marx, puts it, "every individual is therefore in a two-fold sense predetermined by the fact of growing up in a society: on the one hand he finds himself a ready-made situation and on the other he finds in that situation preformed patterns of thought and of conduct." Thus, the sociology of knowledge "does not sever the concretely existing modes of thought from the context of collective action through which we first discover the world in an intellectual sense" (Mannheim 1936: 3). This is so because there is no "epistemology in any absolute sense . . . [a]ctually, epistemology is as intimately enmeshed in the social process as is the totality of our thinking . . . Even a god could not formulate a proposition on historical subjects like $2 \times 2 = 4$, for what is intelligible in history can be formulated only with reference to problems and conceptual constructions which themselves arise in the flux of historical experience" (Mannheim 1936: 79).

Mannheim's claim that knowledge is perspectival, that is always dependent on the position of the observer in a particular social setting, immediately triggered the charge of relativism. If there is no absolute truth that we can eventually achieve or even approximate through many trials and errors, there is no way of adjudicating among different perspectives. Since all we have are perspectives, each of which captures the world through its own partial interests and methods, we are condemned to dwell in a world in which one standpoint is as good as any other and anything goes. In this world, even Mannheim's perspectivism self-deconstructs, since, after all, it is just another perspective. Mannheim tried to answer his critics by proposing a "relationism," a critical self-awareness of one's assumptions and partial worldview in confrontation with the perspectives of others among whom one lives. Since the social world is collectively constructed, individual perspectives are interrelated; they are not self-enclosed standpoints but, rather, they share common patterns that permit localized communication and evaluation. The task of the sociologist of knowledge is, thus, to take advantage of these linkages to take in as many points of view as possible. Such a strategy, in tandem with the awareness of the "narrowness" of his/her own determination, would give her/him "the best chance of reaching an optimum of truth" (Mannheim 1936: 80).

Mannheim's response to the charge of relativism is less than satisfactory, since it assumes that scientists can easily detach themselves from their own positionality and move across other perspectives. Even if social scientists can achieve a measure of detachment, how many perspectives do they need to confront in order to have the optimum of truth? Does the notion of optimum of truth not entail the assumption that one can see the totality of relevant perspectives for a given phenomenon? But how can one have a notion of totality if one is always located in the particular? Even the "comprehensive" standpoint is determined by the knower's particular embeddedness in society.

The specter of relativism will consistently haunt social constructionism, up to the present "science wars."[2] My attempt to deal with cognitive, evolutionary, and ecological approaches to the body in the next chapter, in fact, seeks at least to keep this specter at bay, by offering a non-reductive materialism that is not exhausted by social constructionism: reality is always mediated by our practices and cognitive categories, but it not totally reducible to them. There is a recalcitrant material (i.e., bodily and environmental) surplus that makes possible the emergence of the practices and cognitions with which we engage the world.

Following Durkheim, constructionist sociology of knowledge highlights the crucial role religion plays in generating binding collective representations. "[R]eligion has been the historically most widespread and effective instrumentality of legitimation. All legitimation maintains socially defined reality. Religion legitimates so effectively because it relates the precarious reality of constructions of empirical societies with ultimate reality. The tenuous realities of the social world are grounded in the sacred realissimum, which by definition is beyond the contingencies of human meanings and human activity" (Berger 1969: 32). Religion "cosmicizes" our social constructs by turning them into uncontested sacred realities that have their bases in extra-social and supra-historical process.

Durkheim's methodological holism, his claim that there are social facts that are external to and constraining of the practices of individuals, will also be taken up and elaborated by structuralism. As we shall see later on in the chapters on practice, structuralists such as Lévi-Strauss are not interested in the surface variations of individual behaviors. Rather, they seek the underlying rules or logics that orchestrate the coordinated activities of a particular society and culture. These rules not only have an independent existence from the individuals who perform them, preceding and outliving them, but also determine the types of cognitions, perceptions, and actions that can be generated. Some scholars influenced by structuralism focus on the functions various social structures perform. Thus, a structural functionalist like Talcott Parsons, for example, is interested in the role that religion plays in maintaining social cohesion and homeostasis, by providing a stable and shared set of norms and values. These normative principles, in effect, inoculate the individual against the threat of anomie, against existential crises that might isolate and disorient him/her.

Other scholars, loosely operating under what we might term "late structuralism," a structuralism that is keenly aware of its limitations, emphasize conflict and change in the process of social construction. For example, anthropologist Mary Douglas focuses on the role of culture in creating and maintaining intra- and inter-group boundaries and boundaries between humans and the threatening nonhuman environment. Since these boundaries are contingent, they are precarious and must be constantly reinforced. Attempts to reinforce boundaries against the chaos of nature and social relations, in turn, lead to conflict. Therefore, although Douglas, like Lévi-Strauss, sees culture operating through dualities, she follows Durkheim in understanding these dualities as historically and locally constructed (rather than as structures of the mind). "[I]deas about separating, purifying, demarcating, and punishing transgressions have as their main function to impose system on an inherently untidy experience. It is only by exaggerating the difference between within and without, above and below, male and female, with and against, that the semblance of order is created" (Douglas 1966: 4).

Douglas also argues that the boundaries and hierarchies constructed by the group to control and insulate itself from disorder become inscribed in the bodies of individual members through the search for cleanliness. Thus, she speaks of "two bodies," the social body and the physical body, which coincide in their organizing structures. According to Douglas,

> the human body is always treated as an image of society and . . . there can be no natural way of considering the body that does not involve at the same time a social dimension. Interest in its apertures depends on the preoccupation with

social exits and entrances, escape routes and invasions. If there is no concern to preserve social boundaries, I would not expect to find concern with bodily boundaries. The relation of head to feet, of brain and sexual organs, of mouth and anus are commonly treated so that they express the relevant patterns of hierarchy. Consequently I now advance the hypothesis that bodily control is an expression of social control.... (1982: 70)

The boundaries between what is pure and what is dangerous for the group are performed symbolically and ritually in and through the body, for example, by means of dietary rules that establish what is consumable and, thus, can enter the body and what is toxic or may contaminate body. Similarly, the interaction between social and bodily categories can be seen in the elaborate rites of passage from puberty to adulthood, the segregation of menstruating women, or the burying of the placenta of newborns. In insisting that "the social body constrains the way the physical body is perceived [and that] the experience of the body, always modified by social categories through which it is known, sustains a particular view of society (1982: 65), Douglas is proposing a social constructionist view of the body that foreshadows Michel Foucault's work on the history of modern subjectivity. As we shall see, both Douglas and Foucault will be criticized for their view of the physical body as a passive surface on which society imprints its mechanisms of social control.

The mention of Foucault brings us to the last strand of social constructionism influenced by Durkheim. Durkheimian sociology will also interact with the works of Marx, Nietzsche, and Freud, whom Paul Ricoeur (1974: 148) called the "masters of suspicion," laying the groundwork for contemporary versions of constructionism. Thinkers such as Foucault and Derrida will draw from structuralist readings of Durkheim and from the masters of suspicion to go beyond the limitations of phenomenology's "philosophy of the subject." In the process, these post-structuralist thinkers open the way for us to recover the material density of the body and social practices.

POST-STRUCTURALISM AND THE BODY: FOUCAULT

The development of contemporary forms of social constructionism owes a great deal to a generational change in France: "the passage from the generation known after 1945 as that of the 'three H's' to the generation known since 1960 as that of the three 'masters of suspicion': the three H's being Hegel, Husserl, and Heidegger, and the three masters of suspicion Marx, Nietzsche, and Freud" (Descombes 1980: 3). As we saw in chapter 3, phenomenology was in its apogee in the 1920s and 1930s, serving as the continental counterpoint to the dominance of logical positivism in Anglo-Saxon philosophy. By the end of the War World II, however, doubts began to appear about whether phenomenology's focus on the subject was complicit in the violence and atrocities that accompanied modernity.[3] Modernity was, after all, supposed to bring progress and increasing rationality, to enable humanity to render the world transparent and fully controllable. What had gone so wrong that modernity had instead resulted in Nazism and the Holocaust? Perhaps it was the persistence of the old Cartesian subjectivism, the idea of a unified subject capable of apprehending the world according to his/her own designs that was at the heart of this subversion of modernity's promises.[4] Perhaps the will to dominate was part and parcel of the Cartesian anxiety and temptation of transcendence which still colored Husserlian phenomenology.

To be sure, phenomenology did not disappear from the postwar French intellectual scene, as the towering presence of Jean-Paul Sartre and of other thinkers like Maurice Merleau-Ponty, Albert Camus, and Gabriel Marcel demonstrates. However, a new generation of young French philosophers, including Michel Foucault, Jacques Derrida, and Gilles Deleuze, was hard at work, seeking to extricate themselves from the "tyranny of the subject."

Foucault's first attempt to go beyond phenomenology is his *Madness and Civilization*, published in the early sixties, in which he seeks to show how modern rationality is the product of the physical separation and clinical study of insane people, who had previously moved freely at the edges of medieval society. In the Middle Ages, madness played a eschatological role, being often associated with prophecy, religious mysticism, transgression, and the mysteries of death. From the sixteenth century on, however, mad people were increasingly confined to asylums and hospitals, where an emerging cadre of scientific specialists began to observe and prod them, in an effort to extract the "inner truth" about the conditions that led to their abnormality. This process of "subjectivation," of the construction of the insane person as an analyzable subject, did not depend just on the imposition of scientific classifications and external physical constraints on the bodies of the insane. Rather, in the institutions of confinement,

> [e]verything was organized so that the madman would recognize himself in a world of judgment that enveloped him on all sides; he must know that he is watched, judged, and condemned; from transgression to punishment, the connection must be evident, as a guilt recognized by all: "We profit from the

circumstance of the bath, remind him of the transgression, or of the omission of an important duty, and with the aid of a faucet suddenly release a shower of cold water upon his head . . ." . . . all this must end in the internalization of the juridical instance, and the birth of remorse in the inmate's mind: it is only at this point that the judges agree to stop the punishment, certain that it will continue indefinitely in the inmate's conscience. (Foucault 1965: 214)

Foucault argues that modern rationality and subjectivity (the Cartesian recovery of self-identity through introspection) is born out of these historical, power-laden practices of othering: reason can assert its identity by constructing the identity of its other, its opposite, which now serves as its boundary, its foil. Thus, from the beginning, modern Western rationality and subjectivity were founded on violence and alterity. Indeed, in later works, such as *Discipline and Punish*, Foucault will argue that the disciplinary techniques developed in hospitals, asylums, reform schools, and army barracks eventually spilled into the whole of the social fabric, producing a "panoptical society," built on the surveillance and regulation of "biopower," the somatic energies of entire populations that are placed at the service of the state and capitalism.[5] The birth of Enlightenment rationality, of the Cartesian cogito who can keep madness at bay, therefore, comes at a high price.

It is clear, then, that from the beginning Foucault's work had a constructionist and historicist thrust. However, the early Foucault still retained a kind of essentialism in his attempt to recover madness before it has become mediated by the rational discourses of the Enlightenment. In the preface to *Madness and Civilization*, Foucault tells us that he wants "to return, in history, to that zero point in the course of madness at which madness is an undifferentiated experience, a not yet divided experience of division itself" (Foucault 1965: ix). It is as if Foucault, like Merleau-Ponty, is asking us to go back to experience (madness) in its primal form, outside of the mediating power of reason and language. He seems to be saying that to transcend the tyranny of Cartesianism, we must and can recover foundations that are not socially constructed. As we shall see in chapter 8, Derrida critiques Foucault for engaging in a "metaphysics of presence," a search for origins "outside the text."

Foucault's problematic appeal to innocent origins may explain why he turned to structuralism in works following *Madness and Civilization* (i.e., in *The Order of Things* and *Archeology of Knowledge*). In the wake of Ferdinand de Saussure's work in linguistics, structuralism emerged in France as the main alternative to phenomenology and existentialism's philosophy of the subject. With its claim that signification is the result of differential relations within a system of signifiers rather than the direct correspondence between concepts and extra-mental objects, structuralism decentered the Cartesian subject. Meaning was not the product of the subject's intentionality, of the author seeking to convey a specific feeling or thought that s/he grasps introspectively with full transparency. Instead, following Durkheimian methodological holism, structuralists argue that meaning is created by the orderly play of symbols and social conventions in which the subject is embedded.

Foucault states in no uncertain terms that he does not engage in structuralist analysis in *The Order of Things* and *Archeology of Knowledge*, the two works that follow *Madness and Civilization*. However, in these books he adopts a "method purged of all anthropologism," which unearths the inner logic of underlying historical discursive systems, discontinuous, self-regulating systems of knowledge that he calls epistemes.[6] Each episteme has rules about what counts as valid and truthful statements, about the types of objects that can be grasped and the subjects that can apprehend them. Foucault's key point in reconstructing the "deep structures" and emergence of epistemes through an "archeological" method echoes Durkheim's claim that Western subjectivity is a recent creation. The Cartesian self is the central epistemological figure of the modern epoch. Analyzing Diego de Velázquez's famous painting, *Las Meninas*, where the painter at work is himself an object of representation, a model for the portrait, Foucault argues that the modern epoch is characterized by the dual constitution of the self as both subject and object. This split is made possible by the generalized use of self-reflection, the same kind of optics that accompanied the othering of the mad person. In *Las Meninas*, "Man appears in his ambiguous position as an object of knowledge and as a subject that knows: enslaved sovereign, observed spectator, he appears in the place belonging to the king . . . from which his real presence has for so long been excluded (Foucault 1973: 312).

As we saw in chapter 1, introspection was certainly not invented by Descartes or modernity. St. Paul, the Church Fathers, and particularly Augustine relied heavily on it to build their theologies. In fact, later on we will see that in reconstructing the history of sexuality, Foucault discusses how Christian "techniques of the self"—practices to control carnal temptations, to punish the body for its transgressions, and to ensure an impeccable soul—developed locally, at monasteries and churches, become co-opted by the apparatuses of science, the state, and capitalism to produce the panoptical society. Thus, what distinguishes the modern episteme from the preceding classical epoch is the elevation of the self in its split, subject-object nature, as a foundational "a priori" of knowledge and signification. What defines modernity is "an analytic of finitude," where the human self has taken the place of God, as both the sovereign spectator of the world and the object of his/her own gaze.

We can see, then, that, even in his "structuralist" phase, Foucault retained his constructionist and historicist impetus. However, this social construction-ism was primarily focused on the power of discourse to shape self and environ-ment. During this period, in his desire to overcome the residual subjectivism in *Madness and Civilization*, Foucault seemed to assume a disembodied view of discourse, the rules of which are analyzed for their own sake. While he shed light on the ontogenic power of language, its capacity to give rise to concrete subjects and objects, Foucault disconnected epistemes from institutional, spa-tial, and corporal strategies, losing the rich interplay between, on the one hand, narratives, tropes, and forms of knowledge, and on the other, the practices of exclusion and confinement that gave rise to madness.

Foucault recontextualized and rehistoricized his thought in response to the events of the summer of 1968 in Paris. In May of that year, students engaged in protests against the police tactics used by university administrators allied with the government of Charles de Gaulle. These protests spontaneously mush-roomed into massive street demonstrations attracting not only teachers and workers, but people from all walks of life. Although the movement came very close to overturning the entire status quo, in the end, it dispersed, partially due to the failure of traditional left-wing forces, such as the Communist Party and its associated trade federations, to support it. Foucault's participation in the movement made him aware of the need for a theory of social construction that could account for both the fluidity and fragility of power and its widespread presence and resilience. Structuralism was too static and totalizing (in its claim of recovering the rules of formation for entire systems of thought) to make sense of the protean interplay between domination and resistance. This is why he turned to Nietzsche and his genealogical approach.

As we saw in chapter 2, in *Genealogy of Morals*, Nietzsche had traced the rise of modernity's most cherished values (goodness, individual sovereignty, and truth), to show how, rather than being universal values beyond the contradic-tions of history, they are the products of specific struggles that left their mark on our bodies. Nietzsche, the genealogist of modernity's idols, "refuses to extend his faith in metaphysics . . . he listens to history, he finds that there is 'something altogether different' behind things: not a timeless and essential secret, but the secret that they have no essence or that their essence was fabri-cated in a piecemeal fashion from alien forms" (Foucault 1977a: 143). Thus, to practice genealogy is to "follow the complex course of descent . . . to maintain passing events in their proper dispersion: it is to identify the accidents, the minute deviations—or conversely, the complete reversals—the errors, the false appraisals, and the faulty calculations that gave birth to those things that con-tinue to exist and have value for us; it is to discover that truth or being do not lie at the root of what we know and are, but the exteriority of accidents" (Foucault 1977a: 146).

In order to understand what happened in May 1968, Foucault felt that he needed to identify the myriad of struggles and the unstable foundations upon which modern societies like de Gaulle's France are based. It was no longer a matter of recovering some primal moment when Cartesian reason was about to emerge by othering madness or of assuming that the status quo was simply constituted by deep discursive structures. The task became a genealogical one: to map out how "procedures for the production, regulation, distribution, circulation and operation of statements" are historically deployed and resisted. Foucault had to analyze "regimes of truth," how knowledge is connected with "forms of hegemony, social, economic and cultural" (Foucault 1980: 133).

The concept of regimes of truth underscores Foucault's non-reductive materialism: discursive formations must be studied in action, as they are formed, refined, extended, and contested in interaction with practices that manage bodies and spaces. Although signification and power are inextricably connected with each other, they are not identical. In the application of power, symbols and meanings are the not the only game in town and, thus, social constructionism cannot be equated with textualism, with the idea that all social practices can be understood as texts.[7] For Foucault, "it is necessary . . . to distinguish power relations from relations of communication which transmit information by means of language, a system of signs, or any other symbolic medium. No doubt communicating is always a certain way of acting upon another person or persons. . . . [However,] whether or not they pass through systems of communication, power relations have a specific nature" (Foucault 1982: 217). To give an example, the "scientific" discourses about various types of criminality and about judicial notion of prisoner reform are closely related to architecture of the panopticon, the circular prison where "each comrade becomes an overseer" (Foucault 1980: 152). However, we should not reduce the spatial management and disciplinary practices within the panopticon to the knowledges it generates. The point is to see how material practices marking the physical bodies are linked to the material effects of discourse about those bodies.[8]

To study the connection between truth and power genealogically, Foucault moves away from what he calls a "juridical concept of power," power as a thing that sovereign individuals possess through legitimate delegation (in the democratic process) and with which they constrain the activities of others. Such a view of power is associated with the subject-centered project of the Enlightenment and modernity. Foucault argues that to understand the inner workings of panoptical societies like de Gaulle's France, we need a new relational theory of power: power as the shifting interaction between two or more bodies occupying different positions in the networks that constitute the social field. In this new theory, power is "positive" in the sense that it operates not by directly suppressing, limiting, or denying, but by creating subjectivities. Power is also decentered, since it is not the sole province of the state. Rather, the stability of the state depends on the operation of power in everyday life.

> Power must be analysed as something which circulates, or rather as something which only functions in the form of a chain. It is never localized here or there, never in anybody's hands, never appropriated as a commodity or piece of wealth. Power is employed and exercised through a net-like organization. And not only individuals circulate between its threads; they are always in the position of simultaneously undergoing and exercising this power.
>
> The individual is not to be conceived as a sort of elementary nucleus, a primitive atom . . . on which power comes to fasten or against which it happens to strike, and in doing so subdues and crashes individuals. In fact, it is already one of the prime effects of power that certain bodies, certain gestures, certain discourses, certain desires, come to be identified and constituted as individuals. (Foucault 1980: 98)

This new understanding of power allows Foucault to focus on its "microphysics," the relations and tensions that take place in daily life. These relations are colonized by the state and bourgeoisie to advance collective forms of organization and identity. Rather than assuming that power flows from the top down from a state apparatus that seeks to reproduce itself, we must conduct an "ascending analysis of power, starting, that is, from its infinitesimal mechanisms, which each have their own history, their own trajectory, their own techniques and tactics, and then see how these mechanisms of power have been—and continue to be—invested, colonized, utilized, involuted, transformed, displaced . . . by ever more general mechanisms and forms of global domination" (Foucault 1980: 99). The capillary, polycentric circulation and exercise of power explain the simultaneous fragility and resilience of the de Gaulle regime: regulatory power was "everywhere," but also resisted at every point, since power is relational, all about differentials, about othering. "Where there is power, there is resistance" (Foucault 1978: 95).[9]

Foucault's micro-physics of power foregrounds the body. The starting point for our ascending analysis is not the unified, sovereign Cartesian subject, but the body upon which subjectivity is socially constructed. More concretely, we need to focus on the "infinitesimal mechanisms" of power that operate on the body. Indeed, in our society, Foucault argues that "systems of punishment are to be situated in a certain 'political economy' of the body: even if they do not make use of violent and bloody punishment, even if they use 'lenient' methods involving confinement or correction: it is always the body that is at issue—the body and its forces—their utility and docility, their distribution and submission." The systems of punishment involve power relations that "invest [the body], mark it, train it, torture it, force it to carry out tasks, to perform ceremonies, to emit signs" (Foucault 1977b: 25). To characterize the production of able and disciplined bodies, Foucault uses the metaphor of *dressage*, which in equestrian circles designates the practices by which a horse learns to perform with precision in accordance with its rider's subtle commands. With modernity, the human body enters "a machinery of power that explores it, breaks it down, rearranges it. A 'political anatomy,' which was also a 'mechanics of power,' was being born; it defined how one may have a hold over others' bodies, not only so that they may do what one wishes, but also that they may operate as one wishes, with the techniques, the speed and efficiency that one determines. Thus discipline produces subjected and practised bodies, 'docile' bodies" (Foucault 1977b: 138). One can readily see how modernity became implicated with the Holocaust, for what happened at concentration camps was not some irrational outburst but the rational maximization of the bodies of prisoners before they were systematically exterminated.

For all its plausibility, the genealogical study of the micro-physics of power over the body is not exempt from contradictions. If power has indeed penetrated even to the most intimate crevices of modernity, to the self, on what grounds can we resist the totalizing project of panopticism? Who does the resisting? Does the notion of panopticism not end up undermining Foucault's effort to build a nontotalizing theory of power, beyond the limitations of structuralism? As cultural theorist Fredric Jameson (1984: 57) puts it, the more Foucault succeeds in demonstrating the panoptical character of modern society, "the more powerless the reader comes to feel. Insofar as the theorist wins . . . by constructing an increasingly closed and terrifying machine, to that degree he loses, since the critical capacity of his work is thereby paralyzed. . . ."

To respond to these questions and criticisms, in his later work, Foucault began to deal more directly with the issue of agency. Rather than stressing the social dynamics that shape the body, he turns to the practices of the *rapport à soi* (the relation to oneself), the ways in which individuals fashion themselves into subjects through aesthetics, erotics, and ethics: how individuals adorn their bodies, exercise or starve them to look a certain way, or prepare them to experience pleasures. In particular, Foucault began to focus on "technologies of the self" that have played a key role in the construction of sexuality as the deepest, most secret, and intimate essence of our subjectivity.

Technologies of the self are practices that "permit individuals to effect, by their own means, a certain number of operations on their own bodies, on their own souls, on their own thought, on their own conduct, and this in a manner so as to transform themselves, modify themselves, and to attain a certain state of perfection, of happiness, of purity, of supernatural power" (Foucault 1999: 162).

In religious studies, it is the combination and tension between Foucaultian analyses of the micro-physics of biopower and of the technologies of the self that have proven most fruitful. A good example is Foucault's work on Christian technologies of the self, such as penance and confession, that he saw as two ways through which individuals tell the truth about themselves, thereby constituting themselves as faithful Christians.

> In the Christianity of the first centuries the obligation to tell the truth about oneself was to take two forms, the *exomologesis* and the *exagoreusis*. . . . On the one hand, the *exomologesis* is the dramatic expression of the penitent of his status as sinner, and this in a kind of public manifestation. On the other hand, in the *exagoreusis* we have the analytical and continuous verbalisation of the thoughts, and in this relation of complete obedience to the will of the spiritual father. But it must be remarked that this verbalization . . . is also a way of renouncing self and no longer wishing to be the subject of the will. Thus the rule of confession in *exagoreusis* . . . finds its parallel in the model of martyrdom that haunts *exomologesis*. The ascetic maceration exercise on the body and the obligation of verbalizing the thoughts—those things are deeply and closely related. (Foucault 1999: 179)

According to Foucault, the confession played a formative role in the development of our modern panoptical society. The "hermeneutic of desire," the obligation of deciphering and telling the truth about one's deepest temptations and desires, which, as Augustine had concluded, had to do with the concupiscence of the flesh, comes to full fruition in the Freudian "talking cure." Freud elevates the hermeneutics of the self to new heights, viewing the dynamics of the personality as the historical and individual re-enactment of the universal Oedipal sexual drama. Even dissidents like Carl Jung accept this interiority as an ontological reality.[10] In fact, one can argue that Jung pushes the metaphor of inner depth even further by claiming that there is a collective, transhistorical unconscious that can be accessed through religious mythology, since religion was there at dawn of humanity. Here we see how interiority and selfhood are connected to the search for origins and archetypes in religious studies.

It may seem contradictory to link psychoanalysis with age-old religious practices. After all, psychoanalysis presents itself as means of liberation from the excessive repressive force of religion, internalized in the super-ego. Was it not the goal of psychoanalysis to allow us to speak openly about sex—the sexual drives in children, for that matter!—in order to undo the unnecessary obstacles placed by a puritan Victorian era on the creative expression of psychic energy? Behind what Foucault calls the "repressive hypothesis," the view of religion as neurosis produced by childish fears and fixations, there is "a perverse implantation": the creation of sex, through medical discourses, as an inner essence that defines who we are. By "inciting discourse," by talking endlessly about sex, psychoanalysis does not liberate but rather ties us through a particular type of subjectivity that involves disclosing our deepest secrets. "At issue is not a movement bent on pushing rude sex back into some obscure and inaccessible region, but on the contrary, a process that spreads it over the surface of things and bodies, arouses it, draws it out and bids it speak, implants it in reality and enjoins it to tell the truth . . ." (Foucault 1978: 72). Psychoanalysis is an example of what Foucault means by his clever inversion of the Platonic formula: the modern "soul is the prison of the body" (Foucault 1977b: 30). This modern soul,

> unlike the soul represented by Christian theology, is not born in sin and subject to punishment, but is born rather out of methods of punishment, supervision and constraint. This real, non-corporal soul is not a substance; it is the element in which are articulated effects of a certain type of power and the reference of a certain type of knowledge. . . . On this reality-reference, various concepts have been constructed and domains of analysis carved out: psyche, subjectivity, personality, consciousness, etc.; on it have been built scientific techniques and discourses and the moral claims of humanism. (Foucault 1977b: 29–30)

Along with the construction of sex as a universal drive that gives rise to the self emerged new figures: "the hysterical woman, the masturbating child, the Malthusian couple [the fertile couple upon which the economic reproduction of society depends], and perverse adult" (Foucault 1978: 105). These figures were constructed as "targets and anchorage points for the ventures of knowledge": their bodies had to be observed and classified, their normality and abnormality carefully assessed. We see here how the proliferation of discourses about sexuality creates historical subjects.

It is important to note here that Foucault's claim that sex, the "soul," and subjectivity are socially constructed does not mean that there is no body as such. In the early stages of writing the first volume of *History of Sexuality*, he took sex to be "a pre-given datum, and sexuality figured as a sort of simultaneously discursive and institutional formation which came to graft itself onto sex, to overlay it and perhaps finally obscure it." However, he wondered: "couldn't it be that sex—which seems to be an instance having its own laws and constraints, on the basis of which the masculine and feminine sexes are defined—be something which is on the contrary produced by the apparatus of sexuality? What the discourse of sexuality was initially applied to wasn't sex but the body, the sexual organs, pleasures, kinship relations, interpersonal relations, and so forth" (Foucault 1980: 210).

Although Foucault denaturalizes sex, showing that it is not a fixed biological essence, he seems to leave space for a reality prior to, or least not exhausted by discursive construction. This is not a trivial move. In fact, it is related to his unwillingness to collapse truth and power into each other and to affirm that communication and power relations are indistinguishable from each other. We shall see that social constructionists who emphasize discursivity such as Judith Butler see in this move an equivocation on Foucault's part. Other social constructionists as well as material feminists find in Foucault's appeal to an extra-discursive body a way to rematerialize critical theory.

One of the most explicit applications of Foucault's insights to the study of religion is anthropologist Talal Asad's *Genealogies of Religion* (1993), where he examines the role that disciplinary practices in medieval monasticism—such as fasting, manual labor, and the daily routine of prayers, chanting, and the recitation of texts—played in constituting virtuous Christians. Asad argues that techniques of self such as the Rule of St. Benedict, which prescribed a detailed daily routine for the monks, including precisely timed liturgical exercises and periods of quiet contemplation and physical work, were crucial in the formation of humble and obedient disciples of Christ. Asad contends that obedience and self-denial did not result from the mere imposition of a top-down discipline, which simply repressed the monks' carnal desires. Rather, the point was to encourage a certain kind of desire, the desire to be virtuous, to experience a powerful communion with the sacred. Monastic technologies of the self were self-applied strategies to re-order the soul, to refine and sharpen the body's emotional capacities to have a particular kind of experience of the sacred, one that was not accessible to the laity. What we have here, then, is the construction of an authorized and authoritative religious self through the training of bodies.

> The formation/transformation of moral dispositions (Christian virtues) depended on more than the capacity to imagine, to perceive, to imitate—which, after all, are abilities everyone possesses in varying degree. It required a particular program of disciplinary practices. The rites that were prescribed by that program did not simply evoke or release universal emotions, they aimed to construct and reorganize distinctive emotions—desire (*cupiditas/caritas*), humility (*humilitas*), remorse

(*contritio*)—on which the central Christian virtue of obedience to God depended. (Asad 1993: 134)

The notion of the historical production of religious selves through the management of the body is also developed by authors such as Carolyn Walker Bynum and R. Marie Griffith, who, while not citing Foucault directly, operate within the spaces opened up by his social constructionism. As we saw in chapter 2, Bynum argues that medieval Christian women engaged in voluntary starvation not just because they were dualists and hated the body and therefore wanted to punish it through self-mutilation, but because they wanted to experience "a fusion with the suffering physicality of Christ." Women manipulated their bodies to establish a direct relation with the sacred that subverted, or at least transcended, the limitations placed upon them by the male hierarchy. The ascetic technologies of self that mystic medieval women applied to their bodies represented "a way of criticizing and controlling those in authority. They also provided a distinctive way for women to serve their fellows and meet their God. By their very extravagance, audacity, and majesty, they rejected the success of the late medieval church, rejected—for a wider, more soaring vision—an institution that made a tidy, moderate, decent, second-rate place for women and for the laity" (Bynum 1987: 243). At a time when the church had become too worldly, too compromised with the secular world, these women adopted a radical asceticism that in its glorification of pain and suffering produced an alternative, intense, and embodied way of being religious.

Without denying the power of women to fashion themselves into religious subjects, Griffith's analysis of "somatic indicators of true faith" among Evangelical Christians in the United States shows how "the quest for a particular kind of body is not merely individual matter but holds broad social and cultural implications." In particular, she highlights how Evangelical Christian diet culture disseminates and establishes a "racialized ideal of whiteness, purged of the excesses associated with nonwhite culture" (Griffith 2004: 225). To be a Christian means to be white, and to be white means to be thin, to have the capacity to control the appetites of the flesh in a way that women of color, being closer to nature, could not. Thus, "health and beauty have rarely been separable in white Christianity, where extreme thinness remains the highest standard for women and, as such, a cause for extreme self-loathing among those who fail to achieve it" (Griffith 2004: 237). Moreover, the practices and discourses on fitness among Evangelical Christians intersect with those of global consumerist capitalism, with its emphasis on young, hip, and almost ethereally thin bodies of the cosmopolitan urban class, which sets itself apart from those physically bound by everyday necessities. "Primitivized, eroticized, and excluded, fat persons have become ever more emphatic symbols of peril and filth, the weight of a sinful world that must be purged from Christianity to make way for an army of born-again bodies" (Griffith 2004: 238).

While Griffith and Bynum offer two different readings of the tension between the micro-physics of biopower (the social mechanisms disciplining the body and populations) and the hermeneutics of desire (the practices of the self upon itself) in Foucault, they both point toward the contribution of Foucaultian social constructionism. However, there are thinkers who argue that Foucault did not go far enough, that his references to a pre-discursive body betray an essentialism that was already present in his appeal to an undifferentiated madness in his early work. According to these thinkers, we must be social constructionists all the way down.

BEYOND FOUCAULT? THE SOCIAL CONSTRUCTIONISM OF JUDITH BUTLER

For Judith Butler, the social construction of the body is not a mere theoretical issue. At stake is the imposition of a normative way of being in the world that privileges a male-centered heterosexuality as our inescapable, natural essence. Butler sees the appeal to a gendered essence, to a masculine and a feminine essence distinctive from each other, as the basis for the construction of the sovereign and domineering modern subject. Thus, the problem for Butler is not the historical deployment on the body of certain insidious regimes of knowledge-truth, which the genealogist painstakingly reconstructs to show its excesses and contradictions as a way to resist it. Rather, the problem is more radical—it is an ontological problem: the attempt to naturalize the body, to present it as a given, unified entity, with a fixed, ahistorical nature. The problem is the body itself, which although always the product of our discourses, is said to be the unshakable bedrock upon which we can stabilize subjectivity. For Butler, the oppressive power of male-centered heterosexuality would not be possible without essentializing the body. Thus, feminist and queer studies scholars must go beyond critiquing specific operations of biopower on the body to challenge "the body" itself.

In challenging the givenness of the body, Butler finds that Foucault's social constructionism is incomplete and contradictory. For Foucault, "the body is the site where regimes of discourse and power inscribe themselves, a nodal point or nexus for relations of juridical and productive power. And, yet, to speak in this way invariably suggests that there is a body that is in some sense there, pregiven, existentially available to become the site of its own ostensible construction" (Butler 1999: 307). Although Foucault affirms that the body is a social artifact, that it has become historically sexualized, disciplined, and clinically observed, he seems to assume that there is a thing called body that is "external to its construction."

> [W]hereas Foucault wants to argue—and does claim—that bodies are constituted within the specific nexus of culture or discourse/power regimes, and that there is no materiality or ontological independence of the body outside of any one of those specific regimes, his theory nevertheless relies on a notion of genealogy, appropriated from Nietzsche, which conceives the body as a surface and a set of subterranean "forces" that are, indeed, repressed and transmuted by a mechanism of cultural construction external to that body. (Butler 1999: 308)

For all his efforts to reveal the contingent and precarious character of the values, conducts, identities, and institutions that we take for granted, Foucault, in the end, succumbs to essentialism, an essentialism that reproduces and reinforces the basis for the phallocentric heterosexual order of things. In fact, Foucault's theory of the body replays the strategies deployed by psychoanalysis, which presents itself as liberatory when it is, in reality, inciting us to the truth about ourselves and tying us into a certain type of interiority. Similarly, Foucault "seeks recourse to a prediscursive multiplicity of bodily forces that break through the surface of the body to disrupt the regulating practices of cultural coherence imposed upon that body by a regulatory regime" (Butler 1999: 312). In making this move, however, he ties us to the truth of the body, to the search for pristine origins that transcend our semiotically bound horizons. To avoid this logocentric trap, the same metaphysical longing for unchangeable essences that was behind Descartes's cogito, Butler offers "the culturally constructed body [that] would be the result of a diffuse and active structuring of the social field with no magical or ontotheological origins, structuralist distinctions, or fictions of bodies, subversive or otherwise, ontologically intact before the law" (Butler 1999: 312–13).

For Butler, it is totally contradictory to claim unmediated access to the "real" body. "The body posited as prior to the sign, is always *posited* or *signified* as *prior*. This signification produces as an *effect* of its own procedure the very body that it nevertheless and simultaneously claims to discover as that which *precedes* into own action.... To posit by way of language a materiality outside of language is still to posit that materiality, and the materiality so posited will retain that positing as its constitutive condition" (Butler 1993: 30). As soon as we open our mouths to summon the material body beyond discourse, even if it is to resist patriarchy in the name of maternal qualities,[11] we have simultaneously cancelled its externality, since it appears to us through the socially and culturally determined ways in which our language operates. We shall see in the chapter on textualism at large that Butler's argument is really a subspecies of Derrida's argument that "there is nothing outside the text," the claim that all efforts at finding foundations are shot through with the contingency, relationality, and indeterminacy of the webs of symbols in which we dwell.

It follows that if there is no access to a pre-representational body, the distinction between gender as a socially constructed identity and sex as an ontological reality, a natural endowment upon which gender is constructed, is not tenable. The subject is a contingent artifact through and through. But if the pre-discursive, pre-social, and pre-historical body is a "fiction," what accounts for the durability and cross-cultural presence of this fiction? This is the question that Butler sets out to answer in *Bodies that Matter* (1993) in response to critiques against her earlier work (*Gender Trouble*, published in 1990). Borrowing not only from Derrida but from structural Marxist Louis Althusser and speech-act theorists such as John Searle and J. L. Austin, Butler argues that the materiality of the body is the result of the repetition of the discourses that call it forth.[12] These discourses attain a material density through their constant performance. Their iteration transforms them into taken-for-granted ways of seeing and doing things. As they become institutionalized norms, they gain the power to compel, to produce reality as they name it.

> The presumption that the symbolic law of sex enjoys a separable ontology prior or autonomous to its assumption is contravened by the notion that the citation of the law is the very mechanism of its production and articulation. What is "forced" by the symbolic, then, is a citation of its law that reiterates and consolidates the ruse of its own force.... The process of that sedimentation or what we might call materialization will be a kind of citationality, the acquisition of being through the citing of power, a citing that establishes an originary complicity with power in the formation of the "I." (Butler 1993: 15)

But does the performance of authoritative speech not imply the existence of a subject that controls and uses it? Not for Butler, since the subject itself is an effect of the performance.

> [T]here is no power, construed as a subject, that acts, but only ... a reiterated acting that is power in its persistence and instability. This is less an "act," singular and deliberate; than a nexus of power and discourse that repeats or mimes the discursive gestures of power.

> Where there is an "I" who utters or speaks and thereby produces an effect in discourse, there is first a discourse which precedes and enables that "I" and forms in language the constraining trajectory of its will. Thus there is no "I" who stands behind discourse and executes its volition or will through discourse. On the contrary, the "I" only comes into being through being called, named, interpellated. . . . (Butler 1993: 225)

Butler, then, takes social constructionism to its logical conclusion—she dissolves not only the subject but also the body and matter itself in power-laden webs of signification. As she writes: matter is not a "site or surface, but . . . *a process of materialization that stabilizes over time to produce the effect of boundary, fixity, and surface we call matter*" (1993: 9, italics in the original). Here, she faces a more extreme version of the question about resistance that Foucault encountered in relation to the triumph of panoptical society. If we cannot appeal to the natural body as the ground to resist the imposition of heterosexual hegemony, in the name of what can we reject domination? Since, following Foucault, resistance is "never in a position of exteriority in relation to power," Butler has to rely on the notion of the "abject," the gaps and contradictions within normalized discourse, the points at which discourse breaks down even when applied in its most extreme form, since it inevitably gives rise to a silenced other that permanently haunts it. In performing the heterosexual body as a full, unproblematic presence, we also summon its lack, the homosexual body. The potential for resistance emerges in the tension between presence and absence, a tension which shows the contingent character of what is present. Since in order to have material effects, to produce sexed bodies, a discourse needs to be re-iterated, it is inherently fragile, open to disruption. "The interval between instances of utterance not only makes the repetition and resignification of the utterance possible, but shows how words might, through time, become disjointed from their power to injure and recontextualized in more affirmative modes" (Butler 1997: 15). Resistance, thus, is a deconstructive performance, a parodic exercise in intertextuality that destabilizes the pretensions of a given text to present itself as unified, as an indisputable reality.

Despite all the focus on performance, Butler ends up with a rather thin notion of resistance. Since the abject is nothing but the effect of exclusionary discursive practices, resistance can only be a mere echo of the re-production of normalized systems of signification. Resistance is not the only thin aspect of Butler's theory. Butler, like Foucault, sees herself as a materialist. Yet, Butler's materialism is rather peculiar, since she recognizes nothing but the "materiality of the signifier itself." She seems to conflate the eminently tenable position that discourse always mediates and shapes our experiences, even those that we consider most self-evident and intimate (such as our bodies), with the more problematic claim that "reality" is totally produced by discourse. Butler engages in what philosopher Ian Hacking (1999: 25) calls a "universal social constructionism," descended from "linguistic idealism [which] is the doctrine that only what is talked about exists, nothing has reality until it is spoken of, or written about [or citationaly performed]. This extravagant notion is descended from Berkeley's ideal-ism . . . the doctrine that all that exists is mental."

For all her concern with avoiding Descartes's metaphysics of presence and his quest for a God's-eye view of the world, Butler's partial, overly linguistified materialism relies on a domineering anthropocentric view that insists that whatever is, is discursive and whatever is discursive, is.[13] This thin but curiously arrogant materialism (in the sense that it declares nothing external to itself) fails to acknowledge our embeddedness in nature (even if this is experienced through our constructs) and our continuities with nonhuman animals. As a material process, citationality is but a bleep in chaos of universe, as Nietzsche posited at the end of his *Will to Power*. And how does the discursive emerge in the first place? What are the conditions for its creation and enduring presence? Are these conditions themselves merely sociocultural or are they also biological and ecological? Could it be that "it is the nature of culture to misrecognize culture as nature" by presenting itself as self-sufficient (Kirby 2008: 218)? Perhaps this insistent appeal to the matrix of language is itself an attempt to stabilize, to fix, a protean reality within the safe interiority of human signification.

Without denying the indisputable power of signs to disclose the world to us, a fuller yet humbler materialism must be open to (if never entirely certain of) a materiality not reducible to the discursive. At a very minimum, we must operate at the limits of social constructionism, where its efforts to achieve totality break down before a world that summons us as much as we summon it, as Merleau-Ponty puts it (see chapter 3). In the next chapter, I will try to sketch a social constructionism that allows for the body's multiple materialities, materialities that are surely encountered through but can not be exhausted by discourse. Our willingness and capacity to consider these multiple materialities is crucial in analyzing the range of factors—social, cultural, psychological, neurophysiological, ecological, and evolutionary—that interact in complex, contextual ways to make religious practices and identities possible.

6

Holding Social Constructionism in Check

The Recovery of the Active, Lived Body

Postmodernism is obsessed by the body and terrified of biology. The body
is a wildly popular topic in U.S. cultural studies—but this is the plastic,
remouldable, socially constructed body, not the piece of matter that sickens
and dies. . . . The creature who emerges from postmodern thought is centre-
less, hedonistic, self-inventing, ceaselessly adaptive. He sounds more like a
Los Angeles media executive than an Indonesian fisherman.

—*Terry Eagleton (2003: 185, 190)*

The scandal of Butler's linguisticism, her perceived failure of nerve, lies . . .
in allowing the performance and difference of material life to be located in
the acting human subject and not in the dynamic life of which that subject
is an effect.

—*Claire Colebrook (2008: 69)*

Chapter 5 traced the evolution of social constructionism, highlighting the contributions that its different strands can make to the study of religion and embodiment. I concluded with a critique of Judith Butler's "universal social
constructionism," which is a thin, anthropocentric version of materialism in
disguise. Further, I contended that, in its one-dimensional focus on discursive
practices, this materialism is not helpful in exploring the multiple material factors that condition embodied religious experience. My aim in this chapter is to
provide the outlines of a more open-ended and robust materialism that takes
social constructionism seriously, but without succumbing to the temptation of
positing it as a totalizing interpretive framework.

To open the way for this polymorphous non-reductive materialism, I begin
with critiques of Butler's theories by "material feminists" such as Susan Bordo,
Susan Hekman, and Karen Barad. These critiques point to an alternative
understanding of the body, not as a unified and fixed essence existing outside

culture or as a passive surface that gets inscribed by power, but as dynamic, complex, and intra-active materiality. The implications of this non-reductive materialism for the study of religion are far-reaching. It is not enough for scholars of religion to examine the textual and discursive strategies through which religion is constituted as a field of activity. Scholars of religion must take into account how ecology, biology, psychology, culture, language, and history interact to give rise to particular ways of being religious.

To flesh out what I mean by a non-reductive materialism that recovers the active, lived body, I discuss the work of Gilles Deleuze and Felix Guattari, showing how they recover some of the themes we encountered in Spinoza and Nietzsche in chapter 2. I close by drawing from Donna Haraway's work to propose ways in which a somatically grounded social constructionism may converse with the natural and cognitive sciences on the question of embodied and emplaced religious experience.

BEYOND BUTLER? MATERIAL FEMINISMS
AND THE BODY

Although Susan Bordo, like Butler, is strongly influenced by Foucault, she has been primarily interested in studying the cultural pathologies of the body. Her diagnostic focus on practices connected with eating disorders among women and the physical transformation of body, as well as on the impact on young girls of the images of femininity in mass media and popular culture, has led her to bring "the concreteness of the body (as opposed to an abstract 'theory of' the body)" to cultural studies and philosophy. By portraying the body as an artifact that can be modified at will, postmodern popular culture incites women to "alter [their] bodies without regard for biological consequences, recklessly making them over through yo-yo dieting and plastic surgery and eagerly embracing any technology that challenges [their] various biological clocks. Arguably, we are more in touch with our bodies than before. But, at the same time, they have become alienated products, texts of our own creative making, from which we maintain a strange and ironic detachment" (Bordo 1993: 288).

Bordo recognizes that anorexia and bulimia have been culturally produced. However, she resists "the general notion, quite dominant in the humanities and social sciences today, that the body is a tabula rasa, awaiting inscription by culture. When bodies are made into mere *products* of social discourse, they remain bodies in name only" (Bordo 1993: 35). Bordo's search for the concrete, lived body explains her critique of postmodern theory: "despite its alliance with 'the body,' it often seems to be scaling the heights with pure mind. I am not 'anti-theory.' But my criticism of *certain kinds* of theorizing—as excessively aestheticized, or pretentious, or unhinged from social context—have sometimes been mistaken as indicating that I am." More specifically, the postmodern tendency to "textualize" the body gives "a kind of free, creative rein to *meaning* at the expense of attention to the body's material locatedness in history, practice, and culture" (Bordo 1993: 38). The result is the effacement of lived bodies of particular men and women. In turn, such effacement may lead to the failure to recognize and combat egregious forms of violence against women, some of which, like female genital mutilation, are religiously inflected.[1]

Bordo is quick to acknowledge the invaluable contributions that Butler has made to literary theory and cultural and gender studies: her challenge of entrenched binary notions of what is natural and unnatural. Nevertheless, Bordo feels that Butler's "discourse foundationalism" may easily slide into decontextualized, disembodied theorizing.

> For the discourse foundationalist, insights into our embeddedness in discourse function as a "bottom line," a privileged framework which is used to deconstruct other frameworks of understanding to its own preferred elements (that's why I offer the image of a "theoretical pasta-machine" which converts everything that passes through it into a "trope") and, having done this, dispense with them as so much detritus. Certainly we are embedded in language. We are also creatures with a physiology that limits us, even in the kinds of language we have developed. (Bordo 1998: 89)

The trouble with discourse foundationalism is that it assumes, from the inescapability of semiotic mediation, that "all we are legitimately permitted to talk about is our reality as discourse and representation. . . . [But] what makes 'matter' an 'effect of discourse' and the 'trope' a foundational explanatory concept? The 'trope' has a history, too, [and] is no more 'prior to discourse' than 'matter'" (Bordo 1998: 89). This overly narrow focus on power as discourse, in turn, severely limits our capacity to explore and confront the multiple physical ways (beyond symbolic violence) in which power impinges on the bodies of women.

> My work on the body is more "material" than many because I believe that the study of representations and cultural "discourse"—while an important part of the cultural study of the body—cannot by itself stand as a history of the body. Those discourses impinge on us as fleshy bodies, and often in ways that cannot be determined from the study of representations alone. To make such

determinations, we need to get down and dirty with the body on the level of its practices—to look at what we are eating (or not eating), the lengths we will go to keep ourselves perpetually young, the practices we engage in, emulating TV and pop icons, and so forth. (Bordo 1998: 91)

Thus, like Foucault, Bordo refuses to collapse discursive and nondiscursive practices into each other. Does this refusal not betray a kind of essentialism, since it assumes that there is something beyond discourse, something that is more material? Bordo is aware of the danger of essentialism in the appeal to materiality: "[I]n speaking of materiality, I am neither invoking some 'matter' of the body opposed to its 'form,' nor I am insisting on the primacy of the brute 'matter' of things, or the 'natural' or the instinctual against the culturally over-laid or linguistic. 'Materiality,' for me, is not *stuff*, not substance, not nature" (Bordo 1998: 90).

What, then, is Bordo's notion of materiality and embodiment? She does not use the term material "in the Aristotelian sense of *brute* matter, nor [does she] mean it in the sense of 'natural' or 'unmediated' (for our bodies are necessarily cultural forms; whatever roles anatomy and biology play, they always interact with culture.) [She means] what Marx and, later, Foucault had in mind in focusing on the 'direct grip' (as opposed to the representational influence) that culture has on our bodies, through the practices and bodily habits of everyday life" (Bordo 1993: 16).

Here Bordo's view of materiality echoes Heidegger's and Merleau-Ponty's historicist and materialist phenomenologies, which we encountered in chapter 3.

"Materiality," in the broadest terms, signifies for me our finitude. It refers to our inescapable physical locatedness in time and space, in history and culture, both of which not only shape us (the social constructionist premise, which I share with other postmoderns) but also *limit* us (which some postmoderns appear to me to deny). As Nietzsche rightly insisted, we are always standing *someplace* and seeing from *somewhere*, and thus are always partial and selective thinkers. (Bordo 1998: 90)

Nevertheless, unlike Heidegger and Merleau-Ponty, Bordo goes beyond rec-ognizing the role of humanly constructed materiality. She also explicitly points to the materiality that makes the process of human construction possible. "Our materiality (which includes history, race, gender, and so forth, but also the biology and evolutionary history of our bodies, and our dependence on the natural environment) impinges on us—shapes, constrains, and empowers us—both as thinkers and knowers, and also as 'practical,' fleshy bodies" (Bordo 1998: 91).

In all fairness to Butler, she has explicitly rejected the labels of linguistic foundationalism, monism, or reductionism as misreadings of her work. As early as *Bodies that Matter*, she wrote: "For surely bodies live and die; eat and sleep; feel pain, pleasure; endure illness and violence; and these 'facts,' one might skeptically proclaim, cannot be dismissed as mere constructions. Surely there must be some kind of necessity that accompanies these primary and irrefutable experiences. And surely there is. But their irrefutability in no way implies what it might mean to affirm them and through what discursive means" (Butler 1993: xi). Here Butler seems to be acknowledging that there is a lived body behind discourse after all. Still, she wants to defend the more moderate claim that our experience of the lived body is always discursive. Indeed, "to claim that discourse is formative is not to claim that it originates, causes, or exhaustively composes that which it concedes; rather it is to claim that there is no reference to a pure body which is not at the same time a further formation of the same body" (Butler 1993: 10). She has elaborated more recently: "The claim that a discourse 'forms' the body is no simple one, and from the start we must distinguish how such 'forming' is not the same as a 'causing' or 'determining,' still less is it a notion that bodies are somehow made of discourse pure and simple" (1997: 84). The trouble with these protestations is that they seem to fall into a self-performative contradiction: what if the distinction between forming and causing/determining is as socially constructed as the gender/sex couplet? A consistent deconstructionist would show the contingent character of this distinction to prevent it from being naturalized as hegemonic. The distinction to which Butler appeals only makes sense if "there are modes of embodiment that resist being reclaimed so quickly or so well—that are not the ghostly creatures of 'prior delimitation of the extra-discursive,' much less the residua of certain texts" (Casey 1998: 208). In turn, this would mean that Butler's radical social constructionism will have to be held in check. As she seems to imply in her own disavowals of discursive idealism, "while the body may only be referred to through discourse or representation, it possesses a force and a being that marks the very character of representation" (Colebrook 2000: 77).

A case in point here is the complex understanding of the body in early Daoism. Daoist sages approached the body as a living text, as a configuration of elements like *qi* (vital energy), *jing* (essence), and *shen* (spirit) that could be read through divination. However, some masters also saw the body as a veritable laboratory, a powerful furnace to refine vital elixirs and conduct alchemical transubstantiation in order to attain longevity and, possibly, immortality by becoming a primordial embryo. The success of this inner alchemy (*neidan*) depended on self-cultivation, strengthening and balancing the body through "various forms of calisthenics, psychosomatic exercises, diets, and massages"

(Poceski 2009: 107). Underlying and sustaining both the explicitly hermeneutic practices of divination and disciplinary corporal practices was *de*, the self-moving, spontaneous energy of the universe.

This example shows the polyvocal materiality of the body in Daoism. In Daoism, the body's generativity is not exhausted by signification. Rather, this signification is made possible by the fact that the body, like all matter in the universe, is sheer energy always in the process of flowing and becoming. Thus, we need approaches that can make sense of body's material polyvocality, beyond Butler's provincial focus on the materiality of discourse and textuality. Material feminism offers a promising alternative.

MATERIAL FEMINISM, AGENTIAL REALISM, AND THE BODY

Bordo's proposal for a richer materialism and corporeal feminism is part of a larger effort in feminist theory to recognize that nature has agency. Nature is not only capable of pushing back against our discursive interventions but making our lived experience possible in complex interaction with culture. According to Susan Hekman (2008), constructionist feminism, seeking to avoid the essentialism and foundationalism that served to legitimatize gender oppression, rejects the modernist copy-theory of knowledge, which assumes that reality is out there and that all we need is the right method to be able to capture it once and for all. As we saw in chapter 1 in the discussion of Cartesian epistemology, this representationalism, the idea of a sovereign mind that mirrors reality, presupposes an untenable subject-object dualism. In order to heal this dualism, constructionist feminists such as Butler stressed the unavoidably mediated character of knowledge. The world we experience is necessarily the result of our situated practices, particularly semiotic practices, which create objects and subjects through the process of reiteration, through the institutionalization of shared constructs. Hekman readily acknowledges the fruitfulness of the constructionist move. However, she is concerned that a radical linguistic constructionism does not heal the subject-object split but merely displaces it: only humans, as cultural and linguistic beings, have agency, in contrast with nature, which social constructionists tend to see as an inert or even empty category. Despite totally destabilizing the unified and self-transparent Cartesian subject, constructionisms such as Judith Butler's end up mirroring the Cartesian denigration of matter. For Descartes matter (and the body as constituted by it), in contrasts to *res cogitans*, is purely mechanistic, bound by predictable motions. For Butler, matter is the effect of discourse, the negative trace of signification. In both cases, matter is neither truly active nor affirmative.

Radical feminist constructionists run the danger of reinscribing the culture and nature split, as well as the sharp divide between humans and nonhuman nature. In Hekman's view, this divide has made it difficult for feminists in the humanities and social sciences to dialogue productively with a promising current of feminist studies in the natural sciences.

Echoing Hekman, particle physicist Karen Barad writes: "Language has been granted too much power. The linguistic turn, the semiotic turn, the interpretive turn, the cultural turn: it seems that at every turn every 'thing'—even materiality—is turned into a matter of language or some form of cultural representation. . . . Language matters. Discourse matters. Culture matters. There is an important sense in which the only thing that does not seem to matter anymore is matter" (Barad 2008: 120). It is one thing to recognize that the world discloses itself to us through the contested webs of signifiers we articulate and quite another to assert that language is all there is. "Performativity, properly understood, is not an invitation to turn everything (including material bodies) into words; on the contrary, performativity is precisely a contestation of the excessive power granted to language to determine what is real. Hence in ironic contrast to the misconception that would equate performativity with a form of linguistic monism that takes language to be the stuff of reality, performativity is actually a contestation of the unexamined habits of mind that grant language and other forms of representation more power in determining our ontologies that they deserve" (Barad 2008: 121).

Going beyond Bordo's critique of the linguistic monism or foundationalism in Butler, Barad proposes a fuller concept of performativity that emphasizes the interplay among multiple forms of materiality. Experience and knowledge are possible only through "material-discursive practices" made possible by our physical embodiment, by the interaction of our bodies with the nonhuman environment in which they are embedded and on which they depend for their existence. For Barad, performativity is a "materialist, naturalist, and posthumanist elaboration that allows matter its due as an active participant in the world's becoming." Barad's notion of performativity is not post-human in the structuralist sense, in which the author and subject are dissolved in the play of signifiers. Rather, Barad uses the terms posthumanist performativity to underscore her call to "cut loose [agency] from its traditional humanist orbit. Agency is not aligned with human intentionality or subjectivity" (Barad 2008: 144). She wants to challenge the implicitly dualistic position that views nature as "immutable or passive." To the contrary, matter "does not require the mark of an external force like culture or history to complete it. Matter is always already an on-going historicity" (Barad 2008: 139). Matter has "agential separability," that is, "exteriority within (material-discursive) phenomena," meaning that our practices and matter are mutually implicative, reciprocally disclosing each other (Barad 2008: 143). Along the same lines, material feminist Claire Colebrook (2008: 74) argues that "once nature is accepted as dynamic, active, and unpredictably open, we have arrived at a liberating anti-humanism. The human is not some spiritual substance set over and against matter, nor is it merely material—quantifiable as so much biologically or genetically determinate stuff—for human culture is matter that has acquired organizations so complex as to constitute culture."

Borrowing from Neils Bohr's epistemological framework to explore quantum physics, Barad (2007) calls her approach "agential realism."[2] It is realism because matter does matter, but it is agential in the sense that matter is never passive, as in the copy-theory of knowledge, which holds that the mind simply re-presents what is out there, standing against us. It is agential in the sense that we, as material beings, meet the world through our practices, including semiotic ones, and our artifacts, and the world meets us through its own dynamic impact on bodies. This encounter is always open-ended, complex, often paradoxical, making it impossible to claim access to ultimate essences and foundations. In Barad's own words: agential realism "theorizes agency in a way that acknowledges that there is a sense in which 'the world kicks back' (i.e., non-human and cyborgian forms of agency in addition to human ones) without assuming some innocent, symmetrical form of interaction between the knower and known" (Barad 1999: 2).

I will have more to say about cyborgs later, when I discuss Haraway's work. But from the above, it is clear that agential realism is meant to heal the subject-object split, not by inflating the subject and its cultural productions and erasing the pole of the object as in the case of radical social constructionism, but by refusing the split in the first place, just like Spinoza, Nietzsche, and Merleau-Ponty have done in the past.

> Discursive practices and material phenomena do not stand in a relation of externality to one another; rather, the material and the discursive are mutually implicated in the dynamics of inter-activity. But neither are they reducible to one another. The relationship between the material and the discursive is one of mutual entailment. Neither is articulated/articulable in the absence of the other. . . . Neither discursive practices nor material phenomena are ontologically or epistemologically prior. Neither can be explained in terms of the other. Neither has privileged status in determining the other. (Barad 2008: 140)

Agential realism, thus, underlines the "mutual constitution of entangled agencies" (Barad 2007: 33). That is, the world is the interactive outcome of different forms of materiality—discursive and nondiscursive—which constitute boundaries of various degrees of stability and generalizability. "Reality is not composed of things-in-themselves or things-behind-phenomena, but of 'things'-in-phenomena," where phenomena are "dynamic topological reconfigurations/entanglements/relationalities/(re)articulations" enacted by material-discursive practices (Barad 2007: 135). Sociologist and physicist Andrew Pickering makes a similar point when he argues that scientific objectivity emerges from the "mangle of practice," from the situated, messy, and unpredictable encounter with a "world that makes us in the same process in which we make [it]" (Pickering 1995: 26).[3]

Barad's argument for a "robust account of materialization of all bodies—'human' and 'non-human,'" clears the way for a fully somatocentric theory of religion that does not stop at the genealogical analysis of the textual, discursive, cultural, and social components of religious experience and activity. Instead the task is two-fold: (1) to recover the evolutionary, ecological, and psycho-cognitive conditions for religious life and (2) to understand the complex and diverse ways in which these conditions interact with sociocultural dimensions. As Thomas Tweed puts it (2006: 65, italics in the original), the task is to study religion materialized as "organic-cultural flows" resulting from the "complex interaction of *organic constraints* (neural, physiological, emotional, and cognitive) and *cultural mediations* (linguistic, tropic, ritual, and material)." This will be the focus of the next chapter. For now, I would like to deepen the insights of material feminism by bringing other theorists into the conversation. In particular, I would like to explore further the notion of matter as productive process.

NIETZSCHE'S AND SPINOZA'S RETURN: DELEUZE AND GUATTARI

Arguably, no text marks the birth of postmodern thinking more dramatically than Gilles Deleuze's *Nietzsche and Philosophy*, originally published in 1962. The book challenged the two modernist schools of philosophy that dominated postwar France: structuralism and existentialism. On the one hand, *Nietzsche and Philosophy* offered a way to overcome structuralism's inability to account for change and conflict as well as its drive toward totalizing and reductive models. On the other hand, it provided an alternative reading of Nietzsche that went beyond the subjectivism of Sartrean existentialism. Deleuze's Nietzsche is not primarily about the unencumbered self condemned to make itself anew in every moment of engagement with the world—a modernist view that preserves the Cartesian subject albeit placing the emphasis on passions and actions rather than rationality. Instead, Deleuze highlights the Nietzsche of the will to power, the Nietzsche who saw all reality, including the self and the body, as the ever-changing expression of the tensions among multiple and inexhaustible forces. Reflecting on Nietzsche's view of the body, Deleuze writes:

> What is the body? We do not define it by saying that it is a field of forces, a nutrient medium fought over by a plurality of forces. For in fact there is no "medium," no field of forces or battle. There is no quantity of reality, all reality is already quantity of force. There are nothing but quantities of force in mutual "relations of tension." . . . Every force is related to others and it either obeys or commands. What defines a body is this relation between dominant and dominated forces. Every relationship of forces constitutes a body—whether it is chemical, biological, social or political. Any two forces, being unequal, constitute the body as soon as they enter into relationship. This is why the body is always a fruit of change. (1983: 39–40)

In Deleuze's version of the Nietzschean world, it is becoming all the way down. Down to its subatomic substrata, the cosmos is dynamic and relational, the effect of the endless clash of material forces, of differential quanta of energy that seek to affirm themselves. Therefore, it is not the human subject that is agentic but matter itself—matter organized not around fixed structures but matter as multidirectional flows just like the scattered limbs of Dionysus.

Deleuze brings this active and affirmative materialism to his work with psychiatrist Felix Guattari. In *Anti-Oedipus: Capitalism and Schizophrenia*, Deleuze and Guattari set out to recover Freud's latent materialism against the idealistic turn he took when he introduced the notion of the Oedipal complex. Freud had posited that the source of the personality was the id, fully charged with libidinal energy directed toward the fulfillment of basic organic needs such as survival and reproduction. He had also theorized that the self in formation (in newborns) was "polymorphously perverse," meaning that its psychic energies were not just directed toward sexuality or toward erogenous zones. Rather, the whole body of the infant was invested with raw organic energies, making it almost co-extensive with nature. With the introduction of the Oedipal complex, built on the male child's unfulfilled desires toward the mother, his imagined fear of castration, and his attempts to resolve this tension by imitating the father, Freud, in effect, shackles the multiple powers of unconscious under a hermeneutic device. Moreover, by making this interpretive construct universal, a transhistorical source of humanity's neuroses, Freud essentializes the productive body as a bourgeois subject. "It is as if Freud had drawn back from [the] world of wild production and explosive desire, wanting at all costs to restore a little order there, an order made classical owing to the ancient Greek theater" (Deleuze and Guattari 1983: 54). In the process, Freud "neurotizes everything in the unconscious at the same time as he oedipalizes, and closes the familial triangle over the entire unconscious. Desiring-production is personalized, or rather personologized (*personnologisée*), imaginarized (*imaginarisée*), structuralized. Production is reduced to mere fantasy production, production of expression. The unconscious ceases to be what it is—a factory, a workshop—to become a theater, a scene and its staging" (Deleuze and Guattari 1983: 55).

Religion is a key part of Freud's metanarrative about the self, as we learn in his *Totem and Taboo* and *Future of an Illusion*. Our present predicament lies in the attempt to solve the primal Oedipal event by elevating the murdered father into a repressive God who buttresses the defenses against the id's pleasure principle through morality, taboos, and sacralized rituals. Freud's turn away from the materiality of the libido is, thus, reinforced through an appeal to otherworldly transcendence.

Freud's idealist turn is aggravated by Jacques Lacan's structuralism. Freud proposed that the "cure" for neurosis lay in talking about the Oedipal trauma, in "linguistifying" as much of the unconscious as possible in order to strengthen the ego. Lacan takes this linguistification a step further by claiming that the unconscious is not an unruly sea of forces. Rather, it is structured like language: with the unbridgeable gap between signifiers and the signified (the Phallus) pointing to a lack at the core of the unconscious. Borrowing from Hegel's master-slave dialectic, Lacan (2002: 75–81) understood the formation of the self in early infancy (6 to 18 months) as going through a "mirror stage," when the child identifies him/herself as a distinct "I" by seeing her/his body image reflected on a mirror. This identification is a misrecognition, since the infant fantasizes him/ herself as an integrated self where there is in fact only an inchoate body. What was initially a moment of joyful narcissism, of the discovery of a fully autonomous "ideal I," eventually turns to paranoia and envy, as the infant comes to see the integrated image in the mirror as a rival to his fragmented body. Moreover, as the child sees him/herself reflected in the mother's eyes, s/he becomes aware of his/her unavoidable dependence on others. Because it is dependent on an imaginary order and others for its identity, the self is from its inception unstable and murky. Self-alienation and alterity always haunt the subject.[4]

Lacan's view of the self, then, challenges the Cartesian cogito, the unified and self-transparent thinking thing that has been at the heart of modernity's epistemology and hubris. As Lacan (2002: 157) cleverly puts it: "I am thinking where I am not, therefore I am where I am not thinking." In that sense, Lacanian psychoanalysis provides a valuable critique of the Cartesian notion of self that, as we saw in chapters 3 and 4, made it into religious studies via a one-sided reading of Husserl's phenomenology. Nevertheless, while Lacan's understanding of the development of the "I" preserves both Freud's and Nietzsche's stress on relationality and on the conflictive, precarious, and derivative nature of the ego, it privileges the role of representation in the process.

Against this semiotic reading of the unconscious, Deleuze and Guattari counterpose a "schizoanalysis," which takes the productivity of schizophrenia as its point of departure.

> A schizophrenic out for a walk is a better model than a neurotic lying on the analyst's couch. A breath of fresh air, a relationship with the outside world. While strolling outdoors . . . he [*sic*] is in the mountains, amid falling snowflakes, with other gods or without any gods at all, without a family, without a father or a mother, with nature. "What does my father want? Can he offer me more than that? Impossible. Leave me in peace." Everything is a machine. Celestial machines, the stars or rainbows in the sky, alpine machines—all of them connected to those of his body. He does not live nature as nature, but nature as a process of production. There is no such thing as either man or nature now, only a process that produces the one within the other and couples the machines together. (Deleuze and Guattari 1983: 2)

To restore the organic generativity of the unconscious, schizoanalysis or "materialist psychiatry" reconceptualizes the unconscious as shifting concatenation of "desiring-machines" in connection and tension with surrounding machines.[5] As Deleuze and Guattari put it: "we make no distinction between man [*sic*] and nature: the human essence of nature and the natural essence of man become one with nature in the form of production or industry. . . . Not man the king of creation, but rather as the being who is in intimate contact with the profound life of all forms or all types of beings . . . who ceaselessly plugs an organ-machine into an energy-machine, a tree into his body, a breast into his mouth, the sun into his asshole . . ." (1983: 4–5). For Deleuze and Guattari, desire as production is an underlying immanent principle. Note here that the notions of lack, loss, separation, and representation, so prominent in Lacanian psychoanalysis, give way to metaphors of fullness, connectivity, and production. Because the subject is a protean ensemble of intensities, which overflow boundaries (deterritorialize) to generate new transversal configurations (territorialize), it is relational and decentered without being marked by absence and loss. At the same time, the multidirectionality and polyvocality of the flows produced by the desiring-machines shatters the triangular prison (me-mommy-daddy) in which psychoanalysis has confined the unconscious.

In using the term "machines" to illustrate the operation of the unconscious, Deleuze and Guattari are not falling back on the Cartesian deterministic materialism. Rather, they want to emphasize the creativity of all reality, which is in endless, interconnected, yet nonteleological process of pure becoming. For them, machines are "assemblages" of various energies, "flows of matter-movement," contingent, mobile, and temporary sequences of intertwinings of forces that produce objects and subjects as repetitions within difference. "We will call assemblage every constellation of singularities and traits deducted from the flow—selected, organized, stratified—in such a way as to converge (consistency) artificially and naturally" (Deleuze and Guattari 1987: 406). As in Karen Barad's agential realism, assemblages are non-dualistic. They do not operate in accordance with the subject-object, culture-nature, and discursive-nondiscursive splits. "An assemblage, in its multiplicity, necessarily acts on semiotic flows, material flows, and social flows simultaneously. . . . There is no longer a tripartite division between a field of reality (the world) and a field of representation (the book) and a field of subjectivity (the author). Rather, an assemblage establishes connections between certain multiplicities drawn from each of these orders . . ." (Deleuze and Guattari 1987: 22–23).

The body as we experience it, then, is not the mere product of materializing discourses, as for Judith Butler. For Deleuze and Guattari, the body is a "plane of consistency," what they call the body without organs (BwO), which is criss-crossed, simultaneously territorialized and deterritorialized, striated by nomadic assemblages that eventually form organs, erogenous zones, and forms of subjectivation.[6] In that sense, bodies are "autopoietic," self-generating, self-ordering, and self-sustaining strata or plateaus of organic-inorganic matter. The notion of autopoiesis will be key in the next chapter, as I propose an "enactive approach" (Varela, Thompson, and Rosch 1991) to religion and cognition, an approach that understands religious experience as the nonlinear coupling between dynamic, self-organizing neural systems, sensorimotor processes, and the environment as mediated through our discursive and nondiscursive practices.

Echoing Spinoza, Deleuze and Guattari view the entire universe as a single dynamic principle which expresses itself in infinite ways. "[T]here is no vital matter specific to the organic stratum, matter is the same on all strata. But the organic stratum does have a specific unity of composition, a single abstract Animal, a single machine embedded in the stratum, and presents everywhere the same molecular materials, the same elements or anatomical components of organs, the same formal connections" (Deleuze and Guattari 1987: 45). In fact, Deleuze and Guattari pay homage to Spinoza by equating his philosophy with the world of schizos and children, which is all about pure yet evanescent intensities. "Children are Spinozists. When Little Hans talks about a 'peepee-maker,' he is referring not to an organ or an organic function but basically to a material, in other words, to an aggregate whose elements vary according to its connections, its relations of movement and rest, the different individuated assemblages it enters. Spinozism is the becoming-child of the philosopher" (Deleuze and Guattari 1987: 256).

With Deleuze and Guattari, we come to a body that, while still constructed and de-essentialized (in the sense of not bearing a fixed, transhistorical structure like the Oedipus complex), is fully active, not just the passive effect of discourses that interpellate it. We have here a full somatocentric non-reductive materialism that does not deny the generative power of the semiotic but that recognizes the productivity of other material practices and processes. Material feminist Rosi Braidotti (2002: 15) calls this an "enfleshed materialism."

Given its unequivocal affirmation of immanence and autopoiesis, does this enfleshed materialism leave any space for religion? Deleuze and Guattari would definitely find a lot to like in Daoism's understanding of the body as generative energy flows that are part and parcel of the natural operation of the cosmos. Nevertheless, they see the vertical appeal to God as an authoritarian move that seeks to fix the transversal, rhizome-like operations of the desiring-machines, to create foundational binary oppositions and hierarchies. As we saw in the case of Freud, despite his avowed atheism, he uses religion to support the universality of the Oedipal complex and his tripartite theory of self. "The judgment of God, the system of the judgment of God, the theological system, is precisely the operation of He who makes an organism, an organization of organs called the organism because He cannot bear the BwO [body without organs], because He pursues it and rips it apart so He can be first, and have the organism be first. The BwO howls: 'They made me an organism! They've wrongfully folded me! They've stolen my body! The judgment of God uproots it from its immanence and makes it an organism, a signification, a subject" (Deleuze and Guattari 1987: 158–59). In particular, Deleuze and Guattari (1987: 154) see priests as performing the same idealist move as Lacan: "The priest cast the triple curse on desire: the negative law, the extrinsic rule, the transcendent ideal."

It is clear that Deleuze and Guattari, like Freud, equate religion with unnecessary repression. Furthermore, they see religion as a protagonist in the disembodied idealism that has plagued Western thinking. Nothing can be more opposed to the materiality of the desiring-machines than the notion of a soul, distinct from the body and made in the image of an omnipresent and unchanging God. Poxon (2001) goes as far as characterizing Deleuzian philosophy as "embodied anti-theology." Nevertheless, Deleuze and Guattari's focus on immanent becoming opens the way for the non-reductive study of religious experiences. In the introduction, I argued that we should surrender the quest to find the timeless essence of religion, either in some supra-natural agent or in the unified subjectivity (soul) of the believer, since it is incompatible with a truly enfleshed materialism. As an alternative, I proposed that scholars of religion engage in the situated, fallible, and open-ended yet rigorous analysis of the natural (in the widest sense of the term) conditions that make religious claims possible and binding as well as the material effects that these claims have in everyday life. The focus should fall on the myriad of discourses, practices, environments, and institutions that accompany our experience of this-worldly transcendence, that is, our responses to the insoluble complexity and relative indeterminacy of our existential condition. Rendering it in Deleuzian language: the study of religion is a kind of "transcendental empiricism,"[7] engaged in the painstaking examination of ever-changing assemblages that are part and parcel of the processes of immanent becoming—becoming-human, becoming-animal, becoming-plant, becoming-woman, becoming-man, becoming-god, becoming-convert, becoming-prophet, becoming-saint, or becoming-orixá, and so on. How do we draw and sacralize the embodied striations that constitute our biological-cultural identities? How do these identities come to be recognized as authoritatively religious, capable of generating effective discourses, practices, and contexts that in turn help create ways of being in the world religiously?

There is an ongoing debate as to whether Deleuzian philosophy can be especially helpful in making sense of mystical encounters with nature, which are central to many indigenous religions and new/alternative religious movements. Goddard (2001: 62), for example, thinks that, despite Deleuze's rejection of Henri Bergson's notion of élan vital, (a dynamic principle that dwells in and animates the multiplicity of beings in the world), Deleuzian radical immanentism is compatible with mysticism's "complete immersion in life and in love as a process of metamorphic subjectivation." Certainly, Deleuze's recognition of multiple, interrelated, and shifting biological-cultural becomings resonates with what Brazilian anthropologist Eduardo Viveiros de Castro's calls the "multinaturalism" of Amerindian cosmologies.[8]

I believe that it is possible to construct Deleuze as a religious thinker, just as it is plausible to read Spinoza, and even Nietzsche, as proposing alternative (geocentric and somatocentric) forms of "spirituality." Indeed, George Lakoff and Mark Johnson (1999: 564–67, italics in the original) conclude that immanence may be accompanied by an embodied spirituality that experiences transcendence as "a sense of being part of *a larger all-encompassing whole*, or *ecstatic* participation—with awe and respect—within that whole, and of the *moral engagement* with that experience." Once we realize that "the environment is not an 'other' to us . . . [that] it part of our being . . . the locus of our existence and identity," we develop an "empathetic connection with the more than the human world." This is why they conclude that "a mindful embodied spirituality is . . . an ecological spirituality."

While a non-reductive materialist framework is entirely compatible with this kind of ecological spirituality, it does not require it. A scholar need not be religious or "spiritual" in order to engage in the sensitive yet rigorous study of religion. All that s/he needs is a humility that comes through the awareness of his/her positionality, as well as a keen appreciation of the creativity, complexity, and thrownness of human existence. A naturalistic approach to religion does not necessarily have to make us "critics." And not being a critic does not mean that the scholar is automatically a "caretaker," as Russell McCutcheon (2001) argues. It simply means that the epistemological honesty of non-reductive materialism compels us to be aware of the limits of our efforts to objectify religion or, for that matter, any realm of biological-cultural activity.

From my point of view, there is a more urgent issue in Deleuze's and Guattari's work: their sometimes excessive stress on mobility, fluidity, and chaos. I will argue in chapter 11, where I discuss Thomas Tweed's theory of religion, which is heavily influenced by Deleuze's and Guattari's work, that this stress is neither epistemologically fruitful nor politically strategic in contemporary society. Today, there are not only decentering flows but also powerful forces concentrating resources and imposing stark exclusion and domination. To preserve the agentic materialism of Deleuzian philosophy without falling into an uncritical celebration of disembedded flows, I introduce the notion of networks. Networks simultaneously conduct and restrict flows of goods, capital, people, and religious identities, ideas, and practices across multiple spaces, from the personal to the transnational and global, producing both deterritorialization and reterritorialization. Networks will also figure prominently in the next chapter, particularly in the discussion on religion and neurophenomenology.

In preparation for the next chapter, which explores what the natural sciences can tell us about embodied religion, I would like to close this chapter with a discussion of human-nonhuman relations and of the entanglements of culture and nature that notions such as agentic realism and assemblage illuminate. To do this, I turn to the work of Donna Haraway.

EMBODIED HYBRIDITIES: TOWARD
AN INTERSPECIES MATERIALISM

Like Deleuze and Guattari, Donna Haraway offers a new understanding of machines and their relations to humans. Haraway wants to challenge readings of technology and science built on Cartesian dualisms, the "Great Divides" that characterize modern humanism and posthumanism (Haraway 2008). For the denigration of machines, our perception of them as mere automatons standing against us as agents with free will, and threatening in many a science fiction film to control and disenchant our life-world, is closely implicated with the "fantasy of human exceptionalism," "the premise that humanity alone is not a spatial and temporal web of interspecies dependencies" (Haraway 2008: 11). As we saw in chapter 2, this fantasy of human exceptionalism, which had religious antecedents, led Descartes to elevate the cogito, the disembodied and disembedded thinking thing, above everything else. The chasm generated by this "god-trick," as Haraway (1991: 189) calls it, legitimizes the instrumental understanding of the body and nature. They become the purview of a mechanistic and reductive science, while the cogito can only be properly studied through philosophy and the hermeneutic tools of the humanities. Human exceptionalism transformed into a foundational philosophy, thus, contributes not only to the human-nature split, but the divide between the humanities and the natural sciences and between organic and inorganic life.

We saw above how even those thinkers in the humanities and cultural studies, like Judith Butler, who rightly dethrone and decenter the self, end up reproducing the great metaphysical divides by accepting the notion that biology can only mean determinism and domineering essentialism. We "lose too much" when we view the body as "anything but a blank page for social inscription, including those of biological discourse" and when we reduce "the objects of physics or of any other sciences to the ephemera of discursive production and social construction" (Haraway 1991: 197). For Haraway, as for Barad, this extreme social constructionism is still driven by a Cartesian attitude: nature, both organic and inorganic, is "only matter for the seminal power, the act, of the knower. Here, the object both guarantees and refreshes the power of the knower, but any status as *agent* in the productions of knowledge must be denied the object. It—the world—must, in short, be objectified as a thing not as an agent; it must be a matter for the self-formation of the only social being in the productions of knowledge, the human knower" (Haraway 1991: 197–98, italics in the original).

As an alternative, Haraway advocates for a "Catholic sacramentalism," in which the entire world is animated and in which the word and the intrinsic goodness of matter are intertwined to make transubstantiations possible (2000: 24). As she writes: "[r]aised a Roman Catholic, I grew up knowing that the Real Presence was present under both 'species,' the visible form of the bread and the wine. Sign and flesh, sight and food, never came apart for me again after seeing and eating that hearty meal. Secular semiotics never nourished as well or caused as much indigestion" (2008: 18). For Haraway, thus, our world is constituted by "natural-cultural entanglements," through our practices as "material-semiotic actors," that is, as agents embedded in biological, ecological, and social networks and in conversation with other nonhuman actors. This embeddedness and conversation are, of course, mediated by our metaphors, by our discourses.

Like Barad's agentic realism, the notions of "natural-cultural entanglements" and "material-semiotic actors" are meant to overcome the unproductive subject-object, language-matter, and culture-nature splits without falling into a new kind of foundationalism. By the term "material-semiotic actor," Haraway intends to "[h]ighlight the object of knowledge as an active, meaning-generating axis the apparatus of bodily production, without *ever* implying immediate presence of such objects or, what is the same thing, their final and unique determination of what can count as objective knowledge at a particular historical juncture" (Haraway 1991: 200). As with the reversibility of the flesh in Merleau-Ponty's philosophy, which folds together the inside and the outside, the visible and the visible, and the self and the world (see chapter 3), for Haraway, "bodies as objects of knowledge are material-semiotic generative nodes. Their boundaries materialize in social interaction. Boundaries are drawn by mapping practices; 'objects' do not pre-exist as such. Objects are boundary projects." Our "objective" knowledge of the world is the result of our situated encounter with it, an encounter that is made possible by the simultaneous materiality and discursivity of our bodies. Here by boundaries, Haraway does not mean hard and fast borders, but rather "naturalcultural zones of contact," spaces of "becoming-with" in which the interlocutors meet each other, both with full agency.

To illustrate her alternative ontology, Haraway offers several figures, the most prominent of whom is the cyborg.[9] The cyborg stands as the new subjectivity emerging from recent scientific and technological changes, ranging from in vitro fertilization to organ transplants, gene therapies, transgenics, and the rapid growth of cybercommunications.

A cyborg is a hybrid creature, composed of organism and machine. But cyborgs are compounded of special kinds of machines and special kinds of organisms appropriate to the late twentieth century. Cyborgs are post–Second World War

hybrid entities made of, first, ourselves and other organic creatures in our uncho-
sen "high-technological" guise as information systems, texts, and ergonomically
controlled labouring, desiring, and reproducing systems. The second essential
ingredient in cyborgs is machines in their guise, also, as communication systems,
texts, and self-acting, ergonomically designed apparatuses. (Haraway 1991: 1)

Cyborgs may seem the stuff of science fiction, for example, as in the popular film *Blade Runner*, based on a dystopian world conceived by writer Philip
K. Dick. In this future world, cyborgs are violent and deeply tragic creatures.
In terms of physical appearance, they are indistinguishable from humans.
Yet, they are not fully human. In order to separate them from humans, their
creators in the powerful Tyrell Corporation have given these androids very
short life spans and no memories of their own. They are ahistorical figures
that have not been socialized to express the "normal" range of feelings that
human beings have. This condition drives the cyborgs to fits of anger and to
search for their creator so they can find out why they were made flawed. In
essence, the androids in *Blade Runner* are a retelling of Mary Shelley's
Frankenstein—benighted monsters that warn us of the dangers of playing god
through science.

Haraway presents a different reading of cyborgs. Since they are "compounds of hybrid techno-organic embodiment and textuality," cyborgs are
creative "boundary creatures," "tricksters," who are able to bridge gaps and
cross fixed borders (1991: 3, 212). Cyborgs are not the nightmares of the
future but the promise of the present. "By the late twentieth century, our
time, a mythic time, we are all chimeras, theorized and fabricated hybrids
of machine and organism; in short, we are cyborgs. The cyborg is our
ontology" (Haraway 1991: 150). As "mixed organic-technological hybrids,"
beings constituted of fragments of diverse materials, cyborgs fly in the face
of Western metaphysics' "Great Divides." Although clearly situated, they are
thoroughly relational beings. Cyborgs appear "precisely where the boundary
between human and animal is transgressed. Far from signalling a walling off
of people from other living beings, cyborgs signal disturbingly and pleasur-
ably tight coupling. Bestiality has a new status in this cycle of marriage
exchange" (Haraway 1991: 152).

Haraway's emphasis on the fractured, interconnected, shifting, and generative identities of cyborgs dovetails nicely with Deleuze and Guattari's transcendent empiricism, with their idea of multiple but interconnected immanent
becomings.[10] As Rosi Braidotti (2006: 201) puts it, reading Haraway through
Deleuzian lenses, the cyborg evinces "a radically immanent intensive body
[that] is an assemblage of forces, or flows, intensities and passions that solidify

in space, and consolidate in time, within the singular configuration commonly known as an 'individual' self." The cyborgs' hybridity subverts the naturalized, self-transparent identities we have constructed to keep nature and technology at arm's length. The world of the cyborgs is all about "lived social and bodily realities in which people are not afraid of permanently partial identities and contradictory standpoints" (Haraway 1991: 154). The cyborg calls for an "honest constructionism," one that recognizes

> [t]he worldviews of other species—their knowledge of a given landscape, their own constructions of reality—as sources of insight and change for our own knowledge. We ought to ask whether there are nonhuman ways of being conscious, of having a mind, of acting morally. Perhaps our human ways are unique, but are they the only ways? Are they even the best ways, in terms of the Darwinian notion of fitness as adaptation to a particular niche and way of life? (Peterson 2001: 223)

As with Deleuze and Guattari, it is fair to ask about the limits of Haraway's cyber-materialism. Is it not reductive in the last instance? Is it possible that in her celebration of the cyborg, Haraway has overplayed her hand, endorsing any kind of semiotic and technological intervention in nature? Does this idea that we always encounter nature through our cultural practices and technological prostheses not erase the possibility of transcendence and utopia, resulting in a kind of postmodern version of the Weberian iron cage? Borrowing the title of the Philip K. Dick short story that inspired *Blade Runner*, we can ask: "Do Androids Dream of Electric Sheep?" Can cyborgs have religious experiences? Or are cyberreligious experiences the mere remnants of the ghost in the machine? Why then study them?

While Haraway enjoins us to give up the idea of returning to the Garden of Eden, a myth that is part of human exceptionalism, she is careful not to endorse uncritically all forms of human and nonhuman entwinement. She has consistently denounced the "informatics of domination," the exploitation of organic-technological hybrids by the Tyrell Corporations of the world, by global capitalist interests that commodify cyborg subjectivities, extracting surplus from their bodies. The task for Haraway is to engage in a humble but proactive politics that recognizes interdependence among species and the fragility of our mutual projects. Projects that issue from the illusion of human exceptionalism and sovereignty not only instrumentalize our bodies, other humans, and/or nonhuman species, but also directly contradict our relational ontology. "Our bodies, ourselves; bodies are maps of power and identity. Cyborgs are no exception. A cyborg body is not innocent; it was not born in a garden. . . . The machine is not an *it* to be animated, worshipped, and dominated. The machine is us, our processes, an aspect of our embodiment. We can be responsible for machines, they do not dominate or threaten us. We are responsible for boundaries; we are they" (Haraway 1991: 180).

Furthermore, rejection of the quest for pristine origins or the "god-trick," does not mark the end of religion as the radical experience of futurity. Like Deleuze and Guattari's desiring-machines, the cyborg is a figure that embodies immanent transcendence in a world that simultaneously enables and constrains its actions. The task of the scholar of religion who takes Haraway's work seriously is to explore the grounds and consequences of this "will to transcendence," which is materialized creatively in a myriad of symbols, beliefs, artifacts, practices, and institutions.

CONCLUSION

I close this chapter with Haraway's trans-species materialism because it throws into stark relief the limitations of radical social constructionism. Because radical social constructionism remains anthropocentric, wedded to the fantasy of human exceptionalism, it fails to take seriously the multiple materialities that constitute the body. These multiple materialities are not just the product of iterative discursive practices but rather of the interaction between these practices and matter—including biology and ecology, which is dynamic, agentic, and polymorphously productive—matter that makes possible the production of discourse about it in the first place. Thus, Haraway's non-reductive materialism does not spell the end of social constructionism. Rather, social constructionism is "chastened" or "constrained" (Peterson 2001: 209–11; Hayles 1995: 53). Without surrendering its crucial insight that the world as we experience it is mediated by our practices, it becomes aware of its limits and the conditions for its own existence.

Haraway's careful rethinking of science as situated knowledge and of technology as embodied and open-ended modes of encountering reality paves the way for religion scholars to transcend the widespread anti-natural-science attitude in the field. Its diversity notwithstanding, the dominant hermeneutic and phenomenological traditions in religious studies have consistently been wary of the reductive approaches that explain religion solely in terms of biological and ecological factors. In advocating for an embodied approach to religion in conversation with cognitive science, Edward Slingerland has rightly observed that

[t]raditional humanists continue to accept a world divided between an inert kingdom of dumb objects, governed by deterministic laws, and the real of the free and unconstrained spirit—a metaphysical divide expressed most clearly in German, where the sciences of mechanistic nature (*Naturwissenschaften*) are distinguished from the sciences of the elusive human *Geist* (*Geisteswissenschaften*). Within the confines of such a divided world, it is difficult to see how we humanists can ever escape the solipsistic fate of [Jorge Luis] Borges, endlessly and onanistically spinning stories inside stories. (Slingerland 2008b: 378)

Slingerland is correct in impugning the knee-jerk anti-reductionism of Mircea Eliade. The latter's defense of the study of religion sui generis ends up decontextualizing and dehistoricizing religious discourses, practices, and institutions. Nonetheless, Slingerland is wrong in dismissing the danger of materialist reductionism as a mere "bogeyman." Social constructionism's hermeneutics of suspicion is not only entirely justified but also necessary to construct robust but flexible and reflexive materialist approaches to religion. Thus, against Slingerland, in the next chapter I will argue for an epistemological framework that does not see social and cultural dynamics as mere epiphenomena that emerge from the operation of lower-level neurobiological processes, but that understands discursive and nondiscursive practices as material realities sustaining complex relations of reciprocal determination with physiology and ecology. The choice between the self-defeating relativism of radical constructionism and the naïve and simplistic determinism of physicalism is a false one, yet another version of the dualism that Slingerland wishes to transcend. We want to "say *both, and, neither, nor*" (Haraway 2000: 132, italics in the original).

The real trouble with social constructionism is that it has gone too far. It has become a "linguistic narcissism" (Barad 2008: 42), a totalizing rhetoric that does not allow critique, since nothing (but itself) constrains and resists it. Social constructionism is often portrayed as a nemesis of phenomenology and hermeneutics in the study of religion, since dissolves the self and meaning in the play of social practices in which power is central. However, in their dismissal of the potential non-deterministic or relatively deterministic contributions of biological and ecological factors in the articulation of embodied religious experience, social constructionism, hermeneutics, and classical phenomenology of religion form a common anthropocentric front, reinscribing Cartesian dualism. The secret of religion is always safely protected in the "human" side of the human-nonhuman divide, either in the irreducible inner life of the believer (Schleiermacher, James, and Otto), or in archetypes through which the sacred discloses itself to us (Eliade), or in culture as a systems of symbols (Geertz), or in society, in the dynamics of human solidarity (Durkheim) or economic conflict (Marx). Armed with a holistic but non-reductive materialism that is open to varied "naturalcultural zones of contact," we can now move to explore how evolution, ecology, and neurobiology, as key ingredients of our embodiment, contribute to the emergence of religious experience in interplay with phenomenological and sociocultural realities.

7

A Cultural Neurophenomenology of Religion

Enter the Embodied Mind

[A]ll of our raptures and our drynesses, our longings and pantings, our questions and beliefs . . . are equally organically founded, be they religious or of non-religious content.

—William James (1961: 30)

You can't explain conscious experience on the cheap.

—David Chalmers (1995: 208)

In the previous chapters, I have argued that somatophobia in religious studies has been the result of the appropriation of phenomenology through the prism of Cartesian anxiety. The phenomenology that the discipline of religion has imported is primarily concerned with the quest for essences that can be located in or through the inner life of the irreducible religious subject. Drawing from Heidegger, Merleau-Ponty, and the late works of Husserl, I have argued for an alternative reading of phenomenology that focuses on embodiment and emplacement. Since becoming with and among others is a vital dimension of embodiment and emplacement, social constructionism is central in any integral materialist approach to religious life. Nevertheless, a radical social constructionism, such as that proposed by Judith Butler, is incompatible with an enfleshed non-reductive materialism. In chapter 6, I proposed a constrained social constructionism that, while preserving a powerful deconstructive edge, allows for the recovery of the active, lived body as part of a non-anthropocentric materialism. In this chapter, I will add to this recovery by discussing some of the most exciting research emerging in the neurosciences, cognitive psychology, and evolution. My aim is to show how this research intersects with the materialist insights of phenomenology and social constructionism to articulate a flexible and robust framework for studying religion. In particular, I hope to debunk the perception that taking biology seriously in religious studies leads necessarily to eliminative reductionism: the claim that it is possible and desirable to reduce the complexity and diversity of religious experiences and practices to "nothing but" a single set of variables, usually genetic or neuro-physiological, which can be measured and fully validated empirically. I will argue instead for multiple, localized, and heuristic reductions, overlaps, and exchanges that bring phenomenology, social constructionism, and the cognitive sciences into fruitful conversation. My key contention is that, while religious studies must acknowledge the evolutionary pressures, neurophysiological dynamics, and cognitive constraints that enable and shape religion, these material factors by themselves underdetermine the diversity, creativity, and complexity of everyday religious practices. Thus, in order to offer a more holistic and context-sensitive materialist understanding of religion, the cognitive and neurological sciences must engage psychology, anthropology, sociology, and history, not simply as disciplines that can be ultimately reduced to the lawful behavior of neurons or atoms, but as legitimate fields of knowledge that deal with their own forms of materiality.

This chapter begins with a brief introduction to the origin and development of the cognitive sciences, showing the implications of various theories of cognition for the study of religion. The status of religion in these theories will hinge upon how they conceptualize consciousness, either as an emergent reality with differential degrees of autonomy or as the reflection of brain activity. As in previous chapters, I do not intend to present a detailed account of all the theories, methods, debates, and controversies in the field. Rather, I focus on the epistemologies at stake and on the implications they have for a non-reductive materialist framework in the study of religion.

FROM COGNITIVISM TO EMERGENCE AND ENACTION

The Computational-Representational Model

Cognitive science first emerged in the mid-1950s as a response to the limitations of behaviorism, the then-dominant research program in American psychology. In reaction to psychoanalysis's elaborate speculations about the nature of the psyche, behaviorism tried to understand human activity, without reference to internal states, as the observable coupling of stimulus and response. B. F. Skinner, the leading representative of modern behaviorism, saw consciousness as a "black box" not susceptible to and worthy of scientific study. He understood human behavior as simply the deployment of habits learned through a mixture of rewards, punishments, and positive and negative rein-forcements. While this view was challenged early on, it finally fell into disfavor with the rise of Noam Chomsky's generative linguistics, which demonstrated that children learn languages not through imitation and repetition but by the creative use of innate biological structures, universal rules in the brain that allow for the production of multiple grammatical variations within and across cultures. For Chomsky, the mind is not a tabula rasa that gets imprinted by outside stimuli. Quite the contrary, the mind has an active and determining role in producing knowledge and culture.

Despite offering a more sophisticated theory of mind, Chomsky reproduces the contradictions of Cartesian philosophy. Like Descartes, Chomsky sees lin-guistically mediated thought, the faculty that distinguishes humans from ani-mals, as innate, not as caused by history and culture or affected by the body. The core of Chomsky's linguistics is syntax, formal relations among symbols instantiated in the brain. Once again, we have here the idea of a sovereign cogito removed from society, culture, and nature. This notion of thought as formal language continues to shape cognitive science to this day. It is also evi-dent in cognitive approaches to religion, which tend to focus on the origin and evolution of religious concepts, rather than on embodied practices, material culture, or social institutions. Chomsky's emphasis on universality and innate-ness also carries into the cognitive study of religion, with some scholars hypothesizing that religion is an inherent aspect of the human brain, a fact that explains its durability and widespread presence.

Buoyed by Chomskian linguistics and new research on artificial intelligence and cybernetics, the first generation of cognitive scientists proposed a compu-tational model of the mind. The brain represents the hardware, or in this case the wetware, on which complex software programs are run in response to inputs from the outside. Just like a computer program has a particular syntax, a data structure, and algorithms that allow for the manipulation of informa-tion, the mind operates through a system of symbolic representations (i.e., images, concepts, analogies), each coding for external objects. Thinking hap-pens as these representations are brought into the relation with each other through rule-based computational procedures in order to tackle problems gen-erated by the environment.

While this model rescued the active mind from behaviorism, it preserved some of the latter's assumptions. For one thing, early cognitive scientists main-tained behaviorism's skepticism toward internal psychological processes, defining the mind as primarily an abstract thinking machine manipulating symbols, without reference to emotions and sensorimotor dynamics that could complicate mathematical modeling of behavior. The wetware of the brain "was seen as determining nothing at all about the nature of the program. That is, the peculiarities of the body and brain contributed nothing to the nature of human concepts and reason. This was philosophy without flesh. There was no body in this concept of mind" (Lakoff and Johnson 1999: 76).

As in the case of Chomskian linguistics, early cognitive science is dualistic, setting up an "explanatory gap" (Levine 1983) between mind and brain (body). Early cognitive science fails to explain how subjective experiences such as joy, pain, hope, love, desire, and fear as well as memories and thoughts arise from (or at least are supported by or related to) physical processes in the brain. This is what David Chalmers (1995) calls the "hard problem" in cognitive studies. Cognitive approaches to religion also confront this problem: Is religious experience a complex autonomous reality (with qualia, intrinsic properties), just like consciousness, that cannot be explained by reference to brain states? Or is it the epiphenomenal product of neurophysiological dynamics? Those who espouse the first option have been called "mysterians," since they argue that we might never be able to bridge the explanatory gap and explain consciousness (Searle 1997; McGinn 1999). On the other side of spectrum fall the physicalists and functionalists, sometimes called identity theorists, who believe that we will eventually be able to offer a fully naturalistic understanding of consciousness (Churchland 1986; Dennett 1991). For identity theorists, there is really no mystery or explanatory gap, since the whole experience of an autonomous unified consciousness is but a "useful user illusion" (Patricia Churchland in Blackmore 2006: 62). So, when we talk about consciousness or selfhood, we are operating with a "folk psychology" that is not different from religious worldviews that see nature as animated by spirits.

My own position is closer to philosopher Colin McGinn's "epistemological mysterianism." We might never be able to demystify religious experience fully, not because it is ultimately grounded on some supernatural force or because it is ontologically different (inherently ineffable) from other phenomena, as William James argued, but because our situatedness allows only partial perspectives. The issue then is not dualism (the existence of a "soul" separate from the body, a move that would bring us back to Cartesianism) but hermeneutics. Reductive physicalists engage in a self-performative contradiction: they presuppose the very same thing they seek to deny. As Searle puts it: "The marvellous [sic] thing about consciousness is that if you have the illusion that you're conscious then you are conscious" (quoted in Blackmore 2006: 203). I shall elaborate on this point later in the chapter.

Beyond the mind-body gap, early cognitive science sets up a second dualism. Within their narrow conception of the mind as an abstract thinking machine, early cognitivists, like Chomsky, understood thought as syntax rather than semantics. That is, thinking depends not on the meaning of the mental representations at play but on their formal permutations and differential relations with each other. As a result, what Thagard (2005: 10–12) terms the "computational-representational understanding of the mind (CRUM)" or what critics call cognitivism presupposes an intellectualist representationalism: there is a subject-object split that the mind bridges by representing external reality through discrete syntactic units that acquire meaning as they enter into relations with each other. According to Varela, Thompson, and Rosch (1991: 135) in CRUM, the "cognitive agent . . . is parachuted into a pregiven world."

In all fairness, cognitivism does not espouse a straight copy-theory of representation, whereby the mind simply mirrors extra-mental reality. After all, meaning is generated in the structured manipulation of mental representations. Nevertheless, all forms of cognitivism consider the world as external and independent from the cognitive agent. The latter simply reacts to problems posed by this extrinsic environment, producing functionally adaptive responses.

Connectionism and Neural Networks

In light of the limitations of the classic CRUM position, a second wave of research in cognitive science arose in the 1980s under the umbrella term of connectionism. Whereas cognitivism sees the mind as a digital computer basically functioning according to an input-output logic, connectionism understands it is a system of neural networks operating at multiple levels. These networks are composed of a myriad of neurons or groups of neurons and synapses (links) connected in layers and pathways laid out by the system's history of activity. This history organizes units according to different functions, some dealing with inputs, others with outputs, or mediating between these functions (as in the case of the so-called hidden units). Thinking and meaningful behavior result from widespread emergent patterns of activity throughout the architecture of the neural system. More specifically, mental states are dimensional vectors that result from the total number of neural units activated and inhibited and the frequency of the firing as well as the differential strength (weight) of the connections among these units.

Neural networks have several advantages over the model of the mind as a digital computer. First, they allow us to put the brain's wetware back into the process of cognition by giving us a language to describe and analyze neural dynamics. Second, neural networks approximate more closely cognition in its natural setting, which often involves coordinated multitasking and performance in the midst of all kinds of extraneous background "noise."[1] Because neural networks are flexible and adaptable, they can explain subtle variations in outcomes, which are a feature of human agency. Rather than the 0 or 1 options built into the syntax of computational models, networks show gradations and adjustments in response to changes in the context. Thus, it is possible to track continuity, reactivation, and transformation across the system. Moreover, because the information is stored in the connections as particular weights distributed through the system, there does not have to be a one-to-one relationship between symbols or conceptual categories and neural units. The relationship between the mind and the brain is not one in which a syntactic unit has an isolated neural correlate. Instead, individual conscious phenomena are supported by "massive sequences of synchronized neuron-firings over large areas of the thalamo-cortical system" (Searle quoted in Blackmore 2006: 201). This may explain why even when the system is locally damaged, cognitive processes continue (since they are distributed throughout the connections). The fact that we have to deal with large sectors of the brain (and of the sensorimotor system, as we shall see) and not isolated neural units also means that we need to proceed with caution as we propose explanatory models, shifting to a softer kind of determination rather than a simplistic determinism.

For all the advantages of connectionism over cognitivism, it still cannot resolve Chalmers's hard problem satisfactorily. How does connectionism explain the rise of a unified field of consciousness? The easiest answer is eliminative reductionism: consciousness is nothing but the epiphenomenal effects of the activities of neural networks. This is in fact the answer given by Patricia Churchland (1986) and Paul Churchland (1988). Nevertheless, the model of neural networks entails the concept of emergence, which is at odds with this kind of facile reductive physicalism. Cognition is not the result of neurons operating independently, in a vacuum. Rather, it is the result of the coordinated activities of multiple neural networks. Emergence, thus, refers to the rise of novel and relatively coherent larger structures out of the interconnected activities of smaller units. Under the proper conditions, these new structures may become self-organizing hierarchies whose properties are not reducible to the aggregate activity of the units that comprise them. These new structures may then exert different degrees of downward causation, shaping activity at the micro level. A good example is how amino acids bond with each other to form proteins. The behavior of a given protein is not only dependent on the properties of the linear sequence of constituting amino acids but on the spatial configurations created by the bonds among these units, since these bonds lead the new molecule to fold in particular ways. The shape of the molecule then plays a determining role in the kind of activities it can perform. These proteins interact with each other to give rise to more complex structures such as cell membranes and organelles. Cells then come together to form organs and so on.

Emergent orders may give rise to modules, self-contained specialized macro-units that control domains of activity, for example, memory, vision, imagination, or language comprehension (Fodor 1983). "Control" refers to the role the configuration of the module plays in setting the rules for the selection of specific data from the environment and for the processing of these data. Here connectionism intersects with CRUM's focus on preprogrammed units of syntax.

Although "encapsulated," a module is capable of interfacing with other modules to produce higher cognitive processes and behaviors. Through natural selection over a long time these modules may become genetically specified properties of the brain that account for its integration and systematicity. In turn, these innate structures produce worldwide recurrent cultural patterns. In support of this cognitive Darwinism, social anthropologist Harvey White-house, a leading figure in the cognitive study of religion, points out that "[e]volutionary biology envisages natural selection as short-sighted, favouring genetic mutations that confer immediate, not necessarily long-term, advantages. Consequently, one might expect cognitive capacities to evolve in relatively small parcels—that is, in the form of special-purpose mechanism" (Whitehouse 2001: 6).

The debates on modularity are important from the point of view of religious studies because some scholars have hypothesized that there might be a religion module in the brain, "the seat of an innate human faculty for experiencing the divine or . . . the seat of religious delusions" (Albright 2000: 735). Even cognitive scholars of religion who do not explicitly subscribe to genetically specified modularity tend to focus on the origin, evolution, and transmission of specific representational devices, like memes, that have hitchhiked onto our brains. I shall explore these issues in the next section.

In order to explain the emergence of complex but unified psycho-cognitive phenomena, connectionism relies on an associational model that is still controversial. There is, for example, an unsettled debate about whether the modular model of the brain is too rigid and simplistic. Cognitive anthropologist Dan Sperber posits the "possibility of massive modularity," viewing the brain as multitiered patchwork of modules.[2] "[W]e had better think of the mind as *kludge*, with sundry bits and components added at different times, and interconnected in ways that would make an engineer cringe" (Sperber 2001: 31). Fodor, in contrast, refers to a mixed cognitive system that is modular at the periphery of the mind, that is, for perceptual domains that require fast and fixed processing to ensure survival of the organism, and non-modular (holistic) for higher level processes. Others advocate a "soft modularity" that allows for a combination of constraint, plasticity, and openness (Pyysiäinen 2004: 35). Neurophenomenologists speak not of modularity but rather of "brainwebs," "phase synchronizations" of "scattered mosaics of functionally specialized brain regions" (Varela et al. 2001: 229). In their perspective, unified cognitive moments are the result of transient "neural assemblies" linked by large-scale dynamic reciprocal (top-down and bottom-up) connections. Coherence is thus not a function of the stability of various discrete interfacing modules but of "metaestable patterns"—coordinated "successions of self-limiting recurrent patterns" across the brain (Varela et al. 2001: 237). So, once again, the issue of multiple determination enjoins us to proceed with great caution when making any kind of reductive materialist move. "The moral of all of this is that *you can't explain conscious experience on the cheap*" (Chalmers 1995: 208, italics in the original). You cannot shortchange the task of identifying the complex inter-locking mechanisms that sustain consciousness by prematurely appealing to a single chain of materialist causality.

Furthermore, connectionism has not solved the subject-object split, since it still presupposes an independent external environment that acts as a constraint on the neural networks. Despite all the emphasis on self-organizing systems, connectionism sees the brain as a heteronomous system. Connectionists still "consider information to be a prespecified quantity, one that exists independently in the world and can act as the input to a cognitive system. This input provides the initial premises upon which the system computes a behavior—the output. But how are we to specify inputs and outputs for highly cooperative, self-organizing systems such as brains? There is, of course, a back-and-forth flow of energy, but where does the information end and behavior begin?" In order to bridge the subject-object split and thus embrace a non-dualist materi-alism, "we must move away from the idea of the world as independent and extrinsic to the idea of the world as inseparable from the structure of [the cog-nitive] processes of self-modification" (Varela, Thompson, and Rosch 1991: 139). Cognition involves holistic autonomous systems that do not simply rep-resent an independent external reality but enact it, producing themselves at the same time that they specify the world.

Neurophenomenology and the Enactive Model

With this we have arrived at "enaction," a new perspective introduced by Francisco Varela and associates in *The Embodied Mind* (1991). Enaction shares with connectionism the notion that cognition can be best explained as dynamic emergence. However, enaction finally breaks with representationalism. It departs from the principle that "the mind and the world . . . stand in relation to each other through mutual specification or dependent coorigination" (Varela, Thompson, and Rosch 1991: 150). In contrast to both cognitivism and connectionism, the enactive approach assumes that cognitive systems are autonomous; that is, "cognitive processes emerge from the nonlinear and circular causality of continuous sensorimotor interactions involving the brain, the body, and environment" (Thompson 2007: 10–11). Referring back to Deleuze and Guattari's notion of immanent assemblages, we can say that cognitive systems are autopoietic. They continuously produce themselves as spatially bounded systems (i.e., territorialized identities), distinct from but in close interaction with their surrounding media.[3]

Recalling Haraway's idea of the cyborg, encountering the world through his/her semiotic-enfleshed-technological prostheses, the enactive approach sees cognitive processes as extending "throughout the body and loop[ing] throughout the material, social, and cultural environments in which the body is embedded; they are not limited to the neural processes inside the skull" (Thompson 2007: 12). Cognitive systems operate with information that "depends on being in a world that is inseparable from our bodies, our language, and our social history—in short from our *embodiment*" (Varela, Thompson, and Rosch 1991: 149). Drawing from Heidegger's and Merleau-Ponty's phenomenologies (see chapter 4), the enactive approach understands the context of experience, which cognitivism and connectionism view as independent and external inputs, as the constructed product of our sensorimotor capacities and social practices, our embodied *Dasein*. "Thus the overall concern of an enactive approach to perception is not to determine how some perceiver-independent world is to be recovered; it is, rather, to determine the common principles or lawful linkages between sensory and motor systems that explain how action can be perceptually guided in a perceiver-dependent world" (Varela, Thompson, and Rosch 1991: 173).

The enactive approach's attempt to bridge the subject-object split that has plagued cognitive science parallels the efforts by Karen Barad and Donna Haraway to develop a posthuman, agentic realism, which recognizes the inescapable role of our discourses and practices in mediating the world, while acknowledging the material constraints and capacities entailed by our embodiment and emplacement in the social and natural worlds. Cognitive philosopher Evan Thompson, one of Varela's collaborators, calls this dual recognition "transcendence-within-immanence," a term that echoes once again Deleuze and Guattari's materialism, discussed in the previous chapter.

External events are *really transcendent*, for they are certainly not contained within the system, nor are they mere products of what goes inside the system. Nevertheless, they are *intentionally immanent*, in the following sense: they do not arrive already labeled, as it were, as external events; instead they are constituted or disclosed as such, and with the significance they have, by virtue of the network's autonomous (self-organizing) dynamics. (Thompson 2007: 27)

The enactive approach also goes a long way toward addressing the hard problem of explaining how a physical system can give rise to unified and compelling experiences, to consciousness. If the world is "perceiver-dependent," then it matters what the individual experiences in his/her lived world. As Varela puts it, "lived experience is where we [neurophenomenologists] start from and where we all must link back to, like a guiding thread" (1996: 334). Consciousness then is not a mere epiphenomenon, since it is a key ingredient in the way in which subjects construct data as "intentionally immanent." Indeed, the enactive approach marks a return to the use of first-person data, that is, accounts of sensations and of emotive and mental states by those directly experiencing them, which cognitive science has traditionally dismissed as inherently biased or inaccurate. The enactive approach, however, does not rely on these accounts uncritically. Instead, borrowing analytical tools from Husserl, enaction applies the *epoché*, the phenomenological reduction that brackets the natural attitude, in order to explore experiences more rigorously and systematically. Trained first-person reports are also checked against "third-person" data derived from observation of the external behaviors of experimental subjects and from increasingly sophisticated techniques of brain imaging. These "biobehavioral" data have thus far been the mainstay of neuroscience. Varela and his associates have termed this combination of methods bridging the gap between consciousness and physical processes "neurophenomenology."

Neurophenomenology has other advantages over cognitivism and connectionism. First, it places the full lived body (not just the brain either as an isolated digital computer or self-contained neural networks) front and center in the neurosciences. It goes beyond the "thought as language metaphor, in which reason is conceptualized as linguistic in nature" or "the thought as mathematical calculation metaphor" (Lakoff and Johnson 1999: 472). Instead, cognition involves our emotions, our perceptions as we move through space and time, the experience of internal bodily states, and our multi-sensory encounters with other objects, including other persons. Philosopher Shaun Gallagher, for example, points to how "[m]ovement and the registration of that movement in a developing proprioceptive system (that is, a system that registers its own self-movement) contributes to the self-organizing development of neuronal structures responsible not only for motor action, but for the way we come to be conscious of ourselves, to communicate with others, and to live in the surrounding world" (2005: 1). More specifically, he cites the recent discovery of "mirror neurons" which are activated by both the subject's own movement and by watching the motor activities of others. Thus, the operation of mirror neurons demonstrates how the brain, the body, and the (social) environment are tightly connected (Gallagher 2005: 220–23).

Second, neurophenomenology reintroduces the notion of practice to the study of cognition since it seeks "to describe the process of becoming aware from its very enaction, to describe it as it is carried out" (Depraz, Varela, and Vermersch 2003: 155). Neurophenomenologists go as far as stating that "practice is the privileged site for grasping experience." This is because in the enactive approach "reality is not a given: it is perceiver-dependent, not because [s/he] 'constructs' it at whim, but because what *counts* as a relevant world is inseparable from the structure and history of coupling of the perceiver. Thus cognition consists not of representations, but of *embodied action*" (Depraz, Varela, and Vermersch 2003: 157, italics in the original). Practice enters neurophenomenology through the distinction that pragmatist philosopher John Dewey drew in *Human Nature and Conduct* between know-that, as conceptual knowledge, and know-how, savoir faire, the intuitive skill to perform an activity well. In contrast to knowing-that, which involves deliberate rational analysis, knowing-how has to do with the almost spontaneous deployment of an embodied sense, what (as we shall see in chapter 9) Marcel Mauss and Pierre Bourdieu call a habitus. In knowing-how what matters is not abstract representation but the usefulness and efficacy of a particular strategy. A good example here is ascetical training, which involves "repeated activity, repeated prayer, a consistently affirmed withdrawal, continuous silence, repeated physical acts of fasting, sleep deprivation, and manual labor" (Valantasis 1995: 548). The ascetic repeats these activities until s/he has mastered them, that is, until they become natural components of a new manner of living, a new selfhood.

Because we negotiate our everyday life largely through know-how, neurophenomenologists are particularly interested in exploring how embodied knowledge that is both expressed and inculcated through practices contributes to the process of cognition. "[B]oth philosophers and scientists concerned with mind have grossly overlooked the importance and the central role of the immediacy of practices, skills and their pervasiveness. We should try and impress on ourselves what an enormous part of our lives—working, moving, talking, eating—manifest in know-how. And, concomitantly, what a small part of our lives is spent in deliberate, rational analysis which is symptomatic of knowing-that" (Depraz, Varela, and Vermersch 2003: 158). Here enaction goes beyond the classical cognitive sciences, which have tended to equate thought with knowing-that. This "intellectualist" bias also appears in many of the dominant cognitive approaches to religion.

Third, as part of focusing on lived, situated cognition, neurophenomenology is interested in exploring the contributions of history and culture to the formation of subjectivity. Laughlin and Throop (2006), for example, propose a "cultural neuro-phenomenology" that adds to trained inward introspection and biobehavioral data a careful study of the cultural and historical contexts in which the natural attitude takes shape as well as systematic comparative cross-cultural analysis. As they write (2006: 312): "the effort after truth can be optimized only if we work to reduce bias through simultaneously pursuing a rigorous intrasubjective assessment (the phenomenological *epoché*), intersubjective assessment (the basis of the scientific method), intercultural assessment (anthropological research) and intertemporal assessment (historical analysis)." This interdisciplinary enactive approach shows that culture "in-forms," that is "forms within" neurophysiological pathways and structures that allow for coordination at the level of the subject and for intersubjective communication.

> To become conscious of something in the external world means that the neural network mediating consciousness has been evoked by a chain of networks beginning with those at the peripheral senses. When a child is encultured by his or her society, the development of his or her brain and body—and the somatic structures that mediate his or her consciousness—has been impacted by social conventions and other social processes. It is well to remember that the millions of cells mediating experience and consciousness are themselves part of the extramental world—they are part of our living being-in-the-world. Our actual being is part of the extramental world to which we grow up adapting. (Laughlin and Throop 2006: 317)

In other words, our know-how is "encultured" as embodied generative schemata, as in-formed procedural memory in the body and brain that responds to the socially and culturally mediated environment the individual encounters. This is what researchers in cognition call "neuroplasticity," the capacity of the brain to undergo structural and functional change, to reconfigure neural pathways in the somatosensory cortex and the motor cortex, as it experiences the world.[4]

Cultural neurophenomenology, then, opens the door for a productive exchange between the natural sciences and social sciences, between a biological non-reductive realism and social constructionism. I will return to this exchange but from the angle of social practices in chapter 9.

Given our limited knowledge about the brain, it is not surprising that the jury is still out on strengths and weaknesses of the computational, connectionist, and enactive models. Viable work on each of these research programmes continues, some of which seeks to establish points of cross-fertilization. However, at this juncture, cultural neurophenomenology offers the most flexible-yet-rigorous analytical framework to bring the embodied mind into the conversation about religion. This is because it offers a non-dualistic and non-reductive naturalistic approach to consciousness: it does not dismiss religious experiences and consciousness as illusions (even if they are useful to the user), nor does it disembed the subject from the lived world of history and practices. In the next section, I use this non-reductive materialist framework to evaluate some of the most significant ongoing research on religion in the cognitive sciences. In order to organize a rapidly expanding literature, I have heuristically organized various approaches to the study of cognition and religion in three overlapping but sufficiently distinctive rubrics.

THE COGNITIVE SCIENCE OF RELIGION

While cognitive approaches to religion are diverse, the most prominent lines of research adhere to the epistemology behind the computational-representational understanding of the mind (CRUM), which I outlined above. Just like early versions of cognitivism, which were interested in the manipulation of symbols, cognitive theories of religion tend to understand it as rule-bound systems of representations in the mind. "Religions," as cognitive philosopher Robert McCauley writes, "are not physical things. They are not spatially localizable. Much about them is not readily observable. They seem ineliminably symbolic" (1995: 153). Cognitive theorists see religion as primarily a matter of belief, a perspective that I will argue limits their capacity to give proper weight to material aspects of religion such as practices, institutions, sacred artifacts, and religious architecture. Here the enactive approach that I have sketched above will prove useful to introduce a more embodied (neuro)phenomenological perspective that is compatible with a chastened social constructionism.

Cognitive theories of religion also subscribe to a "selectionism" that focuses on the impact of evolutionary processes on the durability and ubiquity of particular religious patterns. Often a rigid application of this selectionism leads these approaches to underestimate the plasticity and diversity of religious expressions. Again, I will show that enaction offers a better way to account for religious creativity and variation, while acknowledging the recurrence of certain religious patterns across time and cultures. But before I critique dominant cognitive theories of religion (in order to open the space for a nonreductive materialist framework that allows for a dialogue between the natural sciences and the humanities), I need to present briefly their key arguments.

Ontologies, Concepts, and Modules

The most influential cognitive scholars of religion, such as Dan Sperber, Pascal Boyer, and Harvey Whitehouse, are primarily interested in religion as set of conceptual devices that help individuals process information from the environment. Whitehouse, for example, refers back to E. B. Tylor's hypothesis that the origin of religion lies in our ancestors' metaphysical speculations about the line between life and death: what explains the apparition of dead relatives and friends in the dreams, memories, and visions of the living? To resolve this question, Tylor argued that our ancestors posited the idea of spirits, which, while dwelling in our bodies, do not perish with them. Because these spirits are autonomous, that is, they have their own agency, they are capable of informing all aspects of the material world, making it seem animated. Life ends when the spirits abandon the body and the other entities in nature in which they dwell.

Although Whitehouse does not accept Tylor's speculations about the origin of religion, preferring to work with hypotheses that are testable empirically, on the basis of what are the most widespread forms of religion in the world, he concurs with Tylor that the "minimum definition" of religion is "the belief in spiritual beings," including gods, angels, ghosts, witches, and zombies. Thus, the first building block in Whitehouse's cognitive theory is that religion is itself a theory of knowledge based on concepts of supernatural agency, "which seem to lurk in the imagination of humans everywhere" (Whitehouse 2004: 2). From this epistemology, a set of cognitively optimal beliefs and actions issue.

Along the same lines, anticipating cultural relativist critiques that point to the great diversity of religious expressions, philosopher Pascal Boyer writes:

> We have a word for religion. This is a convenient label that we use to put together all the ideas, actions, rules and objects that have to do with the existence and properties of superhuman agents such as God. Not everyone has this explicit concept or the idea that religious stuff is different from the profane or everyday domain. That people do not have a special term for religion does not mean they actually have no religion. In many places people have no word for "syntax" but their language has a syntax all the same. You do not need the special term in order to have the thing. (2001: 9)

Notice here the representational assumptions. There is a thing out there, the essence of which is the belief in supernatural agents, which we represent mentally in our symbolic systems as religion. The existence of this thing out there is like syntax in the sense that it is innate, not affected by our practices, by the idiosyncrasies of how we perform the language.

Once cognitive scholars have defined religion primarily as theories of knowledge based on the existence of supernatural agents, then the question becomes how these epistemologies came to be so widely accepted. What makes beliefs in spirits so widespread, particularly in view that they seem counterintuitive, flying in the face of scientific knowledge or even common sense? This is where Neo-Darwinian evolution comes in: the answer lies in the mental tools that enhance our fitness, more specifically our survival and reproduction as a species. One is these tools is the human tendency to anthropomorphize all aspects of reality, attributing human agency particularly to those entities and processes that we do not understand (Guthrie 1993). This cognitive propensity is very useful to impose some regularity on the profusion of phenomena that confront us. It allows us to draw from our experience of how we behave in order to make predictions about the way the universe works. Besides giving us a set of strategies to deal with immediate unpredictable changes and threats, it enables us to think of the cosmos as purposeful and thus meaningful. The beliefs in supernatural agents is, thus, "another Good Trick, an evolutionary innovation—like eyesight itself, or flight—that gives us the ability to "divide detected motion into banal (the rustling of the leaves, the swaying of seaweed) and the potentially vital: the 'animate motion' (or 'biological motion') of another agent, another animal with a mind, who might be a predator, or a prey, or a mate, or a rival conspecific" (Dennett 2005: 109).

Cognitive psychologist Justin Barrett calls this mental tool "agency detection device" (ADD), which is prone to "hyperactivity," since in terms of evolutionary fitness it is better to over-detect agency than to underreact to potential external threats. The Hypersensitive agent detection device (HADD), however, was not a mental tool restricted to our ancestors, who were particularly vulnerable to natural phenomena and were dominated by superstitions. Experimental work with children has found this tendency to identify animals, plants, and even inorganic objects as agents. And any adult who has been beset by problems with computers can attest to how easily we look for the "ghost in the machine" to deal with bafflement. According to Barrett (2004: 33):

When HADD perceives an object violating the intuitive assumptions for the movement of ordinary physical objects (such as moving on non-inertial paths, changing direction inexplicably, or launching itself from a standstill) and the object seems to be moving in a goal-oriented manner, HADD detects agency. Gathering information from other mental tools, HADD searches for any known agents that might account for the self-propelled movement. Finding none, HADD assumes that the object itself is an agent. Until information arrives to say otherwise, HADD registers a nonreflective belief that the object is an agent, triggering a ToM (Theory of Mind) to describe the object's activity in terms of beliefs, desires, and other mental states.

Religion (i.e., the belief of supernatural agents, as defined by Barrett and other prominent cognitive scientists) thus appears as a natural outcome of the way in which our brain works. There is nothing strange about the emergence of religion. "[B]elief in gods arises because of the natural functioning of completely normal mental tools working in common natural and social contexts" (Barrett 2004: 21). Nor can the origin of religion be identified with a particular historical event, as in Freud's theory of the primal parricide. Religion is rather a generalized habit of mind which, because of its functionality, is transmitted from generation to generation and across cultures.

But is it not possible to break a mental habit or to "break its spell," as Dennett puts it, especially when it is patently wrong? And if that were the case, would religion not have ceased to be compelling after the Copernican and Newtonian revolutions? Religious concepts, however, are more complex than outright absurdities. It is true, as Boyer tells us, that "*religious concepts invariably include information that is counterintuitive relative to the category activated*" (Boyer 2001: 65). Here, counterintuitive does not mean "strange, inexplicable, funny, exceptional or extraordinary." Rather, Boyer means "counterontological": religious concepts violate some of the expectations derived from our ontological categories. For example, the Yekuana in lower Amazonia believe that the crimson-crested woodpecker is the powerful spirit of Wanadi, a mythical hero and the first shaman at the beginning of time (Guss 1989). Clearly, the biological properties that accompany the ontological category of animal do not stipulate that a bird (which is an entry under the mental folder labeled animal) would have eternal life. So, the Wanadi myth is counterontological. Nevertheless, when you ask a Yekuana why Wanadi is associated with the crimson-crested woodpecker, you are likely to hear that it is because Wanadi is the spirit of light and the woodpecker normally appears at dawn in the forest. Here the Wanadi myth is does not violate the expectations of how a bird like the crimson-crested woodpecker should behave. In fact, it confirms commonsense expectations. The myth does not claim that Wanadi is a woodpecker because the latter grows poisonous leaves out of its beak. Everyone knows that birds do not do that. They soar to the heaven, just like Wanadi does.

This example demonstrates that the "religious concept preserves all the relevant default inferences except the ones that are explicitly barred by the counterintuitive element" (Boyer 2001: 73). What is the significance of the limited violation of our ontological categories and the preservation of the default inferences that follow from our concepts? This combination, cognitive scholars of religion argue, is what makes the acceptance and transmission of certain religious ideas possible. Those religious concepts that do not violate enough of the properties in our default reasoning are not very likely to grab our attention or to make enough of an impact that we would commit them to memory. As a result, these concepts will have a very transitory existence and thus have little possibility of circulating widely within and across cultures. On the other hand, concepts that radically violate our intuitive ontological knowledge are very likely to be unintelligible, unbelievable, and difficult to communicate to others. Religious notions that are likely to stick and spread are "minimally counterintuitive (MCI) concepts. These MCIs may be characterized as meeting most of the assumptions that describers and categorizers generate—thus being easy to understand, remember, and believe—but as violating just enough of these assumptions to be attention demanding and to have an unusually captivating ability to assist in the explanation of certain experiences. These MCIs commonly occupy important roles in mythologies, legends, folktales, religious writings, and stories of people all over the world" (Barrett 2004: 22).

The underlying argument here is that the origin, selection, and transmission of religion is cognitively constrained, shaped by the universal properties of the human mind. "Our cosmologies, eschatologies, ethics, ritual exegeses and so on, are all firmly constrained by what we can encode, process, and recall" (Whitehouse 2004: 16). The fact that there are recurrent, cross-cultural patterns of religious activity points to the determining role of the architecture of our minds, which, while allowing variation, does not permit an anything-goes logic. The analysis of minimally counterintuitive religious concepts, then, allows for a truly comparative study of religion beyond the vague metaphysical category of archetypes used by Eliade and other historians of religion. "[W]hat is MCI in one culture is MCI in any other culture. A person who can walk through wall is MCI anywhere. A rock that talks is MCI anywhere. This independence from cultural relativism enables identification as an MCI to be a valuable tool in making pan-cultural predictions and explanations" (Barrett 2004: 22).

Now that we know that some MCIs are more likely to be transmitted, we can ask about the actual mechanisms of this transmission. Here there is divergence among theorists of cognition. Dan Sperber (1996, 2001), for instance, defends a nativist perspective. Echoing Chomsky, he argues that the cognitive biases we consistently find in religion have to do with the modularity of the brain. Religious concepts are like bacteria or viruses. Here Sperber resorts to epidemiological terms,[5] not to put religion down, implying that it is necessarily a negative natural phenomenon, but to map out the dynamics of religious and cultural transmission within and across human populations. Religious representations are like viruses and bacteria because they spread in epidemics, with successfully engineered representations spreading by contagion as humans come into contact with each other. Some of these representations may not circulate very widely. They may even die out, without leaving much of a trace. Others may spread slowly but become persistent in a certain region, becoming in effect endogenous to that culture. Still others attain even wider circulation, cutting across generations and environments. Sperber hypothesizes that the representations that attain wider circulation are those that have from the outset a closer elective affinity with the innate mechanisms of the brain. Here his argument dovetails with Boyer's and Barrett's on counterintuitive ontologies. Sperber, however, takes a stronger nativist stand, stressing the modularity of the process. As our species evolves over a long period, these religious representations become incorporated into our brain as part of its modular development, as enriched content for genetically prespecified and specialized domains, which, in turn, allow for the generation of more representations and behaviors that reproduce its underlying structure. In that sense, Sperber's understanding of religion parallels Chomsky's view of language as competence supported by a deep, innate generative grammar that all humans share.

Neurotheology

Sperber is careful not speak of a religion module or a "God Module," as it has been dubbed by the popular press (Begley 2000).[6] However, neuroscientist V. S. Ramachandran points to how epileptic seizures in the left temporal lobe and certain brain injuries trigger vivid experiences that subjects have described as mystical. Ramachandran's patients report "deeply moving experiences including a feeling of divine presence and the sense that they are in direct communion with God. Everything around them is imbued with cosmic significance" (Ramachandran and Blakeslee 1998: 179). This could mean that there is a particular region of the brain that has become specialized to support religious experience. Indeed, there is a whole field called "neurotheology" that uses noninvasive techniques of neuroimaging, such as positron emission tomography (PET) and functional magnetic resonance imaging (fMRI), to map out the differential levels of activity across brain regions when subjects, such meditating

Buddhist monks or Franciscan nuns in deep prayer, report to be having experiences associated with religion (Newberg, d'Aquili, and Rouse 2001; Persinger 1987). These studies confirm strong activity in the temporal lobe, leading neurotheologians to claim that experiences of the divine are non-pathological mini-seizures located in this particular brain region.[7] Geneticist Dean Hamer (2005) adds another piece to the puzzle by arguing that there is a "God gene" (VMAT2) that enables the brain to sustain religious experiences. This gene codes for a cell membrane protein that allows neurotransmitters such as dopamine, serotonin, and norepinephrine to bind with neurons. These neurotransmitters produce powerful moods, sensations, and emotions, many of which are associated with religious ecstasy. Hamer hypothesizes that the presence of this gene provides an evolutionary advantage: it enhances our sense of well-being and supports an optimistic outlook necessary for self-transcendence.

Neurotheology's main value has been to demonstrate that science can no longer dismiss religious experiences as mere delusions invented and propagated by religious ideologues, a position which, as we shall see below, is more along the lines of Richard Dawkins's.[8] There are real, cerebral bases to these experiences. Beyond that, neurotheology has been extremely controversial. It is one thing to state that there is a correlation between localized activity in the brain (or atrophy of a brain region) and religious feelings and quite another to claim that these neural processes cause a sense of the supernatural.[9] Acknowledging that there are biological bases for human spirituality—a fairly uncontroversial position that is as old as William James's psychology of religion—is not the same as holding that religious experience is nothing more than neurological activity encoded in our genes. Paradoxically, by insisting that religious experience can be fully explained in terms of neural activity, neurotheologians reproduce a version of the Cartesian disembodied mind. They leave "by the wayside the rest of the organism and the surrounding physical and social environment . . . and also leaving out the fact that part of the environment is itself a product of the organism's preceding actions" (Damasio 1994: 251). A more holistic materialism would recognize that "the mind is embodied, in the full sense of the term, not just embrained" (Damasio 1994: 118).

To hypothesize that a gene has been placed there by God to maintain communication with him/her is even less tenable,[10] given the wealth of evidence in support of naturalistic explanations of the evolution of the brain. Hamer himself recognizes that, if anything, "[t]here are probably many different genes involved, rather than just one" (2005: 8). Moreover, he is prepared to admit that spirituality might the result of "gene-environment" interactions, as is the case for other evolutionary traits. In any case, the debate about a neurogenetic

God is beyond the purview of a rigorous non-reductive materialist framework for the study of religion.

Against the unwarranted eliminative reductionism of neurotheology, Michael Trimble and Anthony Freeman have shown that patients with temporal lobe epilepsy who assiduously attend religious services are more likely to report having intense mystical experiences than regular churchgoers without the disease or epileptic patients who expressed no interest in religion. These reports were accompanied by different patterns of brain activity. For example, "the hyperreligious patients were much more likely to have bilateral EEG changes, in keeping with the other main finding, namely, the history of postictal psychosis. The latter usually relates to a bilateral expression of the postseizure state" (Trimble and Freeman 2006: 413).[11] Clearly, there is a complex feedback between neurology and culture taking place here that calls for a non-eliminative sort of materialism. The hyperreligious subjects in the study are experiencing distinctive brain patterns, which they might be interpreting and shaping through the frameworks provided by their religious involvement. The interplay between neurology and culture is clear in one of Trimble's patients.

> Patient 2 said, "I became a Christian after attending a healing meeting where I believe I heard the voice of God calling to me saying 'Come to me and I will heal you.' From that point on everything started to change." The patient then had epilepsy surgery. "I personally believe that God was in the theater watching over me and changing my life. It seemed as if I woke up, a new creation, with a fresh start in life." (Trimble 2007: 149)

As anyone who has worked with Evangelical Christians knows, patient 2 is constructing a standard narrative of conversion to make sense of the neurophysiological states s/he is undergoing. The brain events that s/he experiences come to be construed as meaningful religious experiences through an embodied cultural hermeneutics.[12] Religion is not simply a set of neural and biochemical processes that take place inside the skull. At best, we can claim that certain genetic and neuronal configurations may predispose some individuals toward experiences and moods that are lived as religious. This predisposition is mediated by social discourses and practices. Ann Taves makes precisely the same point in her study of the evolving understandings of religious experience from John Wesley to Williams James. Whether experiences such as trances, glossolalia, or visions were understood as the "indwelling of the Spirit" or as the expression of animal magnetism, mesmerism, or hysteria was the result of the interplay between, on the one hand, practitioners located in competing religious "communities of discourse and practices" and, on the other, the "traditions of discourse and practice" used by intellectual elites to study these phenomena (Taves 1999: 4).

Trimble (2007: 175) recognizes that "[a]t present there are few hard and fast data to call upon in the area of neurotheology, and most writers on the subject recycle the same results from a small number of disparate investigators." If neurotheology is to advance beyond claims based on mere correlations it needs to "answer some core questions: Just how common is this form of [temporal lobe] epilepsy? How often does it lead to religious behaviour? How socially conditioned is such manifestation of religion? From which anatomical structures do these seizures originate? What is the effect of treating the seizures? Is there any distinction from the religiosity of those without epilepsy?" (Coles 2008: 1957).

To add more credibility to the personal reports of its experimental subjects, neurotheology would do well to follow the example of neurophenomenology. The latter focuses on subjects like Buddhist monks, who not only have developed a keen awareness of their mental and bodily processes during "religious" states of consciousness but, more importantly, who have been trained in the phenomenological methods of introspection (Harrington and Zajnoc 2003). For example, Lutz, Dunne, and Davidson (2007) have begun to develop a detailed inventory of Buddhist meditative practices and states (whether they rely on breathing manipulation, chanting, particular postures, or focused attention on an object or different parts of the body, or whether the practitioner favors clarity, stability, emptiness, or balance, etc.) and their neural and physiological counterparts. The operative word in this kind of research is "neuroplasticity," how brain pathways are activated, remodeled, and strengthened by controlled types of experiential input. I will return to the notion of neuroplasticity in the next chapters on practice, since experiential inputs are controlled through embodied religious training. Further, religious training, as anthropologist Talal Asad (1993) shows, is closely connected with the exercise of social and cultural power. Here we are back to the notion of cultural realism that I presented in the introduction. As emergent realities, the products of human practice have some causal efficacy over the neurophysiological conditions that made them possible.

Evolution and Memes

An alternative perspective on the selective transmission of religious categories comes from the notion of memes. Biologist Richard Dawkins argued in his influential *The Selfish Gene* that the unit of natural selection and the driving force behind the evolutionary process is the gene trying to reproduce itself. Therefore, behaviors from aggression to altruism could be explained as "phenotypic effects" generated by genes attempting to propagate themselves in response to environmental pressures, including competition with other genes. These effects are not necessarily favorable to the individual or groups of individuals (even species) who carry the genes. In fact, some of these genes may sustain a parasitical relationship with their carriers, only utilizing them as "survival machines" that ensure the genome's presence in future generations (Dawkins 1989: 19–20). In other cases, the relationship between the gene and the organism might one of mutuality or of neutrality (with the gene having neither a positive nor a negative impact on the individual).

Dawkins extended his gene-centered view of evolution to culture by introducing the concept of memes. Memes are efficient "replicator" units in culture. They are discrete cultural traits, concepts, metaphors, narratives, musical tunes, ritual behaviors, habits, and biases that copy themselves across human populations.

> Just as genes propagate themselves in the gene pool by leaping from body to body via sperms or eggs, so memes propagate themselves in the meme pool by leaping from brain to brain via a process which, in the broad sense, can be called imitation. [So that] [w]hen you plant a fertile meme in my mind you literally parasitize my brain, turning it into a vehicle for the meme's propagation in just the same way a virus may parasitize the genetic mechanism of the host cell. (Dawkins 1989: 192)

Just as for DNA, since the replication process is error prone or it might involve recombination with other units, the copying of memes is not perfect. Memes, in fact, seem more prone to mutation. Or they may combine to form "memeplexes," meme complexes, in order to enhance their chances of future survival in the face of intermemetic competition. Recombinations, mutations, and errors in transcription give rise to variation within continuity.

Dawkins considers religions particularly aggressive, virulent memeplexes that have invaded our minds and are now reproducing themselves endlessly, saturating all societies. Religion functions like a Trojan, a computer virus that, operating invisibly, instructs the machine to copy it until the hard drive crashes, but not before infecting other computers. Thus, the task of all critical thinkers, such as Dawkins, is to put a stop to this process of replication gone awry. But how does the Trojan of religion invade our brains? It has to do with the education of children. "Natural selection builds child brains with a tendency to believe whatever their parents and tribal elders tell them (Dawkins 2006: 12).

This "programmed-in gullibility," which is a valuable resource in the acquisition of language and survival strategies from the elders, is very easily subverted by religious authorities who advance ideas about omniscient and wrathful gods in order to preserve their power and privilege. This power and privilege are, in turn, necessary for the reproduction of the religious memes.

While Dawkins also uses epidemiological metaphors to talk about culture and religion, his views on selection and transmission differ substantially from Sperber's and Boyer's. Whereas Dawkins considers the organism (and thus the brain) as a tabula rasa, a mere vehicle that genes orchestrate to replicate themselves almost mechanically, Sperber and Boyer stress the active role of neurophysiology constraining the kind of cultural units that are selected and communicated. Memes, thus, do not just replicate themselves or simply copy themselves into the minds of individuals. Rather they are creatively reworked, enriched, and extended by our cognitive apparatuses. "[C]ultural concepts are not 'downloaded' from one mind to another. They are built by inferences from cultural input. . . . [T]his has important consequences. The processes in question do not reduce to 'decoding' other people's thoughts from their over gestures or utterances. They create new representations. . . . The way this happens is massively constrained by prior assumptions in memory" (Boyer 2000: 97). Paradoxically, Dawkins brings us back to the simplistic models of mind with which our account of cognitive science started.

This is admittedly a brief and impressionistic sketch of the variegated landscape of the cognitive study of religion. However, even with this limited treatment, we can begin to evaluate the epistemological assumptions and stakes in the ongoing debates.

FROM RELIGIOUS REPRESENTATION TO RELIGIOUS ENACTION

The overarching strength of the various research strands within the cognitive studies of religion lies in their capacity to hold cultural relativism and social constructionism in check. In one way or another, all of these strands convincingly demonstrate that because religions are embodied phenomena, they have developed within the biological constraints that have shaped our bodies. Religions are not exempt from evolutionary pressures and neurophysiological dynamics that simultaneously enable the production of a diversity of ideas, symbols, and practices and constrain the types of religious discourses and activities that are likely to persevere across generations and cultures.

However, hardcore genetic selectionism of the sort advocated by Dawkins has its limits. It is not entirely successful in explaining the durability, ubiquity, and diversity of religion. In *The Origin of Species*, Darwin challenged teleological readings of evolution, arguing that the diversification and specialization observed in contemporary species was not the necessary fulfillment of a predetermined telos. Rather, it was the result of "slight modification[s], which in the course of ages chanced to arise" (Darwin 1982: 131). Nevertheless, Darwin opened the door to quasi-normative understandings of evolution, such as that offered by Dawkins, when he affirmed that in the face of fierce intraspecies competition, "we may console ourselves with the full belief, that the war of nature is not incessant, that no fear is felt, that death is generally prompt, and that the vigorous, the healthy, and the happy survive and multiply" (Darwin 1982: 128). Natural selection "works solely by and for the good of each being, all corporeal and mental endowments will tend to progress towards perfection" (Darwin 1982: 459). If that is the case, then, religion, having persisted across cultures for thousands of years, even against the challenges of science and secularization, has more than demonstrated if not "perfection," at least remarkable vigor. Following Darwin's logic, this vigor implies religion has played and continues to play a useful, adaptive role for humans. But this conclusion flies in the face of Dawkins's attempts to debunk religion in the name of science. Dawkins recognizes this contradiction:

> Knowing that we are products of Darwinian evolution, we should ask what pressure or pressures exerted by natural selection originally favoured the impulse to religion. The question gains urgency from standard Darwinian considerations of economy. Religion is so wasteful, so extravagant; and Darwinian selection habitually targets and eliminates waste. Nature is a miserly accountant, grudging the pennies, watching the clock, punishing the smallest extravagance. (Dawkins 2006: 163)

As we saw above, Dawkins explains the durability and ubiquity of religion as the maladaptive byproduct of the fitness-enhancing process of imitation. This explanation, nevertheless, reproduces a subject-object split that explains biological regularity "as an optimal fit or optimal correspondence" between genes and "pregiven dimensions of the environment" (Varela, Thompson, and Rosch 1991: 193). This dualism is open to teleological readings of the evolutionary process: the mere existence of the current phenotype proves that it must be the fittest.[13] This potential for rendering the present state of affairs as the inevitable, natural outcome of iron-clad material processes is precisely what raises the hackles of social constructionists. They would like to "identify the accidents, the minute deviations—or conversely, the complete reversal—the errors, the false appraisal, and the faulty calculations that gave birth to those things that continue to exist and have value for us" (Foucault 1977a: 146). The trouble is that social constructionists oftentimes push their deconstructive genealogies to an extreme, denying any kind of determination beyond language and culture. This denial, as we have seen, leads to anthropocentric exceptionalism, the denial that we are part of the natural world.

How do we overcome the dualism behind hardcore selectionism without falling into human exceptionalism? We have to move from a "prescriptive" evolutionary logic to a "proscriptive" one. That is, we shift from

> the idea that what is not allowed is forbidden to the idea that what is not for-bidden is allowed. In the context of evolution this shift means that we remove selection as a prescriptive process that guides and instructs in the task of improving fitness. In contrast, in a proscriptive context natural selection can be seen to operate, but in a modified sense: selection discards what is not compatible with survival and reproduction. Organisms and the population offer variety; nat-ural selection guarantees only that what ensues satisfies the two basic constraints of survival and reproduction. (Varela, Thompson, and Rosch 1991: 195)

We should not think of evolution as selecting for specific phenotypes in a one-to-one interaction between a set of environmental conditions and a genetic unit or complex. Instead, "selection operates as a broad survival filter that admits any structure that has sufficient integrity to persist" (Varela, Thompson, and Rosch 1991: 196). The evolutionary process is proscriptive because it functions under the logic of "satisficing" rather than optimizing, with the result that "what an organism looks like and is 'about' is completely *underdetermined* by the constraints of survival and reproduction."[14] Evolution in this sense would be "bricolage, the putting together of parts in complicated arrays, not because they fulfill some ideal design but simply because they are possible. Here the evolutionary problem is no longer how to force a precise trajectory by the requirements of optimal fitness; it is, rather, how to prune the multiplicity of viable trajectories that exists at a given point." (Varela, Thompson, and Rosch 1991: 196, italics in the original).

A proscriptive view of evolution would allow us to rethink Darwin as a the-orist of contextualized immanent becoming, of emplaced variability, differ-ence, and convergence (Grosz 2008).[15] Such a view would also go a long way toward explaining the persistence of "extravagant" and "wasteful" religion. A proscriptive reading of evolution is not only a critique of Dawkins's simplistic Neo-Darwinism, but it also has important implications for cognitive approaches to religion. "Just as evolutionary theory imagines that the specifications of organic form, coded in genes, can be passed down the generations independently of the process of development, so cognitive science imagines that cultural knowledge, coded in words or other symbolic media, can be passed on independently of its practical application in particular tasks and contexts" (Ingold 2001: 139). While Boyer, Barrett, Atran, and others are quite correct in pointing to cognitive ontologies that establish the boundaries of what is possible (the cognitive contours of the "broad survival filter"), they are missing the main sources of cultural and religious creativity. The sorts of agents, categories, devices, and templates that the dominant cognitive theories of religion stipulate *underdetermine* the production, circulation, and consumption of religious practices and artifacts. The real issue is not to demonstrate that there are deep recurring patterns of religious life. Rather, the task is to understand how religious diversity emerges in interaction with and supported by cognitive and evolutionary constraints. We need to think of cognition as a two-way street, with diversity pushing back against the relatively malleable cognitive constraints that prune it, and thus, reworking however gradually our categorical lenses. Although the human brain shows definite innate regional specialization, contact with the natural and social environment mediated by our bodies leads to continual and widespread rewiring of its neural networks, especially during infancy, childhood, and adolescence. As such, we should speak of a "natural drift," a "conjoint history" in which "the organism is both the subject and object of evolution," rather that the quasi-teleological movement of hypostasized genes and memes (Varela, Thompson, and Rosch 1991: 185–204).

Because a myriad of religious discursive and nondiscursive practices can satisfy the parameters of minimally counterintuitive ontologies, we must find another way to specify why a given religion takes the forms that it does at a particular time and space. How can we attain this level of specificity, examining religions as they are actually lived? Following the enactive approach, we must introduce a richer notion of cognition into the strongly representational epistemology that has dominated the cognitive study of religion. This richer notion of cognition would bring the full body into the conversation, as well as human praxis as a central social, cultural, and historical force in specifying the trajectory of particular religious formations. To provide a rich materialist description of a religious phenomenon, it is certainly necessary to recognize its neurocognitive bases, but it is not sufficient. We must study how neurocognitive networks and processes interact with social and cultural practices, which have a material density in and of themselves (Margolis 2001). A certain religious concept may be pervasive because it is minimally counterintuitive (and thus it is easy to remember and transmit), but it gains its authority through social practices and institutions that sanction it not only as a legitimate way to see the world, but as orthodoxy. By the same token, memes, as Boyer and Sperber rightly note, do not just download themselves onto our brains, but they are inculcated into our bodies through contested practices that articulate certain kinds of subjects.

The most serious obstacle to introducing an enactive and embodied approach to the cognitive study of religion is unquestionably the continued reliance on the representationalist epistemology that characterizes CRUM. Religion is primarily understood as thought and thought as language, but not in the sense of a living language, language in action, but language as an abstract system of symbols. Religion, however, is much more than thoughts and beliefs, or rather religious thoughts and beliefs are entwined with the sensorimotor, with a profusion of smells, sounds, sights, tastes, emotions, and movements. Religion is about "the force of belongingness" that has been critical to the evolutionary success of humanity (King 2007). In addition, religion is closely linked to domination and resistance and to the pleasures of motion, of experiencing intense emotions and physically creating and transforming spaces. It is not clear how we go from HADDs and MCIs to the tactile-kinetics of religion, to material culture, architecture, dance, music, pilgrimage, fasting, and body scarification. How can we explore the interactions between religion, politics, and economics with cognitive approaches in mind?

It is not that cognitive theorists have not tried to build a more holistic theory of religion. Whitehouse (2004), for example, has developed the intriguing notion of "modes of religiosity." According to him, there are "two modes of religious experience and action." The "most ancient" is the imagistic mode of religiosity, built on exceptional, high-arousal, sometimes traumatic experiences, which activate an "episodic memory," imprinting powerful and detailed flashbulb memories of the climatic event. Since this mode of religiosity relies on the spontaneous and raw power of the event, it is hard to replicate, thereby limiting its capacity to spread, normalize into orthodoxy, or be the basis for the development of a hierarchical cadre of specialists. In tension with this mode of religious experience is what Whitehouse calls the "doctrinal mode of religiosity." It "tends to be highly routinized, facilitating the storage of elaborate and conceptually complex religious teachings in semantic memory, but also activating implicit memory in the performance of most ritual procedures. These cognitive features are linked to particular social morphology, including hierarchical, centralized institutional arrangements, expansionary potential, and dynamic leadership" (Whitehouse 2004: 65–66). The diversity of religions is the result of the oscillation between these two modes of religiosity, since Whitehouse makes clear that very rarely do we find "ideal types" of each of the modes.

Whitehouse's theory of modes of religiosity represents a promising effort to blend cognitive approaches with psychological, sociological, and anthropological perspectives (including Weber's concepts of routinization of charisma and bureaucratic rationalization). The theory certainly makes significant strides toward bringing emotion, motivation, ritual, and social morphology into dialogue with cognitive work on the origin and transmission of religion. One can examine, for example, the tension between the religion of the elites, which tends to be heavily doctrinal and invested in the production of dogma with universalist pretensions, and the popular religions that are often localized, syncretic, and involved powerful episodes of individual and collective devotion.

Nevertheless, Whitehouse still continues to think of memory, which is the defining core of the two modes of religiosity, as if it is a matter only "from the neck up" (Csordas 1999: 150). For example, he fails to bring in the pragmatist notion of know-how. The knowledge incorporated in know-how is not simply conceptual, nor is it just a matter of arousal at retrieving stored images. The knowledge with which we engage everyday life is primarily sensorimotor skill, inculcated through dwelling with and among social practices. "[W]e learn to perceive not by taking on board mental representations or schemata for organizing the raw data of bodily sensation, but by a fine-tuning or sensitization of the entire perceptual system, comprising the brain and peripheral receptor organs along with their neural and muscular linkages, to particular features of the environment" (Ingold 2001: 142). Bringing the full body back into the theory of modes of religiosity would mean, then, that we would have to develop a richer analysis of the ways in which society and culture shapes our cognition, along the lines of a non-reductive cultural neurophenomenology.

Going back to the example of the Yekuanas in Venezuela and Brazil, young men learn what they need to know to become adult members of the group not by studying a doctrine nor by engaging dramatic events (even though there indeed are intense rites of passage). Instead, boys acquire this knowledge primarily by performing everyday domestic chores that prove to the parents of their brides that they have the skills to take care of their own new families. More specifically, the young men learn the Watunna, the collection of Yekuana myths, by singing it as they weave a series of increasingly more intricate baskets, which contain the symbols of powerful animals in the forests. These baskets will hold the food that the young Yekuana and his bride will ingest, making them, literally, vessels for the physical incorporation of the natural world purified through their singing and weaving (Guss 1989).

This example shows how the transmission of religion involves more than mental categories. Or rather, it demonstrates how mental categories are part of a holistic "mode of inhabiting the world" as embodied beings (Csordas 1999:

144). The underlying problem with even those cognitive approaches to religion that are open to enaction is that they continue to understand practice as a second moment in the cognitive process. At worse, practice is a merely instrumental implementation of preexisting codes; at best, it is a performance that falls in line with but never transforms our mental representations. Cognitive philosopher Robert McCauley, for example, is interested in how we acquire ritual competence. However, he defines competence not in terms of embodied skills, but as syntax, as the ability to make judgments about the ritual form, about the proper relationships among practices. While he recognizes that this ability to judge is based on tacit knowledge, what he means here is not a sensorimotor know-how, but a structuralist notion of deep, built-in principles that can be accessed intellectually.[16] In his quest for the generative rules of ritual practice, McCauley fails to take full account of the effervescence and material efficacy of rituals. As Durkheim rightly argues, effervescence and material efficacy are not just products of judgment or the enactment of predetermined scripts, but of the viscerality of the event, the raw religious energy that envelops both performers and audience. Effervescence and efficacy also emerge out of the embeddedness of the performance in contingent social and cultural power asymmetries that give rituals authority, that is, the sanctioned power to bind, summon, purify, or to set things apart.[17] Contrary to McCauley's declaration above, religions are physical, material things. They are holistic and spatially located modes of being-in-the-world.

The bottom line is that, for all the fruitful insights they have provided, the dominant theories of religion and cognition have been hampered by a heavy reliance on representationalism. In order to overcome this limitation, they need to engage more closely the notions of emergence and enaction. Such a conversation will lead cognitive theorists of religion to take history, culture, society, phenomenology, and embodiment more seriously and to explore the complex interaction these realms of human existence and practice sustain with evolution and the dynamics of the mind-brain. Given this complexity, reductive moves will themselves have to be constrained.

CYBORGS NOT ROBOTS: ON THE RELATIVE INDETERMINACY OF RELIGIOUS LIFE

The relationship between the natural sciences and the humanities and the issue of reduction have been most recently broached by Edward Slingerland (2008a). He rightly decries the often-radical separation between the "postmodern relativism" that still dominates the study of culture and the objectivism and eliminative physicalism of the natural sciences. On the one hand, the humanities assume that "humans are fundamentally linguistic-cultural beings, and that our experience of the world is therefore mediated by language and/or culture all the way down. Inevitable corollaries of this stance are a strong linguistic-cultural relativism, epistemological skepticism, and a 'blank slate' view of human nature: we are nothing until inscribed by the discourse into which we are socialized, and therefore nothing significant about the way in which we think or act is a direct result of our biological endowment" (Slingerland 2008a: 15). On the other hand, the natural sciences sometimes assume a naïve representationalism that holds that, given the proper tools and methodology, we can find universal facts or laws independent of our mind, facts which determine all reality, including society and culture.

Echoing Dennett, Guthrie, Boyer, Barrett, and Whitehouse, Slingerland attributes this separation between *Geisteswissenschaften* and *Naturwissenschaften* to an ontological dualism that is a built-in tendency in our cognitive apparatus. Because we naturally impute anthropomorphic agency to objects in our environment in order to predict, explain, and control their behavior, we come to think that all reality, including ourselves, is informed by souls that are irreducible to matter. This ontological dualism, while serving adaptive purposes, has eventually led to a disembodied view of culture—culture is only the product of culture and texts only refer to others texts. This radical linguistic-cultural reductionism, in turn, accounts for the fierce resistance that the humanities put up against any attempt to bring evolutionary biology, genetics, or the neurosciences into the discussions about the source and transmission of culture. Paradoxically, humanists resist frank dialogue with the natural sciences in the name of combating reductionism, while engaging in a totalizing maneuver of their own.

In order to overcome ontological dualism, Slingerland steers a middle course between postmodern relativism and rational objectivism. He argues for a pragmatist view of knowledge that recognizes that "absolute, disinterested objectivity is an illusory goal" (2008a: 70). Instead, knowledge is situated enaction, whereby we perceive the world through our own categories. But these categories are not totally arbitrary; they are constrained by our own materiality, leading thus not to an anything-goes kind of relativism but to relatively stable phenomena upon which we can build a fallible but robust science. The key to this science lies in the concepts of emergence and vertical integration. Social and cultural phenomena are not disembodied self-referential realities. They are complex emergent effects of more basic biological, chemical, and physical processes. As emergent higher level realities, society and culture have their own logics, which are not totally reducible to lower level dynamics. In other words, "mutually autonomous levels of explanation" coexist, with the social and natural sciences developing appropriate tools to study human-level structures (Slingerland 2008a: 27). Nevertheless, because higher level structures are dependent for their existence on lower level ones, a vertically integrated model gives "precedence to the physical" (2008a: 262). According to Slingerland (2008b: 382–83), "the human mind is coterminous with the human body (especially the brain), and this body-brain is no more than a very complex physical thing, a product of millions of years of evolution. Human thought is not a ghostly, disembodied process, but rather a series of body-brain states—a series of physical configurations of matter—each causing the next in accordance with the deterministic laws that govern the interaction of physical objects" (Slingerland 2008b: 383).

Slingerland sees vertical integration as offering the best opportunity for what biologist E. O. Wilson (1998) calls "consilience," the unity of knowledge. Slingerland envisions the coming together of the disciplines into a "rough explanatory hierarchy, with the lower levels of explanation (such as physics) setting the limits on the sorts of explanations that can be entertained at the higher levels (such as biology). To move forward as a field of human inquiry, the humanities need to plug themselves into their proper place at the top of this explanatory hierarchy, because the lower levels have finally advanced to the point that they both need to hear from us [scholars in the humanities] and have many interesting things to say in return" (Slingerland 2008a: 299).

I am sympathetic to Slingerland's diagnosis of the unproductive separation between the natural sciences and the sciences of the spirit, although he sometimes overplays the bogeyman of postmodern relativism, equating it with every form of social constructionism. In addition, he is right on target when he singles out human exceptionalism as the most intransigent obstacle to a truly interdisciplinary dialogue. He puts it well when he observes that "we generally have no problem with vertical integration when it comes to most parts of our bodies . . . but we are deeply troubled by the idea that anything we take to be fundamental about us as human beings—our ability to reason, to make decisions, to feel emotions, to make commitments—is part of our evolutionary design" (Slingerland 2008a: 251). As we saw in the previous chapter, taking the materialist turn requires viewing culture as the result of not just discursive and nondiscursive practices but also biological processes. Evolution applies to our bodies as well as to our minds. Thus, any materialist account has to be careful not to reinscribe a human exceptionalism that makes consciousness a sui generis entity. I also agree wholeheartedly with Slingerland's proposal to take an enactive perspective on knowledge. Finally, I share his belief that the concept of emergence is key to the understanding of the complex relations between biology and culture.

Where I part ways with Slingerland is in the linear and unidirectional way in which he understands the notion of emergence and the integration of nature and culture. Beyond bottom-up causal explanatory chains, Slingerland only recognizes endogenous horizontal causation within each of the emergent levels. This narrow understanding of causation leads him to conclude that "we are robots designed to be constitutionally incapable of experiencing ourselves and conspecifics as robots—or, for that matter, to really believe that we live in a robotic world—since our theory of mind module seems to be overactive, causing us to project agency into the world at large as well as onto other 'agents'" (2008a: 26).

Slingerland seems to have missed the point that the enactive approach represents a radical rethinking of the notion of causation. Emergent processes are not simply the product of unidirectional, aggregative interactions but of non-linear dynamics. "Non-linear interactions are nonadditive or nonproportional. They give rise (by definition) to systems whose activities cannot be derived aggregatively from the properties of their components" (Thompson 2007: 419). As we saw above, the nonlinear enactive view of cognition proposes auto-poietic systems of coevolution and codetermination between the full-bodied organism and her/his environment. Autopoiesis requires system causation, that is, downward causation by higher level emergent realities and the system itself over the local and lower level processes that have become integrated to produce it.

Because the enactive perspective considers cognitive systems in non-dualist terms and views the "processes crucial for consciousness [as] cut[ting] across the brain–body–world divisions, rather than being brain-bound neural events" (Thompson and Varela 2001: 418), culture and society can not be understood as simply higher level structures that are ultimately reducible to biochemical or atomic processes. As integral parts of the system, culture and society enter into the dynamic interplay of bottom-up and top-down influences. In its most rad-ical version, the enactive approach to cognition operates with a "relational holism," a fully processual view in which

[e]verything is process all the way "down" and all the way "up," and processes are irreducibly relational—they exist only in patterns, networks, organizations, or webs. For the part/whole reductionist "down" and "up" describe more or less fundamental levels of reality. In the process view, "up" and "down" are context-relative terms used to describe phenomena of various scales and complexity. There is no base level of elementary entities to serve as the ultimate "emergence

base" on which to ground everything. Phenomena at all scales are not entities or substances but relatively stable processes, and since processes achieve stability at different levels of complexity, while still interacting with processes at other levels, all are equally real and none has absolute ontological primacy. (Thompson 2007: 440–41)

While Slingerland places emergence at the center of his proposal, he still continues to work with an atomistic metaphysics (reality made up of chains formed by the addition of basic units), rather than with processual notions of emergent fields, networks, webs, and large-scale synchronizations. As a result, he ends up with a simplistic and deterministic view of cognition. One does not have to accept Thompson's radical dissolution of explanatory hierarchies to advocate for more flexible materialism. "New Mechanicists" and "Heuristic Interlevel Theorists," for example, show that oftentimes straight bottom-up explanations are neither possible nor desirable because there is "level-hopping" and intense but patchy intra- and inter-level interaction shaped by the contexts in which cognitive processes take place (Bechtel 2007; Machamer, Darden, and Craver 2000; McCauley and Bechtel 2001). Because "the causal rubber meets the road at many places" when it comes to cognition, neuropsychologist Huib Looren de Jong argues for a robust methodological pluralism à la Feyerabend. "As they say in Texas, 'don't fence me in.' . . . Let's forget the single-level fixation, and be careful about simplistic interpretations of interlevel relations" (2006: 442).[18]

The significance of this complex view of causation for the cognitive study of religion is that nonlinear dynamics recognize the materiality and determining power of religious practices in a way that vertical integration does not. And this recognition comes without positing some external source, be that God, a soul, or an irreducible sacred, that warrants our exceptionality vis-à-vis the rest of the natural world. The reason Slingerland subscribes to vertical integration is that he wrongly believes that acknowledging any top-down determination would necessarily result in reintroducing dualism and, thus, denying full embodiment. However, there is no need to appeal to ontological dualism here or to fall back on the "folk psychology" that takes consciousness for granted, as a pre-given, unified, and sovereign reality. Following Karen Barad's agential realism (see chapter 6), it is entirely tenable to hold that consciousness is a dynamic emergent reality made possible by the "intra-action" of multiple materialities, ranging from the ecological and neurophysiological to the psychological and social, while affirming its causal efficacy in everyday life. The determining power of consciousness and religious experience does not come from the fact that they are immaterial or transcendental, but from being differently material. Religious phenomena have a materiality mediated by practices that give it "agential separability," that is "exteriority-within-phenomena" (Barad 2008: 140), grounding it on but not reducing it to the physicality of the brain-body. Religion's causal efficacy comes from its integration as discourses, practices, institutions, and artifacts into nonlinear self-organizing systems of perception, cognition, and action. If there is a "mystery" to religion, or consciousness for that matter, it is in the impossibility of disentangling totally, once and for all, the clear "chains of causation." This impossibility is merely the result of our embodiment. Just as we cannot take a God's-eye view of the world, we cannot assume that we will be totally transparent to ourselves.

> If we acknowledge that the source of the mystery lies in the structure of human intelligence, then we can avoid being drawn into religious mysticism about consciousness. For we can explain the sense of mystery without postulating magical processes in the world. The source of mystery lies in our given cognitive limits, not in a supernatural dimension of the universe. We do not therefore need to become embroiled in mystical absurdities and dead-ends. (McGinn 1999: 70)[19]

As we set out to understand complex autopoietic systems, we need to understand that "no methodological approach to experience is neutral; they all inevitably interpret their phenomenal data. The hermeneutical dimension of the process is inescapable: every examination is an interpretation, and all interpretation reveals and conceals at the same time. But it does not follow that a disciplined approach to experience creates nothing but artifacts or a 'deformed' version of the way experience 'really' is" (Depraz, Varela, and Vermersch 2003: 9). As Heidegger's and Merleau-Ponty's materialist phenomenologies tell us, our embodiment conditions us to grasp ourselves and the world in situated, open-ended, always intentional, pluralistic-yet-relatively-stable ways without falling into the nihilism of a radical social constructionism.

There is no question that complex autopoietic systems complicate the search for the unity of knowledge.[20] They certainly challenge the idea that the disciplines can be and should be ordered in a straightforward explanatory hierarchy. Perhaps consilience should be defined in a more flexible way, as the collaboration and convergence among various disciplines in dealing with common pressing problems, in producing fallible but effective materialist explanations of recurring saliences across time and space. The robustness of these explanations will depend on how far they can be extended and on the fruitful cross-fertilizations they sustain with other conceptual devices. It is very likely that the intervening disciplines will constrain and cross-fertilize each other (in their methodologies, levels of analysis, conceptual frames, etc.) to varying degrees, depending on the obduracy and affordance[21] of these saliences.

The notions of emergence, autopoiesis, downward causation, and relational holism are not without their critics. Philosopher Jaegwon Kim (2006), for example, argues that the combination of downward causation and upward determination makes non-reductive physicalism incoherent. Kim's objections, however, may apply only to relatively simple, reactive Newtonian systems and not to quantum and living systems. These debates show that the nature of consciousness and the role of culture are far from being settled with the certainty that Slingerland's model of vertical integration implies. One can take the natural sciences seriously in the study of culture and religion without resorting to the sort of parts-whole reductionism that Slingerland proposes. The metaphor of the robot is too conceptually impoverished to make sense of the complexity and malleability of cognition and religion, unless by robot one means Donna Haraway's cyborgs, who are integrated and shifting bits of materiality, of semiotic, animal, technological assemblages of various kinds. While cyborgs are clearly grounded in and determined by their carnal and machinic realities, they are not just vertically integrated. For them, integration and determination is multidirectional, contextual, and shaped by their own practices as they summon and are summoned by the world.

CONCLUSION

Humanists and scholars who approach religion through the social sciences and cultural studies have nothing to fear and much to gain from a frank conversation with the cognitive sciences, particularly with enactive models of cognition. The focus on the biological bases of and cognitive constraints on religious experience need not lead to an eliminative reductionism that dismisses the centrality of history and culture in the co-articulation of religious life. Notions such as autopoiesis and dynamic emergence do not discount the vividness and coherence of religious experiences, nor do they cancel out the power of discursive and nondiscursive practices to interpellate situated religious subjects. Quite the contrary, embodied cognition enriches the materiality of phenomenology and praxis by enfleshing it, by foregrounding the complex relations of mutual determination they sustain with neuropsychological processes. Conversely, we saw how cognition and evolution need a rematerialized humanities and social sciences to be able to specify the local diversity, complexity, and rich cross-fertilization of religious life, without losing sight of broad ecological, genetic, and neurophysiological constraints that give rise to cross-cultural and cross-generational regularities.

These reciprocal relations demonstrate the need to go beyond Slingerland's model of vertical integration toward a non-reductive, non-dualist materialism that allows for links among ecology, neurophysiology, psychology, culture, and history, which carry various weights and directions (vertical, horizontal, parallel, sequential, recursive, etc.). The choice then is not between being robots, whose multiple behaviors are reducible to isolatable naturalistic phenomena, or being angels, totally exempt from the enabling and constraining power of biology and society. Rather, borrowing from Donna Haraway, I suggested that we are cyborgs, determined by different but networked forms of materiality. The task of the religion scholar is to study how the relatively fluid interaction among these forms of materiality makes possible symbols, beliefs, affects, practices, object, institutions, and environments that come to be lived as religious.

Dewey's notion of know-how opens the door for a richer understanding of cognition that goes beyond the study of mental representations, pointing to the fact that practices do not just serve the instrumental roles of expressing, reinforcing, or transmitting these representations. Placing know-how at the center of everyday processes of cognition means taking practice "as the privileged site for grasping experience" (Depraz, Varela, and Vermersch 2003: 155). In the next two chapters, I hope to complement the insights of enaction by approaching the topic of religious materiality from the perspective of social practices.

PART II
Practice

8

The Eclipse of Practice

Textualism at Large

Interpretive anthropology is very practice oriented so texts are performed. That is why I say what I say about texts analogues. I've read the cockfight as a text. Now that's an action, and I textualize it perhaps, but I've tried to look at it as a Balinese text. I have tried to see how the Balinese make sense of this.

—*Clifford Geertz (in Panourgiá 2002: 427)*

In the extent to which what is called "meaning" (to be "expressed") is already, and thoroughly, constituted by a tissue of differences, in the extent to which there is already a text, a network of textual referrals to other texts, a textual transformation in which each allegedly "simple term" is marked by the trace of another term, the presumed interiority of meaning is already worked upon by its own exteriority.

—*Jacques Derrida (1981: 33)*

By the late 1960s, the Eliadean synthesis of history of religions and phenomenology of religion began to show signs of exhaustion. Scholars of religion realized that, if the task was merely to identify and catalogue sacred archetypes across different cultures and eras, the Eliadean approach ignored the creativity and multiplicity of local religious practices and institutions. Innovation and diversity were very much evident at the close of the sixties, as baby boomers founded and experimented with new, often "syncretic" religious movements. At the same time, postcolonial voices began to challenge the totalizing pretensions of Western scholarship, demanding to be heard on their own terms.

Working within the Boasian tradition of American anthropology, Clifford Geertz provided a way out of the Eliadean model of the eternal recurrence of the sacred, offering rich ethnographies of distinctive local symbolic systems. Geertz brought semiotics, hermeneutics, and practice into the study of religion, making it possible to explore how particular peoples construct shared yet contested worldviews. As such, Geertz's anthropology, masterfully exemplified in his highly influential *Interpretation of Cultures* (1973), contributed to a very salutary contextualization and historization of the study of religion. However, this materialization was only partial, since Geertz focused almost exclusively on the meaning-making dimensions of religious practices. This focus exacerbated some of the idealist tendencies in the phenomenology of religion.

In this chapter, I discuss Geertz's approach to religion in detail to demonstrate that, despite offering a much-needed break from Eliade, he ended up distorting certain aspects of the linguistic turn in the social sciences and humanities. In the process, he contributed to a semiotic reductionism, which construed not only representational practices but all forms of sociocultural activity as texts to be read and decoded. I argue that, in conjunction with structuralism and deconstruction, Geertz gave rise to a strong version of "textualism," a perspective that understands all human practices through the prism of representation and signification. Because this textualism gave scholars of religion a legitimate social-scientific language to continue talking about their enduring concerns with meaning, belief, and experience in the face of secularizing processes and naturalistic theories, it came to dominate religious studies from the 1970s on. I conclude the chapter by exploring the limitations of textualism to set the stage for a fuller practice approach, which will be the focus of the next chapter.

THE TROUBLE WITH GEERTZ

Many materialist anthropologists consider Clifford Geertz a precursor to postmodernism.[1] Indeed, Geertz's preference for "blurred genres" to describe fluid and localized cultures, over and against the search for fixed cross-cultural patterns, seems to echo Jean-François Lyotard's critique of modernity's teleological grand narratives and his defense of "local language-games." Moreover, when Geertz writes that anthropological writings are "interpretations . . . fictions" or that "cultural analysis is intrinsically incomplete . . . and [that] the more deeply it goes the less complete it is" (1973: 15, 29), he appears to foreshadow deconstructionism's claim that all texts are ultimately undecidable and thus open to endless self-referentiality.

While there are definite affinities between Geertz's interpretive anthropology and postmodernism, this reading ultimately misses the mark. In reading culture, Geertz does not advocate an anything-goes approach, where one ethnographic description is as good as any other, or where the anthropologist's positionality inevitably produces a partial account, incommensurable with other positioned representations. Rather, Geertz subscribes to a modified version of modernist verisimilitude. As he puts it: "cultural analysis is (or should be) guessing at meanings, assessing the guesses, and drawing explanatory conclusions from the better guesses, not discovering the Continent of Meaning and mapping out its bodiless landscape" (Geertz 1973: 20). We may not be able to unlock all the mysteries of a culture, as structuralists sought to do by uncovering cultural algorithms, the permutations of humanity's foundational cognitive dualities. Nevertheless, we can strive hard to produce increasingly nuanced, cogent, and rigorous "thick descriptions" of particular forms of local life. We can understand and, thus, translate for Western audiences the inner logics of a public event such as a Balinese cockfight. The latter cannot be read as a timeless Freudian struggle between the eros and thanatos, the life and death instincts, or between the ego and the id, as Balinese masculinity is formed. Nor can it be simply seen as a functionalist ritual that resolves social conflict and integrates the collective. The Balinese cockfight is primarily not about money, or even status. Geertz seems quite sure when he enjoins us to read the fight as literary text, as a symbolic system that is "saying something of something" (1973: 448). According to him,

> What sets the cockfight apart from the ordinary course of life, lifts it from the realm of everyday practical affairs, and surrounds it with an aura of enlarged importance is not, as functionalist sociology would have it, that it reinforces status discriminations ... but that it provides a metasocial commentary upon the whole matter of assorting human beings into fixed hierarchical ranks and then organizing the major part of collective existence around that assortment. Its function, if you want to call it that, is interpretive: it is a Balinese reading of Balinese experience, a story they tell themselves about themselves. (Geertz 1973: 448)

Geertz, then, means his ethnographies to be authoritative, to tell us as richly as possible how the local actors see themselves and the world around them. When it comes to culture, then, Geertz is a realist of sorts. Studying culture is not a matter of getting into the mind of the native in an exercise of intuition and divination à la Schleiermacher. In fact, Geertz dismisses this approach as "subjectivism" and "cabbalism" (1973: 30). Rather, it is the task of analyzing public symbols that are "material," that is, expressed in and through everyday life. Because these symbols are there, sustaining intersubjectivity and organized as a meaning-giving system that locals often take for granted, they are accessible to the anthropologist. That is why "the whole point of a semiotic approach to culture is ... to aid us in gaining access to the conceptual world in which our subjects live so that we can, in some extended sense of the term, converse with them" (Geertz 1973: 24).

Geertz's realism should give some pause to those who think of him as a post-modernist. This realism turns into a quasi essentialism and quasi universalism when it comes to religion. Geertz's influential definition of religion as a cultural system grows organically out of his many years of fieldwork. It is not imposed from above as procrustean archetypes that reduce religious diversity to recurrent morphologies of the sacred in time and space, a strategy more akin to Eliade's ahistorical and decontextualized history of religions approach. Nevertheless, Geertz's definition is not meant to be just another localized language game, applicable only to the Javanese or Balinese. For Geertz, what makes religion tick is its capacity to provide ever-changing cognitive, emotional, motivational, and behavioral (in the sense of shaping an ethos) resources to deal with issues of ultimate concern, as theologian Paul Tillich would put it. These are existential issues common to all humanity: bafflement, moral evil, and suffering and death. Thus, while local religious symbols, practices, and institutions are always contested and in constant flux, the phenomenological-hermeneutic core of religion remains unchanged, setting it apart from other symbolic systems and from social structures. In insisting "that religion has an autonomous essence—not to be confused with the essence of science, or of politics, or of common sense," Geertz "invites us to define religion (like any essence) as a transhistorical and transcultural phenomenon" (Asad 1993: 28).

In this chapter, I am not concerned with Geertz's universalization of religion per se. My focus here is on what is being universalized: the notion that religion is "a cluster of sacred symbols, woven into some sort of ordered whole" (Geertz 1973: 129). It is the idea that religion, like any other text, is primarily about communication, signification, conceptualization, values, and meaning-making.

As Asad sees it, what Geertz universalizes is a "modern, privatized Christian" conception of religion that "emphasizes the priority of belief as a state of mind rather than as constituting activity in the world." Moreover, beyond this internalist view of religion, Geertz reduces religion to signification, to its semiotic function, which becomes a precondition for meaningful practice. For Geertz, the power of religion is not in the situated practices that authorize it as an autonomous and efficacious field of human activity, but in its capacity as an ordered system of symbols, with its own internal logic, to "establish powerful, pervasive, and long-lasting moods and motivations" (Geertz 1973: 90). The secret of religion lies in the way in which the symbolic web that constitutes it links a worldview with a particular way of life, a "moral and aesthetic style and mood," which Geertz calls ethos. Thus, "whatever else religion may be, it is in

part an attempt (of an implicit and directly felt rather than explicit and consciously thought-about sort) to conserve the fund of general meanings in terms
of which each individual interprets his experience and organizes his [*sic*] conduct" (Geertz 1973: 127). Put more plainly, "sacred symbols . . . relate an
ontology and a cosmology to an aesthetics and morality" (126) that is shared
and territorialized in a particular locality, and expressed and reproduced publicly in and through practices.

What we have here, then, is a conception of religion as an ontogenic text, a
text that generates practices and renders them meaningful. Such a conception
has its roots in the notions that "social reality is fundamentally symbolic" and
that our apprehension of the world is not immediate and complete, but always
uncertain and partial, always "mediated by the whole of explanatory procedures which precede it and accompany it" (Ricoeur 1979: 99). Both of these
principles lie at the core of the linguistic turn in the social sciences.

The linguistic turn emerged as early as the 1930s as a critique to the logical-
positivist and unity of science approach of the Vienna Circle.[2] Although there
was diversity within the Vienna Circle, its members shared some form of representationalism, a theory of knowledge that holds that ideas, when formulated
correctly, reflect extra-mental reality. The task of epistemology, then, was to lay
the foundations of science by recovering an observational language held
together by minimal grammatical structures and devoid of metaphysical conceptions that cannot be verified or falsified in confrontation with sense experiences. For the Vienna Circle, philosophy should strive toward a logically perfect
and transparent language, modeled after the logic of the natural science and
mathematics. This language was basically a concatenation of single proposi-
tions, such as "all swans are black," which can be empirically tested. Logical-
positivists, thus, held an atomistic view of language.

The linguistic turn stands for a broad movement that showed the impossibility of deriving this representational language, pointing instead to the ways in
which all human activity, including science and philosophy, is embedded in the
ambiguities and contingencies of history and everyday life. Against logical-
positivism's atomism, the linguistic turn offered a holistic view of language as
an ever-changing web of signification that defines the limits of what appears to
us. Arguably, no one contributed more to the linguistic turn than Ludwig Wittgenstein, a Vienna Circle fellow traveler. In his early work, he had advanced an
influential version of representationalism.[3] In his later work, however, Wittgenstein offered a radically contrasting view of language.[4] The meaning of a
word is not the thing it supposedly stands for on a one-to-one basis. Rather, it
is given by the rules for the use of that word. These rules, in turn, are determined by convention and habit, by the relatively stable ways in which the

community of speakers uses the word among other words to mean something in a particular setting. Therefore, for Wittgenstein in his late period, the search for a transhistorical and transparent language that mirrors the world once and for all is a dead end. Instead, philosophy should study language as it is practiced, as individuals engage in rule-governed, context-dependent, and purposive meaning-making activities, which he called "language-games."[5] Each of these language-games has its own internal logic, particularly its own criteria for what counts as valid and intelligible. This notion of language-games as localized, holistic, yet fluid life forms was central to Geertz's understanding of culture as situated systems of public symbols that can only be approached through a thick description.

The overall effect of Wittgenstein's Copernican turn was to redirect the focus in the social sciences and humanities away from the quest to replicate the logic of the natural sciences and toward hermeneutics, to the interpretive study of practices whereby we make meaning. This shift is the basis for Paul Ricoeur's famous heuristic suggestion that the metaphor of the text *may* be a useful "paradigm for the so-called object of the social sciences" (Ricoeur 1979: 74). Like texts, social actions are rule-governed and context-dependent externalizations of psychic life that, once expressed, gain autonomy vis-à-vis intentions of the author, allowing for multiple, open-ended interpretation (Ricoeur 1979: 88). "Like a text, human action is an open work, the meaning of which is 'in suspense.' It is because it 'opens up' new references and receives fresh relevance from them, that human deeds are also waiting for fresh interpretations which decide their meaning" (Ricoeur 1979: 86). In deciding this meaning, we can apply some of the same interpretive strategies we use to make sense of texts.

This "softer" use of the analogy of the text, as *one* methodological strategy to disclose (and foreclose) certain aspects of human activity, continues to be of vital importance. Indeed, understood in this relativized way, the linguistic turn is enormously salutary, fruitfully stressing the role of creativity, practice, context, self-reflection, positionality, and symbolic mediation in human activity. It should not be conflated with the textualism that I seek to overcome. Such a textualism is rather the result of Geertz's exaggeration of some aspects of the linguistic turn, particularly of Ricoeur's text analogy. Geertz's interpretive anthropology clearly partakes of the salutary elements of this turn. He understands specific behaviors and events not as separate units whose ultimate truth can be discovered by looking at facts, but rather as practices embedded in larger forms of life that are symbolically mediated. Nevertheless, Geertz pushes the recognition of the mediated nature of understanding to its breaking point, positing that what makes humans distinctive is the fact that we are *Homo symbolicus*. Geertz makes this move to break with the functionalism of Malinowski,

Durkheim, and Parsons, who see culture's and religion's primary roles as integrating the various social components. Functionalism fails to acknowledge that cultural systems have their own internal dynamics (which Geertz understands as essentially expressive) that are not reducible to the requirements of social structures. This is why he writes:

> the [Balinese] cockfight . . . makes nothing happen. The cockfight is 'really real' only to the cock—it does not kill anyone, castrate anyone, reduce anyone to animal status, alter the hierarchical relations among people, or refashion the hierarchy; it does not even redistribute income in any significant way. [Rather] . . . it catches up [the] themes . . . [of] death, masculinity, rage, pride, loss, beneficence, chance . . . and, ordering them into an encompassing structure, presents them in such a way as to throw into relief a particular view of their essential nature. An image, fiction, model, a metaphor, the cockfight is a means of expression; its function is neither to assuage social passions or heighten them . . . but, in a medium of feathers, blood, crowds, and money, to display them. (Geertz 1973: 443–44)

The trouble is that Geertz's anti-functionalism runs the risk of decontextualizing cultural systems.

Geertz's assumption that we are fundamentally symbol-making creatures essentializes symbolic systems and our need to read them as meaningful texts as humanity's "second nature." According to Geertz (1973: 140), the human beings are "symbolizing, conceptualizing, meaning-seeking animal[s]." For them, "the drive to make sense out of experience, to give it form and order, is evidently as real and as pressing as the more familiar biological needs." This is because humans are, "incomplete" and "unfinished" animals, whose DNA has not been pre-programmed to deal with the multiple and evolving demands of their survival. In contrast to other animals, which come with more specified "intrinsic" templates for action in their genes, humans require "extrinsic sources of information" provided by culture to apprehend and transform the world around them. Indeed, "undirected by culture patterns—organized systems of significant symbols—[human] behavior would be virtually ungovernable, a mere chaos of pointless acts and exploding emotions, his experience virtually shapeless. Culture, the accumulated totality of such patterns, is not just an ornament of human existence but—the principal basis of its specificity—an essential condition for it" (Geertz 1973: 46). Furthermore, the unavoidable interaction between intrinsic and extrinsic sources of information shapes the evolution of *Homo sapiens*. "Between the cultural pattern, the body, and the brain, a positive feedback system was created in which each shaped the progress of the other, a system in which the interaction among increasing tool use, the changing anatomy of the hand, and the expanding representation of the thumb on the cortex is only one of the more graphic examples. By submitting himself [*sic*] to governance by symbolically mediated programs for producing artifacts, organizing social life, or expressing emotion, man determined, if unwittingly, the culminating stages of his own biological destiny" (Geertz 1973: 48).

Political scientist and historian William Sewell, who has been strongly influenced by Geertz, argues that the Geertzian view of the biological necessity of culture is a "brilliant piece of materialist argumentation. It transcends the material/ideal dichotomy not by some verbal formula but by a substantial, scientifically based account of the inescapable complementary of 'material' and 'ideal' in the human condition. It enables us to recognize the simultaneous rootedness of culture (or 'mind') in bodily needs and its irreducibility to bodily needs" (Sewell 1999: 45). Such a reading is plausible. The trouble is that, when it comes to religion, Geertz fails to follow through with this materialist and relational view of culture, body, and society. In "Religion as a Cultural System," for instance, he contends religion offers both "models of" and "models for" reality, that religion always sustains relations of reciprocal determination with society and biology, simultaneously mirroring life conditions (as a cognitive map, a worldview) and shaping them (as a template, an ethos). However, at the end of the same essay, Geertz concludes that "the anthropological study of religion is . . . a two-stage operation: first, an analysis of the system of meanings embodied in the symbols which make up the religion proper, and second, the relating of these systems to socio-structural and psychological processes" (1973: 125).

This position is significantly more idealist and static than that advocated by Max Weber in *The Protestant Ethic and the Spirit of Capitalism*, long considered a classic in *Verstehen* sociology and a precursor to "Religion as a Cultural System." After arguing that certain theological conceptions (worldviews), such as those of calling and predestination, contributed to the emergence of a this-worldly asceticism (an ethos) that, in turn, served as the psycho-behavioral fuel for the wealth accumulation necessary to set modern capitalism in its tracks, Weber is quick to acknowledge that he has studied religious ideas in themselves as a purely heuristic exercise, to be able to highlight their power to change the course of history at given junctures. Weber (1958: 183) writes: "Here we have only attempted to trace the fact and the direction of [Protestantism's] influence to their motives in one, though a very important point. But it would also further be necessary to investigate how Protestant Asceticism was in turn influenced in its development and its character by the totality of social conditions, especially economic." And this is, in fact, what Weber does in *Sociology of Religion*, where he claims, for example, that enchanted religions are more likely to thrive among peasants because of the latter's reliance on an unpredictable nature, which leads them to posit capricious spirits that must be placated through magic and rituals. It is difficult to think of a more materialist position. Weber seems to be saying: "tell me what your life conditions are and I will tell you the extent to which your religion is rationalized."[6]

Weber, thus, can be read as a non-reductive materialist, attempting to correct crude and reductive appropriations of Marx. As he tells us at the end of *The Protestant Ethic*, "but it is, of course, not my aim to substitute for a one-sided materialistic an equally one-sided spiritualistic causal interpretation of culture and of history. Each is equally possible, but each, if it does not serve as the preparation, but as the conclusion of an investigation, accomplishes equally little in the interest of historical truth" (Weber 1958: 183). In contrast, when it comes to religion, Geertz seems to suspend this dialectic view of the relation between culture and society. For Geertz, the symbol takes precedence. The first analytical operation of interpretive anthropology is to set religion apart as a reality that can be studied sui generis. This setting apart of religion is not a heuristic or even a simple preparatory move to foreground certain dynamics, which certain forms of materialism and functionalism ignore. It is, above all, a synchronic strategy, an attempt to retrieve religion's authentic ontogenic core: the public meanings and personal emotions expressed the symbolic systems that orient meaningful action.

Geertz's semiotic reductionism is evident in his treatment of practice as the performance of texts. He recognizes that "interpretive models are not only textual. Some are textual, but again there is the dramatic model, I use the theater model sometimes. So I don't want to identify textual things with interpretive models" (Panourgiá 2002: 427). The relativization of the text analogy seems to point to Ricoeur's softer and more plausible version of the linguistic turn, while the reference to the dramatic model appears to indicate that Geertz is aware of the centrality of practice. Indeed, Geertz affirms that "interpretive anthropology is very practice oriented so texts are performed. That is why I say what I say about text analogues. I've read the cockfight as a text. Now that's an action, and I textualize it perhaps, but I've tried to look at it as a Balinese text. I have tried to see how the Balinese make sense of this. So behavior is read by the people who are involved in it" (Panourgiá 2002: 427). Notice here, however, how the text precedes and grounds practices, how practices are the enactments of texts, and how these enactments are themselves read as texts. Practices are essentially media for the externalization and internalization of texts. Texts are the alpha and omega of practices.[7]

As we saw in chapter 4, a materialist phenomenology of embodiment runs counter to the ontogenic view of texts that Geertz wishes to defend. "Bodily activity is not a way of expression or objectifying meanings first formed in the mind. The meaning of a bodily action is not *given to* the action by some external agent [such a self-contained symbolic system] but is *in* the action itself." In other words, "the meaning of praxis and practical knowledge lies in what is accomplished through it, not in what conceptual order may be said to underlie or precede it" (Jackson 1996: 32, 34). If this is the case, embodiment, as the non-dualistic ground of being-in-the-world, as the emplaced interplay of biology and culture, individual and society, symbol and power, and discursive and nondiscursive practices, offers a more fruitful "paradigm" to explore the richness of religion than the metaphor of the text (Csordas 1990). This metaphor retains some of the Cartesian disembodied mentalism that I tried to expose in chapter 1.

In the end, despite the focus on locality, everyday life, and cultural complexity, Geertz's excessive symbolicism ultimately yields a one-dimensional view of religion. He sees religion primarily as a set of expressive texts to be enacted and decoded, not as shifting clusters of embodied practices emplaced in social and ecological fields. To do ethnography for him is not to submerge oneself in the physicality of practices, but to read culture and religious texts "over the shoulders of those to whom they properly belong" (Geertz 1973: 452). As a result, "both the anthropologist and the culture he or she is trying to grasp seem to be floating in thin air. This disembodied stance is reiterated in Geertz's . . . image of humanity 'suspended in webs of significance'" (Lee and Ingold 2006: 83). Geertz, thus, may have overcome the subjectivism of early hermeneutics and Eliade's ahistorical search of archetypes. Nonetheless, his theory of religion is burdened by a semiotic reductionism that obscures crucial aspects of religious activity.

To overcome the limitations of viewing religion as self-contained semiotic phenomena, texts that scholars must endlessly decode or aesthetically experience, Asad suggests an alternative focus on historical, contested practices, with religion representing activities embedded in and interacting with fields of action. The boundaries of religion as a range of sanctioned activities, which include discursive as well as nondiscursive practices, change constantly in interaction with other types of (nonreligious) practices. That is why "there is nothing essentially religious, nor any universal essence that defines 'sacred language' or 'sacred experience'" (Asad 2003: 25). As Asad (1993: 53) puts it, "religious symbols—whether one thinks of them in terms of communication or of cognition, of guiding action or of expressing emotion—cannot be understood independently of their historical relations with non-religious symbols or of their articulation in and social life, in which work and power are always crucial."

In all fairness to Geertz, the problem is not that he ignores power in favor of a "sociological aestheticism," which he himself condemns (1973c: 30; Panourgiá 2002: 427). After all, he argues that culture is "a set of control mechanisms— plans, recipes, rules, instructions (what computer engineers call 'programs')— for governing behavior" (Geertz 1973f: 44). The issue is rather that Geertz understands both culture and power primarily in cognitive and affective terms (Asad 1993: 44). Geertz understands power as the struggles around cultural "programs," around representation and emotion. In the case of religion, the stakes of those struggles are higher since those representations are "clothed" with such a strong "aura of factuality that the moods and motivations seem uniquely realistic" (Geertz 1973a: 90). In contrast, Asad suggests a genealogical approach that focuses on the material conditions, both bodily and sociopolit- ical, that make representations and certain forms of subjectivity (with emo- tions tied to them) possible in the first place and give them their ontogenic power, the power to produce factuality. What Asad would like to see is "an anthropology of practical reason—not in the Kantian sense of universalizable ethical rules, but in that of historically constituted practical knowledge, which articulates an individual's learned capacities," and forms "a precondition for varieties of religious experience" (Asad 1993: 76–77). Asad's focus is on the training of religious bodies, on the disciplinary practices that allow the individual to create and recognize binding representations and feel in given ways. The power of the representations or "programs" does not lie in the inner logic of their symbolic structure, as Geertz assumes when he tells us that anthropology of religion must first analyze "the systems of meaning embodied in the symbols which make up the religion proper." Instead, representational power is predicated on authorizing practices that render certain symbols effec- tive. What is missing in Geertz's definition of religion is "a concept of culture as material social process" (Roseberry 1989: 25).

THE DURKHEMIAN LEGACY: STRUCTURALISM AND ITS CRITICS

If we follow Asad, to study religion's efficacy is to move from textualism to practice; it is to avoid reducing context to a mere text analogue. This shift from textualism to practices characterizes the most exciting work emerging in reli- gious studies. Nevertheless, this movement does not occur in a vacuum. A lively, albeit ambivalent, materialist, praxis-oriented countercurrent exists among classical approaches to religion. For instance, Durkheim, who is often counterposed to Marx as an idealist focused on independent existence and the social power of collective representations, stressed the centrality of ritual in producing the effervescence and cohesion that is religion's hallmark.[8] "[W]hoever has really practiced a religion knows very well that it is the cult which gives rise to these impressions of joy, of interior peace, of serenity, or enthusiasm which are, for the believer, an experimental proof of his beliefs. The cult is *not simply a system of signs by which the faith is outwardly translated*; it is a collection of the means by which this is created and recreated periodically. Whether it consists in material acts or mental operations, it is always efficacious" (Durkheim 1965: 464, my emphasis).

Like Weber, Durkheim offers a subtle theory about the relation between ideas and matter, and between symbol and practice. If the task is to study the sacred as an effective force, as "objectified sentiments," then it does not make sense to separate cognition from practice and text from context. After all, "to consecrate something, it is put in contact with a source of religious energy, just as to-day a body is put in contact with a source of heat or electricity to warm or electrize it; the two processes employed are not essentially different. Thus understood, religious technique seems to be a sort of mystic mechanics" (Durkheim 1965: 467). Once again, the talk of mechanics, techniques, and tangible energies in the shape of heat and electricity could not be more materialist. However, Durkheim's social Kantianism—the attempt to ground sociology through the search of socially constructed a prioris irreducible to biology and psychology—undermines his materialist thrust. The sacred's material "maneuvers," Durkheim tells us, "are only the external envelope under which the mental operations are hidden." He continues: "It is sometimes said that inferior religions are materialistic. Such an expression is inexact. All religions, even the crudest, are in a sense spiritualistic: for the powers they put in play are before all spiritual, and also their principal object is to act upon the moral life" (Durkheim 1965: 467).

Durkheim's ambivalence toward the materiality of religion and his ultimate surrender to an Aristotelian kind of idealism, in which ideas are foundational but must be always expressed materially, defines much of the structuralist-functionalist research programme he inaugurated, giving rise to two approaches in tension with each other. In the rest of chapter, I focus on the Durkheimian line of inquiry that is in direct conversation and feeds into Geertzian interpretive anthropology, reinforcing the textualism that has been dominant in the study of religion. I will discuss the second current of the Durkheimian research program in the next chapter, since it provides a counterpoint to the emphasis on symbolic systems, making possible the recovery of a richer and more dynamic understanding of religious practices. The semiotic line of the Durkheimian research program was developed by Lévi-Strauss, who, seeing language as the inescapable precondition and foundation for thought, modeled the study of all cultural production on the most advanced linguistic theories of his time.

Drawing from linguists Roland Jakobson, N. S. Trubetzkoy, and Ferdinand de Saussure, who argued that signification is grounded not on the purely idiosyncratic performance of language (*parole*) but on its deep formal grammar (*langue*), Lévi-Strauss sought to uncover the underlying universal structures of culture, not its historically contingent variations. For Lévi-Strauss, culture, like language, is organized as a system of irreducible units that enter into relations with each other according to specific rules, just as a meaningful sentence is constituted by arranging nouns, verbs, adjectives, and prepositions in particular ways. So, if for language there are phonemes, the irreducible units of sound that within human vocal range are marked as intelligible in specific combinations, for culture and religion, there are mythemes, stable ways of structuring relations between actors and their actions in mythical narratives. What accounts for this stability is the fact that these bundles of differential relations are themselves anchored on oppositional pairs that define the deepest structures of the human mind. According to Lévi-Strauss, anthropology's task is to search for transhistorical homologies in the symbolic and cognitive operations by which humans negotiate tensions such as those between the raw and the cooked, insider and outsider, male and female, and others that ultimately have to do with the chasm between culture and nature. He writes in *Tristes Tropiques* that

> the customs of a community, taken as a whole, always have a particular style and are reducible to systems. I am of the opinion that the number of such systems is not unlimited and that—in their games, dreams or wild imaginings—human societies, like individuals, never create absolutely; but merely choose certain combinations from an ideal repertoire that it should be possible to define. By making an inventory of all recorded customs, of all those imagined in myths or suggested in children's games or adult games . . . one could arrive at a sort of table, like that of the chemical elements, in which all actual or hypothetical customs would be grouped in families, so that one could see at a glance which customs a particular society had in fact adopted. (Lévi-Strauss 1973: 178)

Even though Lévi-Strauss starts from ethnographic experience, he "always aimed at drawing up an inventory of mental patterns, to reduce apparently arbitrary data to some kind of order, and to attain a level at which a kind of necessity becomes apparent, underlying the illusions of liberty" (1969: 10). As we shall see, this hermeneutics of suspicion directed against the foundational and intentional subjectivity that phenomenology elevates became part not only of Derrida's deconstructionist arsenal, but also of Foucault's archaeologies of knowledge and Bourdieu's theory of practice.

Lévi-Strauss's textualist approach to culture—culture as an ordered system of signifying differentials—was crucial in overcoming the limitations of phenomenology, which dominated the French philosophical scene from the 1920s to the 1950s.[9] Arguably, the most striking incarnation of this phenomenological tradition is Jean-Paul Sartre's early existentialism, which posited a totally unencumbered self who makes him/herself anew with every act. In locating the self within a web of relations that not only transcends him/her but determines his/her identity, structuralism contextualized the phenomenological self. However, this contextualization was incomplete because it lost the historical dimension of practice, which was seen as a mere reproduction of culture's deeper grammar. This loss is behind Lévi-Strauss's startling assertion that structuralist anthropology's task is not "to show how men [sic] think the myths, but rather how the myths think themselves out in men and without men's knowledge" (1969: 46). The underlying codes (i.e., the text) do all the work, as they undergo their regulated permutations. Individuals are mere "carriers" of structures.[10]

Geertz's work, then, emerged as an attempt to recover the subject and its creative praxis (Ortner 2005). Referring to structuralism, Geertz (1973: 17) writes: "Culture is most effectively treated, the argument goes, purely as a symbolic system (the catch phrase is, 'in its own terms'), by isolating its elements, specifying internal relationships among those elements, and then characterizing the whole system in some general way—according to the core symbols around which it is organized, the underlying structures of which it is a surface expression, or the ideological principles upon which it is based." Such an approach runs the danger of "schematicism": "locking cultural analysis away from its proper object, the informal logic of actual life." Borrowing from Wittgenstein's work on the embeddedness of language in ordinary life, Geertz argues that interpretative anthropology must attend to behavior, "because it is through the flow of behavior—or more precisely, social action—that cultural forms find articulation." A symbolic system has meaning "in an on-going pattern of life, not from any intrinsic relationships [its elements] bear with one another" (1973: 17). In fact, Geertz is at his best when he explores symbolic systems as they are being used, particularly in "deep plays," in collective dramas so charged with emotion that the participants learn their culture's ethos. The most illustrative example is his famous treatment of the Balinese cockfight.

Through this powerful display of "animal savagery, male narcissism, opponent gambling, status rivalry, mass excitement, [and] blood sacrifice," Balinese men form and discover their "temperament and [their] society's temper at the same time" (1973: 449, 451). Here Geertz is a theorist of practice par excellence.

Unfortunately, as we saw above, when it comes to religion, Geertz fails to follow through on his injunction to embed religious symbolic systems within the larger *Lebenswelt*. Thus, despite the welcomed critique of structuralist schematicism and the emphasis on performance, he still preserves a textualism that understands religion proper synchronically, as an autonomous system of signification. Culture is not a cluster of shifting, power-laden practices, but an ensemble of texts. Geertz brings practices back in but reifies them as semiotic artifacts. Meaning-making and communication precede and shape all other kinds of activity.

TEXTUALISM AD INFINITUM: DERRIDA

"Performative textualism" is also found in Jacques Derrida's deconstruction. Despite the fact that hermeneutics, as a strategy of recovery, is often opposed to deconstruction's decentering of texts, these two traditions have reinforced each other in their textualist approach to religion. Like Lévi-Strauss's structuralism, Derrida's deconstruction is a critique of phenomenology's attempt to go back to the things as they really present themselves to us, beyond surface appearances that we construct through the naïve and taken-for-granted intersubjective world in which we are embedded. Husserl, the key figure in the development of modern phenomenology, had hoped to succeed where Kant failed, retrieving the a prioris of apperception through a series of philosophical moves that would increasingly neutralize time and history. These a prioris would then provide solid foundations for the sciences, which Husserl perceived to be in crisis. By foregrounding our inescapable "fallenness" in our structures of signification, Derrida challenges the possibility of recovering transcendental sources of legitimation.[11]

Beyond the critique of phenomenology, Derrida offers a salutary deconstruction of the "metaphysics of presence" that has dominated Western thought: the notion that, with the right epistemological moves, we can find an Archimedean point upon which we can stand, free of all the limitations of the flesh—our historicity and contingency—and move the universe. Deconstruction shows the folly of the search for a God's-eye's view of the world, through which all things are immediately given, fully transparent, their essence revealed once and for all. Thus, in contrast to Eliade, who expressed a strong nostalgia for origins, for *illo tempore*, the time when the gods walk side-by-side with us, when all reality was imbued with the power of the sacred, Derrida posits the impossibility of return to the logos. At best, *homo religiosus* can only reenact lack endlessly. We cannot go back to pristine origins, because we are always suspended in a web of signification in which, as Saussure had argued, signs do not relate to a pre-symbolic reality but to other signs. Our interpretive horizons are uncertain because they are always intertextual, or as Derrida (1976: 158) is often quoted as saying, "there is nothing outside the text." Here it is worth quoting Derrida in one of his most lucid moments:

> In the extent to which what is called "meaning" (to be "expressed") is already, and thoroughly, constituted by a tissue of differences, in the extent to which there is already a text, a network of textual referrals to other texts, a textual transformation in which each allegedly "simple term" is marked by the trace of another term, the presumed interiority of meaning is already worked upon by its own exteriority. It is always already carried outside itself. It already differs (from itself) before any act of expression. And only on this condition can it constitute a syntagm or text. Only on this condition can it "signify." (Derrida 1981: 33)

Derrida departs from Lévi-Strauss, and thus earns the designation of poststructuralist, in his rejection of the possibility of achieving a total and final reading of a symbolic system, of finding once and for all the underlying laws that define its permutations. Lévi-Strauss "seeks to decipher, dreams of deciphering a truth or an origin which escapes play and the order of the sign, and which lives the necessity of interpretation as an exile" (Derrida 1978: 292). Against this quest, Derrida counter poses an interpretation that "is no longer turned toward the origin, affirms play and tries to pass beyond man [*sic*] and humanism, the name of man being the name of that being who, throughout the history of metaphysics or of ontotheology—in other words, throughout his entire history—has dreamed of full presence, the reassuring foundation, the origin and end of play" (Derrida 1978: 292). In simple terms, whereas Lévi-Strauss is "totalitarian," Derrida wants to show the radical openness of the hermeneutic process.

Nevertheless, Derrida's appeal to the endless dissemination of meaning hides a totalitarianism of its own. For what he offers is another version of the universalization of intertextuality and of the interpretive task, this time pushed to a dizzying intensity that not even Geertz's hermeneutics would prescribe. If Lévi-Strauss wants to bring the work of the human sciences to a closure by pinning down the algorithms of culture and Geertz seeks increasingly thicker and more coherent but never complete descriptions of symbolic systems, Derrida traps us in an insoluble, bottomless labyrinth of signs. One of the clearest examples of Derrida's strong version of semiotic reductionism is his analysis of Michel Foucault's *Madness and Civilization*. In Derrida's reading, "Foucault wanted to write a history of madness *itself*, that is madness speaking on the basis of its own experience and under its own authority, and not a history of madness described from within the language of reason, the language of psychiatry *on* madness . . . on madness already crushed beneath psychiatry, dominated, beaten to the ground, interned, that is to say, madness made into an object and exiled as the other of a language and a historical meaning which have been confused with logos itself" (Derrida 1978: 34). The problem is that, in giving voice to the silenced madness, Foucault cannot but assume the "language of reason." Foucault is trapped in the same discursive field that has confined madness and forced it to reveal the truth about itself. Thus, Derrida asks rhetorically: "Does it suffice to stack the tools of psychiatry neatly, inside a tightly shut workshop, in order to return to innocence and to end all complicity with the rational and political order which keeps madness captive?" He answers his own question: "Nothing within this language [of Western reason], and no one among those who speak it, can escape the historical guilt—if there is one, and if it is historical in the classical sense—which Foucault apparently wishes to put on trial. But such a trial may be impossible, for by the simple fact of their articulation the proceedings and the verdict unceasingly reiterate the crime" (Derrida 1978: 35). His radical gesture notwithstanding, Foucault engages in a metaphysics of presence that seeks to go back to the "zero point" where reason splits from madness (in the Cartesian cogito), in order to recover madness, even if only in its halting speech.[12]

Foucault's response to Derrida illustrates how theorists of practice react to the excesses of textualism. It is beyond the scope of this essay to discuss the fine points of the Derrida-Foucault debate. For our limited purposes, it is sufficient to highlight that for Foucault (1998: 395) the "stakes of the debate are clearly indicated: Could there be anything anterior or exterior to philosophical discourse? Can its conditions reside in an exclusion, a refusal, a risk avoided, and, why not, a fear?" Is there anything outside the text, outside the discursive practices that Derrida has textualized and universalized in an attempt to flee context? Foucault views Derrida as "the most decisive modern representative" of a "system in its final glory":

> the reduction of discursive practices to textual traces; the elision of the events produced therein and the retention only of marks for reading; the invention of voices behind texts to avoid having to analyze the modes of implication of the

subject in discourses; the assigning of the originary as said and unsaid in the text to avoid placing discursive practices in the field of transformations where they are carried out.

I will not say that it is a metaphysics, metaphysics itself or its closure which is hiding in this "textualization" of discursive practices. I'll go much further than that: I shall say that what can be seen here so visibly is a historically well determined little pedagogy. A pedagogy that teaches the pupil there is nothing outside the text, but that in it, in its gaps, its blanks and its silences, there reigns the reserve of the origin; that it is therefore unnecessary to search elsewhere, but that here, not in the words, certainly, but in the words under erasure, in their grid, the "sense of being" is said. (Foucault 1998: 416)

Behind Foucault's angry response is the same point that Asad formulated against Geertz's concept of religion. Despite the emphasis on performance and playfulness, both Derrida and Geertz seem to be engaged in a kind of genesis amnesia about their interpretive practices, a failure to understand the sociohistorical conditions that have enabled their discourse about the primacy of symbols and texts. This forgetfulness of the contingent but effective link between knowledge and power is possible because symbols and texts have become so self-referential that they leave no possibility of relativizing them, of embedding them in time and space. They become so detached from their contexts of production, circulation, and consumption that they appear to be animated in themselves, in much the same way as the fetishism of commodities that Marx (1978a: 319–29) described. This is why I referred to Derrida's approach as a performative textualism: a textualism for textualism's sake, where the text gains prestige "proportionate to its unreality, its gratuitousness, its sovereign indifference," and its subversive playfulness (Bourdieu 1984: 495).[13] It is no wonder, then, that Foucault thinks that Derrida's little pedagogy gives to "the master's voice the limitless sovereignty that allows it to restate the text indefinitely."[14] The religion scholar caught in the textualist attitude acts as the authorized interpreter of texts and the endless discourses on them, or of the deepest feelings and beliefs of the faithful. S/he becomes the sovereign master of a discursive field that is not conditioned by historical processes of othering like those Foucault traced in *Madness and Civilization*.

Overcoming textual reductionism would mean, then, challenging the taken-for-granted assumptions that signifying, meaning-making practices always have ontological primacy and that the metaphor of text is always helpful in understanding all types of practices. To avoid these two assumptions, we must not detach texts and discursive practices from the larger matrix of ordinary life in which they are created, circulated, and consumed. Because practices are poly-functional, that is, they have multiple functions that cannot be reduced to just representing or communicating ("saying something about something"), it is essential to study the tight interplay between signifying, meaning-making practices and other types of practices that are, at a particular moment, not strictly or primarily semiotic. In Foucaultian terms, it is to explore from one's strategic position the specific historical relations among discursive and nondiscursive practices, without presupposing that there is a universal formula that makes certain kinds of practice "models of or for" all the others. To break down what he meant by discursive and nondiscursive practices, Foucault used in his later works the term "technologies," clusters of operations individuals deploy strategically to constitute themselves and the world around them. He identified four major types of technologies, each with its own power-knowledge nexus:

> (1) technologies of production, which permit us to produce, transform, or manipulate things; (2) technologies of sign systems, which permit us to use signs, meanings, symbols, or signification; (3) technologies of power, which determine the conduct of individuals and submit them to certain ends or domination, an objectivizing of the subject; (4) technologies of self, which permit individuals to effect by their own means and with the help of others a certain number of operations on their own bodies and souls, thoughts, conduct, and ways of being, so as to transform themselves in order to attain a certain state of happiness, purity, wisdom, perfection, or immortality. (Foucault 1988: 18)

Foucault's move, then, is not to jettison the analysis of semiotic technologies, but to nest it in a larger exploration of the concrete relations these technologies sustain with other practices at a particular point in time. Here, Foucault stands firmly in the second strand of the Durkheimean research program, which has made embodied practice, not consciousness or collective representations, the point of departure for the study of religion. In the next chapter, I turn to this alternative research programme, reconstructing its genealogy and main presuppositions as a way to foreground the shift from textualism to practice.

9

"Ceci n'est pas un texte"

From Textualism to Practice

Social life is essentially *practical*. All mysteries which mislead theory into mysticism find their rational solution in human practice and in the comprehension of this practice.

—*Karl Marx (1978e: 145)*

It is not enough to say that the subject is constituted in a symbolic system. It is not just in the play of symbols that the subject is constituted. It is constituted in real practices—historically analyzable practices.

—*Michel Foucault (1984: 369)*

The world of the text is really not the world.

—*Robert Orsi (2005: 164)*

Having characterized the textualism that has dominated religious studies in the last thirty years, I now turn to the sources of the shift toward practice. Like the debates on the relationship between mind and body, the concept of practice has a long history. Aristotle used the term *praxis* to describe intentional, rational activity which is its own end. He distinguished it from *theoria*, contemplative activity directed toward truth, and *poeisis*, whose end goal is making, production (*techne*). Praxis is, then, from the beginning reflexive and requires holistic involvement. It is the creative recursive activity of free individuals who fulfill their potential through the process of acting. Whereas *poeisis* is for Aristotle the skillful implementation of already established schemas, rules, or plans in order, for example, to produce a perfect boat or to craft an eloquent speech, praxis involves *phronesis*, a practical wisdom that allows one to negotiate with others, balance competing interests, and adapt to the specific demands and possibilities of the environment at hand in order undertake the right action. This is why Aristotle sees praxis and *phronesis* as closely connected with politics, virtue, and the common good.[1]

Although helpful, the distinction between *theoria*, *poeisis*, and praxis should not be overdrawn. As I argued in my discussion of phenomenology, even the theoretical attitude depends on our embeddedness in the life-world constituted by our practices. Production, for its part, no matter how rule-bound, is not mere reproduction. It always involves a measure of creativity. This fact explains why from Aquinas on, the distinction between *poeisis* and praxis became increasingly blurred in such a way that the latter came to stand for all forms of actions.[2]

Seeking to highlight the creative and situated dimensions in the Aristotelian notion of praxis and to bring attention to the power of individuals to transform their surroundings, educating and elevating themselves in the process, the Left Hegelians, particularly Marx, rethought the concept of praxis along historicist and constructionist lines. For Marx, praxis follows naturally from our species-being (*Gatungswessen*) as *homo faber* (makers). Human beings find their self-realization by externalizing their creativity, giving rise to history and culture, which, in turn, are internalized to serve as the basis for new forms of activity. Any socioeconomic arrangement that thwarts the expression of this dialectical creativity is built on alienation, the distortion and projection of our essence so that it now stands outside, against us, as an extraneous object that controls us. This modern understanding of praxis makes its way to the contemporary social sciences and cultural studies.[3]

Standing with Marx, I also emphasize the dynamic nature of praxis against the contemplative and "poeitic" (in the Aristotelian sense) force of textualism, which sees practices as just the reenactment of already constituted symbolic systems, "models of" or "models for," to quote Geertz. Texts should not be treated as "fetishes," acting independently of the practices by which we produce, circulate, consume, and authorize them. However, building on my earlier discussions on embodiment and going beyond Marx and other social constructionists, I would like to recognize that praxis is enabled and constrained not just by the sociocultural context but by biology, by our natural environment, and our physicality.

Armed with this preliminary definition of praxis, let us now explore its applications in religious studies. Along the way, a more refined notion of practice will emerge to inform the non-reductive materialist framework I wish to advance.

THE ALTERNATIVE DURKHEMIAN LEGACY: APPROACHES TO RITUAL

In the discipline of religion, a praxis approach emerged early on, in conversation and tension with the approaches laid out by Max Müller and E. B. Tylor.

Whereas Müller placed language, particularly (mis)naming turned into myth, at the root of religion, Tylor traced the latter's origin to cognition, to the primitive man's philosophical speculations about immortality (i.e., animism). In response, biblical scholar William Robertson Smith offered a focus on religious practices that would not only influence James Frazer's pioneering work on magic, but also Durkheim's sociology of religion and Freud's analysis of totemism.[4] In approaching the "religions of the Semites," Robertson Smith starts with a remarkable reflexive move, a critique of the habits and practices of religion scholars that resonates powerfully with Asad's reading of Geertz.

> Our modern habit is to look at religion from the side of belief rather than that of practice; for, down to comparatively recent times, almost the only forms of religion seriously studied in Europe have been those of the various Christian Churches, and all parts of Christendom are agreed that ritual is important only in connection with its interpretation. Thus the study of religion has meant mainly the study of Christian beliefs, and instruction in religion has habitually begun with creed, religious duties being presented to the learner as flowing from the dogmatic truths he is taught to accept. (Robertson Smith 1973: 155)

Like Asad, Robertson Smith argues that this focus on beliefs and creed is counterproductive when studying "antique religions." For the latter "had for the most part no creed; they consisted entirely of institutions and practices." In contrast to our contemporary understanding of religion as a "matter of individual conviction and reasoned belief," the "ancients" saw religion as "part of the citizen's public life, reduced to fixed forms, which he was not bound to understand and was not at liberty to criticise or to neglect." Thus, "so long as the prescribed forms were duly observed, a man [*sic*][5] was recognised as truly pious, and no one asked how his religion was rooted in his heart or affected his reason. Like political duty, of which indeed it was part, religion was entirely comprehended in the observance of certain fixed rules of outward conduct" (Robertson Smith 1973: 156).

One may fault Robertson Smith for overstating the stability of practices, as they are shared with others in the same space and time or passed from generation to generation. In fact, the relative stability of habitual practices is one of the central tensions in praxis approaches, as we shall see later in relation to Bourdieu's work. Nevertheless, Robertson Smith makes an invaluable contribution when he breaks with modern prejudices about the nature of religion, prioritizing the study of situated practices, such as sacrifice, and institutions, including the priesthood, over myth, doctrine, and grand philosophical speculations about the nature of the gods. He was one of the first theorists of religion who challenged the Reformation's excarnation and disenchantment of reality, the hegemony of word over deed and text over ritual, which, as we saw in previous chapters, made its way into the early phenomenological and hermeneutical study of religion. Robertson Smith began to restore the efficacy and performative generativity of ritual.[6] "We shall find that the history of religious institutions is the history of ancient religion itself, as a practical force in the development of the human race, and that the articulate efforts of the antique intellect to comprehend the meaning of religion, the nature of the gods, and the principles on which they deal with men, take their point of departure from the unspoken ideas embodied in the traditional forms of ritual praxis" (Robertson Smith 1973: 159).

In other words, all the existential concerns that Geertz thinks are at the heart of religion are for Robertson Smith not foundational but the post facto intellectual justification and refinement of certain kinds of practices through which individuals relate to their material surroundings. We do not have to accept Robertson Smith's theory of the origin of religion to see the genius of his stress on practices. The issue is not whether ideas or practices gave rise to religion in the first place. Conceptualizing the issue in this way makes it either insoluble or leads to reductionism, whether of the idealist or materialist species. Rather, my aim here is to trace a genealogy of the praxis approach to religion, productive insights and dead ends included. Robertson Smith's notion that religion is closely connected to embodied habit and practice is picked up by Marcel Mauss, another important scholar, who, despite his seminal collaborative work with Durkheim, is not afforded sufficient recognition. In a landmark lecture he delivered at the Society of Psychology in 1934, Mauss stressed the centrality of the body in the creation and transmission of shared cultural and religious knowledge. Foreshadowing Foucault's and Bourdieu's work, Mauss proposed the concept of "techniques of the body" to characterize "the ways in which from society to society men know how to use their bodies" (1979: 97). He elaborates: "I call technique an action that is *effective* and *traditional* (And you will see that in this it is no different from a magical, religious, or symbolic action). It has to be *effective* and *traditional*. There is no technique and no transmission in the absence of tradition. This above all is what distinguishes man from animals: the transmission of his techniques and very probably their oral transmission" (Mauss 1979: 104). What makes culture possible, as a reservoir of knowledge shared across generations and within groups, is the transmission, not of disembodied ideas, symbols, texts, or even minimally counterintuitive concepts (as posited by many cognitive theorists). Instead, the glue that holds together societies is the "art of using the human body," that is, the ways in which tradition is inculcated in the bodies of individuals, who then produce and reproduce practices that are effective to the degree that they are in sync with that particular sociocultural and physical setting. "Body techniques can be classified according to their efficiency, i.e., according to the result of training," which is a certain dexterity, to enable "those people with a sense of the adaptation of well-co-ordinated movements to a goal, who are practiced, who 'who what they are up to'" (Mauss 1979: 108).

To characterize inculcated tradition and foreground cultural creativity and diversity, Mauss borrows from Aristotle and uses the term *habitus*, instead of habit or custom, both which suggest a fully unreflective, mechanical reproduction of certain types of activities. Mauss sees habitus as "acquired abilities" and "faculties" which "do not vary just with individuals and their imitations; they vary especially between societies, educations, properties and fashions, prestiges. In them we should see the techniques and work of collective and individual practical reason rather than, in the ordinary way, merely the soul and its repetitive faculties" (Mauss 1979: 101).

Mauss, in effect, renders Robertson Smith's understanding of habitual practice more flexible, more open to change and creativity. More importantly, he has rematerialized Durkheim, demonstrating that social cohesion goes beyond sharing vague collective representations or group sentiments, the most general and powerful of which are religious. Solidarity requires the imprinting of socially constructed skills, practical competences, and predispositions on the body through socialization and imitation.[7] In the process, Mauss contributed to an understanding of practice as the interplay among sociology, psychology, and biology. Indeed, he tells us that, in order to understand society, we need a "triple viewpoint, that of the 'total man,'" which focuses on "indissolubly mixed together" "physio-psycho-sociological assemblages of actions" (Mauss 1979: 120). Here, Mauss is articulating a non-reductive materialist position.

But how is this different from Geertz's idea of ethos and of culture as "control systems"? Perhaps Geertz's textualism is not radically different from Mauss's praxis approach after all? The key distinction is that, while Mauss and other practice theorists who follow are interested in the ethos (and the behavior it generates) as a multivocal and multiply determined reality, Geertz is primary interested in its representational and expressive aspects. Thus, for medieval Christian monks performing liturgical services,

[r]itual is . . . directed at the apt performance of what is prescribed, something that depends on intellectual and practical disciplines but does not itself require decoding. In other words, apt performance involves not symbols to be interpreted but abilities to be acquired according to rules that are sanctioned by those in authority: it presupposes no obscure meanings, but rather the formation of

physical and linguistic skills. Rites as apt performances presuppose codes—in the regulative sense as opposed to the semantic—and people who evaluate and teach them. (Asad 1993: 62)

If we accept, with Robertson Smith and Mauss, that practices and habitus are central to religion, then the metaphor of the text, with its concern only for meaning and communication, is much too limiting to explore their variegated operations. This is why Arnold Van Gennep, another important practice theorist, understands rituals not just as signifying events but as "magico-religious ceremonies." Religion in this synthesis designates the theories of reality—be they dynamism, the belief in a monistic impersonal principle or mana, or animism, a dualistic perspective that sees the world as infused with power personified in plants, animals, or human beings. Magic, on the other hand, has to do with the "techniques (ceremonies, rites, services)" involved. "Since the practice and the theory are inseparable—the theory without the practice becoming metaphysics, and the practice on the basis of a different theory becoming science—the term I will at all times use is the adjective magico-religious" (Van Gennep 1960: 13).

Van Gennep continues the materialization and historization of the Durkheimian legacy. He embeds religious ritual and culture in the natural world in ways that prefigure Mary Douglas and also brings process and change to the fore, greatly influencing Victor Turner, whom I will discuss shortly. Process, change, and embeddedness in nature are mutually implicative, since "man's life resembles nature, from which neither the individual nor the society stands independent. The universe itself is governed by a periodicity which has repercussions on human life, with stages and transitions, movements forward, and periods of relative inactivity" (Van Gennep 1960: 3). Thus, "for groups, as well as for individuals, life itself means to separate and to be reunited, to change form and condition, to die and to be reborn. It is to act and to cease, to wait and rest, and then to begin again, but in a different way. And there are always new thresholds to cross: the threshold of summer and winter, of a season or a year; of a month or a night; thresholds of birth, adolescence, maturity, and old age; the threshold of death and that of the afterlife—for those who believe in it" (Van Gennep 1960: 189–90).

The main problem with Van Gennep's approach is that he applies his preliminal-liminal-postliminal process not just to rites of passage but to all rituals, reducing the multiplicity of forms and contexts to a recurring pattern that is then applied top-down by subsequent scholars. As the pattern becomes universalized, it loses most of its analytical power. Durkheimian sociology has been traditionally beset by the twin threats of teleological evolutionism in the

movement from mechanical to organic solidarity and structural holism, positing homeostatic social holes in which conflict is pathology. By making change
part and parcel of social and religious life, Van Gennep goes a long way toward
addressing these dangers. However, because he is not interested in understanding particular rites, Van Gennep's historization of Durkheim remains
incomplete.

Victor Turner picks up where Van Gennep left off. He elaborates on the
dynamics of ritual practice by relating it to the movement between structures,
which goes through breakthrough periods of liminality and communitas,
where there is a momentary inversion or flattening of dominant hierarchical
relations. Because these periods of liminality and communitas are not norm-
governed, but spontaneous, undifferentiated, and raw in their energy, they are
dangerous and must be negotiated properly though elaborate ritual practices
(Turner 1969: 94–130). And, since Turner sees liminality and communitas as
crucial cultural mechanisms by which groups deal with internal group changes
(in response to shifting patterns of social relations) and the external environment, he, like other practice theorists, situates religion within a holistic context. Describing his fieldwork among the Ndembu people of Zambia, Turner
writes: "I could not analyze ritual symbols without studying them in a time
series in relation to other 'events,' for symbols are essentially involved in social
processes" (1968: 20). Notice here how Turner succeeds where Geertz ultimately fails. Turner sees symbols as inextricable ingredients of "events,"
unfolding practices, not simply as "products," codes or scripts. For Turner,
rituals are embedded in social dramas, "processual units" which, "unlike atemporal structures (including 'conceptual,' 'cognitive,' and 'syntactical' structures), [are] organized primarily through relations in time rather than in space,
though, of course cognitive schemes are themselves the result of a mental
process and have processual qualities" (Turner 1974: 35–36). By atemporal
structures, Turner means "models of what people 'believe they do, ought to do,
or would like to do,'" which seems to offer a veiled critique not only of structuralism but Geertz's more subject-centered approach.

Turner applies his praxis approach successfully to various religious phenomena including carnivals, pilgrimages, and millenarian movements. All
these phenomena involve movement or changes of status, "a breach of regular
norm-governed social relations" (Turner 1974: 38). Carnival, for example,
may mean the temporary inversion of class distinctions, with poor people
dressing and acting as kings and queens, or the loosening of moral restrictions,
allowing all the excesses of carnality—drinking, eating, nudity, and sexuality.
Pilgrimages, for their part, require the movement from profane to sacred
spaces and back. Millenarian movements, in turn, posit alternative and utopian

ways of being in the world in conflict with the larger society. Given the tensions involved, individuals and groups navigate these phenomena through the performance of a plethora of stabilizing yet contested ritual metaphors. These ritual metaphors are not sets of rules or prescribed texts that actors simply enact. They are, instead, intense embodied "rhythms" that make possible the safe passage across social and religious statuses or roles. Thus, the pilgrim, for instance, might carry a heavy stone on his/her back, or walk barefoot or on his/her knees for long distances, while praying, chanting, or fasting. And while the reasons for undertaking the pilgrimage and the actions during the journey may be deeply personal, they derive a great deal of their power from their social embeddedness, from the collective effervescence (communitas) of all pilgrims involved. Immersed in social dramas that engage the self in its fullness, pilgrims draw from age-old practices, improvising to be able to construct emotions and behaviors that respond to the particular relation they have with the objects and beings considered sacred, that is, whether the pilgrim is repaying a vow, seeking a blessing, or demonstrating total loyalty.[8]

As Turner moves from ethnography to performance, from ritual to theater, in his later works, he offers an even more radical critique of anthropological textualism. "If anthropologists are ever to take ethnodramatics seriously, our discipline will have to become something more than a cognitive game played in our heads and inscribed in—let's face it—somewhat tedious journals. We will have to become performers ourselves, and bring to human, existential fulfillment what have hitherto been only mentalistic protocols" (Turner 1982: 101). In conversation with historian and theorist of hermeneutics Wilhelm Dilthey, Turner understands the task of a transformed anthropology as the recovery of "structures of experience."

> Structures of experience, for Dilthey, are not the bloodless "cognitive structures," static and "synchronic," so beloved of the "thought-structuralists" who have dominated French anthropology for so long. Cognition is, of course, an important aspect, facet, or "dimension" of any structure of experience. Thought clarifies and generalizes lived experience, but experience is charged with emotion and volition, sources respectively of value-judgments and precepts. Behind Dilthey's world-picture is the basic fact of the total human being (Lawrence's "man alive") at grips with his environment, perceiving, thinking, desiring. As he says, "life embraces life." (Turner 1982: 13)[9]

Turner's vitalist-praxis perspective is meant as a critique of the Lévi-Straussian–Derridean textualism that I sketched above. However, the critique also applies to Geertz when he underplays dramas and emotions and stresses symbolic systems (with drama as a mere performance of a text that precedes and shapes practices) as the key interpretive tool. By appealing to the concept of experience, Turner recovers the embodied and practical dimensions of religion from the stifling textualism that emerged in the humanities and social sciences at the intersection of structuralism, hermeneutics, and deconstruction.

ENTER MARX AND HISTORICAL MATERIALISM

For all the strengths of his approach, Turner's view of the "total human being" tends to concentrate on the ludic dimensions of our structures of experience, avoiding sustained analysis the interplay between experience and power (in the form of domination and resistance).[10] This is not surprising, given than Turner was attempting to overcome Alfred Radcliffe-Brown's legacy of hard structural-functionalism in British social anthropology. This is where "middle" Marx offers an important corrective. At his best, Marx offers a nuanced picture of humans as *Homo faber*, as creative producers who, in the process of external-izing their capacities to generate social and cultural reality, transform themselves by internalizing (learning from and finding fulfillment in) the products of their own labor. In this dialectical process of externalization, objectivation, and internalization, we enter into unavoidable relations with fellow human beings, giving rise to an organized "mode of production." "This mode of production must not be considered simply as being the reproduction of the physical existence of the individuals. Rather it is a definite form of activity of these individuals, a definite form of expressing their life, a definite mode of life on their part. As individuals express their life, so they are" (1978c: 150).

By introducing the notion of practice, Marx is able to go beyond a crude materialism that sees individuals as simply reacting to the physical demands of survival. That is why in his rightly celebrated *Theses on Feuerbach*, he argues that "the chief defect of all hitherto existing materialism—that of Feuerbach included—is that the thing, reality, sensuousness, is conceived only in the form of the object or of *contemplation*, but not as *human sensuous activity*, *practice*, not subjectively" (Marx 1978e: 143). Humans are not just passive recipients of the blind force of nature. Rather, they encounter internal and external nature and relate to each other as embodied beings through their practices, through the creative use of their culture—their ideas, symbols, tools, inculcated skills, and dispositions. Thus, "the materialist doctrine that men are products of cir-cumstances and upbringing, and that therefore, changed men are products of other circumstances and changed upbringing, forgets it is men who change circumstances and that it is essential to educate the educator himself. The coincidence of the changing of circumstances and of human activity can be conceived and rationally understood only as revolutionising practice" (Marx 1978e: 144).

Marx here is laying the groundwork for a non-reductive materialism that focuses on the interplay between social structure and individual agency, tradition and change, ideas and matter, and culture and nature. This dialectical, open-ended praxis approach, however, is sadly lost in subsequent interpretations of Marx, particular of the Second International, as the political demands for a shorthand revolutionary formula and the drive to build a scientific Marxism modeled along the natural sciences (through a crude and teleological evolutionary paradigm) forces simplification. Instead of thinking of the mode of production as a holistic, multifaceted mode of life, dialectically relating structure and agency, and ideas and material reality, later Marxisms increasingly fall into the reductive dichotomy of "a determining base and a determined superstructure" (Williams 1981: 31). Cultural production then becomes merely epiphenomenal, the phantom and inverted reflection of economic production, which determines all human expressions with an iron grip. This view is prefigured even in the early Marx's work, in the famous affirmation in *A Contribution to the Critique of Hegel's Philosophy of Right* that "religion is the opium of the masses." And this is the view that scholars of religion have traditionally and unproductively set against the idealism of Weber's *The Protestant Ethic and Spirit of Capitalism*.

The point is not to deny the presence of a problematic reductive materialism throughout Marx's work. Rather, I am interested in highlighting those elements in Marx's thinking that have contributed to the emergence of a promising praxis approach. Marx's attempts to offer a holistic anthropology reconciling the historical dynamism of the Hegelian *Geist* with the Feuerbachian stress on embodiment and material reality influenced not only the work of a countercurrent of "warm Marxism" of Antonio Gramsci, the Frankfurt School, Raymond Williams, E. P. Thompson, and Stuart Hall, but also Pierre Bourdieu's theory of practice.[11]

BOURDIEU'S THEORY OF PRACTICE: ANALYZING REPRODUCTION AND DOMINATION

Seeking to bridge the gap between an objectivism that posits self-standing social structures that reproduce themselves through the activities of individuals and a subjectivism that construes action as issuing from sovereign agents entering into haphazard interactions with each other, Bourdieu constructs one of the most sophisticated theories "of the mode of generation of practices, which is the precondition for establishing an experimental science of *the dialectic of internalization of externality and the externalization of internality*, or more, simply, of incorporation and objectivation" (Bourdieu 1977: 72). The echoes of Marx's praxis approach are unmistakable. To construct his theory, Bourdieu adds specificity to Mauss's notion of habitus, which acts as a hinge in the dialectic between incorporation and objectivation. Bourdieu defines habitus as "systems of durable, transposable dispositions, structured structures predisposed to function as structuring structures, that is, as principles which generate and organize practices and representations that can be objectively adapted to their outcomes without presupposing a conscious aiming at ends or an express mastery of the operations necessary in order to attain them" (1990: 53). As embodied and historical agents, individuals act always embedded in socially structured situations, amid already-established power relations, which condition their needs and interests, provide them with specific resources, skills, and propensities, open and/or close possible courses of action, and delimit the horizons of the possible and impossible.

Socially structured situations do not impose themselves mechanically on individual agents—this would be simply reinstating social ontology of objectivism. Rather, the position of an individual vis-à-vis others in the same social space enables "generative principles of regulated improvisations," whereby social agents can craft their own personal style, while producing behaviors that are appropriate to the situation (Bourdieu 1977: 78). The socially structured context inculcates in the individual not particular behaviors that s/he must reenact endlessly, as Robertson Smith and Mauss implied in their definition of ritual and habitus, but an embodied "sense of place," "a feel for the game," a "practical reason" that is not just cognitively expressed—knowing the rules, risks, and goals of the game—but manifested in gestures, manners, tastes, and dexterities that allow effortless "invention within limits" (Bourdieu 1977: 96).[12] In producing through habitus behaviors in sync with structures they find, individuals sustain and transform those structures, which then become the basis for new praxis.

Bourdieu's understanding of practice through the prisms of the habitus connects nicely with my previous discussions of the body, for, unless education is institutionalized through the production of an orthodox canon, knowledge is "transmitted in practice, its practical state, without attaining the level of discourse." This is the reason why in the learning process

> the child imitates not "models" but other people's actions. Body hexis [the body's disposition in space] speaks directly to the motor function, in the form of a pattern of postures that is both individual and systematic, because linked to a whole

system of techniques involving the body and tools, and charged with a host of social meanings and values: in all societies, children are particularly attentive to the gestures and postures which, in their eyes, express everything that goes to make an accomplished adult—a way of walking, a tilt of the head, facial expressions, ways of sitting and of using implements, always associated with a tone of voice, a style of speech, and . . . a certain subjective experience. (Bourdieu 1977: 87)

The in-corporation of the habitus is not merely superficial, a thin veneer of culture added onto biology. The habitus is an "incorporated principle of classification which governs all forms of incorporation, choosing and modifying everything that the body ingests and digests and assimilates, physiologically and psychologically" (Bourdieu 1984: 190). Habitus is what makes taste possible, since it shapes the individual's relation to his/her body, "a way of treating it, caring for it, feeding it, maintaining it" (190).

The notion of habitus, thus, can be very useful to study embodied religious practices. For instance, constructing Hindu identity in diaspora is not simply or, even primarily, about demonstrating intellectual mastery of the complex metaphysics of the great sacred texts, the Vedas or the Upanishads. Rather, it is all about *rasa*, a particular way of carrying oneself, an embodied aesthetic or poetics of life, a kind of naturalized joie de vivre, a proper sensitivity and disposition to taste reality in its gustatory, visual, olfactory, tactile, and kinetic intensities (Ram 2000). In diaspora, *rasa* maybe inculcated through what Narayanan (2003) calls "embodied cosmologies," the performance of shared narratives connected with ethnic or national identities through dance and theater. In the staging of the *Ramayana* or the *Mahabharata*, for example, the movements of the actors are as important as the lines they utter. Or rather, there is no dichotomy between form and content, for the content is lived through the enactment.

Rasa in diaspora is but a recent expression of age-old practices of knowledge transmission beyond those of the literate Brahmin elites. According to religion scholar Susan Schwartz (2004: 4), for the vast majority of people in India, "the study of texts was not the main component of transmission. To this day, oral tradition remains the primary mode of teaching in the arts of India, as it is in so many other areas of the culture." Schwartz points to ancient writings, such as the *Natyashastra*, a seminal treatise on dance, drama, and aesthetics, that describes how gurus taught their disciples. "Sources often maintain that very little talking was done. Rather the guru would provide, in measured doses, lessons by example, which the student would absorb, copy, and rehearse until the teacher was satisfied. The atmosphere in which teaching and learning took place was oral/aural/kinesthetic" (Schwartz 2004: 5). The result was a different kind of pedagogy. Knowledge is literally "ingested," it "becomes, like food, part of one's cell structure." It is precisely this strongly embodied, material dimension of *rasa* that makes the term applicable not only to a dance performance but to the flavor of a tasty stew or a juicy fruit. "Where taste, sound, image, movement, rhythm, and transformation meet, therefore, the experience of *rasa* is possible" (Schwartz 2004: 5–6). The experience of *rasa* is doubly non-dualistic, for it not only involves the performance through a multisensory habitus by the dancer, but it requires that the spectator too savor the mood, the full emotional charge of the drama through his/her own bodily dispositions and incarnate memories. "The aesthetic breakthrough of *rasa* . . . depends on the moral cultivation of the spectator as well as on features of the aesthetic object" (Higgins 2007: 45).

Clearly, Bourdieu's notion of habitus-mediated practice is helpful to capture the complexity of *rasa*, as it is to understand the embodied "dancing wisdom" of African-based religions such as Haitian Vodou and Brazilian Candomblé, which, as we saw in chapter 3, is built on the exposure to and performance of repetitive ritual sequences (Daniel 2005: 265–66). Bourdieu enriches the notion of habitus with that of social field. One's embodied competences, dispositions, and aspirations are determined by one's shifting positions in various intersecting fields of power. In particular, one's class—one's access to economic resources—conditions one's social capital (the quantity and quality of contacts that can be mobilized at a particular moment), cultural capital (the educational opportunities and access to legitimate knowledge), and symbolic capital (the capacity impose one's view authoritatively as a group's taken-for-granted worldview). Nevertheless, Bourdieu breaks with Marxist economism in two ways. First, he does not understand class as a fixed, brute structural condition given by one's objective relation to the means of production. Bourdieu adopts a more Weberian theory of class, as a relatively fluid, negotiated position in the field of sociocultural production. Thus, class positions are always constructed through symbolic processes that lead individuals in the same social space to (mis)recognize through cultural markers some groups as "naturally" dominant and others as necessarily subaltern. Second, Bourdieu argues that the logic of the game allows the players to exchange and convert the various forms of capital to enhance strategically their relative position at a given juncture. Thus, no single form of capital takes precedence at all times.

The notion of symbolic power has especial relevance in the study of religious practices, since it is the power "to impose the principles of the construction of reality—in particular, social reality" as doxa, that is, as received opinion, a common sense that "goes without saying because it comes without saying" (Bourdieu 1977: 165, 167). Symbolic power and doxa are central to the effectiveness and legitimacy of religion since they help to create the "illusion of absolute autonomy, which tends to have us conceive the religious message as a spontaneously generated product of inspiration" (Bourdieu 1987: 125), an unconditioned expression of the deepest beliefs, thoughts, and feelings of the religious actor. Thus, the charisma of a religious specialist, to use Weberian language, resides in his/her ability to hide the contextual conditions that have given him/her the competence and right to speak with authority and to present this charisma (against that of competitors) as grounded extra-historically, standing above the profane practices of everyday life and thus not subject to dispute. This doxic misrecognition of the religious specialist's situated subjectivity is what allows him/her to present what is a positioned perspective as a universal and binding message. Therefore, religious production often involves the "principle of *ideological alchemy* by which the transfiguration of social relations into supernatural relations operates and is therefore inscribed in the nature of things and thereby justified" (Bourdieu 1991: 5, italics in the original).

For Bourdieu, (mis)recognition of legitimate religious power is not one-directional, exerted from the top by the religious expert. Instead, the prophet(ess) or priest(ess) draws from his/her habitus to generate practices that respond to the needs, competences, and aspirations of his constituency. The effectiveness of a religious product issues from the alignment of habituses and from the resonance these habituses have with the socially constructed structures in which they are embedded. On the basis of this alignment and resonance, the constituency then recognizes of the legitimate power of the prophet(ess) or priest(ess), charging him/her with charisma.[13]

From Bourdieu's perspective, Asad's critique of Geertz aims at demonstrating how, in presenting religion as a transhistorical, autonomous, and textualized expression of the existential self, the latter fails to take into account the situated practices that make possible religion's obliteration of its context of production, circulation, and consumption. Rather than studying religion critically, Geertz naïvely perpetuates the doxa that he insists must be decoded before it can be related to structural conditions. Geertz ignores how habitus, in both the religious specialist and his/her followers, generates the religious goods (rituals, texts, material culture, etc.) which are considered legitimate. Furthermore, he ignores his own anthropological habitus, which predisposes him to seek what is authentic in the native's experience.

It is important to note that religious habitus is not simply the product of a given position in the economic field. Marx's affirmation that the "ideas of the ruling class are in every epoch the ruling ideas: i.e., the class which is the ruling material force of society, is at the same time its ruling intellectual force" (1978c: 172), is too crude to make sense of the genesis of religious doxa. This is because the religious field has its own dynamics, its own regimes of production, institutions, training sites, specialists, audiences, sanctioned commodities, vectors of dissemination, and hierarchies and interests attached to various groups in these power differentials. The key is not to reduce religion to economic and political power, but to elucidate in a given situation the ways in which the dynamics of the religious field reinforce or stand in tension with the logics of other fields of social action. Here, Bourdieu stands with the non-reductionist materialism of Weber: we must grasp religious symbolic systems "simultaneously in their function, structure, and genesis." After all, Bourdieu (1998: 57) writes: "Weber reminds us that, to understand religion, it does not suffice to study symbolic forms of the religious types, as Cassirer or Durkheim did, or even the immanent structure of the religious message or of the mythological corpus, as with the structuralists. Weber focuses specifically on the producers of religious messages, on the specific interests that move them and on the strategies they use in their struggle (for example, excommunication)" Moreover, going beyond Marx's economism (which equates labor with manual or industrial transformation of raw materials) but preserving a materialist lens, Bourdieu calls for the study of *"religious labor* carried out by specialized producers and spokespeople invested with power, institutional or not, to respond to a particular category of needs belonging to certain social groups with a definite type of practice or discourse" (1991: 5, italics in the original).

Overall, Bourdieu offers one of the most sophisticated theories of practice available today. Nevertheless, this theory shows significant weaknesses. Although Bourdieu highlights the role of the body in practice, he tends, like many of the social constructionists we encountered in chapter 5, to view the body as a kind of blank slate that is marked and molded by history and culture. Against Bourdieu, Foucault, and Douglas, anthropologist Jean Comaroff (1985: 5–9) argues that the body is active, with its physiological realities, such as birth, death, and sickness, not only establishing the limits of the possible but also providing metaphors to frame cultural production. Edward Slingerland goes even further. He faults Bourdieu for leaving "unanswered the much more basic and important questions of *how habitus* is formed, *how* fields are perceived and interacted with by agents, or what constraints there might be on *habitus* and field formation" (Slingerland 2008a: 95, italics in the original). According to Slingerland, by focusing on the trajectory of individuals in the social field, Bourdieu only sees the "tip of the cognitive iceberg." He does not go *"far enough back* in his conception of history. The deposited layers of history that form our schemas of perception and motivation . . . go back into *evolutionary* time, into the history of interactions between creatures more and more like us trying to make their way through a complex world" (Slingerland 2008a: 95, italics in the original).

As I wrote in chapter 7, I disagree with Slingerland's prescriptive view of evolution. Borrowing from the enactive approach to cognition, I presented an alternative proscriptive version of evolution that moves away from teleological, unidirectional determinism, seeing evolution rather as a broad drift that allows for diversity, creativity, and complex emergence within relative stability. Nevertheless, Slingerland is correct in criticizing Bourdieu for not adopting a more robust view of embodiment, one that seeks to explore the relations of reciprocal determination among structured social contexts, the flexible architecture of the human brain, and the sensorimotor apparatus. The notion of habitus has to be brought into conversation with cultural neurophenomenology, particularly around the notion of enaction, which offers a holistic view of practice as a dynamic interplay of neurophysiological, cultural-historical, and ecological networks. This conversation is just beginning to happen around ongoing work on neuroplasticity, the capacity of the neural networks to establish new connections and thus alter the architecture of the brain in response to experience. This research shows, for instance, that "the brain of an expert, such as a chess player, a taxi driver, or a musician, is functionally and structurally different from that of a non-expert. London taxi cab drivers have larger hippocampi than matched controls, and the amount of time the individual has worked as a cab driver predicted the size of the posterior hippocampus" (Lutz, Dunne, and Davidson 2007: 522). Similar relations of reciprocal determination among structured environments (created by practices), embodied skills and propensities, and neurophysiology might be at work among those engaged in disciplined Buddhist meditation. In a recent study, "cortical brain regions associated with attention, interoceptive, and sensory processing were found to be thicker for a group of mid-range [meditation] practitioners than for matched controls" (Lutz, Dunne, and Davidson 2007: 523).

But it is not just the brain that is involved. Performance theorist Richard Schechner has shown that "rasaesthetics" involves the stimulation of the "brain in the belly," the enteric nervous system. *Rasa*, like "Asian medicine, meditation, and martial arts," engages "the region in the gut between the navel and the pubic bone [that] is the center/source of readiness, balance, and reception" (Schechner 2003: 349). In all these performances, as in African-based or shamanic dances and trances, "the actor is engaged in his total being in a psychophysical process where his internal energy, aroused in his vital center below the navel, then directed into and through the embodied forms of external gesture" (Zarrilli 1990: 143). This projected energy is what enables *rasa*'s co-participatory embodied enjoyment by actor and audience.

All these examples, then, show that Bourdieu's notion of embodied habitus needs to be supplemented by and critiqued through a richer understanding of the body's physicality. From the constructionist side, Bourdieu's theory of practice also shows some limitations. Despite his critique of objectivism, he understands the logic of practices a bit too statically. Like Foucault, he tends to stress reproduction and domination over production and resistance. According to Sherry Ortner, an advocate of practice theory in anthropology, in sharing Lévi-Strauss's effort to uncover the "underlying illusions of liberty" behind social action, Bourdieu subscribes to a post-structuralist "anti-humanism [that] poses real problems for an anthropology that wishes to understand not just the workings of power, but the attempts of subalterns (in the Gramscian sense) to attain the privilege of becoming subjects in the first place" (Ortner 2005: 33).[14] Doxa, for example, can only be challenged at moments of crisis when objective conditions change abruptly and mental schemas lag behind, no longer mapping onto them. Then taken-for-granted opinion breaks into orthodoxa, which must affirm its authority consciously and vigorously, without ever succeeding in "restoring the primal state of innocence of doxa," and heterodoxa, which openly disputes the validity of received tradition.[15] The result of this break is the simultaneous hardening of clerical power and acceleration in the production of written canons as well as the emergence of (oral) heresies and prophetic or millenarian movements among the laity.[16] In contemporary societies, the tension among doxa, orthodoxy, and heterodoxa intersects closely with class struggles. "The dominated classes have an interest in pushing back the limits of *doxa* and exposing the arbitrariness of the taken for granted; the dominant classes have an interest in defending the integrity of doxa or, short of this, of establishing in its place the necessarily imperfect substitute, *orthodoxy*" (Bourdieu 1977: 169, italics in the original).

While this is a useful synthesis of Weber's notion of breakthroughs (periods of great upheaval when the priestly office is challenged by prophetic authority)[17] and the Marxist notion of ideology, it is ultimately an impoverished theory of religious change. It fails to capture what Robert Orsi (1997: 8) calls the "everyday miracles": how "religious ideas and impulses are of the moment, invented, taken, borrowed, and improvised at the intersections of life." To formulate a theory of practice that has a well-developed analytics of domination but incorporates the creative dynamism of Dilthey's *Erlebnis* and Turner's ethnodramatics and recognizes the subtle of ways in which religion is produced, negotiated, and contested in everyday life, we need to enhance Bourdieu's "constructivist structuralism" or "structuralist constructivism" (1990: 123).

PRACTICE AND RESISTANCE

Michel de Certeau's exploration of the practices of everyday life offers one way out of the one-sided emphasis on domination and the implication that religious innovation takes place primarily in periods of dramatic change. Rather than focusing on the "strategies," whereby the powerful "capitalize acquired advantages" to place the dominated in "readable spaces" in which the latter can be classified and disciplined, de Certeau concentrates on the "multitude of 'tactics' articulated in the details of everyday life." His goal "is not to make clearer how the violence of order is transmuted into a disciplinary technology, but rather to bring to light the clandestine forms taken by the dispersed, tactical, and makeshift creativity of groups or individuals already caught in the nets of 'discipline'" (de Certeau 1984: xiv–xv). An excellent example of what de Certeau means by tactics is what the French call "*la perruque*" (literally "the wig"), through which a worker takes advantage of company time and resources to do his/her own activities. *La perruque* functions as a diversionary tactic because it diverts time "from the factory for work that is free, creative, and precisely not directed toward profit. In the very place where the machine he must serve reigns supreme, [the worker] cunningly takes pleasure in finding a way to create gratuitous products whose sole purpose is to signify his own capabilities through his *work* and to confirm his solidarity with other workers . . ." (de Certeau 1984: 25).

Tactics are, therefore, the "art of the weak," calculated actions that while operating in the space of the dominant other, creatively subvert or trick the system (de Certeau 1984: 37). Because tactics operate in the crevices left by disciplinary practices, they are unlikely to overturn the status quo wholesale. However, their flexibility, mobility, and ingenuity make possible localized resistances that may be articulated at some point into a transformative movement.[18]

Bringing the discussion back to religion: doxa is never fully established, as Bourdieu seems to imply, because the religious goods generated by experts through their structured and structuring habitus are not consumed blindly by their followers. Rather, in the exercise of consumption, the followers stamp religious goods with their own idiosyncrasies and introduce potentially heretical uses, implicitly challenging the specialists' claim to a monopoly over the production of sanctioned symbolic goods. In today's pluralist religious fields, consumers may even mix and match religious goods from diverse sources of legitimation, which circulate in global circuits, to produce their own artifacts in response to their personal and local needs. Therefore, there does not need to be a major socioeconomic or ecological crisis for religious change to take place. Innovation, contestation, and hybridization are as much part and parcel of practices of everyday religious life as are domination and reproduction. This is why de Certeau argues that we need to engage in a "polemological analysis" of religion (1984: xvii), an analysis of how religious symbols, myths, texts, rituals, institutions, and spaces are deployed and actively negotiated by multiple actors embedded in shifting but always asymmetrical fields of force.

For de Certeau, consumption is not passive. It always entails a complex cluster of situated maneuvers and ruses where consumers use their practical wisdom to "compose the network of an antidiscipline" (1984: xv). I will explore the embedding of resistance in social networks and fields more fully in chapter 11. Notice how de Certeau's resistances are not those of an unconditioned Sartrean subject "condemned to be free." De Certeau preserves a keen awareness of the power regime in which practices occur, while allowing them a wider range of creativity and innovation than Bourdieu's constructivist structuralism does.

This brings us to the second tactic to revise Bourdieu's theory of practice. Echoing de Certeau's emphasis on conditioned resistance, historicist Marxists, influenced by Gramsci's notions of hegemony and the organic intellectual, have built on Marx's concept of praxis. Gramsci's problem was to explain why capitalism had not collapsed when objective economic contradictions in the 1920s seemed, as Marx and Engels had written in *The Communist Manifesto*, to spell its inevitable end. Instead of the automatic rise of communism, a powerful fascist movement emerged and led the working classes in advanced European economies like Germany to sacrifice their lives in World War II. Gramsci attributed this anomaly to the ability of official intellectuals in the Nazi state apparatus to mobilize the means of mass communication to articulate an "ideology," understood not in the pejorative sense of pure false consciousness but as a coherent "conception of the world," a "philosophy of life" that resonated with the culture and interests of the subaltern classes and "cements" them into a collective historic subject. When this ideology becomes common sense, it constitutes hegemony, a power relation in which the subaltern classes voluntarily consent to their subordinate role in society. Fascist intellectuals had succeeded in using socioeconomic upheavals in Europe to appeal to the nationalistic and belligerent sentiments of the working class, while communists waited for capitalism to collapse on its own. However, since "all men are philosophers," building conceptions of the world out of their own language, common sense, popular religiosity, and "folklore," it is possible for intellectuals to emerge "organically" from the subaltern class to articulate a counterhegemony, a critical perspective of the world that can be counterposed to dominant ideology. Gramsci was particularly impressed with the power of the Catholic Church to serve as the lingua franca for all Italians on the basis of symbols, traditions, and rituals that offer a universal message of salvation. The task for the "philosophy of praxis"—the code term that Gramsci used to refer to Marxism from his prison cell—was to turn this lived religious cosmology into a critical point of view capable of grasping the totality of power relations, beyond the sectoral perspective offered by the dominant classes as the way things are. As Gramsci (1971: 331) writes:

> A philosophy of praxis cannot but present itself at the outset in a polemical and critical guise, as superseding the existing mode of thinking and existing concrete thought (the existing cultural world). First of all, therefore, it must be a criticism of "common sense," basing itself initially, however, on common sense in order to demonstrate that "everyone" is a philosopher and that it is not a question of introducing from scratch a scientific form of thought into everyone's individual life, but of renovating and making "critical" an already existing activity.

Like Bourdieu, Gramsci recognizes how economic exploitation and political subjugation require the imposition of a doxa. However, like de Certeau, Gramsci chooses to stress the creative consciousness and effectiveness of the praxis of the subordinate classes, demonstrating how work on resources for their day-to-day life can be the basis for social change at various scales. Marxist cultural theorist Raymond Williams elaborates on Gramsci's focus on the transformative power of everyday life, while de-emphasizing the problematic notion of the organic intellectual, which arguably laid the groundwork for the dominance of a centralizing Communist Party in many socialist societies. For Williams, what is at stake in the struggle between hegemony and counter-hegemony is not a phantom ideology that hangs like an obfuscating fog above the hard realities of economic exploitation. Rather, the struggle takes place in the "structures of feelings" of society. Structures of feeling refer to a practical consciousness that is "almost always different from official consciousness, and this is not only a matter of relative freedom or control. For practical conscious-ness is what is actually being lived, and not only what it is thought is being lived. Yet the actual alternative to the received and produced fixed forms is not silence: not the absence, the unconscious, which bourgeois culture has mythi-cized. It is a kind of feeling and thinking which is indeed social and material, but each in an embryonic phase before it can become fully articulate and defined exchange" (Williams 1977: 130–31). More concretely, a structure of feeling is "concerned with meanings and values as they are actively lived and felt, and the relations between these and formal or systematic beliefs are in practice variable.. . . We are talking here [not of] feeling against thought, but thought as felt and feeling as thought: practical consciousness of a present kind, in a living and interrelating continuity. We are then defining these elements as a 'structure': as a set, with specific internal relations, at once interlocking and in tension. Yet we are also defining a social experience which is still in *process . . ."* (Williams 1977: 132).

Williams offers a theory of practice that combines Dilthey's historical phenomenology with Marx's concept of material praxis and Gramsci's concern for the creative power of popular culture. Cross-fertilized with the post-structuralist analytics of reproduction, Williams' synthesis provides a promising approach to practice. It can reveal domination down to its most surreptitious mechanisms and, simultaneously, recognize the ways in which subjects not only resist but creatively use the determining power of their cultural and religious artifacts, including symbols, values, emotions, texts, and beliefs, to change their conditions of existence.

STUDYING RELIGION THROUGH PRACTICE

The cross-fertilization of Marx's, Bourdieu's, and Foucault's analytics of power with cultural studies approaches that focus on everyday life and resistance has, in fact, proven critical to the best works on the interaction between religion and society. For example, political scientist James Scott shows how Muslim peasants in Malaysia publicly express compliance but behind the scenes subvert power relations, pilfering resources, foot dragging, gossiping, mocking or feigning exaggerated deference toward authority figures, and generally deploying the "weapons of the weak."[19] More specifically, poor villagers strategically appeal to a shared "moral economy," using *zakat* (charity)—one of Islam's five pillars—together with the threat of shame and misfortune, to "encourage" the rich to distribute some of their wealth. Anthropologist Jean Comaroff demonstrates how Zion churches in South Africa simultaneously facilitate the proletarianization of the Tshidi, contributing to individualism and the breakdown of traditional kinship arrangements, and serve as the source for a discourse of protest against the excesses of commodification of the life world.[20] Historian E. P. Thompson points to the ways in which Methodism provided the discipline necessary to harness the productive power of the nascent working classes in England, while, at the same time, offering millenarian and utopian ideals that rejected the sins of capitalism and ills of industrialization.[21] Another historian, Reynaldo Ileto (1979) explores how *cofradías* (Catholic brotherhoods) in the Philippines drew "idioms of protest" from narratives and ritual re-enactments of Jesus Christ's passion that Spanish missionaries had brought with colonization. These idioms cosmicized the suffering and struggles of the rural poor, contributing to the formation of collective consciousness and mobilization. Because many brotherhood leaders read human and divine history as intertwined, as traditional popular Catholicism taught them, they rose as prophets and messiahs against the Spanish colonial rule.

In religious studies, the concern for the practices of everyday life has been picked up by at least two important lines of inquiry: the emerging studies on the relation between religion and the visual and performing arts, including drama, dance, and music, and the so-called lived religion school. A good example of the former is Vasudha Narayanan's work on the "embodied cosmologies." Studying how Hinduism is transmitted under diasporic conditions, she shows how narratives that are considered central to the articulation of Hindu identities and sacred localities are materialized and reinscribed through practices, by sculpting these narratives in temples and stupas, performing them in dance, staging them in films, soap operas, and the Internet, mapping them onto home altars, and circulating them through icons that immigrants carry as they engage in transnational social fields. The performed narratives often are not the great Brahmanical sacred texts such as the Vedas or the Upanishads, which Max Müller considered the core of Hinduism as a religion. Instead, it is the vernacular *bhakti* poetry that is consider crucial in constituting Hindu habituses, in inculcating embodied *rasa*, that is, ways of being Hindu, of dressing, eating, experiencing pain and pleasure, and relating to the deities. These narratives are not mere scripts that are reenacted and displayed à la Geertz, but religion-in-the-making, transformed by the contested ways in which they are embodied and emplaced. Thus, in order to capture the multiplicity of ways of living and transmitting "Hinduism," Narayanan suggests that we decolonize our methodologies, no longer "privileging . . . the written text and beliefs by the dominant, hegemonic cultures [that] lead to the marginalization of other ways of knowing, other sources of knowledge. The lived experience, the experiences of space and time—through performing arts, art, and architecture—and food are all significant and not just topics for the department of anthropology or the school of fine arts. I am arguing for valorizing what we call interdisciplinary and multidisciplinary methods and to look beyond traditional Eurocentric constructions of fields and disciplines" (Narayanan 2003: 516).

The lived religion school, which has emerged as a more-or-less cohesive praxis-oriented countercurrent within American religious history, shares many of Narayanan's concerns. It marks a shift

> away from the denominational focus that has so preoccupied scholars of American religions, toward a study of how particular people, in particular places and

times, live in, with, through, and against the religious idioms available to them in culture—all idioms, including (often enough) those not explicitly their "own." The shared methodology [in this approach] is radically or phenomenologically empiricist, concerned with what people do with religious practice, what they make with it of themselves and their worlds. It is further assumed . . . that religious practice is polysemous and that it is constituted—assembled—by cultural bricolage. (Orsi 1997: 7)

As I have argued elsewhere, the lived religion approach has been particularly helpful in understanding how increasing numbers of immigrants from Africa, Asia, and Latin America are transforming the religious field in the United States post-1965.[22] These immigrants are bringing with them new artifacts, rituals, beliefs, and (transnational) forms of organization, dwelling, and belonging that challenge "Protestant" understandings of religion— religion as text-centered, heavily doctrinal, and cognitive—and call for a more contextualized, materialized, and dynamic theory of religion. Nevertheless, because of its "empiricism," the lived religion approach leans too heavily toward the phenomenological dimensions of practice, being more concerned with how believers materialize intimacy with the sacred in everyday life and how religion scholars experience the practices and structures of feeling of religious people. Orsi, for instance, has been concerned with demonstrating "the realness of sacred presence in the imaginations and experiences of religious practitioners and its fate in the modern world" (2005: 10). Thus, he explores how immigrant adults "worked fervently to render the interiority of Catholic faith visible and materially substantive for children— and for themselves" (2005: 109).[23] The effort to understand how religion provides "existential vocabularies" to experience, transform, and endure "the necessary material realities of existence—pain, death, hunger, and sexuality," all part of our common humanity, lead Orsi to call scholars of religion to question their habitus, which distances them from their "subjects." We need "to include the voices of our sources more clearly—and disruptively—in our texts, inviting them to challenge and question our interpretations of them, to propose their own alternative narratives, to question our idioms from the perspective of their own, and, in general to break into the authority of our understandings and interpretations and to reveal their tentative character" (Orsi 2005: 175). This is because "lived religion refers not only to religion as lived by others but also to life as lived by those who approach others' everyday experience to learn about culture and history; it refers, in other words, to the conjuncture of two lived worlds in the study of religion" (Orsi 1997: 18).

In this sense, the lived religion approach shares Geertz's quest to produce vivid and thick descriptions of the native's life-world. As a result, we find in lived religion approaches some of the same weaknesses that afflicted interpretive anthropology.[24] More specifically, because Orsi holds (2005: 167) that "religious cultures are local and [that] to study religion is to study local worlds," the lived religion perspective places a heavy emphasis on micro-descriptions and self-reflections, running the danger of failing to connect localized practices to the larger context in which they are embedded, which includes national, transnational, and global economic, political, cultural, and environmental processes.

To be sure, power figures more prominently in lived religion approaches than in the work of Geertz or even Turner. As Orsi writes: "scholars who work on lived religion in the United States have become . . . theorists of relative cultural freedom" (1997: 13). He observes that since "lived religion appears as a space of resistance par excellence in the United States since the colonial period," a new understanding of American religion necessarily "emphasizes dissent, subversion, and resistance, rather than harmony, consensus, and social legitimation" (Orsi 1997: 15). However, he cautions us not to "overlook religion's complicity in sustaining structures and patterns of alienation and domination" (15). Schmidt puts it well when he states that the "notion of lived religion is itself intended to break down further the already crumbling oppositions between popular and elite, high and low, official and vernacular, the social and the religious, while preserving space for critical analysis of the issues of power, domination, and hierarchy . . ." (Schmidt 1997: 73).

All of this resonates with the practice approach I have developed, except that domination and resistance tend to be analyzed locally, within the native's horizon of experience, without the benefit of an "ascending analysis" that places the religious practices of concrete individuals in larger sociocultural fields that include the modern nation-state, global capitalism, and (post)colonialism.[25] In other words, the power analytics that Asad, Foucault, Bourdieu, Gramsci, Williams, and globalization theorists offer have not been yet fully incorporated into the lived religion framework.

In this regard, lived religion approaches in the United States can learn a great deal from the best works on religion and society in Latin America. Responding to the towering presence of Gramsci in Latin America, these studies show how popular religiosity, from "folk" Catholicism and liberation theology to Pentecostalism and African-based religions like Candomblé and Santería, is both powerfully lived at the personal and local levels and embedded in structural and systemic power arrangements reproduced and contested through class-, race-, and gender-based struggles. Amid these struggles, lived religion serves both to impose hegemony and animate resistance, sometimes simultaneously.[26]

CONCLUSION

The different emphases in the United States and Latin America indicate that the practice-centered approach is a big and diverse tent. My account here is thus not meant to be canonical. Still, my incomplete genealogy shows some general trends. Taking a practice-centered approach does not mean that texts, in their various forms, are not important, nor that we must abandon rigorous textual analysis. Although scholars of religion can use archeology, geography, and material culture to study civilizational forms no longer present to us in the same way as, for example, the practices of the twentieth-century Hindu diaspora or of pre-Conciliar Catholics, texts of various kinds are often key components of these cultures and religions. Moreover, as Narayanan argues, contemporary cultures also appropriate age-old texts and produce new ones, both of which are central to their lived religion in the form of embodied and emplaced cosmologies. It would, then, be a folly to surrender the valuable exegetical tools that we have developed over the years.

What a practice-centered approach demands, rather, is that we always place texts in their contexts of production, circulation, and consumption. Referring to the "social life" of commodities, Appadurai (2006: 15) writes: "all things are congealed moments in a longer social trajectory. All things are brief deposits of this or that property, photographs that conceal the reality of the motion from which their objecthood is a momentary respite." In the same way, he claims "all art is a momentary assemblage of mobile persons and things and . . . art objects, assemblages, events, and performances vary only in the intensity of their interest in denying or celebrating the social trajectory to which all things are subject" (Appadurai 2006: 16). A similar volatility and "illusion of permanence" and autonomy apply to texts.

As we saw in the previous chapter, Ricoeur has argued that texts, whether they be manuscripts, oral testimonies, inscriptions in *stupa*s, tattoos, or web pages, are material realities in their "being-thereness." While this is a useful insight, the fact that texts are objectified activity should not lead us to forget their processual character. And while it is legitimate and fruitful to explore how texts "say something about something," we should be careful not to reduce their materiality to signification. Texts are always the result of (and we always meet them through) practices of production and consumption. These practices point to: (1) the habituses of their authors and competing audiences; (2) the selection of materials (e.g., the types of parchment, binding, and ink used); (3) manipulation (miscopying them, generating apologias or polemics around them, and bowdlerizing or even banning them); and (4) appropriation (since texts are not just interpreted but also memorized, chanted, decorated, paraded down the streets, and even worn, as in the case of *tefillin* in Judaism). Texts, thus, should not be opposed to or even separated from religious practices or artifacts. Instead, texts are the relatively stable albeit open-ended products of practices of "religious mattering," text-making and text-consuming practices, including those of the religion scholar.

To highlight the materiality and visuality that texts share with religious objects among which they circulate and with which they often cross-fertilize, David Morgan (2005: 64–68) uses the term "imagetexts." He illustrates what he means by this term with the example from Islam, a religion of the Book par excellence, which has strong injunctions against idolatry (*shirk*). Knowing that they cannot worship any created beings or things, the disciples of a popular Sufi Sheik in Senegal have filled the contours of his image with a beautifully calligraphed text praising Allah. This juxtaposition transforms "what one sees into a devotional reading, implying, perhaps, that the body of the saint is the Word of God as well as kind of visual presence, since the devout viewer of the image is also the reader of the text and worshipper of God" (Morgan 2005: 67).

The best textual scholarship already takes a practice-oriented approach. For example, scholar of early Christianity Karen King analyzes the production of Gnosticism as a set of heretical texts against an emerging, contested Christian canon. By reconstructing the ways in which texts have been produced, manipulated, and appropriated not only by various Christian groups but also by academy, she wants to show the contingent character of the term Gnosticism and to open spaces for an appreciation of the diversity and difference of early Christian practices. Rather than uncritically relying on essentialized notions of orthodoxy and heresy, King "aims to get at practice . . . not a fixed and essentialized categorization of early Christian multiformity. The result of this historiographical method would be to demonstrate where and how the 'textual' sources, cultural codes, literary themes, hermeneutical strategies, and sociopolitical interests of various rhetorical acts of Christian literary production, theological reflection, ritual and ethical practices, and social construction simultaneously form multiple overlapping continuities, disjunctures, contradictions, and discontinuities, both locally and translocally" (King 2008: 80–81).

The appropriation of texts by situated actors, ranging from institutions invested in maintaining orthodoxy to individuals at the margins of society, contributes to the reproduction of sedimented practices and the creation of new ones. Some of these practices will, at a given juncture, have specific semi-otic and expressive functions, while others will not be primarily interpretive. It follows, then, that "text" is not the only metaphor to understand the richness of human activity. There are other productive tropes, such as territory, flows, networks, and embodiment, that we can use to explore this complexity. As a corollary, signifying, meaning-making, and discursive practices cannot be privileged a priori, as preconditions for the study of the essence of religion, but rather they must be studied in their inevitable interplay with other types of practices. Practice-centered approaches also explore religion in all its histo-ricity, as a holistic process, not a simply a product, of either symbolic systems or economic structures. Neither symbolic systems nor socioeconomic struc-tures are autonomous units that stand above the flow of history and the lived experiences of concrete individuals, who produce and reproduce them. Thus, praxis approaches reject reductive, mono-causal readings, foregrounding instead overlapping levels of determination that sustain persistent power asym-metries. Because of their holism, practice-centered approaches see religion as embodied and emplaced, as a praxis that is made possible by the interaction among society, culture, psychology, and biology. Finally, practice-centered approaches are generally interested in how religion shapes and is shaped by everyday life, and how this lived religion is connected with the exercise of dom-ination and resistance among actors sharing local, national, transnational, and global social spaces.

In the next section, I will focus more closely on the interaction between religious practices and the production of multiple spaces.

PART III
Emplacement

10

Expanding the Conversation on Emplaced Religion

> A critique could be carried out of this devaluation of space that has prevailed
> for generations. . . . Space was treated as the dead, the fixed, the undialectical,
> the immobile. Time, on the contrary, was richness, fecundity, life, dialectic.
>
> —*Michel Foucault (1980: 70)*

In contrast to the ambivalence toward the body and practice in religious studies, the category of space has consistently occupied a prominent position in the discipline.[1] Such a prominence is particularly notable in light of the way in which the social sciences have, until recently, neglected spatial dynamics. Critical geographer Edward Soja, for example, has shown how disciplines such as sociology and anthropology have persistently understood space in static terms, as the mere passive background, the empty container, in which or against which individuals perform their activities. Soja attributes this failure to recognize that space is agentic, that it acts upon individuals just as it is shaped by their practices, to an Enlightenment-based bias in favor of time.

In its drive to liberate humanity from the imposition of control from outside the rational self, the Enlightenment construed space as part of nature, an external material limit to be transcended or, at the minimum, civilized through human action. Partaking in the Enlightenment's stress on self-legislation, the social sciences were born as an attempt to go beyond religious revelation and to explain the social by the social, as Durkheim demanded in *The Rules of Sociological Method*. The social sciences, particularly critical social theory, have emphasized the processes through which historical individuals generate cultures and build societies. Moreover, just as the Enlightenment espoused a faith in progress, the social sciences often bought in evolutionary, even teleological, views of social action, hypothesizing that modernity would necessarily result in increasing complexity, social differentiation, rationalization, and secularization. This historicist perspective meant that space was at best something to be harnessed by human praxis as individuals transformed nature, including "human nature," into culture and society. And "it is precisely the critical and potentially emancipatory value of historical imagination, of people 'making history' rather than taking it for granted, that has made it so compulsively appealing. The constant reaffirmation that the world can be changed by human action, by praxis, has always been the centerpiece of critical social theory" (Soja 1989: 14). As we shall see later in the chapter, starting in the late 1960s, this historicist bias has given way to a "spatial turn," the result of the unsettling of traditional, dichotomous notions of time and space brought about by globalization.

Whereas the social sciences have embraced a "space-blinkered historicism" (Soja 1989: 11), religious studies has been weary of it, associating it with the process of secularization that would eventually evacuate religion for the public sphere, virtually erasing the discipline's object of study. In fact, Mircea Eliade goes as far as to argue that sacred time is utterly different from linear profane time. Because sacred time is circular, referring back to the paradigmatic actions of the gods who created meaningful space out of chaos, the historicism of the social sciences cannot be but reductive, erasing the spatial distinctions that are central to the religious experience.

In this chapter, I will show that, while Eliade was wrong in his ahistorical and decontextualized reading of the production of sacred spaces, his strong focus on the spatial dimensions of religious experience provides an invaluable corrective to the biases of the social sciences. The recognition of the centrality of space in religious life complements the preceding discussions on embodiment and practice. As we saw in chapter 3, in my reconstruction of a materialist phenomenology, embodiment is *Dasein*, "being-thereness," existing concretely not just in time, but in space, among others with whom we build life-worlds through our situated practices. Thus, a non-reductive materialist approach to religion makes space a core epistemological category. I understand space not as an inert condition, opposed to the dynamism of history and practice, but as tightly entwined with time, mobility, organic evolution, ecological interconnectedness, and the contested construction of individual and collective identities. The task is not to defend religion from "the terrors of history" by taking human practice out of the process of sacralization. Rather, it is to put practice in place, to articulate a "practical theoretical consciousness that sees the life-world of being creatively located not only in the making of history but also in the construction of human geographies . . . [such that] social being [is] actively emplaced in space *and* time in an explicitly historical *and* geographical contextualization" (Soja 1989: 11, italics in the original).

This chapter begins with an analysis of the notion of space among seminal scholars of religion, such as Eliade and Durkheim. It then maps out how the work of critical theorists as diverse as Foucault, de Certeau, Lefebvre, Soja, and

Harvey can enrich the conversation in religious studies. This conversation has its own internal logic and interlocutors, ranging from J. Z. Smith, Sam Gill, Edward Linenthal, David Chidester, Kim Knott, to Thomas Tweed.

SPACE AS A KEY CATEGORY IN RELIGIOUS STUDIES

Perhaps the clearest evidence of the centrality of space in the study of religion from its early days is found in Durkheim's work. He argues (1965: 52) that religion is relational, universally defined by the tension between the sacred and the profane: "All known religious beliefs, whether simple or complex, present one common characteristic: they presuppose a classification of all the things, real and ideal, of which men [sic][2] think, into two classes or opposed groups, generally designated by two distinct terms which are translated well enough by the words *profane* and *sacred* (*profane, sacré*)." As a good social constructionist, Durkheim sees the sacred-profane distinction as the product of social structures and divisions, reflected as collective emotions and representations, which are then projected into various objects, both animate and inanimate. "Religious force is only the sentiment inspired by the group in its members, but projected outside of the consciousnesses that experience them, and objectified. To be objectified, they are fixed upon some object which thus becomes sacred; but any object might fulfil [sic] this function" (Durkheim 1965: 261). Thus, sacrality as a marker of separateness from the profane is extrinsic, contingent, and polyvalent property, which takes a virtually infinite number of material expressions. "[T]he sacred character assumed by an object is not implied in the intrinsic properties of this latter: *it is added to them*. The world of religious things is no one particular aspect of empirical nature; *it is superimposed upon it*" (Durkheim 1965: 261, italics in the original).

Despite the sociohistorical contingency of the sacred, Durkheim sees the contrast between sacred and profane as "universal." Moreover, he views the contrast as absolute. In language that Eliade would later echo, albeit giving it a different twist, Durkheim construes the relation between sacred and profane as one characterized by "heterogeneity." Nonetheless, "this heterogeneity is sufficient to characterize this classification of things and to distinguish it from all others, because it very particular: it is absolute. In all the history of human thought there exists no other example of two categories of things so profoundly differentiated or so radically opposed to each other" (Durkheim 1965: 53).

This is precisely where space comes into Durkheim's theory of religion. Because the distinction between sacred and profane is universal and absolute, it informs the totality of the individual's worldview and experiences, as well as society's structures. The sacred and profane are not simply "two distinct classes . . . [but also] two worlds between which there is nothing in common" (Durkheim 1965: 54). In other words, the sacred-profane duality is spatial, separating two "worlds," "kingdoms," "domains," "universes" by erecting a variety of sanctioned symbolic and physical barriers, thresholds that must be crossed in prescribed ways in order not to violate the distinction. As the group projects its social effervescence into a particular object, it marks this object in space, separating and elevating it to a realm utterly different from "daily life [which] drags wearily along" (Durkheim 1965: 250). But here Durkheim makes an even bolder claim: religion is not only inextricably spatial; it is, in fact, the source of the category of space in the first place. By universally setting "things apart and forbidden" in the minds of early humans, religion generates the conditions through which we can experience space meaningfully. Building on but going beyond Kant's idea of space as a priori of cognition, Durkheim writes:

> space is not the vague and indetermined medium which Kant imagined; if purely and absolutely homogeneous, it would be of no use, and could not be grasped by the mind. Spatial representation consists essentially in a primary co-ordination of the data of sensuous experience. But this co-ordination would be impossible if the parts of space were qualitatively equivalent and if they were really interchangeable. To dispose things spatially there must be a possibility of placing them differently, of putting some at the right, others at the left, these above, those below, at the north of or at the south of. . . . That is to say that space could not be what it is if it were not, like time, divided and differentiated. But whence come these divisions which are so essential? (Durkheim 1965: 23–24)

The answer to the last question is that these divisions are of "social origins." According to Durkheim, "it is the rhythm of social life which is at the basis of the category of time; the territory occupied by the society furnished the material for the category of space; it is the collective force which the prototype of the concept of efficient force, an essential element in the category of causality. However, the categories are not made to be applied only to the social realm; they reach out to all reality" (Durkheim 1965: 488). Moreover, since "the first systems of representations with which men have pictured to themselves the world and themselves [are] of religious origin," Durkheim concludes that religion is at the root of human spatial imagination. Because "nearly all the great social institutions have been born in religion," the duality between sacred and profane serves an epistemological role, giving rise to the spatial distinctions at work not only in everyday life but in philosophy and science.

Joining space and religion in such a dramatic and foundational fashion has the powerful effect of sensitizing scholars of religion to spatial dynamics in unique ways. Indeed, the structuralist and post-structuralist legacy of Durkheimian sociology of religion and culture shows an abiding interest in questions of space, from Mary Douglas's focus on the religiously inflected construction of boundaries within and among groups, to Van Gennep's and Turner's work on rites of passage and liminality, Foucault's treatment of subjectivation in the confessional and panoptical society, and Pierre Bourdieu's notion of body hexis.

The close connection between space and religion in Durkheim is also picked up by Mircea Eliade. Like Durkheim, Eliade considers the distinction between the sacred and profane as essential to religious experience. He also stresses how the sacred breaks with the homogeneity of profane space, giving rise to meaningful dwelling.

"For the religious man, space is not homogeneous; he experiences interruptions, breaks in it; some parts of space are qualitatively different from others. . . . There is, then, a sacred space, and hence a strong, significant space; there are other spaces that are not sacred and so are without structure or consistency, amorphous" (Eliade 1959a: 20).

Eliade, nevertheless, rejects Durkheim's sociological reductionism, the latter's claim that, while the sacred-profane duality is universal and absolute, the sacred is a purely relational and contingent category, invested with power by the changing dynamics of the social group. For Eliade, it is not just the duality that is universal and absolute, but the sacred itself has ontogenic power, the power to give rise to reality, to space and time, and, thus, to make possible the emergence of the social, which Durkheim falsely considers as the independent variable. Here Eliade reinterprets Durkheim through the lens of Rudolf Otto's notion of "the Holy"—the sacred is the numinous, the "wholly other," Being-itself which has the power to create an ordered cosmos out of chaos. He writes that for the "archaic man," whom Eliade regards as the clearest expression of the timeless *homo religiosus*, "the *sacred* is equivalent to a *power*, and in the last analysis, to *reality*. The sacred is saturated with *being*. Sacred power means reality and at the same time enduringness and efficacy. The polarity sacred-profane is often expressed as an opposition between real and unreal or pseudo-real. Thus, it is easy to understand that religious man deeply desires *to be*, to participate in *reality*, to be saturated with power" (Eliade 1959a: 13, italics in the original).

The sacred demonstrates its agency through hierophanies, manifestations that break into amorphous time and space, turning the event into a paradigmatic "primordial act" that is ritually reenacted by the religious person and setting apart the territory in which it takes place. The hierophany sets sacred space apart not just by investing it with ontological power and elevating it above the undifferentiated routine of profane space, but also by centering, transforming it into an enduring pivot that connects immanence with transcendence. We could say that the experience of sacred space makes possible the "founding of the world: where the sacred manifests itself in space, the real unveils itself, the world comes into existence. But the irruption of the sacred does not only project a fixed point into the formless fluidity of profane space, a center into chaos; it also effects, a break in plane, that is, it opens communication between the cosmic planes (between earth and heaven) and makes possible ontological passage from one mode of being to another" (Eliade 1959a: 63). The creation of sacred space entails the emergence of an *axis mundi* connecting the heavens and the earth.

For Eliade, thus, sacred space is inextricably connected with world-centering. "A universe comes to birth from its center; it spreads out from a central point that is, as it were, its navel" (Eliade 1959a: 44). Surrounding this navel is chaos, "uncosmicized because unconsecrated space, a mere amorphous extent into which no orientation has yet been projected, and hence no structure has yet arisen—for religious man, this profane space represents absolute nonbeing" (64).

Notice that, in addition to seeing religious creativity as synonymous with ordering, Eliade holds that world-creating and world-centering are not the by-products of the consecrating activities of historical and social individuals. Rather, they are powers inherent to the sacred. Eliade acknowledges that "every manifestation of the sacred takes place in some historical situation" and that "[e]ven the most personal and transcendant mystical experiences are affected by the age in which they occur" (Eliade 1996: 2). However, in the end, he defends the "autonomy of hierophanies: the sacred expresses itself according to the laws of its own dialectic and this expression comes to man *from without*" (Eliade 1996: 369). This autonomy helps explain why certain morphologies of sacred space recur across history and culture, a phenomenon that Durkheimian sociological reductionism cannot explain, since it claims that the process of sacralization is purely contextual.

In contrast to Durkheim's social constructionism, Eliade does not view sacred space as the mere product of human praxis. "In actual fact, [a sacred] place is never 'chosen' by man; it is merely discovered by him; in other words, the sacred place in some way or another reveals itself to him" (Eliade 1996:

369). As hierophanies manifest themselves in time and space, they provide the blueprint for human activity, for the implementation of spatial and temporal distinctions in the present. The construction of widely recognized sacred spaces "was based on a primeval revelation which disclosed the archetype of the sacred space in *illo tempore*, an archetype which was then indefinitely copied and copied again with the erection of every new altar, temple, or sanctuary" (Eliade 1996: 371–72). In this way, "the altar . . . becomes a microcosm existing in a mystical space and time quite distinct in nature from profane space and time. To speak of building an altar is, in the same breadth, to speak of a repetition of the creation of the world" (Eliade 1996: 372). Human-made space has meaning only in so far as it reproduces sacred archetypes. "[T]he world which surrounds us, civilized by the hand of man, is accorded no validity beyond that which is due to the extraterrestrial prototype that served as its model. Man constructs according to an archetype" (Eliade 1954: 10).

Eliade is here basically arguing that in order to understand fully the centrality, uniqueness, and power of space in the study of religion, the scholar must suspend history, or, rather, linear profane time. Like all "archaic societies" that he constructs from afar, Eliade's work is driven by "the will to devaluate time" (1954: 85). According to Eliade, we must understand that "sacred time is reversible in the sense that, properly speaking, it is a primordial mythical time made present. Every religious festival, any liturgical time, represents the reactualization of a sacred event that took place in a mythical past, 'in the beginning'" (1959a: 68–69). By introducing a cyclical notion of time, time as the eternal return to mythical and pristine origins, as a "continual" or "atemporal present," Eliade effectively immunizes religious studies against the bias toward time that has led to the neglect of space in the social sciences.

The powerful impact of Eliade's understandings of sacred space and time is undeniable. For example, Davíd Carrasco effectively uses Eliadean categories such as the *axis mundi* and the myth of the eternal return to illuminate the place of ceremonial centers in Aztecs cosmology. These centers emplaced "the parallelism between the microcosmos, in the form of architectural assemblages, and the macrocosmos expressed in the myths about the realms of the gods and their associated conceptions" (Carrasco 1999: 43–44). As such, these centers served as "world-founding," "world-centering," and "world-renewing spaces," where Aztec priests performed rituals such as the New Fire Ceremony, which involved human heart sacrifice, reenacting the original sacrifice by the gods that gave rise to the ordered universe. These sacrifices were meant to keep civilization and cycle of life going, avoiding collapse into chaos (Carrasco 1999: 96–105).

Eliade's work also resonates with humanistic geographer Yi-Fu Tuan's distinction between space and place, a distinction that became central in the study of human environmental experience. According to Tuan, space is undifferentiated and undetermined, just as Eliade saw space before hierophanies. "Space lies open; it suggests the future and invites action. On the negative side, space and freedom are a threat. To be open and free is to be exposed and vulnerable. Open space has no trodden paths and signposts. It has no fixed pattern of established human meaning; it is like a blank sheet on which meaning may be imposed" (Tuan 1977: 54). In order to become meaningful, space has to become a place and this process of becoming involves centering. "Compared to space, place is a calm center of established values" (Tuan 1977: 54).[3] Where Tuan parts ways with Eliade is in his insistence that the process of turning space into place is not the result of some supernatural or supra-historical intervention but a quintessential human endeavor. "What begins as undifferentiated space becomes place as we get to know it better and endow it with value" (Tuan 1977: 6). Moreover, unlike Eliade, Tuan does not give ontological privilege to place over space, equating the latter with non-being. Rather, for Tuan, "the ideas of 'space' and 'place' require each other for definition. From the security and stability of place we are aware of the openness, freedom, and threat of space, and vice versa" (Tuan 1977: 6). In fact, "human beings require both space and place. Human lives are a dialectical movement between shelter and venture, attachment and freedom" (Tuan 1977: 54). As we shall see, in his emphasis on human praxis and the dialectic relation between space and place, Tuan is closer to J. Z. Smith's critical reworking of Eliade. The focus on the dialectical movement between venture and shelter also foreshadows Thomas Tweed's notions of crossing and dwelling.

At the epistemological level, Eliade's most important legacy is in empowering religious studies to resist the teleologies of secularization, which have blinded much of the social sciences to the enduring and widespread vitality of religion. Nevertheless, this contribution comes at a very high cost. For Eliade has left unchallenged the untenable dichotomy between space and time, merely switching the duality around, privileging space, particularly the foundational center, against the corrosive power of historicity and change. The result is an essentialist theory of religion that flattens the diversity of religious phenomena across history and cultures. Despite Eliade's remarkable erudition, his history of religions does not seek to provide fully contextualized analyses of changing forms of religious emplacement and materiality. Instead, Eliade summons a myriad of religious practices as surface expressions of underlying transhistorical or supra-historical patterns that are endlessly reenacted. This search for deep, universal "Platonic forms" flies in the face of his own anti-reductionist efforts.[4]

The challenge, then, is to retain Eliade's fruitful insight about the significance of space in religion and his warning not to reduce the emergence of sacred space to social activity, while, at the same time, reintroducing historicity and practice in full force. As Durkheim rightly claims, the production of sacred space is always mediated by the social context. However, the social and cultural contexts do not exhaust all that goes on in the process of inhabiting and consecrating spaces. Just as we always live our bodies within a web of narratives but cannot reduce our physicality—the neurobiological and cognitive dynamics that make the production of culture possible—to a mere cluster of discourses, we experience space in the complex, open-ended interplay between cultural and ecological dynamics. Therefore, we need not appeal to some transcendental, ontological category of the sacred in order to build a non-reductive theory of religious emplacement. Transcendence is immanent, part of our own untotalizable but still binding materiality. In the rest of this chapter, I will discuss some of the concepts and methods that can serve as the building blocks for such a theory.

J. Z. SMITH: THE LOCATIVE AND THE UTOPIAN

One of the first critics of Eliade's approach to sacred space was Jonathan Z. Smith. Smith notes that, although Eliade uses Durkheimian categories, Eliadean history of religions "implies a fundamental reversal" of Durkheim's social Kantianism. For Eliade, "world creation and world founding are not anthropological categories expressive of human freedom. Rather, they are to be understood as ontological (perhaps even theological) categories. Man's fundamental mode is not freedom and creativity but rather repetition. Or, perhaps more accurately man's creativity is repetition" (Smith 1978: 92). In order to reintroduce history, context, and human creativity, Smith challenges Eliade's privileging of primordial order and the center, both of which are implicit in the notion of foundational archetypes. Smith offers "a phenomenology of rebellion," which highlights how the paradigm of the center is an oppressive ideology. Smith also focuses on the role of the anti-structural "periphery" in the construction and maintenance of sacred spaces (Smith 2004: 15).

Smith asks: "Is chaos best understood as the equivalent of the profane, that which is neutral, that which is unreal? I would suggest that chaos is never profane in the sense of being neutral." Echoing Yi-Fu Tuan, Smith continues, "chaos *only* takes a significance within a religious world view. Chaos is a sacred power; but it is frequently perceived as being sacred 'in the wrong way.' It is that which is opposed to order, which threatens the paradigms and archetypes but which is, nevertheless, profoundly necessary for the very creativity that is characteristic of Eliade's notion of the sacred" (Smith 1978: 97). Beyond the unwarranted privileging of order against chaos, Smith also faults Eliade for reading the category of the center "too narrowly ... in literalistic terms of geographical symbolism" (98). That is, Eliade confuses a certain map of reality which reflects his exultation of the center for Being-itself, for territory itself.

Pointing to examples of the building of temples and palaces as centers of religious and political power in Ancient Near Eastern religions, Smith argues that "the language of 'center' is preeminently political and only secondarily cosmological. It is a vocabulary that stems, primarily, from archaic ideologies of kingship and royal function. In any particular traditions, it may or may not be tied to cosmological and cosmogonic myths" (1987: 17). The elevation of the center as sacred paradigm is not necessarily "celestial [but rather] relentlessly terrestrial and chthonic" (Smith 1987: 12). It is a mode of inhabiting the world, a "locative" vision that responds to the interests of a particular, situated group of people, namely, political and religious elites that derive their power from the boundaries and divisions they sacralize. "A temple is built at a central place, the place where a king or god happens to have decided to take up residence. Perhaps this is because temple here is always a royal function, and the power of kingship is such that it constitutes a place as central sheerly by being *there*" (Smith 1987: 22, italics in the original).

This locative, centralized, and centralizing map is not the result of an innocent revelation or a discovery of a transcendent sacred. It is "an imperial figure. It is a map of the world which guarantees meaning and value through structures of congruity and conformity" (Smith 1978: 292). Locative maps achieve the ubiquity that Eliade confuses for universality because they are produced by ruling groups that, in controlling the means of legitimate cultural production and circulation, impose hegemonic ideas. As Smith writes:

> the very success of these [locative] topographies should be a signal for caution. For they are largely based on documents from urban, agricultural, hierarchical cultures. The most persuasive witness to a locative, imperial world-view are the production of well-organized, self-conscious scribal elites who had a deep vested interest in restricting mobility and valuing place. The texts are, by and large, the production of temples and royal courts and provide their raison d'être—the temple, upon which the priest's and scribe's income rested, a "Center" and microcosm; the requirements of exact repetition in ritual and concomitant notion of ritual as a reenactment of divine activities.... In most cases one cannot escape the suspicion that, in the locative map of the world, we are encountering

a self-serving ideology which ought not to be generalized into the universal pattern of religious experience and expression. (1978: 293)

In reintroducing political and economic power to the articulation of sacred space, Smith returns to Durkheim's understanding of religion. He has succeeded in retaining Eliade's keen sensitivity toward the spatial in religious studies, while bringing back the dimensions of practice and change to the study of sacred spaces. Citing anthropologist Mary Douglas's *Purity and Danger*, Smith states that "there is nothing that is inherently or essentially clean or unclean, sacred or profane. There are situational or relational categories, mobile boundaries which shift according to the map being employed" (Smith 1978: 291). The sacred is a "category of emplacement" (Smith 1987: 104), through which individuals situate themselves vis-à-vis others, marking differences and power asymmetries by erecting boundaries, establishing centers and peripheries, and generating classifications and hierarchies. Religion is not the unfolding of some ontological, supra-human principles in history, but "an inextricably human phenomenon." It is "a distinctive mode of human creativity, a creativity which both discovers limits and creates limits for humane existence. What we study when we study religion is the variety of attempts to map, construct and inhabit such positions of power through the use of myths, rituals and experiences of transformation" (Smith 1978: 291).

I argued above that Smith's emphasis on practice and human creativity dovetails nicely with the insights of humanistic geographers such as Yi-Fu Tuan. By adding a strong focus on power, Smith's approach also resonates with the work of Michel Foucault, as well as of critical geographers such as Henri Lefebvre. For example, Lefebvre (1991: 37) calls for geography to shift its focus "from things in spaces," in a Euclidean-Cartesian mode, "to the actual production of space," to the actual processes through which humans build "lived spaces." The production of space, in turn, mediates and is shaped by the logic of capitalist social relations (Lefebvre 1991: 227–28).

If the sacred is a relational category, what is set against it? Smith suggest that there is another mode of mapping the world, "a utopian" worldview "in which the categories of rebellion and freedom are to the fore; in which beings are called upon to challenge their limits, break them, or create new possibilities, a centripetal world which emphasizes the importance of periphery and transcendence" (Smith 1978: 101). Whereas the carriers of the "central-locative" religious vision have been priests and kings, the protagonists of the "peripheral-utopian" mode of being in the world are people in motion, in diaspora, "god-men, saviors, or religious entrepreneurs," who shift the mode of religious activity from "celebration to initiation. Rather than being born into a divinely established and protected land whose glories one celebrated, one was initiated (reborn) into a divine protector who has ties to no land." This is the reason why "[d]iasporic religion, in contrast to native, locative religion, was utopian in the strictest sense of the word, a religion of 'nowhere,' of transcendence" (Smith 1987: xiv).

Smith's distinction between locative and utopian constructions of sacred space is very helpful in explaining, for example, the explosive growth of Charismatic Christianity throughout the world. This type of Christianity is very often carried by itinerant prophets, healers, and religious entrepreneurs who highlight the power of a Holy Spirit that knows no territorial boundaries or class, racial, or gender distinctions. In a globalized world characterized by widespread and intense flows of ideas, capital, goods, and people, Christianities animated by a deterritorializing and deterritorialized Holy Spirit seem to have the upper hand over locative Christian modes of dwelling, such as the traditional Catholic Church anchored on fixed parishes. Charismatic Christianities appear to have the creative adaptability to operate in multiple peripheries, among poor women in Africa, people of African descent in Latin America, or undocumented Latin American, African, and Asian immigrants in the United States and Europe.

However, as I will argue in the rest of the chapter and in the next one, Smith's distinction needs to be fleshed out, elaborated, and nuanced in light of changing cartographies of the sacred that are accompanying contemporary processes of globalization. Smith (1978: 101) himself calls for preserving "a sufficient sense of the experiential character of [the] dichotomy and resist[ing] imposing even an implicit evolutionary scheme" into the model. The locative-utopian tension cannot be read mechanically or teleologically, as if the two terms are mutually exclusive. Rather "[b]oth have been and remain coeval existential possibilities which may be appropriated whenever and wherever they correspond to man's experience" (Smith 1978: 101). Further, Smith has more recently introduced three spatial categories that scholars of religion can cross-reference with locative and utopian tendencies to provide more detailed maps of religious practices and institutions. He talks about a "(1) the 'here' of domestic religion, located primarily in the home and the burial sites; (2) the 'there' of public civic and state religions, largely based in temple constructions; and (3) the 'everywhere' of a rich diversity of religious formations that occupy an interstitial space between these two loci, including a variety of religious entrepreneurs and ranging from groups we term 'associations' to activities we label 'magic'" (Smith 2004: 325). While each of these spatial levels of religious experience and practice may have a close affinity with either locative or utopian visions, the "contestations, permutations, and combinations generated by these two *ethoi*, whether within or between any particular tradition, constitute what we take to be the history of religions" (Smith 2004: 334).

Smith's attempts to elaborate his cartographies of the sacred point to the need to specify the meanings and operations of the locative and the utopian. I now turn to the work of Michel Foucault and Michel de Certeau to shed some light how we can study the imperial figure of the locative and the transgressive tactics of the utopian.

RELIGION, SPACE, DOMINATION, AND RESISTANCE

In the previous section, we saw how J. Z. Smith associates the locative with the figure of the king. Foucault too argues that up until the advent of modernity, the most dramatic demonstration of power was the ritualized public torture of the bodies of those who had challenged the king's sovereignty. "The dissymmetry, the irreversible imbalance of forces were an essential element in the public execution. A body effaced, reduced to dust and thrown to the winds, a body destroyed piece by piece by the infinite power of the sovereign constituted not only the ideal, but the real limit of punishment" (Foucault 1977b: 50). However, toward the late 1700s, with the birth of the clinic and prison, a new way of applying power emerged that relied not on the spectacular and excessive application of punishment, but on the internalization of surveillance and discipline by the modern subject. This form of power did not seek to obliterate bodies, but to reform souls and to extract inner secrets of individuals as way to produce "docile bodies." It was a power that worked the body "'retail,' individually . . . exercising upon it a subtle coercion . . . obtaining holds upon it at the level of the mechanism itself—movements, gestures, attitudes, rapidity—an infinitesimal power of the active body." This power "implies an uninterrupted, constant coercion, supervising the processes of activity rather than its result, and it is exercised according to a codification that partitions as closely as possible time, space, movement" (Foucault 1977b: 137).

With the advent of modernity, power enters the locative vision in more complex ways than proposed by Smith, who is, after all, working with Ancient Near Eastern materials. According to Foucault, the model for production of social space from the late 1700s on is philosopher Jeremy Bentham's panopticon, a penal architectural device that allowed simultaneously for the global and individualized surveillance of prisoners.

The principle was this. A perimeter building in the form of a ring. At the center of this, a tower, pierced by large windows opening on to the inner face of the ring. The outer building divided into cells each of which traverses the whole thickness of the building. These cells have two windows, one opening on to the inside, facing the windows of the central tower, the other, outer one allowing daylight to pass through the whole cell. All that is then needed is to put an overseer in the tower and place in each of the cells a lunatic, a patient, a convict, a worker or a schoolboy. The back lighting enables one to pick out from the central tower the little captive silhouettes in the ring of cells. In short, the principle of the dungeon is reversed; daylight and the overseer's gaze capture the inmate more effectively than darkness, which afforded after all a sort of protection. (Foucault 1980: 147)

The panopticon, thus, completes the imperialism of the center. It seeks to erase utterly the "peripheral-utopian" mode of being in the world. Or better said, in the panopticon the locative becomes the utopian (or dystopian, depending on your view of modernity), fulfilling the dream of the Enlightenment to be able to shed light onto the whole of society. For Foucault, "Bentham was the complement to Rousseau. What in fact was the Rousseauist dream that motivated many revolutionaries? It was the dream of a transparent society, visible and legible in each of its parts, the dream of there no longer existing any zones of darkness, zones established by the privileges of royal power or the prerogative of some corporation, zones of disorder" (Foucault 1980: 152). Moreover, the panopticon's spatial configuration makes the center omnipresent: everyone within the architectural device carries the center, internalized as a technology of the self, as an essential part of their subjectivities. "There is no need for arms, physical violence, material constraints. Just a gaze. An inspecting gaze, a gaze which each individual under its weight will end by interiorizing to the point that he is his own overseer, each individual thus exercising this surveillance over, and against, himself" (Foucault 1980: 155).

According to Foucault, by the eighteenth century, the spatial, surveillance, and disciplinary strategies illustrated by the panopticon began to be implemented in schools, barracks, hospitals, asylums, and factories, buttressing the emergence of a modern panoptical society, in which the state, in both its capitalist and socialist versions, applies a "biopower," the ability to control, classify, and extract surplus and knowledge from populations. But what does this understanding of the relationship between space, power, and knowledge have to do with religion? Foucault argues that mechanisms of power and subjectivation at work in the panoptical society are secular deployments of old religious technologies of the self. More specifically, Foucault points to Christian ideas of the soul, particularly of the means to reform it in order to save the individual, as the precursors of the panoptical gaze. Before there was biopower there was "pastoral power" (Foucault 1999: 135–52), the power to individualize before God, which is essential for the development of modern forms of "governmentality."

Foucault readily recognizes that the quest for self-knowledge was already part of the Greco-Roman world in which Christianity flourished. However, whereas for the Hellenistic world this quest was at the service of the mastery of the self and the judgment of how to constitute oneself as a citizen, a member of the polis, in Christianity, self-knowledge becomes the means to recognize and confess sin. According to Foucault, "Christianity appropriated two essential instruments at work in the Hellenistic world: self-examination and the guidance of conscience. It took them over, but not without altering them considerably" (1999: 143). In Christianity, these two instruments become part of an institutionalized confessional asceticism that makes the care of the soul not just a matter of personal concern but of a hierarchical organization.

> Christian pastorship implies a peculiar type of knowledge between pastor and each of his sheep. This knowledge is particular. It individualizes. It isn't enough to know the state of the flock. That of each sheep must also be known. . . . [T]he shepherd must be informed as to the material needs of each member of the flock and provide for them when necessary. He must know what is going on, what each of them does—his public sin. Last and not least, he must know what goes on in the soul of each one, that is, his secret sins, his progress on the road to sainthood. (Foucault 1999: 142–43)

Foucault, then, gives a new twist to Durkheim's claim that religion is "the womb of civilization." The assorted techniques of disciplining and mortifying the body used in cloisters and monasteries in order to combat concupiscence and produce "total obedience, knowledge of oneself and confession to someone else" provided the raw material for the emergence of modernity, with its simultaneously totalizing and individualizing "regime of truth" (Foucault 1999: 157). Foucault points specifically to Council of Trent in the mid-1500s. It introduced "a new series of procedures developed within the ecclesial institution for the purpose of training and purifying ecclesiastical personnel. Detailed techniques were elaborated for use in seminaries and monasteries, techniques of discursive rendition of daily life, of self-examination, confession, direction of conscience and regulation of the relationship between director and directed" (Foucault 1980: 200). However, this was not an exclusively Catholic phenomenon, for Quakers such as William Tuke (1732–1822) introduced practices of self-examination and moral reform to asylums and prisons. He "created an asylum where he substituted for the free terror of madness the stifling anguish of responsibility; fear no longer reigned on the other side of the prison gates, it now raged under the seals of conscience" (Foucault 1973: 247).

Christianity thus introduced a confessional "hermeneutics of the self," in which "the problem is to discover what is hidden inside the self; the self is like a text or like a book that we have to decipher" (Foucault 1999: 168). After all, Christians face "the possibility that Satan can get inside your soul and give you thoughts you cannot recognize as satanic, but that you might interpret as coming from God" (Foucault 1984: 361). As we saw in chapters 8 and 9, Asad (1993) argues that we continue to suffer the consequences of this confessional hermeneutics of self in textualist and privatist understandings of society, culture, and religion, from Geertz to Derrida. What is important to note here is that Foucault shows us how locative religion is tightly connected with the production of the emplaced self via the power-knowledge nexus. But it is not just about the implementation of the "self-serving ideologies" of kings and priests. It is also about how religious practitioners constitute themselves and others as subjects through spatialized and spatializing techniques. "Ritualized disciplines of the body, which regulate its gestures and rhythms, its speaking, eating, and excreting, situate embodied practices in place" (Chidester and Linenthal 1995: 10). This is the case, for example, for medieval Christian monks, whose life was ordered through daily emplaced tasks, including routine praying, chanting, and working. Monasteries and convents not only served as spaces to train docile, ascetic Christian bodies. They were also "authorizing spaces," spaces that consecrated subjects with the power of orthodoxy (Asad 1993: 83–124).

The constitution of religious subjects through spatialized and spatializing techniques is also evident in the evolution of domestic spaces.[5] Colleen McDannell, for instance, describes how "[c]onservative Protestants, through home schooling, articulate a domestic ideology that shapes their Christian piety, political orientations, and attitude toward their local churches" (McDannell 1995b: 189). Home schooling enables these Protestants "to create a Christian space within the home," which, in turn, fulfills the "goal of creating neighborhoods to train 'our whole race for heaven.'" Home schooling "does not merely socialize children. It teaches their parents how to be Christian" (MacDannell 1995b: 190).

As a final example, in *Globalizing the Sacred*, Marquardt and I also drew from Foucault to show how former members of Salvadoran youth gangs who have converted to Pentecostalism creatively deploy religious narratives and practices to respond to the dislocation produced by neo-liberal capitalism and a geopolitical civil war. Through these practices and narratives, the new converts emplace themselves in multiple spaces, rearticulating the spaces of the self and the congregation as protective zones of intimacy and catharsis against the depraved surrounding world, while, at the same time, entering the transnational social field created by churches operating in the United States and El Salvador (Vásquez and Marquardt 2003: 119–44).

Despite his invaluable insights into the way religion contributes to the production of spatialized selves, Foucault gives us very few tools to explore what J. Z. Smith calls the utopian religious vision. In fact, in spite of his rejection of the Enlightenment's naïve historicism, Foucault's analysis ultimately succumbs to a totalizing, static logic at odds with his critique of undialectical views of space. He "never explains what space it is that he is referring to, nor how it bridges the gap between the theoretical (epistemological) realm and the practical one, between the mental and the social, between the space of the philosophers and the space of the people who deal with material things" (Lefebvre 1991: 4). By viewing space only as heteronomous, as only producing docile bodies, Foucault ends up constructing a theory machine as suffocating as the panopticon.

In order to recover the full force of situated practices, their ambivalent and shifting power to subjugate and to resist, we need to return to Michel de Certeau. In the previous chapter, I drew from de Certeau's work to strengthen the dimension of resistance and creative innovation in Bourdieu's theory of practice. Here I would like to elaborate on his notions of strategies and tactics to highlight the contested nature of social spaces. De Certeau recognizes that space and domination are closely connected, particularly in what he terms "strategies." Strategies are the "triumph of place of over time" (de Certeau 1984: 36). They are locative in the sense that they freeze actors in an asymmetrical power relation, similar to Foucault's panoptical practices.

> I call a strategy the calculation (or manipulation) of power relationships that becomes possible as soon as a subject with will and power (a business, an army, a city, a scientific institution) can be isolated. It postulates a place that can be delimited as its own and serve as the base from which relations with an exteriority composed of targets or threats (costumers or competitors, enemies, the country surrounding the city, objective and objects of research, etc.) can be managed. (de Certeau 1984: 35–36)

In contrast to strategies, there are tactics, which are nomadic practices of contestation. A tactic "is a calculated action determined by the absence of a proper locus. No delimitation of an exteriority, then, provides it with the condition necessary for autonomy. The space of a tactic is the space of the other. Thus it must play on and with a terrain imposed on it and organized by the law of a foreign power" (de Certeau 1984: 37). The tactic does not operate as part of a totalizing spatializing machine but in "isolated actions, blow by blow." Therefore, a tactic "must vigilantly make use of the cracks that particular conjunctions open in the surveillance of the proprietary powers. It poaches them. It creates surprises in them. It can be where it is least expected. It is guileful ruse" (de Certeau 1984: 37).

To illustrate how the tension between locative and centralizing strategies and translocative and peripheral tactics can help us understand the production of space, de Certeau gives us two visions of the city. One is the perspective of the "voyeur-god," the city planner who watches the flow of people in the streets from the windows of his shining high-rise building in the heart of the business district. This disembodied vision is "a way of keeping aloof, by the space planner urbanist, city planner or cartographer. The panorama-city is a 'theoretical' (that is, visual) simulacrum, in short a picture, whose condition of possibility is an oblivion and a misunderstanding of practices" (de Certeau 1984: 92–93). Set against this "celestial eye," this "eye of power," to use Foucault's expression, is the walker who jaywalks or takes shortcuts over the manicured lawns, resignifying and reappropriating the normalized spaces laid out by the urban planners. "The ordinary practitioners of the city live 'down below,' below the thresholds at which visibility begins. They walk . . . they are walkers . . . who bodies follow the thicks and thins of the urban 'text' they write without being able to read it." "Escaping the imaginary totalizations produced by the eye," the everyday spatial practices of the walker point to another spatiality, a "poetic and mythical experience of space . . . and to an *opaque* and *blind* mobility characteristic of the bustling city. A *migrational*, or metaphorical, city . . ." (de Certeau 1984: 93).

By focusing on "multiform, resistant, tricky, and stubborn procedures that elude discipline without being outside the field in which it is exercised," de Certeau is offering us a "theory of everyday practices, of lived space, of the disquieting familiarity of the city" (de Certeau 1984: 96). This theory manages to retain the powerful tools Foucault has given us to analyze the relation among space, domination, and subjectivation, while not surrendering to an absolutist panoptical machine. De Certeau takes to heart Foucault's asserting that "where there is power, there is resistance."[6] Chidester and Linenthal pick up on the interplay of domination and resistance in the construction of sacred space. Whereas domination operates through strategies of appropriation and exclusion, through the efforts of a person or group to have monopoly over the legitimate access to sacred space, resistance relies on tactics such as inversion and hybridization. These tactics "lend themselves to projects of reversal, or innovation, or even to the kinds of 'desecration' that symbolize alternative relationships to sacred space" (Chidester and Linenthal 1995: 19). Inversion reverses "a prevailing spatial orientation—the high becomes low, the inside becomes outside, the peripheral becomes central." Hybridization, in turn, mixes and scrambles what dominant strategies have tried to naturalize as taken-for-granted sacrality, transgressesing the sharp boundaries and distinctions made in the name of that sacrality. Here we are back once again to J. Z. Smith's effort to recognize the creative anti-structural power of the peripheral-utopian religious vision.

De Certeau's emphasis on everyday practices also bears important affinities with the contemporary interest in the religions of the subaltern, more specifically, on popular religions and lived religion, which I explored in the previous chapter. Orsi (1997: 15), for example, states that "some notion of resistance to power is central to the theory and phenomenology of lived religion. The sacred is reconceptualized as the place not simply where things happen, but where the circulation of power short-circuits." Lived religion, he continues, "appears as the space of resistance par excellence in the United States since the colonial period." Along the same lines, following Antonio Gramsci's insight that "all men are philosophers,"[7] Isambert (1982) characterizes popular religion as a "terrain" opened up by the counter-hegemonic beliefs and practices of peasants and the urban working class.

Rather than focusing exclusively on the doctrines and disciplining practices of the institutional Catholic Church, the scholar of religion who follows de Certeau's lead might study the devotional practices built around Juan Soldado, a soldier in Tijuana borderlands who was accused and executed in the late 1930s for the rape and murder of a little girl and was then turned into a vernacular saint and martyr by the local population (Vanderwood 2004). The devotion toward Juan Soldado has carved an alternative sacred space of practice at the "borderlands" of Catholicism, a space in which believers who still see themselves as closely connected with the institutional church and its normalizing strategies engage in transgressive devotional tactics.

De Certeau's theory of spatial tactics, then, provides a way to specify and build on J. Z. Smith's notion of the "peripheral-utopian" religious world view. But it does so primarily at the local, micro level. De Certeau sets up a sharp dichotomy between strategies and tactics that "polarizes macro-micro relations," privileging and taking for granted the emancipatory force of "the intimacies of the local, the body, the street, the everyday. These are powerful and revealing positionings, but at the same time they close off too much, unnecessarily reducing the scope and power of critical spatial imagination" (Soja 1996: 314). De Certeau fails to acknowledge that practices are emplaced in multiple—sometimes overlapping, sometimes contradictory—contexts and that they have multi-scalar effects. Quotidian tactics, then, may be implicated in large-scale domination while institutional strategies do not always function to reproduce social order, control, exclusion, or inequalities. Religious studies scholar Kim Knott puts it well when she writes that "mundane places like the high street, are also loci of global and diasporic interconnections, with their Internet cafés, phone and fax centers, and travel agents. In being home to recent migrants from many parts of the world, the high street is a hub of international communications: religious blessings and messages, no less than more mundane social exchanges, are transmitted" (Knott 2008: 1110).

Although de Certeau talks about the space of tactics as "migrational" and nomadic, as characterized by a myriad of eccentric trajectories, he does not tell us much that can help us flesh out Smith's bold claim that the peripheral-utopian religious vision is often diasporic, "a religion of 'nowhere,' of transcendence." We need a way to emplace the spatial practices of everyday life within larger global dynamics that are redefining our notions of space and time.

GLOBALIZATION, THE TRANSLOCATIVE, AND THE ABSOLUTE

According to anthropologist Arjun Appadurai, his discipline must confront "some brute facts about the world of the twentieth century." Key among these facts is "the changing social, territorial, and cultural reproduction of group identity. As groups migrate, regroup in new locations, reconstruct their histories, and reconfigure their ethnic project, the ethno of ethnography takes on a slippery, nonlocalized quality. . . . The landscapes of group identity . . . around the world are no longer familiar anthropological objects, insofar as groups are no longer tightly territorialized, spatially bounded . . ." (Appadurai 1996: 48). Operating through dramatic changes in transportation and communication technology that allow a faster and more intense and widespread circulation of goods, capital, ideas, and people across multiple spatial scales, globalization today is transforming our "cognitive maps," the ways in which we experience time and space (Jameson 1984).

Although contemporary globalization is a complex cluster of economic, sociopolitical, and cultural phenomena, at its core is a tensile interplay between what geographer David Harvey (1989) calls "time-space compression" and what sociologist Anthony Giddens (1990) terms "distantiation." On the one hand, there has been a shift in the hegemonic economies from a "Fordist-Keynesian" regime of production anchored on energy-intensive, heavy industries powered by a national working class and centered in the great cities to a flexible regime heavily reliant on service and knowledge-based sectors informed by the logic of deterritorialized networks. The new flexible economic regime has radically sped up the production and consumption of commodities throughout the world, accentuating the "volatility and ephemerality of fashions, products, production techniques, labour processes, ideas and ideologies, values and established practices" (Harvey 1989: 285). Thus, the new flexible regime of production amounts to an "annihilation of space through time" (Harvey 1989: 293). As the global mass media, the Internet, and culture industries touch even the most remote parts of the world, promoting a deluge of commodities often produced through decentered assembly lines spread throughout the world, we are now literally in each other's backyards. The ultimate "dematerialization of space" is cyberspace, which allows for instantaneous and simultaneous interaction among physical spaces that may be thousands of miles apart (Harvey 2000: 62).

As Harvey sees it, the faster pace of production and consumption has a close elective affinity not only with the postmodern skepticism toward grand narratives and its emphasis on the local, but also with the renewed public visibility of religion. Both postmodernism and religion offer re-territorializing and re-centering strategies, resources to gain a sense of (spatial) orientation in an increasingly baffling world.

> Deeper questions of meaning and interpretation . . . arise. The greater the ephemerality, the more pressing the need to discover or manufacture some kind of eternal truth. . . . The religious revival that has become much stronger since the late sixties and the search for authenticity and authority in politics (with all the accoutrements of nationalism and localism and of admiration for those charismatic and "protean" individuals with their Nietzschean "will to power") are cases in point. (Harvey 1989: 292)

Parallel to a drastic time-space compression, globalization also disembeds or deterritorializes social relations, rendering them independent of face-to-face interactions in specific locations. Through disembedding, social relations are "lifted out . . . from local contexts of interaction" and are "restructur[ed] across indefinite spans of time-space," giving rise to new, recombined cultural artifacts (Giddens 1990: 21). For example, transnational immigrants who have come in great numbers to work in the service sectors in New York or London often sustain close relations with their families in their countries of origin, forming what immigration scholars call transnational social fields that link multiple localities. These transnational social fields facilitate not only the movement of remittances, but also cultural and religious ideas, practices, identities, and institutional forms that change local ways of life in both the country of settlement and of origin (Levitt 2001).

Anthropologist Roger Rouse's work on Mexicans who have migrated from Aguililla, Michoacán, to Redwood City in Silicon Valley is illustrative of the simultaneous disembedding of social relations and spatiotemporal compression. Rather than seeing this migration as a linear movement between two distinct "communities," two spaces that are not coeval—Aguililla, a small farming town in the so-called Third World, and Redwood City, a thriving urban center in the postmodern informational economy—Rouse speaks of a transnational circuit. "Today, it is this circuit as a whole rather than any one locale that constitutes the principal setting in relation to which Aguilillans orchestrate their lives. Those living in Aguililla, for example, are as much affected by events in Redwood City as by developments in the *municipio* itself, and the same is true in reverse. Consequently, people monitor what is happening in other parts of the circuit as closely as they monitor what is going on immediately around them" (Rouse 1991: 14).

Religious organizations often provide the institutional infrastructure to make transnational livelihoods possible, serving as polycentric networks where diverse religious goods circulate, including audiotaped sermons, charismatic pastors or prophets, missionaries, sacred music, and relics. These ubiquitous, fluid, and polymorphous networks challenge the venerable congregational approach to religion, since this approach still assumes that lived and popular religions are, for the most part, circumscribed to the territorialized space of a congregation, itself anchored around the "axis mundi" of the temple, mosque, or synagogue. Furthermore, globalization's relentless dialectic of de-territorialization and re-territorialization has released religion from the constraints of the personal sphere and the container of the secular nation-state. Local religious practices such as shamanism now enter global flows, cross-fertilizing among themselves to give rise to new free-floating configurations such as New Age religions. Simultaneously, global religious movements like Pentecostalism become nucleated in diverse ways in the vernacular, offering personal salvation, self-improvement, or communal renewal, which the secular utopias of modernity have not been able to fulfill (Vásquez and Marquardt 2003; Vásquez 2005).

Given the wholesale spatiotemporal changes, we can no longer theorize space through the traditional modernist tools of the social sciences. According to Appadurai (1996: 32), "the new global cultural economy has to be seen as a complex, overlapping, disjunctive order that cannot any longer be understood in terms of existing center-periphery models (even those that might account for multiple centers and peripheries)." We need to move beyond not only Eliade's obsession with the center, but also beyond theories of the production of space, such as Smith's, which still rely on the simple interplay and tension between center and periphery. Appadurai (1996: 33–36) suggests that we need to understand emerging spatial configurations as shifting and irregular landscapes generated by the disjunctive, perspectival relationships among at least five global cultural flows. First, there are "ethnoscapes," landscapes "of persons who constitute the shifting world in which we live: tourists, immigrants, refugees, exiles, guest workers. . . ." Second, Appadurai points to "technoscapes" through which "technology, both high and low, both mechanical and informational, now moves at high speeds across various kinds of previously impervious boundaries." The third cluster of "scapes" are "financescapes," which highlight the hypermobility of capital. Fourth, "the distribution of the electronic capabilities to produce and disseminate information . . . now available to a growing number of private and public interests throughout the world" points to proliferating "mediascapes." These mediascapes "tend to be image-centered, narrative accounts of strips of reality" that are providing the raw cultural materials out of which increasing numbers of people throughout the world fashion their identities and life-worlds. Finally, there are "ideoscapes," "also concatenation of images, but they are often directly political and frequently have to do with the ideologies of states and the counterideologies of movements" vying for power.

What are the implications of Appadurai's alternative way of conceptualizing space for the study of religion? The fact that religions do not figure among his list of flows should not preclude fruitful use of his framework by religious scholars. In fact, Elizabeth McAlister has coined the term religioscapes to refer to "the subjective religious maps (and attendant theologies) of diasporic communities who are also in global flow and flux" (1998: 156). Along the same lines, Tweed introduces "sacroscapes" to refer to the traces, trails, and landscapes that religious flows sketch as they transform "peoples and places, the social arena and the natural terrain" (2006: 61, 62).

The lesson to be learned from Appadurai's notion of globalization as multiple, interactive and often contradictory flows and landscapes is that space and time are not opposed to each other. "Space is not static, nor time spaceless" (Massey 1994: 264). Moreover, "we need to conceptualize space as constructed out of interrelations, as simultaneous coexistence of social interactions and interactions at all spatial scales, from the most local level to the most global." This relational and dynamic view is necessary because "[s]pace is created out of the vast intricacies, the incredible complexities, of the interlocking and non-interlocking, and the networks of relations at every scale from local to global. What makes a particular view of these social relations specifically spatial is their simultaneity" (Massey 1994: 265).

Thus, religious studies scholars need to think of religion as a multi-scalar phenomenon, as dynamic discourses, practices, and deterritorializing and re-territorializing institutions that link the local and the translocal. Religion is simultaneously locative and mobile, involved in place-making at different scales from the personal, domestic, everyday, and community levels to the urban, national, regional, transnational, global, and cosmic scales (Knott 2008). The task of the religion scholar is to map out the operation of religion in each scale, elucidating the connections, tensions, and cross-fertilizations among scales. Rather than a frozen abstraction or an absolute reality, a particular sacred space is a relatively stable but contested moment at the intersection of multiple power-laden social relations.

Because lived space is not an abstraction, but a situated, time-bound convergence of relations, it is always a particular kind of space. There is a myriad of spaces: gendered, racial/ethnic, and class-inflected spaces, architectonic (built) or "natural" spaces, national or diasporic spaces, secular and religious spaces (Low and Lawrence-Zúñiga 2003). But what is the confluence of relations that make a space religious or sacred? Globalization scholars do not tell us much about this. We even saw above how David Harvey views religious place-making as a cluster of purely reactive practices in the face of the widespread dislocation produced by globalization. If religious practices are not granted their determinative power, how can the scholar analyze the interaction of spaces experienced or imagined as religious/sacred with other types of lived spaces?

In order to recover the determinative power of religion in multi-scalar analyses without appealing to the Eliadean sacred, Henri Lefebvre's notion of absolute space might be helpful. "Considered in itself—'absolutely'—absolute space is located nowhere. It has no place because it embodies *all* places" (Lefebvre 1991: 236). A religious space can readily become absolute space through its radically deterritorializing appeal to transcendence. This appeal may turn the locative micro-cosmos into a reflection of an imagined macro-cosmos or erase through a violent millenarian irruption other times and places, which are seen as contingent,. What makes religious spaces unique is that they present themselves not merely as localitive and translocative spaces, that they negotiate the tension between the local and the global, but that they invoke supra-historical or transhistorical transcendence. Very often, religion adds a powerful utopian, millenarian, and even apocalyptic dimension to lived spaces, imagining a radical, perhaps even violent, inversion of the present, a rectification of all the traumas and unfulfilled longings, and a return to a timeless state of grace.

Is Lefebvre not falling back on Eliade's theory of the ontological power of the sacred? Not so, because for Lefebvre, absolute space is "religious as well as political." It is a thing of this earth, a matter of transcendence within history, the paradoxical insertion of u-topia (a place that is a non-place in the ordinary sense) by emplaced bodies. Absolute space is not revealed from above, but produced and mobilized by situated social actors who attach it to particular landscapes and material objects through boundary-making rituals. However, the fact that absolute (religious) spaces are manufactured does not render them indistinguishable from any other socially constructed space. That absolute space is summoned through a cosmic imagination does not make it less effective. Quite the contrary, absolute space derives its totalizing power, its power to set things apart, to generate and overturn classifications and hierarchies, from the fact that it is imagined as utterly de-territorialized and de-territorializing. In the production of religious space as absolute space, "the imaginary is transformed into the real" (Lefebvre 1991: 251). This is the reason why for Lefebvre the absolute space of religion is not a mere epiphenomenon of other social processes. Rather this space is "both imaginary and real," "at once and indistinguishably mental and social" (Lefebvre 1991: 240, 251). Religious spatial practices have their own determinative power as they enter multi-scalar relations with other spatial practices.

A good example of how Lefebvre's notion of absolute space helps make sense of the specificity of religion's contribution to place-making is Sam Gill's genealogy of the Mother Earth concept in Native American Religions. When European Americans moved west, they brought with them a strong sense of manifest destiny, understanding their travels and settlement as a civilizing mission. This civilizing mission was predicated on a locative vision of space; space had to divided, settled, and distributed under the logic of private property, as spelled out in treaties. Against this "secular" locative vision, Native American groups constructed a religious perspective. They appealed "to the actions of a creator figure who established the proper order in the act of creation. This creator existed before the earth. This creator made the earth. This creator, sometimes using elements of the earth, made the people and all things living on earth and named them, thus giving them identity and responsibility" (Gill 1987: 64). Because the creator did not divide the land during the act of creation and because it gave Native Americans "chieftainship of the land," a special responsibility to guard the proper order of things, the locative claims of European Americans are not legitimate. Ultimate authority rests with the creator. "No other authority can supersede this, not even that of the president of the United States" (Gill 1987: 65).

Native American groups thus articulated a counter-hegemonic supra-locative religious view, appealing to the absolute space of creation that contains all spaces, that erases the personal spaces carved out by the settlers. However, Gill is clear that this vision was enmeshed in history and implicated in the politics of encounter. Although relying on a supra-locative authority, the appeal to absolute space is part of a political hermeneutics. What was initially a narrative that Native Americans constructed around the metaphor of motherhood, as a trope for interdependence and care, in order to establish "some commonality with their oppressors by which to communicate effectively their reluctance to be severed from their lands," eventually, as European American encroachment intensified, became a distinctive divinity—Mother Earth (Gill 1987: 66). Gill notes that the concept of Mother Earth is relatively new among Native Americans: "the earth was not formally referred to as a mother figure or goddess until the twentieth century" (1987: 145). By transforming "metaphor into divinity," or as Lefebvre would put it, transforming the imaginary into the real, Native Americans were able to build an effective pan-indigenous identity that could resist the secular locative practices of the European American settlers.

> Mother Earth as an Indian goddess serves a need for the alliance of peoples whose cultural identities have faced enormous crises and transformations, often due to loss of land or the forced revision of their ancestral relationships with land. Mother Earth gives a primordial and spiritual base, and thus religious authority and responsibility, to the Indian identity. She is the basis on which Indians articulate the superiority of their way of life over against "White Americans. . . ." (Gill 1987: 148)

This example shows how religion enables transcendence within history through absolute space. Absolute space results from the appeal to u-topia—the place that is no place because it is all places—by embodied, emplaced beings. That absolute space emerges in the midst of human history and culture does not mean that it lacks its own ontogenetic power, that it is the mere reflection of social dynamics. Quite the contrary, the introduction of the absolute space of religion has the power of ethnogenesis, the power of creating a new social formation, a pan-indigenous people. This power, however, need not rest on Eliade's notion of a supra-historical sacred.

Religion, in sum, generates distinctive and effective forms of spatiality, which while not reducible to other dynamics of place-making, are immanent to the life-world. Religion is not only locative and translocative, but also supralocative, capable of expressing transcendence, absolute space, in the midst of the spaces of everyday life. I would like to close this chapter by discussing a current approach to religion that takes into account all these spatial operations and integrates the concepts, methods, and debates I have explored thus far.

THOMAS TWEED: BRINGING IT ALL TOGETHER

One of the most fruitful contemporary attempts to build a framework for the multi-scalar study of religion is Thomas Tweed's work on diasporic religions. He explores the spatial practices of Cuban immigrants in Miami who have left

Cuba in successive waves following the revolution in 1959. Because these immigrants feel they cannot return to Cuba until the end of the Communist government, they have built an exilic space, mapping through architecture and rituals a re-memorialized Cuban cartography into Miami. In the process, they have constructed a powerful collective identity as authentic Cubans, the defenders of true Cuban culture and history, which the revolution has usurped. Tweed calls this collective identity a "diasporic nationalism" that fuses the here with the there and the present with the past and future, dwelling in the present in United States and crossing the Bay of Biscayne to imagine themselves in Cuba as it was before the revolution and as it will be once more.

Some of the key landmarks in the transposed imagined Cuban identity are religious. For example, Cuban Americans have built a shrine to Our Lady of Charity, the patroness of Cuba. Inside the shrine there is a huge mural representing Cuban history (minus Fidel Castro) with the Virgin at the center, in effect, sacralizing the narrative that Cuban exiles have constructed.

> At the zenith of the mural, two angels ascend to heaven through the clouds, wrapped in the Cuban flag. There is nothing subtle about all this, and few Cuban American visitors to the shrine fail to notice the links established between the Virgin and Cuban soil.
>
> There are less explicit but still powerful expressions of attachment to homeland embedded in the shrine's natural and built environment. The shrine stands only yards from the bay, and water recalls both the geography of their island nation and the legend of their patroness. The shrine also was designed so that the statue of the Virgin would stand in a direct line with Cuba. (Tweed 1999: 144–45)

To make sense of the rich and complex ways in which Cubans in Miami draw from religion to deal with their existential predicament, Tweed borrows from J. Z. Smith. Cuban diasporic religion is locative, since it helps the exiles carve out a place, a space of livelihood, in the midst of a country that often does not understand and fully accept them. This diasporic religion is also translocative and transtemporal because it allows a strong, immediate spiritual, emotional, and embodied connection between two places that are physically separated in time and space. Finally, going beyond Smith and echoing Lefebvre's notion of absolute space, Cuban diasporic religion is supralocative in the sense that it establishes a vertical link between human and sacred histories, between the desire for a Cuba returned to its mythical state of harmony and abundance and the transcendent power of Our Lady of Charity. This vertical link endures beyond the contingencies of secular history, buttressing hope in its eventual eschatological fulfillment. As in the case of Mother Earth for Native

Americans, the supralocative contributes to ethnogenesis. Pushed to the limits, the vertical link may dissolve human time and distinctions altogether, generating sheer u-topia: Cuba as the New Jerusalem.

In Tweed's multi-scalar perspective, "religions can map and inhabit worlds of meaning in at least three ways. These might be described as *locative*, in which religion is associated with a homeland where the group now resides; *supralocative*, which names the inclination in later generations of some diasporic peoples to diminish or deny the significance of both the homeland and the adopted land in their religious life; and *translocative* . . . which refers to the tendency among many first- and second-generation immigrants to symbolically move between homeland and new land" (Tweed 1997: 94–95).

Tweed's work on the spatiotemporal dynamics of diasporic religion has been very influential. Paul Christopher Johnson (2007), for example, builds on Tweed's insights to explore the practices of Garifuna shamans. He adds the notion of "multiple diasporic horizons," the ability of these shamans to bring into focus the multiple homelands of Africa, St. Vincent, Honduras, Belize, and more lately New York City, as they jostle with each other to establish the authenticity and authority of their rituals. Johnson also stresses the materializing practices that accompany the process of mapping religion onto new territories. Artifacts that have been brought from the homeland become supercharged with nostalgia, desire, hope, and the power to awe. When these objects are not present, practitioners sacralize other artifacts in the new place of settlement. This selection and sacralization operates through what Johnson calls "metaphoric, metonymic, and synecdochic hooking" (2007: 55). As in the case of the shrine to Our Lady of Charity, Garifuna shamans chose new ritual objects and sacred spaces that are similar to those in the imagined homeland, trigger buried, embodied topophilic memories, or condense all previous religious signification and emotion.[8]

In his latest work, Tweed radicalizes the multi-scalar impetus of his ethnographic work among Cuban Americans. Drawing from Appadurai, Deleuze, Guattari, and anthropologist James Clifford,[9] he proposes a "hydrodynamics of religion" (Tweed 2006: 172), the study of how multidirectional religious flows converge with other organic-cultural flows to form a "swirl of transfluvial currents that enable people to dwell in particular places and move across space." He writes: "I decided . . . that two . . . orienting metaphors are most useful for analyzing what religion is and what it does: spatial metaphors (*dwelling* and *crossing*) signal that religion is about finding a place and moving across space, and aquatic metaphors (*confluences* and *flows*) signal that religions are not reified substances but complex processes" (Tweed 2006: 59).

The strengths of this spatial approach are many. To begin with, Tweed takes seriously the idea that space is not opposed to time. For him, space is truly dynamic and agentic. This dynamism issues from the fact that, in Tweed's theory, religious mobility is "spatialized," shown to carve out various landscapes of livelihood, "to map, construct, and inhabit ever-widening spaces: the body, the home, the homeland, and the cosmos" (Tweed 2006: 84). Simultaneously, the theory "mobilizes" space through the notion of protean place-making and space-crossing flows. Note here how far we have gone from J. Z. Smith's still-dualistic metaphors of the "central-locative" and "peripheral-utopian" visions of the world.

Second, the metaphor of multidirectional, convergent flows enables scholars to explore the "mutual intercausality of religion, economy, society, and politics" (Tweed 2006: 60). Religion is thus properly recontextualized and rematerialized, embedded in the diversity of human practices that are part and parcel of *Dasein*, of "being in the world." While religion is not reducible to other more foundational flows, Tweed does not give it any privileged ontological status. Along these lines, the use of aquatic metaphors "avoids essentializing religious traditions as static, isolated, and immutable substances, and so moves toward more satisfying answers to questions about how religions relate to one another and transform each other through contact" (Tweed 2006: 60). Aquatic metaphors, thus, make it possible to examine the multiple roles of religion in the interaction between the global and the local, and all the meso-levels within this tensile pair. These metaphors give us powerful analytical tools to study how religion enters contemporary and age-old processes of globalization and transnationalism.

Finally, Tweed's theory of religion also decenters the theorist, providing him/her resources to resist the Cartesian anxiety, the need to find an Archimedean point and a panoptical divine eye that could capture the totality of religious phenomena. For Tweed, theory is "embodied travel," a "purposeful wondering," that is not a "stationary view of a static terrain. It is not geography or chorography—or even localized topography of indigenous mapmakers. It is more like 'dynography,' a term used in medicine to describe the computer-generated representations of blood flows through arteries or of the bodily movement of children with spastic cerebral palsy" (Tweed 2006: 11). As an embodied, emplaced being, the theorist is caught in and enabled by place-making and space-crossing flows. His/her theories are themselves organic-cultural flows, shifting metaphors that make it possible to encounter the world from a particular perspective. Like Appadurai's notion of scapes, Tweed's hydrodynamics of religion are inescapably perspectival.

With Tweed we have a fully reflexive, non-reductive materialist spatial theory of religion. As he puts it, "[a]s spatial practices, religions are active verbs linked with unsubstantial nouns by bridging prepositions: *from, with, in, between, through,* and, most important, *across.* Religions designate where we are *from,* whom we are *with,* and prescribe how we move *across*" (Tweed 2006: 79).

In the next chapter, I build on and challenge Tweed's hydrodynamic theory of religion, focusing on two key dimensions that he acknowledges but does not develop sufficiently. First, there is the issue of power and resistance, which was central to theorists such as Smith, Foucault, and de Certeau. The question is whether the heavy reliance on aquatic metaphors may render Tweed's theory excessively anti-structural, blinding it to powerful and proliferating processes of spatially mediated control, surveillance, and exclusion that are accompanying globalization today. Then, I return to the matter of the body and nature, particularly to the ways in which religious and cultural flows are enabled, constrained, and channeled by ecology. I will argue that the notion of networks provides a salutary corrective to the anti-structural force of Tweed's notion of flows, while preserving the dynamism and open-endedness of his theory.

11

Mobility, Networks, and Ecology

Nature, society, and culture mutually condition and codetermine each other
as a result of the nonlinear dynamics of networks.

> —*Mark C. Taylor (2007: 30)*

What will nature permit us to do here? What will nature help us to do here?

> —*Wendell Berry (1987: 146)*

The previous chapter explored the ways in which religion is intimately connected with the production of multiple spaces. We saw that the spatial turn in
the humanities and social sciences, precipitated by contemporary globalization's dialectical interplay of time-space compression and distantiation, has
made necessary and possible the multi-scalar study of religion. In particular,
geographers, such as Yi-Fu Tuan, Henri Lefebvre, Edward Soja, David Harvey,
and Doreen Massey, in conversation with J. Z. Smith, Sam Gill, David Chidester,
Edward Linenthal, Kim Knott, Thomas Tweed and other religion scholars
working on spatial matters, provide useful tools to construct a dynamic, relational, and holistic view of religious spaces. These scholars show us that, on the
one hand, it is important to study the religious practices of everyday life in their
richness, creativity, and diversity through the thick ethnographic description
of congregations, urban ecologies, and other lived spaces. On the other hand,
we need to document how local religious practices are embedded in, connected
to, and reflective of translocal religious and nonreligious flows and processes.
We need to understand how globalization in its multiple dimensions becomes
territorialized in local settings, through the practices of situated individuals
who reproduce and/or contest it.

I concluded chapter 10 with a discussion of Tweed's hydrodynamics of religion as an example of a promising emerging synthesis of (1) the long-standing
concern for sacred space in religious studies; (2) the analysis of practice,
power, and resistance in the process of place-making in critical geography;
and (3) the growing literature on mobility from globalization, transnationalism,

and diasporic studies. Tweed fruitfully combines the spatial metaphors of crossing and dwelling with aquatic tropes, including flows and confluences, to emplace religion in non-essentialist ways. In this chapter, I build on and go beyond Tweed's hydrodynamics of religion by taking a closer look at mobility and embeddedness. I am concerned that in his justified drive to challenge static and essentialist readings of religion, Tweed is in danger of falling into what scholars of immigration Andreas Wimmer and Nina Glick-Schiller (2003) call an excessive "fluidism," which reproduces the view of globalization as a totalizing and inevitable reality, a reality where all social identities and boundaries have become ephemeral and all power asymmetries have been erased.[1] The task is to acknowledge that complexity, connectivity, and mobility are preponderant features of our present age without ignoring strong counter-vailing logics of segregation, surveillance, and control that also accompany today's globalization.

I close this chapter by returning to the emplaced body, more concretely to the body embedded in nature, in order to refine, extend, and add specificity to Tweed's claim that religions are "confluences of organic-cultural flows that intensify joy and confront suffering by drawing on human and suprahuman forces to make homes and cross boundaries" (2006: 54). I elaborate Tweed's notion of the "organic" further in order to bring ecology into the conversation on religious emplacement.

NOT THE "BODY WITHOUT ORGANS": A NEW GLOBAL MOBILITY REGIME

For the past five years, I have been co-directing a study of Latino immigrants who are settling in new destinations like Siler City, North Carolina; Omaha, Nebraska; and Marietta, Georgia.[2] In contrast to immigrants who came to the traditional gateway cities of New York, Los Angeles, and Miami, Latino immigrants in new destinations cannot rely on established networks to facilitate their integration, to assist them in the process of crossing and dwelling. These recent immigrants are especially vulnerable to the power of local, state, and federal agencies that are harassing them as part of a growing anti-immigrant climate. In this context, the religious organizations that immigrants build become ever more crucial to their survival, very often providing the only spaces where immigrants can find protection, solidarity, intimacy, and spiritual and financial help. It is precisely this reality of control and exclusion as well as resistance that I wish to underscore as I reflect on Tweed's valuable work.

From the point of view of these immigrants, Tweed's theory of religion over-emphasizes mobility. Since the first of July, 2007, Latino immigrants in Georgia, both documented and undocumented, report a generalized climate of fear and uncertainty as the state began to implement SB 529, the Georgia Security and Immigration Compliance Act (Lovato 2008). Among other things, this law empowers the local police to check the legal status of any suspicious person and to report any undocumented person directly to ICE (Immigration and Customs Enforcement). Many of the immigrants we have interviewed told stories of police officers hiding by traffic lights, waiting for any Latino-looking individuals to make small mistakes, such as going slightly over the speed limit or not putting on the turn signal when switching lanes, so they can stop drivers and check papers. Our informants also tell us of the fear they have when driving without a license, since the law makes it impossible for any undocumented immigrants to secure one. Under these conditions, a fender-bender could result in spending days in a local jail and being deported while their children, who often are U.S. citizens, can only stand by helplessly. Many immigrants tell us that they now go out only to do what is necessary to survive: they leave home to go to work, buy groceries, pick up kids from school, or maybe to attend church, where they feel a small measure of safety. However, even churches are not safe places anymore. In Oklahoma, which has adopted another harsh law (HB 1804), there are reports that enforcement officials, knowing that centrality of religion for Latin Americans, have intercepted immigrants entering churches (Scaperlanda 2008).

There continue to be flows of all kinds among immigrants in Georgia and Oklahoma. They are still sending remittances to their home towns in Oaxaca, Chiapas, and Huehuetenango, often to build the local Catholic Church or to support the transnational ministry of Pentecostal churches. In fact, some of our interviewees tell us that, given their precarious legal status, they have been working harder, often taking two or three jobs, to send more money to Mexico, Guatemala, and Brazil, knowing that they might get caught and get deported at any moment. Nevertheless, these flows are strikingly susceptible to the panoptical control of the state. The mobilities that are a normal part of everyday life have become perilous.

The issue of undocumented immigration is a complex one, and reasonable people may disagree on how to solve it in a comprehensive and humane fashion. Nonetheless, our fieldwork raises an unavoidable question: how can we theorize fluidity and mobility while taking into account what, borrowing from Foucault, I call transnational biopower, the increasing power of nation-states to monitor, regulate, exclude, and exploit migrant populations? Thus far, the globalization literature has tended to stress movement, heterogeneity, paradox, and hybridity. This emphasis is a much-needed corrective to readings of globalization that present it as an inevitable economic process that flattens all differences and localities. Tweed's hydrodynamics of religion represents a valuable contribution to this correction.

However, as the example of the immigrants we are studying shows, globalization is not just about cultural mélange; it is also about the radical concentration of wealth in the metropole, the reinvigoration of the national-security state, and the emergence of virulent nativist movements. The case of undocumented Latino immigrants in the United States is neither insignificant nor unusual. Rather, it is part of much larger and widespread power configurations. Today's world is not like Deleuze and Guattari's "body without organs" (1987: 149–66). On the contrary, it is a body full of striations, open wounds, and scars. Mobility and connectivity have been accompanied by an exacerbation of socioeconomic inequalities. For example, in 1960 the per capita GDP of the twenty richest countries in the world was eighteen times that of the twenty poorest countries. By 1995, the gap more than doubled, to thirty-seven times (World Bank 2001). "The picture that emerges is increasingly one of two very different groups of countries: those that have benefited from development, and those that have been left behind. An unprecedented number of countries saw development slide backwards in the 1990s. In 46 countries people are poorer today than in 1990. In 25 countries more people go hungry today than a decade ago" (Robinson 2004).

How then do we study religion in motion without uncritically celebrating mobility or falling back on the old static, essentialist, and functionalist models of society and culture? Arjun Appadurai's characterization of globalization as the disjunctive interaction among scapes and Tweed's readings of religions as a "swirl of transfluvial currents" are insufficient. Following theorists such as Michael Hardt, Antonio Negri, and Zygmunt Bauman, I argue that today's globalization can be better characterized as a "mobility regime." Today, global capitalism thrives as much as on mobility and deterritorialization as on the operation of integrated systems of surveillance, control, and containment (Hardt and Negri 2000: 45). On the one hand, globalization encourages people to migrate by undermining local ways of life and beaming cosmopolitan images of wealth and success in the metropole. On the other hand, as the tightening of immigration laws from the United States to Europe to South Africa demonstrates, globalization involves limiting the movement of people. This interplay between mobility and containment/closure allows for a new global bio-politics, the extraction of surplus from dislocated individuals, who, as "illegal" immigrants, provide cheap and disposable labor without the right to demand any recognition and political power from their host societies.

According to Shamir (2005: 200), "the engine of the contemporary mobility regime is a 'paradigm of suspicion' that conflates the perceived threats of crime, immigration, and terrorism (hence the notion of 'integrated risk management'), and . . . the technology of intervention that enables it is biosocial profiling." The result is a "gated globe" in which selective osmosis regulates and monitors the flows of people (Cunningham 2004). "Thought of in spatial terms, globalization is a process constitutive of a global mobility regime that aspires to screen those substances (viruses, people, and hazardous materials) that may cross the boundaries of some designated social containers (e.g., national borders and gated communities) from those that may not" (Shamir 2005: 208–9). This is why Bauman claims that today "mobility has become the most powerful and most coveted stratifying factor, the stuff of which the new, increasingly world-wide, social, political, economic, and cultural hierarchies are daily built and rebuilt" (1998: 9).

Since the post-9/11 gated globe is characterized by "enclosed mobilities, regulated transnationalisms, and monitored rather than simple flexible sovereignties" (Cunningham 2004: 332), the dialectic of domination and resistance must be front and center in our social analyses of religion in motion. To account for this dialectic, Tweed's theory of religion must be enriched with relational metaphors beyond the aquatic tropes. For example, Tweed writes:

> Sacrospaces, as I understand these religious confluences, are not static. They are not fixed, built environments—as the allusions to landscape in the term might imply—although religions do transform the built environment. I have in mind much more dynamic images. Imagine the wispy smoke left by a skywriter, the trail of an electron, the path of a snowball down a steep icy hill, or the rippled wake left by a speeding boat. Whatever else religions do, they move across time and space. They are not static. And they have effects. They leave traces. They leave trails. (2006: 62)

At stake in today's globalization are not just traces or trails but sharp boundaries, fortified borders, stipulated and illicit paths, strategies of inclusion and exclusions, and postcolonial practices for generating and managing difference. And while the boundaries and borders created may be permeable, contingent, and contested, they are binding. They have the power to mark bodies, create (criminal) alien subjects, and channel flows of goods, ideas, money, and people in certain directions, according to certain power logics. Tweed is certainly careful not to celebrate flows uncritically. He readily acknowledges that "sometimes trails are sites for mourning." He also refers to "compelled passages and constrained crossings," in which religions may "justify the forced or coerced migration of peoples, as with slavery to the United States and Latin America, where slavery's Christian advocates in the Atlantic World appealed to sacred narratives to defend their practices" (Tweed 2006: 135). However, most of the metaphors Tweed uses to illustrate how religion moves tend to underplay how social and religious practices are both "structured" and "structuring," as Bourdieu (1977: 72–95) would put it.

I suggest that the notions of networks and the associated concept of social fields can provide a good counterpoint to the excessive anti-structuralism of hydraulic models. Tweed himself mentions networks throughout *Crossing and Dwelling*. He even cites Michael Mann's point that "societies are constituted of multiple overlapping and intersecting sociospatial networks of power" (Mann 1986: 1) as a helpful reminder that "power as well as meaning is involved" (Tweed 2006: 210). However, in the end, Tweed concludes that "flow is a better metaphor than network for cultural analysis" (2006: 210). For him, networks are derivative traces of motion, relatively stable reifications of flows. "To say that religions are organic-cultural flows, then, is to suggest they are confluences of organic channels and cultural currents that conjoin to create institutional networks that, in turn, prescribe, transmit, and transform tropes, beliefs, values, emotions, artifacts, and rituals" (2006: 69). This understanding of networks as residual, structuralist moments in the process of religious generativity runs the danger of representing flows as disembedded and decontextualized realities, without particular agents, vehicles, trajectories, and targets. Even Deleuze and Guattari, who rely heavily on aquatic metaphors, see flows as produced, circulated, and consumed by machinic assemblages, networks of interconnected desiring-machines. In the same manner, religious flows are always produced by individuals and institutions embedded in sociocultural and ecological networks of relations, which shape and are shaped by confluences. Praxis and structure are not separate dimensions of our life-world, with one preceding the other. They are mutually implicative. Further, mobility does not undermine this recursive relation by heightening the itinerancy of practices against the staticity of reified networks and institutions, which then seek to control flows post facto. Mobility only underscores how much practices and structures are from the outset dependant on each other to provide a relative measure of stability to our experience.

Tweed is aware of the limits of his "hydrodynamics of religion." Toward the end of *Crossing and Dwelling*, he asks:

> if religious flows are nonlinear systems, like heart rhythms or faucet drippings, does that mean that the only appropriate aim is interpretation, not prediction or control, as some scholars who have pondered the implications of chaos theory

for the humanities and social sciences have argued? If so, what would that interpretation entail, for example in historical analysis? . . . [I]f we try to trace the complex flows that emerge from "initial conditions" will interpreters be washed away while trying to chart the transfluence of innumerable causal currents? . . . Which flows should the interpreter follow, and if the answer is all of them, and more, then would that ever allow analysis of more than a single event, and even then only with the sense that surely we have missed some of the transverse currents that have propelled religious history?" (Tweed 2006: 173)

In other words, if the world is nothing more than an ever-changing sea of amorphous flows, how can we study it? Paradoxically, the hydrodynamics of religion is in danger of washing the positioned scholar away and ultimately succumbing to the Cartesian anxiety by offering "the view from everywhere at once or nowhere in particular" (182). According to Cunningham (2004: 334), "one of the central fallacies of the turn to a porous world and an emphasis on cultural flows has been the assumption that flow connotes mobility and, consequently, fluid, unpredictable interconnection. Flows, of course, can equally connote boundedness, exclusion and the systematic regulation of movement." Moreover, can chaos theory, to which Tweed tentatively points, provide sufficient tools to identify, analyze, and critique persistent, egregious, and intransigent forms of power, such as those that many immigrants face in their daily lives? In a gated globe, regulated by panoptical regimes of mobility and characterized by selective osmosis, we need metaphors that do not "overtheorize" globalization "in terms of social openness and undertheorize [it] in terms of social closure" (Shamir 2005: 214). I turn to the notion of networks as an epistemological and methodological move to re-emplace global flows and Tweed's hydrodynamics of religion.

TOWARD A NETWORKS APPROACH TO RELIGION: THE BUILDING BLOCKS

The concept of networks is, of course, hardly novel. Network analysis has a long trajectory in the social sciences (Mitchell 1969; Granovetter 1973; Castells 1996). It has also had a distinguished career in the sociology of migration (Boyd 1989; Portes 1995; Menjívar 2000). In the study of immigrant religions, the concept of networks is emerging as tool to enrich and critique work on territorially bounded congregations, which has been the dominant paradigm in the field (Ebaugh and Chafetz 2002; Vásquez and Marquardt 2003).

From the perspective of religious studies, the language of networks may appear reductionist and anti-humanist, failing to take into account the symbolic, affective, and axiological aspects of religious life. "[T]he structure of a network itself says very little about the qualitative nature of relationships comprising it [or, for that matter, the experiences embedded in them]" (Vertovec 2003: 647). There is also the danger of functionalism, the assumption that networks work primarily to unify and balance self-contained systems. Finally, we must confront the contradictions of a hardcore methodological holism, which hypothesizes networks as not only self-generating agents, but unitary actors with their own consciousness and intentionality. This is a version of the long-standing problem of agency: "networks research typically rests on a default conceptualization of human beings acted upon by networks rather than acting on them and through them" (Smilde 2005: 758).

To avoid these dangers, we must reconceptualize networks. Rather than assuming that they are always closed, linear systems that automatically integrate constituent parts in a harmonious whole, we need to realize networks take different morphologies that evolve across time and space. While some networks will, at particular junctures, be relatively simple and unidirectional, others will be flexible, highly dynamic, nontotalizing, and multidirectional structures of relationality. For example, Brazilian immigrants in Pompano Beach in South Florida sustain durable relations not just with various communities in Brazil, each with its own regional flavor, but also with groups in Boston, New York, and New Jersey as well as with growing Brazilian populations in Orlando and Atlanta. Interacting business and church networks are crucial in linking these various locations, facilitating movement and exchange across state and national boundaries. To cite another, more visible example: "Structured around dispersed nodes that communicate with one another in nonlinear space, the al-Qaeda network relies on neither hierarchical chain of command nor conventional rules of engagement. Rather it mobilizes nimble, dispersed, and highly elusive units capable of penetrating and disrupting, or even destroying, massive structures" (Cooke and Lawrence 2005: 25).

Networks mark relatively stable but always contested differentials of power, of inclusion and exclusion, of cooperation and conflict, of boundary-crossing and boundary-making. Networks are sociopolitically, culturally, and ecologically embedded relational processes that constrain and enable practices as diverse as place-making and identity-construction (Dicken et al. 2001). The worldviews, beliefs, and behaviors of particular individuals cannot be mechanically read from their location in a given network. Referring back to the work of theorists of practice discussed in chapter 9, including Marx and Bourdieu, we must acknowledge that a networks approach can only allow us to explore how positionality in a field of power differentials shapes and is shaped by relatively stable and embodied dispositions, propensities, and competences to act in certain ways. At their best, network approaches are anti-essentialist. They allow us to analyze "processes in terms of patterned interrelationships rather than on the basis of individual essences" (Wellman and Berkowitz 1988: 4). Network analysis enables us to take a praxis-oriented approach, focusing on how individuals engage in "invention within limits" (Bourdieu 1977: 96) by drawing from resources available to them through the shifting fields of relations and webs of exchanges they sustain.

Bourdieu's notion of social fields enhances further networks analysis, adding a macro-contextual dimension. Social fields are relatively bounded domains of intermeshed practices inhabited by individuals with differential access to resources of various types, including economic, political, educational, and religious. A social field is "a set of multiple interlocking networks of social relationships through which ideas, practices, and resources are unequally exchanged, organized, and transformed" (Levitt and Glick-Schiller 2004: 1009). In this sense, a social field is both "an arbitrary social construct" and "objectified history" (Bourdieu 1990: 66, 67). In it, "individuals do not move about . . . in a random way, partly because they are subject to the forces which structure this space . . . and partly because they resist the forces of the field with their specific inertia, that is, their properties, which may exist in embodied form, as dispositions, or in objectified form, in goods, qualifications, etc." (Bourdieu 1984: 110). Networks and social fields define "probable trajectories" for individuals and groups. They delineate the horizons of what is possible in any given juncture.[3]

As Foucault (1980) has demonstrated, power is intertwined with the production of knowledge and articulation of selfhood. Networks, therefore, are not just shifting and multicentered capillaries through which power and economic, social, and cultural capitals circulate. As temporal and spatialized forms of relationality, they are also negotiated "phenomenological realities" (White 1992), consisting of narratives, practices, cognitive maps, and micro-histories. Meaning, orientation, and intentionality are not just commodities that circulate but are constitutive of the networks themselves (Emirbayer and Goodwin 1994). Within and through networks, actors carve out spaces to dwell, itineraries, and everyday routines, drawing from religious symbols and tropes to reflect on and orient their own praxis and to "sacralize" nature and built environments.

The insight that networks are phenomenological realities can be traced as far back as Marcel Mauss's pioneering work on the gift. He argues that practices like potlatch among indigenous peoples in North America and kula in

Papua New Guinea are not simply the aggregation of individual transactions. They entail dense networks or "systems of total exchange of services," which bind the participants into a shared moral economy that obligates them to give, receive, and reciprocate. The objects that circulate in these networks are highly charged with moral and emotional energy, as the participants deposit bits of themselves in these objects, animating them, giving them "a magical or religious hold." In "the things exchanged during the potlatch, a power is present that forces gifts to be passed around, to be given, and returned" (Mauss 1990: 43). These things have "productive power itself. It is not a mere sign and pledge; it is also a sign and a pledge of wealth, the magical and religious symbol of rank and plenty" (Mauss 1990: 44). Networks of exchange shape individual and group identities through the distribution of honor, prestige, status, and authority. Thus, these networks are necessarily invested with conflict, competition, and the power to include and to exclude. Despite the fact that in today's world, exchanges have come to be dominated by the contractual, calculative, and utilitarian logic of the capitalist market, Mauss (1990: 69) observes that networks are not totally disenchanted. They still strong hold moral and "sentimental" value, reflected in "the joy of public giving; the pleasure in generous expenditure on the arts, in hospitality, and in the private and public festival."[4]

Extending Mauss's seminal insights, I would like to highlight the spatial dimensions of the moral economies networks create. Borrowing from American religious historian Amy DeRogatis (2003), I argue that networks may embody and produce moral geographies, "maps of piety and behavior." As an illustration, let us go back to the example of Brazilians in Pompano Beach, Florida. These immigrants lack the established immigrant organizations available in Miami and face a decentered exurban space of sprawling shopping malls and gated communities connected only by busy thoroughfares. They thus try to carve out defensive spaces anchored in the domestic sphere. More specifically, they map out their homes in South Florida as "slices of Brazil abroad" (*pedaços do Brasil na distância*) through the prominent display of Brazilian flags and other symbols of the homeland. Alternatively, they sacralize their domestic spaces, turning them into "bits of heaven" (*pedaços do céu*), marked by homemade altars to their patron saints. As part of this sacralization, Brazilians set their homes, as realms of peace, safety, and intimacy, against the evil space of the street, which is construed as dangerous, cruel, and impersonal. For Brazilian Pentecostals, this moral map, built on the good-evil and purity-danger axes, dovetails with a Manichean cosmos that opposes those who have been baptized in the Spirit (the church) against the temptation-filled outside world.

Central to the Brazilians' sacralization of the home is the weaving of interpersonal networks with relatives and friends from the same village in Brazil.

These networks, which are often imbued with intimacy, trust, emotional attachment, and meaning, render the sacred domestic space mobile and transportable, stretching it over the hostile and baffling exurban environment. This explains why many of our informants told us that their churches are like their "home away from home," both in Florida and Brazil, or like "my mother's house, where I feel accepted and safe." However, this process of sacralization and extension of the domestic space is inflected by power and conflict, since many times Brazilian immigrants are forced to live in crowded apartments, where "no one knows each other" and "everybody works all the time." In situations like these, the "home" in Florida becomes a space of alienation and mistrust, the antithesis of the remembered home in Brazil. Moreover, narratives of home among Brazilian women in the immigrant networks are often different from those among Brazilian men, stressing the never-ending, unrecognized struggles to keep the family fed and healthy rather than celebrating the warmth of the domestic space.

We should, thus, not assume that intimacy, trust, and emotional attachment are automatic ingredients of all networks. Sometimes constraints, proximity, or lack of resources compel people to enter into networks on the basis of competition or antipathy. This is often the case for Evangelical Protestant churches in their missionary work among immigrants. Immigrants may circulate among various churches despite strong attempts by pastors to disqualify each other as not upholding a sufficiently orthodox message.

Still, even in the midst of conflict, the Brazilian example demonstrates that narratives, meaning, emotion, and morality are constitutive of the religious networks immigrants build. This is precisely where the non-reductive materialist study of mobile religion can benefit from the insights of thinkers working in the hermeneutic tradition, such as Paul Ricoeur (1974).[5] As immigrants move and encounter obstacles across the networks, they "emplot" their experiences drawing from narratives of exile, conversion, spiritual pilgrimage and renewal, homecoming, or the coming of reign of God. These narratives often provide the motivation to migrate as well as the cognitive and affective frames to render movement and settlement meaningful. As one Brazilian Catholic told our research team: "[When I came to this country,] I did not have anyone to rely on: my childhood friends, my family, or the certainty [*segurança*] of being in my own country. Well, I thought, now I can only rely on God. I have to hold on to him to be able to keep going. And so once I saw myself alone in an ocean, shipwrecked, and he was my only life raft."

Given the intersubjective meaning inherent in religious networks, they can generate "counter-publics" (Fraser 1997), alternative spaces of sociability in tension with the normalizing power of the state. Often these spaces nurture discourses and practices that contest dominant secular readings of civil society and citizenship. For instance, religious movements such as Charismatic Christianity and the Islamic revival in the so-called Third World and among immigrant communities in Europe and the United States can be partially understood as transnational "popular publics," "intentionally organized relational context[s] in which a specific network of people from popular classes seek to bridge to other networks, form coalitions, and expand the influence of its discourses" (Smilde 2004: 181). In the case of the Islamic revival movement, the new popular publics challenge not only taken-for-granted constructions of masculinity and femininity, but also the stress on unencumbered individualism as well as the private-public split at the heart of Western bourgeois civil society. As with any social reality, these publics are "not liminal 'free spaces' but structured relational contexts in which new articulations of structure can occur" (Smilde 2004: 181).

STUDYING RELIGION IN MOTION THROUGH NETWORKS: THE AGENDA

To avoid fetishizing the concept of networks, we need to specify the morphologies that religious networks adopt. How are the conduits configured? Are these conduits gendered? Is access to them mediated by variables like class, race, ethnicity, time of arrival, and status? More generally, who are the key actors involved in the transnational, global, and diasporic religious networks? Are they religious elites, missionaries, itinerant pastors, pilgrims, and/or religious tourists? In what spatiotemporal scales do they operate? By what specific mechanisms? Informal exchanges or formalized chains? What kind of media are involved (from familial or kinship-based networks to electronic media)? What is flowing? Is it commodities, gifts, texts, relics, saints, theodicies, (video-) taped sermons, money, or bodies?

To tackle these questions, we can borrow from commodity-chains analysis, which maps the circulation of cultural artifacts across space and time, taking into account the contexts of production and consumption (Appadurai 1986; Haugerud et al. 2000; Hughes and Reimer 2004). For example, if we are investigating the circulation of religious elites, say Buddhist monks or Christian missionaries, we might study the locales and institutions in which they are trained and invested with legitimate authority as they incorporate a particular orthodox habitus. We might also study how religious elites adapt doctrines and ritual practices to particular localities and how locals creatively appropriate the teachings, opening the way for "heresies" and other forms of religious innovation. We can then trace how these recreated teachings are fed back to the "core" areas of religious training. A similar commodity-chain analysis can be undertaken for other religious phenomena as diverse as conversions, glossolalia, missions, textual canons, myths and narratives of origin, dietary and sexual taboos, initiation rites, and notions of community and schools of law (for example, *umma* and schools of *shari'a* in Islam). In this way, we can explore the interplay between "text" and "context": among (1) doctrines, symbols, tropes, and beliefs; (2) rituals, institutions, material cultures, and political economies; and (3) religious subjects. Sociologists Michel Callon's and Bruno Latour's "actor-network theory" (ANT) takes a similar approach to show how scientists, living organisms, and scientific instruments intermingle and act upon each other in heterogeneous "semiotic-material" networks that "stabilize" biological reality (Callon 1986; Latour 2005).

Since networks mark both inclusion and exclusion, flows and closures, we can use the analysis of chains of religious goods to find the points at which power is applied and resisted, to identify "zones of awkward engagement" (Tsing 2005: xi), sites in which religion is a key factor in the negotiation of difference and diversity. In other words, the question is who has access to sanctioned religious goods? Who is denied this access? How does this differential access interact with other power dynamics based, for example, on class, race, ethnicity, and nationality?

In addition to the synchronic study of networks, we need to develop historically rich genealogical studies of the development of particular linkages. At a more abstract level, we need to ask how religious networks come to be constituted and rooted in a particular space and time. How do different kinds of ties come together to form transnational social fields? Here we should not assume that the development of networks is necessarily a linear process, moving smoothly to increasing complexity and interconnection. There might be periods of disjuncture where the morphology, density, intensity, and content of religious networks can shift radically, in response to events ranging from natural disasters and the introduction of religious innovation to changes in migration regimes and conflicts in the articulation of collective (ethnic, national, imperial, and regional) identities. In reconstructing the genealogy of various networks, we need to ask how global, transnational, and diasporic religious linkages that are salient today compare to and contrast with age-old extensive mercantile (both overland and maritime), pilgrimage, missionary, military, and scholarship circuits such as the Silk Road, the Atlantic Slave Trade, the Spice Routes, and the Inca trail system (Hourani 1951; Ray 1994; Risso 1995; Foltz 1999; Klein 1999; McEwan 2006). For example, the Iranian Revolution of

1978–79 depended on the mobilization of preexisting Shia "mosque networks," which involved

> time-honored practices such as training, communication, financial donations, and pilgrimage, including ritualized formulas for the expression of respect, condolence, congratulation, and other routinized interactions. The structure of the network was expressed in hierarchies of master-pupil relationships, formalized through the granting of *ijazat* (licenses), the collection and distribution of *zakat* (religious taxes), and the recognition of *maraji'-i taqlid*, the handful of religious scholars deemed by laypersons and others scholars to be "sources of imitation." (Kurtzman 2005: 70–71)

One of the distinctive aspects of contemporary mobile religion is its relation to the restructured but still binding modern nation-state. Although it has been relativized by globalization processes, the state still plays a central role in the way networks are nucleated, deploying a whole host of legal, social scientific, ideological, bureaucratic, military, and geographic apparatuses to project itself globally and to extract surplus from transnational migrants. For instance, Ong (2003: 9) argues that Cambodian immigrants to the United States are constituted into "self-motivated, self-reliant, and entrepreneurial citizen-subjects" through "technologies of governmentality," which rely on "a network of welfare offices, vocational training schools, hospitals, and the workplace." These technologies aim to override traditional Buddhist ethics and produce autonomous, individualistic, and disciplined yet flexible "entrepreneurs of the self," entirely compatible with neo-liberal capitalism. A parallel dynamic may be at work in some of the discourses of global neo-Pentecostalism, which appear to legitimate U.S. hegemony by imagining the world as the arena where a cosmic struggle between Jesus and the devil is taking place and by celebrating a strongly individualistic prosperity gospel in line with the American Dream. In the meantime, the U.S. economy is more and more dependent on the cheap labor of undocumented workers who, in the post-9/11 nativist climate, have become criminalized (Glick-Schiller 2005). This is the obverse side of networks as "popular publics."

Religiously inflected networks today also use different media to establish connectivity. For instance, the vitality and ubiquity of the Hindutva movement is due in large part to the activities of successful Indian entrepreneurs, doctors, software engineers, journalists turned freelance scholars in diaspora, who have the resources and technological competence to spread their message through the Internet. They are able to combine racial and religious primordialism, that is, the recovery of an imagined ancestral land and a unified people with a glorious myth of origins, with hypermodernist, deterritorialized, and decentered cyberspaces. Another example of how today's media shapes networks in distinctive ways is the recent massive demonstrations against the draconian immigration reforms proposed in the U.S. House of Representatives. More than half a million marchers appeared to materialize out of thin air in Los Angeles, while other impressive demonstrations took place in cities as diverse as Chicago, Omaha, Phoenix, Dallas, Atlanta, Salt Lake City, and New York. At the heart of these mobilizations were diffuse networks of grassroots immigrant-advocacy groups, including Catholic and Evangelical Protestant churches, which worked closely with Spanish-language radio hosts and TV news anchors. In between playing salsa, *reggaetón*, or popular *telenovelas*, these media personalities encouraged their listeners and viewers to turn up for the various public demonstrations, instructing people to carry the U.S. flag and those of their nations of origin in order to mark their multiple belonging (Flaccus 2006). Instead of the Internet, which is not readily accessible to many Latino immigrants, a rapidly expanding Latino cultural industry provided the media to articulate and mobilize local and national networks and to mark the simultaneous embeddedness that is the hallmark of transnationalism. The size and organization of the protests surprised the mainstream media and English-speaking public because they had not been paying attention to the growth of this Latino cultural industry, which includes a mixture of entertainment, business, community service, and religious organizations (since many of the local radio stations are owned by Evangelical churches). The examples of Hindutva and Latino protests show that, when studying networks today, we need to be sensitive to the differential access to and use of media. We will have to be attentive to issues like the digital divide, which is conditioned by factors such as class, gender, race, and immigrant status.

The production, circulation, and consumption of religious goods have always interacted with the dynamics of "profane" economies. For instance, historian Peter Brown shows how the dissemination of relics in late antiquity and early medieval Christianity, including the physical remnants of saints, offered a way to relocalize the sacred, that is, to make it present in everyday life at the margins of the Christian world. Simultaneously, the movement of relics contributed to the rise of a politically and religiously powerful class of "impresarios" operating through "intricate systems of patronage, alliance and gift-giving that linked the lay and the clerical elites of East and West in the late Roman Empire" (Brown 1981: 89–90). The transfer of relics from one community to another became part of "a network of 'interpersonal acts,' that carried the full overtones of late-Roman relationships of generosity, dependence, and solidarity . . . [coming] to link the Atlantic coast [of Europe] to the Holy Land; and, in so doing, these 'interpersonal acts' both facilitated and further heightened the drive to transmute distance from the holy into the deep joy of proximity" (Brown 1981: 90).

In the wake of a global neo-liberal capitalism driven by the instantaneous production, circulation, and consumption of cultural goods, the imbrication of "sacred" and "profane" has intensified to such an extent that it is blurring the boundaries separating religion and economics. Religious symbols and practices are increasingly detached from their local contexts of production and incorporated into profane global networks driven by the cash nexus, as seen in Madonna's use of Kabbalah and yoga in her music videos. Conversely, David Chidester persuasively argues that globalization charges consumer products like Coca-Cola, McDonald's and Tupperware with transcendence, with omnipotence and omnipresence. "In the production and consumption of popular culture, even ordinary objects can be transformed into icons, extraordinary magnets of meaning with a religious cast. In conjunction with these objects of popular culture, the term religion seems appropriate because it signals a certain quality of attention, desire, and even reverence for sacred materiality" (Chidester 2005: 34). Moreover, neo-liberal capitalism itself is often sacralized, presented as a this-worldly eschatology in which endless consumption is the mark of grace (Comaroff and Comaroff 2001). A networks approach to religion can help us track these kinds of transmutations, which Marx (1978c: 319–29) described so presciently as "fetishism of commodities," allowing us to identify the specific processes, actors, and contexts that make the sacred and profane convertible to each other.

One last aspect that is unique to the concept of networks in relation to spatial and hydraulic tropes is the linkage between sociocultural processes and physiological and neurocognitive dynamics, which I explored in chapter 7. In *Crossing and Dwelling*, Tweed makes the provocative and fruitful assertion that religions are confluences of organic-cultural flows. For him, "interpretations of cultural trajectories like religion cannot ignore 'the micro-mechanism of cognition and communication.' At the same time, interpreters cannot obscure and minimize the ways that macro-cultural processes are at work in the religious lives of women and men" (Tweed 2006: 65). Tweed rightly seeks to overcome the mind-body and culture-nature dualisms. However, this attempt is only partially successful, since he understands the organic through the metaphor of constraints while he views the cultural as mediations. According to Tweed (2006: 65), "religion scholars . . . can only do their best to acknowledge the complex interaction of organic constraints (neural, physiological, emotional, and cognitive) and cultural mediations (linguistic, tropic, ritual, and material)."

Throughout this book, I have been articulating a non-reductive materialism that recognizes density, relative stability, and causal efficacy of multiple but cooperative forms of materiality that give rise to complex and dynamics auto-poietic systems. In this non-reductive materialism, religion is not just a "shifting cultural current" canalized by "constraining organic channels," as if these channels were external to and always determining in the last instance of historical-cultural praxis. Religion and culture as embodied practices, artifacts, institutions, and environments may also play a co-originating role, crossing with organic processes through the body's reversibility, through the chiasm that is the flesh, to enable and constrain our being-in-the-world. In order to characterize the complex biological-cultural processes that make possible religious experiences, Tweed needs a more fine-grained trope than undifferentiated flows. He needs a trope that can help identify and study the specific mechanisms of interaction among different forms of materiality. Here the relational tropes of networks, webs, and pathways, which have been the mainstay in connectionism and enactive cognitive approaches, may prove very useful. These relational tropes may help us link embodiment, emplacement, and practice in the study of religion, since religious ideas, emotions, practices, and identities are produced by relations of reciprocal determination among the net-like neural infrastructures of cognition, ecological webs, and power-laden networks of social relations.

I will have more to say about ecology, emplacement, webs, and religion later in this chapter. Now, I turn to how the concept of networks may further the conversation on the cognitive foundations of the transmission of religion.

RELIGIOUS TRANSMISSION, NETWORKS, AND COGNITION

We saw in chapter 7 that there is promising research identifying cross-cultural patterns in ritual action, belief fixation, conversion, memory, and religious transmission, as well as seeking to answer the question of the origin of religion (Boyer 2001; Pyysiäinen 2001; Whitehouse 2004; Barrett 2004; Dennett 2006). Suspicious of social constructionism, this cognitivist-evolutionist research program still has not yielded models flexible enough to deal with variation, creativity, innovation, and fluidity, all hallmarks of mobile religions. For example, there is evidence that the kind of religion that enters hyper-accelerated global, transnational, and diasporic networks with the greatest ease shares many features with what anthropologist Harvey Whitehouse (2004) calls an "imagistic mode of religiosity," including a stress on high levels of arousal, iconicity, multivocality, and episodic memories. This is made clear in the recent controversy around the cartoons of the Prophet Mohammed published by a Danish newspaper. Unable to hold the Danish government accountable, leaders of the Muslim Danish community circulated the cartoons across their networks, skillfully using a combination of face-to-face lobbying and cell phone and Internet messaging. Eventually, the caricatures achieved extensive publicity in the Middle East, Indonesia, Malaysia, Nigeria, and the Philippines. The "memorable" images generated emotionally charged waves of intense social cohesion among aggrieved Muslims across the globe. In turn, the Muslim reaction entered the global networks anchored in the West in selected powerful images of trampled Danish flags, burning consulates, and violence against Christians. Note here that imagistic transmission stands in complex interaction with a "doctrinal mode" of religiosity, as many Arab governments used the controversy to blunt the challenge of growing Islamic rectificationist movements by showing that they are defending the purity of faith against the secular West. Here the tendency is to centralize, codify, and homogenize Islam.

This example contradicts Whitehouse's cognitive model of religious transmission, which hypothesizes that the imagistic mode of religion is less portable than the doctrinal mode. As we saw in chapter 7, according to Whitehouse the mode of religiosity that is best suited for transmission across multiple spaces and times is the doctrinal because of its routinization into narratives, texts, theologies, and ethics, all of which can be presented as universal. From these universal precepts follow standardized ritual practices, which can be deployed anywhere. In contrast, the imagistic has to rely on the face-to-face contact to reignite the intense but fragmentary event on which it depends (that is why Whitehouse calls the memory involved here an "episodic" or "flashbulb" memory"). It then more difficult to replicate in different contexts the particularism of imagistic religion. In fact, Whitehouse goes as far as saying that "unlike the beliefs and practices of the doctrinal mode, traditions operating in the imagistic mode do not spread widely" (2004: 73).

One of the key factors that explains this contradiction is the nature of the communication and transportation networks involved. Whitehouse's failure to account for the great portability of imagistic modes of religiosity, such as the controversy over the cartoons of the Prophet Mohammed or of Charismatic Christianities that rely on spectacular exorcisms of the devil, has to do with the fact that he is still in caught in a modernist, representationalist mind-set that considers print media as the key vehicle for the spread of religion. However, imagistic modes of religion today, including African and Latin American Pentecostalisms, circulate through other media. Their worldwide diffusion is rather the result of the practices of transnational networks of missionaries that rely heavily on the widespread use of electronic, image-heavy media, like TV, videos, films, and the Internet. Through this media, these religious actors render the imagistic mode of religiosity translocal, no longer only the province of small, localized communities, but rather of transnational "communities of feeling" (Appadurai 1996: 8). While these fraternities and sodalities of emotion may be located in London, Johannesburg, or São Paulo, they feel part of a global church of the saved.

Canadian sage Marshall McLuhan wrote in *Understanding the Media* (1964) that the new technologies that are emerging are literally changing our brains, in some ways stretching our neural networks to envelop the whole world. While he might have overstated his case, he is correct in highlighting how cybernetworks are redefining the interface between embodiment and culture, between the neural and the cultural. We live in a society that is awash in images that circulate at blinding speeds and are mixed and remixed endlessly, a "society of the spectacle" (Debord 1994), a global society of "permanent simulacra" (Baudrillard 1995). This society nurtures what Georg Simmel called "a blasé attitude": the "incapacity to react to new sensations with the appropriate energy." For the "blasé person" in the global metropolis of cyberspace, things appear in "an evenly flat and gray tone; no object deserves preference over any other" (Simmel 1950: 414). In the "dessert of the real," amid the 24/7 flood of images that saturates our senses, what stands out, is remembered, and thus, is more likely to be transmitted is the stark, the spectacular that sets itself apart from the profane world. And what can be more spectacular than apocalyptic and millenarian messages, narratives of a cosmic struggle between God and the Devil that is enacted every time an exorcism takes place in a neo-Pentecostal church. In our postmodern world, where the social seems to have imploded, where signs seem to point only to other signs (Baudrillard 1995), it is imagistic religion, particularly as expressed in vivid, life-or-death encounters with traveling spirits, that is more memorable and transportable.

The bottom line is that while the cognitivist-evolutionary research program has some valuable things to teach us about mobile religion, it does not tell us enough about the specifics of the selection of images, forms of collective action, and the situational "oscillation" between imagistic and doctrinal modes of religiosity. Here this research program can be augmented and critiqued through the judicious use of the notion of interactive networks of different forms of materiality. In the case of cartoon controversy, the choice and oscillation are conditioned by many contextual factors, including the nature of Western media, the morphology of Muslim networks, Orientalism as an ideology of othering, and the construction of sovereign subjectivities (with an unalienable freedom of conscience and expression) that are central to the idea of the modern secular nation-state. To take into account all these contextual material factors, we need a network theory of religious transmission that is more nuanced that what Whitehouse has proposed.

Ongoing work on modularity, emergent properties, and autopoiesis in Multiagent Systems (MAS) and Complex Adaptive Systems (CAS), in which "intelligent" networks are involved, shows some promise (Gros 2008). Borrowing from research on the architecture of the brain, distributed artificial intelligence, and other complexes consisting of large numbers of mutually interacting yet asynchronous individual components that form dynamic self-organizing systems, we may be able to derive probabilistic models to map the turbulence of mobile religions (M. Taylor 2007). More ambitiously, research on cultural neurophenomenology, particularly the work of Francisco Varela, Evan Thompson and associates (see chapter 7), may lead to a richer understanding of the nonlinear interactions among networks operating at various scales and crossing multiple forms of materiality, from the micro in the human brain to the macro, such as the Internet, capitalist world system, and biosphere.

In placing networks front and center and exploring more systematically their analytical potential, my aim in this section has been to offer an approach, which for the lack of a better term, I will call "structured and structuring dynamism."[6] This approach provides a different, possibly complementary, angle to Tweed's theory of religion in motion. I have focused on networks as a way to underline the fact that religions on the move entail the activity of specific individuals and groups that are located in and connected through shifting but binding differentials of power. Although networks are deterritorializing—deeply implicated in globalization's time-space compression and distanciation—they are always territorialized and prone to hierarchization. In that sense, networks are completely compatible with the spatial metaphors that are emerging in the study of religion, since it is the configuration of networks that lays the contours of the landscapes we inhabit. Networks, nevertheless, go beyond the locating of religion in particular nodes. They allow for multi-scalar relationality, movement, and connectivity without falling into the radical anti-structuralism implicit in flow metaphors. As Mark Taylor argues, we can take seriously the post-structuralist challenge against totalitarian staticity without falling into the "night in which all cows are black,"[7] by understanding that structures can "act as wholes without necessarily totalizing" (M. Taylor 2007: 12).

Network analysis offers both a robust social epistemology, enabling erudite "ascending analyses" of the "infinitesimal mechanisms of power," as Foucault (1980: 99) puts it, and a politically astute strategy. It helps us understand power not just the capacity negotiate meaning, carve contested sacred geographies, and invent hybrid identities, but also as control over life, over the need, means, and ability to move. Networks can help us to account for mobile religion's flexibility, mobility, connectivity, and innovation, without ignoring how it is often implicated in the hard realities of exclusion, exploitation, and subjugation, which are also part and parcel of globalization.

ECOLOGY AND EMPLACEMENT

Most discussions of emplacement and mobility in religious studies have ignored ecology. When Tweed refers to organic-cultural flows, the term organic signifies primarily the body, including the neuro-cognitive processes that I explored in chapter 7. Thus, Tweed highlights religion's role in the formation of corporeal "biological and cultural clocks" and "neural and cultural compasses" that help us manage time and navigate space. Similarly, although Slingerland frequently appeals to evolution in his quest to embody religion and culture, he seldom mentions the environmental processes that constrain, enable, and interact with our brain and in-skilled body. It is as if materiality stopped at the body's dermis. But, as Abram (1996: 46–47) tells us, "the boundaries of a living body are open and indeterminate; more like membranes than barriers, they define a surface of metamorphosis and exchange. The breathing, sensing body draws its sustenance and its very substance from the soils, plants, and elements that surround it; it continually contributes, itself, in turn, to the air, to the composting earth, to the nourishment of insects and oak trees, ceaselessly spreading out of itself as well as breathing the world into itself, so that it is very difficult to discern, at any moment, precisely where the living body begins and where it ends." Despite this mutuality, the literature on place-making in the humanities and social sciences has tended to sweep the part of "nature" that refers to the ecological webs and geophysical realities with which our bodies are tightly intertwined under the catch-all term of "landscape."[8]

The notion of landscape is certainly useful in understanding processes of place-making. Drawing from his research among the Apache, anthropologist Keith Basso (1996) has, for example, shown how having a sense of place entails the coming together of the physical terrain and the "landscape of the mind." Particular aspects of the physical topography become heavily invested with memories and emotions, producing an enduring wisdom "that sits in places." Places, then, are neither naked, impenetrable geophysical realities without any moral and cognitive valence, nor are they anything we can make of them at a particular moment. Rather, they carry the sedimented yet dynamic weight of tradition. They condense the narratives, lived experiences, and histories of those who have come before us. So, even though the sensing of place is a creative activity, "a kind of imaginative experience, a species of involvement with the natural and social environment, a way of appropriating portions of the earth," this appropriation is not decontextualized (Basso 1996: 143). It is made possible by the durable wisdom that already dwells in places.

Despite its undeniable value in emplacing religion and culture, the notion of landscape remains trapped in an anthropocentrism that does not allow full embeddedness in ecology. For instance, Colleen McDonnell, a pioneer in the study of material Christianity, equates "cultivated nature" with landscape. She tells us that the "natural environment undergoes a transformation when trees are planted, roads paved, houses built, and churches constructed. Like a chair is made by human hands or a human-designed machine, landscapes are shaped by human intent. People manipulate nature, sometimes subtly and frequently powerfully, to express their communal and personal values" (McDannell 1995a: 3). Put this way, the notion of landscape is well suited to highlight embodied praxis and the social construction of space, but at the cost of preserving a notion of human exceptionalism that, in separating us from the non-human animals (as uniquely intentional and meaning-making beings), carries traces of Cartesian dualism. Notice in McDannell's reading of the notion of landscape how humans have agency while nature is the passive object of our practices.

Theologian Belden Lane tries to overcome this anthropocentrism. Building on Basso's insight, he pushes back against radical versions of social constructionism that view space and nature as a tabula rasa that can be sacralized and de-sacralized at will. A "sacred place is a 'storied place.' Particular locales come to recognized as sacred because of the stories that are told about them" (Lane 2001: 15). However, while sacred places are always narrativized, they "also participate in the entire array of sensory exchanges that play across the land, reaching beyond the impact of human influence alone." According to Lane, the sacred place "demands its own integrity, its own participation in what 'becomes' its own voice. A sacred place is necessarily more than a construction of the human imagination alone" (Lane 2001: 4). When studying the landscapes of the sacred, Lane calls for scholars to move "beyond cognitivism," toward a non-dualistic phenomenology that recovers the wholeness of place.

A sacred place is not simply a unique site magically "possessed" by chthonic forces. Nor is it a topographical wax nose that can be culturally twisted into anything one makes of it. A difficulty with both approaches is that the perceiver largely ignores the actual particularities of the place itself. It becomes a blank slate on which divine or human meaning are arbitrarily inscribed—by means of luminous revelation on the one hand or cultural construction on the other. (Lane 2001: 52)

Neither the Eliadean approach built around hierophanies nor J. Z. Smith's constructionist line, which we encountered in the previous chapter, tells the whole story about emplacement. In fact, taken together, these two approaches tend to cancel each other out or to set unhelpful dichotomies. Confronting these approaches with neurocognitive processes, as Tweed does, definitely begins to break the dualistic logjam, expanding the scope of the materialist phenomenology of place. However, it is still insufficient. Lane argues that religion scholars need also to take into account the work of ecological psychologists and anthropologists, such as James Gibson and Tim Ingold, which shows that the process of emplacement is "relentlessly interactive." A sacred place is "'known' only to the extent that we participate in the various affordances it offers, responding to the striking geographical features it projects, adjusting to changing visual, auditory, olfactory, and kinesthetic qualities" (Lane 2001: 53). In Merleau-Ponty's words, the flesh of the world and our flesh touch each other to make possible our being-in-place.

While Lane moves the study of emplacement and mobility beyond the anthropocentrism, he does not specify the ways in which our enmeshment in ecological webs and flows affords our perception and sense of place. Furthermore, Lane sometimes slides into Eliadean, supernaturalistic language that falls beyond the purview of a materialist phenomenology. For example, building on Eliade's claim that a "sacred place is not chosen, it chooses," he writes that a "[s]acred place . . . is a construction of the imagination that affirms the independence of the holy. God chooses to reveal himself only where he wills" (Lane 2001: 19). I would like in the last part of this chapter to explore more in depth the notion of affordances, which I mentioned in chapter 7 in relation to the inculcation of body schemas, as way to foreground ecology's active role, in interplay with human practice, in religious place-making and mobility.

As anyone who has dealt with the interaction between ecology and religion knows, it is difficult to approach this topic without making reference to the work of Roy Rappaport. Building on Durkheim's understanding of religion as social cement and anthropologist Gregory Bateson's notion of cybernetic systems, Rappaport offered valuable insights into the ways in which ritual cycles function to codify and regulate the interaction between social structures and ecological processes, ordering and providing meaning to complex matter and energy transactions that make possible the subsistence of human populations. Rappaport was one of the earliest and most articulate advocates of "a more holistic human involvement in the natural environment, which includes the engagement of unconscious aspects of the human mind, as in religion, ritual, and aesthetics" (Hornborg 2001: 177). This holism enabled him to give religion causal efficacy against the claims of mechanistic materialists such as Marvin Harris, who considered religious ideologies as mere superstructures. In contrast, Rappaport argues that ritual is "a very old if not primordial mode of production," fully "commensurable with feudalism, capitalism, and oriental despotism" (1979: 73).

Rappaport goes even further in asserting the material density and causal power of religion, suggesting that it has played a key role in humanity's evolutionary adaptiveness. According to him, the notion of the sacred is simultaneously universalizing and empty, that is, capable of attaching itself to any object, landscape, practice, or institution. Because of this dual nature, the sacred offers "ordered flexibility combined with differential responsiveness" (Rappaport 1999: 427). The sacred can then "sanctify" regulatory hierarchies, giving them the authority to operate on ecological and social conditions to produce well-being for the group. If the regulatory hierarchies fail to generate well-being or if they are seen as oppressive by the group, those in subordinate positions may "desanctify" them. In those cases, the subordinate groups can refuse to participate in the ritual cycles or engage in desecration, thereby interfering with the sacred's potential to generate *communitas*. Prophets may rise up to challenge the status quo, offering new sources of sanctification. These struggles allow for the creative readjustment of the regulatory hierarchies, ensuring once again the adaptation and well-being of the group. This is what Rappaport calls the "cybernetics of the Holy": "The structure of sanctification, and thus of authority and legitimacy, is 'circular,' a cybernetic 'closed loop'" (1999: 430).

Rappaport's cybernetics of the Holy resonates with the work of some of the practice theorists we have discussed, such as Marx, Weber, Turner, and Bourdieu. Moreover, his emphasis on ecological-social holism reinforces the need to embed the body and religion in nature. However, the specter of functionalism haunts Rappaport's work. Although he acknowledges that cultural-ecological systems contain widespread maladaptations and interlevel contradictions, Rappaport's view of ecology carries heavy teleological assumptions. He places a strong emphasis on the system's capacity for self-regulation and self-reproduction, assuming that its telos is equilibrium. In contemporary scientific theories, this view of ecology has given way to one that stresses complexity. In this new perspective, many natural processes are nonlinear or even stochastic, and they involve multiple, often loosely coupled variables, which produce results oscillating over wide ranges (Worster 1994: 407–33). The variable activities of humans, which now affect virtually all ecosystems, only add more perturbations. According to Solé and Bascompte (2006: 217–18), "[a] detailed description of a complex ecosystem is an impossible goal: Each species by itself involves too many variables to deal with. But . . . at some levels of description, statistical models of multispecies communities are able to explain the origins of ecological complexity and how it changes over time." They suggest that a focus on "patterns emerging from network dynamics and topology" gives us considerable explanatory power, since "[c]omplex ecosystems have a network structure that pervades their behavior and response against perturbations" (Solé and Bascompte 2006: 14). The combination of the analysis of ecological and social networks and the study of complex spaces is precisely what this chapter seeks to advance as a supplement to Tweed's hydrodynamics of religion.

As an alternative to Rappaport, following Lane's advice, I turn to James Gibson's and Tim Ingold's work. Both Gibson and Ingold retain Rappaport's stress on embeddedness, relationality, and interactivity, while underscoring the creative role of emplaced and embodied practice.[9] Gibson's work focuses on the ecology of perception: how is it that human beings come to perceive the environment in which they are emplaced? To answer this question, Gibson suggests that we take our concepts not from mathematics and physics, which operate through Cartesian dualism, but from ecology. Perception does not result when disturbances generated by external objects impact our sensorium, triggering mental associations. Nor does it emerge from just the imposition of a prioris of apperception innately lodged in the subject. As in the enactive approach to cognition, Gibson seeks to transcend the subject-object split, arguing that perception is a cooperative, interactive process. Things have "affordances," that is, they have spatial and spatiotemporal properties that they furnish to observers. While affordances are real, they are always relational, always *for* the embodied subject. "I assume that affordances are not simply phenomenal qualities of subjective experience. . . . I also assume that they are not simply the physical properties of things as now conceived by physical science. Instead, they are *ecological*, in the sense that they are properties of the environment relative to an animal" (Gibson 1982: 404, italics in the original).

The fact that affordances are perceived relative to the animal opens the way for a post-humanist materialism, the kind of the "agential realism" Karen Barad seeks to articulate in which the self and his/her surroundings "intra-act," engage with each other not as independent entities but as agents within a single material matrix of becoming (see chapter 6). "Different subjects—a human, a dog, a rat—construct different worlds through their embodied interactions with it. Each construction is positioned and local, covering only a tiny fraction of the spectrum of possible embodied interaction" (Hayles 1995: 58).[10] Thus, while a vertical solid surface in a landscape may afford collisions or falling, bar foot locomotion, or furnish the possibility of climbing using ropes for a human being, for a bird, it may afford flight and unobstructed vision. In turn, the presence and activity of other animals is part of the affordances humans encounter. Beavers and ants, for example, often transform the landscapes in which we and they dwell. More radically, archeological and paleontological research shows that the part of the human brain that controls hearing and our sense of smell shrank around the same time as we began to domesticate dogs. "Dog brains and human brains specialized: humans took over the planning and organizing tasks, and dogs took over the sensory tasks. Dogs and people coevolved and became even better partners, allies, and friends" (Grandin and Johnson 2005: 306).[11]

It follows then that "[t]he meaning or value of a thing consists of what it affords. . . . What a thing affords a particular observer (or species of observer) points to the organism, the *subject*" (Gibson 1982: 407). What a thing is and what it means are inseparable. They both are the result of the encounter between the embodied creature and its surroundings. "The affordances for behavior and the behaving animal are complementary" (Gibson 1982: 410). Embodied practices, with all the interacting neurocognitive, physiological, and cultural processes that make them possible, and a terrain's affordances are complementary.

Indeed, for Gibson, humans encounter affordances in their surrounding environments through practical engagement. The sense of a particular place is a perception of the "*practical* lay-out, not *theoretical* lay-out," that is, not of its Cartesian coordinates. What the subject sees when s/he encounters a place, sacred or otherwise, is not Euclidean geometry, but "possibilities of support, of falling, of resting, of sitting, of walking, of bumping into, of climbing, of taking shelter, of hiding, of grasping, of moving movable things, of tool using, and so on and on" (Gibson 1982: 415). The subject encounters these possibilities and constraints over time, as s/he moves around and across lived spaces. Environments "are perceived not at successive points but rather along paths of observation . . . the knowledge of inhabitants is not so much built up as forged along lines of movement, in the passage from place to place and the changing horizons along the way" (Ingold 2007: 204). Knowing is a set of "inscriptive practices" on both the body and the environment, a kind of "wayfaring," a tracing of routes in which individuals adjust and fine-tune "their pace, posture, and orientation in response to an on-going perceptual monitoring of their surroundings" (Ingold 2007: 203). Their adjustment and fine-tuning, in turn, transform the surroundings, opening a spiral of codetermination.

Time, mobility, and practice are thus central to place-making, as Tweed has rightly concluded. "What the perceiver looks for are constancies underlying the continuous modulation of the sensory array as one moves from place to place" (Ingold 2000: 166). The affordances that become salient are "invariant combinations of properties of things (properties at the ecological level) taken with reference to a species or an individual . . . with reference to its needs (biological and social) as well as to its action-systems and its anatomy" (Gibson 1982: 410).

Gibson's "ecological optics" has several implications. First, we must resist the radical constructionist temptation to understand place-making as a purely sociocultural, semiotic act. Spaces do not become "storied" places in a vacuum or purely at random. Nor is emplacement only a matter of bringing in the body via its neural and cognitive dynamics. We must also take into account what the environment affords our bodies. Ecology is central in any fully materialist reading of religious emplacement. The questions that Wendell Berry (1987: 146) asks about farming and human economies are also very relevant for religion: "What will nature permit us to do here? . . . What will nature help us to do here?" Affordances play an important role in determining the kinds of places that consistently become sacralized, become storied, charged with powerful memories and emotions that set them apart from other places.

It is not that only those places with unique or unusual affordances become sacralized. As Lane correctly observes, often sacred mountains are not necessarily the highest or most massive, and holy waters are often not those of the most pristine or fastest flowing rivers. Further, "the sacred place is very often an ordinary place, ritually set apart to become extraordinary. Its holiness resides not in certain inherent marks of external significance or obvious distinction. It is, instead, only declared to be different, heterogeneous, discontinuous from the commonness of the surrounding terrain" (Lane 2001: 25). Here Lane puts the notion of sacramentality to good use. Just as for Catholics the Eucharist is the transubstantiation of bread and the wine, the sacralization of place often involves a radical transformation of unexceptional spaces.

Instead, I am suggesting that we take a non-dualistic or, rather, holistic albeit nontotalizing approach to religious place-making. Sacralization of a place is a complex process that cannot be reduced to geophysical properties afforded to the believer. Nor can it be understood as a purely social and semiotic act. It is rather an interplay among multiple materialities: social construction and the environment afford each other.[12] A place owes its sacred character to "the experiences it affords those who spend time there—to the sights, sound and indeed smells that constitute its specific ambiance. And these, in turn, depend on the kinds of activities in which its inhabitants engage. It is from this relational context of people's engagement with the world, in the business of dwelling, that each place draws its unique significance" (Ingold 2000: 192).

Whether it is Mount Fuji, the Ganges, or a crossroads at a city park where food has been left for the Orichas, the similarities scholars observe among sacred places across cultures and epochs need not be the result of the structure of hierophanies, of an ontological sacred that presents itself as axis mundi. Rather, these family resemblances may be the result of the interaction between the affordances of certain places, the culturally in-skilled embodied schemas through which we encounter and engage these affordances as salient, and the myths, tropes, and symbols we use to tell each other about these encounters. Religious emplacement is an ecological, corporeal, practical, and semiotic-cognitive process. And to the extent that we also modify these places through our technologies, as in the creation of cyberspaces, it is also a machinic process, as Haraway argues.

Second, we must understand ecology, not as external reality standing against the subject, but as part of an integrated process of being-with and being-in-the-world. As Ingold (2000: 19) puts it, "[a] properly ecological approach . . . is one that would take, as its point of departure, the whole-organism-in-its-environment. In other words, 'organism plus environment' should denote not a compound of two things, but one indivisible totality." This would be a thoroughly embodied ecology, an "ecology of life," as Ingold terms it, that does not set mind against matter, culture against nature, practice against structure, mobility against emplacement. In this ecology, "we do not have to think of mind or consciousness as a layer of being over and above that of the life of the organisms, in order to account for their creative involvement in the world. Rather, what we may call the mind is the cutting edge of the life process itself . . ." (Ingold 2000: 19).

Third, the lived, emplaced body is key in the subject-object integration. This is so because the body is simultaneously crisscrossed by ecological networks operating at multiple levels and in-skilled by a socially mediated habitus that allows it to be attuned to the environment, to perceive, give valence, and work upon affordances. The kinds of posture, attention, locomotion, and manipulation of objects in which we can engage are made possible by the reciprocal activity of the body (including the dynamic architecture of the brain) and its surrounding environment. Structured and structuring praxis generated by incorporated cultural and religious wisdom goes hand-in-hand with the environment as we make places our home or as we sacralize them.

The discussion of the "ecology of life" brings us full circle in the attempt to rematerialize religion, linking the three majors themes that have guided this book: embodiment, practice, and emplacement/mobility. The ecological perspective offers "the simple observation that the human species is, after all, a species among species and that, as such, humanity's relations with its physical and biotic environments are, like those of other animals, continuous, indissoluble, and necessary" (Rappaport 1979: 61). In that sense, as Bateson (1972) recognized long ago, "biological epistemology" challenges the disembodied, detached, and purely rational Cartesian subjectivity that has been the foundation of Western thinking and has made its way into religious studies via a misreading of phenomenology. Bringing ecology back in highlights the non-anthropocentric, networked, flexible, and immanentist materialism I have tried to advance. It holds in check both a mechanistic materialism that reduces complex emergent properties to the lawful behavior of atoms and the "hungry metaphor" of textualism, the notion that self-referential semiotics systems are the only way of being in the world. The scholar of religion who takes ecology seriously avoids reductionisms, semiotic or not, and takes into account the multiple, intra-active forms of materiality that make possible those experiences, practices, artifacts, and institutions practitioners and scholars call religious.

By the Way of a Conclusion

One question that needs sustained exploration is this: What does it mean to be a material being living in a material world?

—Owen Flanagan (2007: 4)

For me, there are "realities" at all levels of the human endeavor: biological-evolutionary, cultural-social, individual. These overlap and interplay. To assert a connection between the ethological, the anthropological, and the aesthetic is not to deny local individual variation and uniqueness.

—Richard Schechner (2003: xii)

The goal of this book has been to lay the epistemological bases for a flexible yet rigorous non-reductive materialist framework for the study of religion. I sought to overcome disabling dichotomies in religious studies that have privileged beliefs over rituals, the private over the public, text and symbol over practice, and mind and soul over the body. I tried to overcome these dichotomies not simply by reversing their valence and privileging the terms that have been hitherto denigrated. It is not that doctrines and personal beliefs, texts, and symbols do not matter or carry their own material density. Rather, I have argued that we can only appreciate their full materiality if we contextualize and historicize them, if we approach them as phenomena produced, performed, circulated, contested, sacralized, and consumed by embodied and emplaced individuals. Only when we see these discourses, beliefs, symbols, and texts as mobile yet relatively stable artifacts operating among and interacting with other material objects within the times and spaces constructed by the practices of situated individuals and groups can we avoid the threat of textualism, the temptation to make semiotic systems purely self-referential. Religious practices are "'multimedia events.' . . . where speech, vision, gesture, touch, and sound combine" (McDannell 1995a: 14).

I have also argued that in order to adopt a holistic and honest materialism, it is necessary to be keenly aware of the limits of social constructionism. We must recognize that, although our experience of the world is mediated through our discursive and nondiscursive practices, we cannot reduce to human texts the materiality of our bodies and the world in which and through which we live. We always confront "the stubbornness of the materiality of things" (Appadurai 2006: 21). Nature, however, is not opposed to culture, as an utterly external naked reality standing against us or as a mere passive or empty surface upon which we inscribe our meanings. Nor is nature a mere artifice of reiterated, reified discourses. These attitudes betray a Cartesian dualism and the underlying anxiety to establish human exceptionalism, both of which have fed modernity's and religious studies' somatophobia. Rather, in culture and nature we find mutually implicative protean forms of materiality, each with its efficacy and dynamism, intra-acting with each other in complex ways that can be partially grasped but are never totally accessible. As sociologists of science associated with the actor-network theory remind us,

> [k]nowledge . . . is embodied in a variety of material forms. But where does it come from? The actor-network answer is that it is the end product of a lot of hard work in which heterogeneous bits and pieces—test tubes, reagents, organisms, skilled hands, scanning electron microscopes, radiation monitors, other scientists, articles, computer terminals, and all the rest—that would like to make off on their own are juxtaposed into a patterned network which overcomes their resistance. In short, it is a material matter but also a matter of organising and ordering those materials. So this is the actor-network diagnosis of science: that it is a process of "heterogeneous engineering" in which bits and pieces from the social, the technical, the conceptual and the textual are fitted together, and so converted (or "translated") into a set of equally heterogeneous scientific products. (Law 2003: 2)

Religions too are products of heterogeneous engineering. Like Donna Haraway's cyborgs, religions are hybrid products of "differential patterns of mattering" (Barad 2008: 140), involving embodied practitioners and scholars, discursive matrices, and social, neural, and ecological networks. The experience of transcendence that characterizes religion as well as other forms of being-in-the-world emerges in the immanent interplay of these relatively open forms of materiality, with emergent effects and properties that are not always reducible to lower level components and activities. This immanent transcendence humbles us, making religious studies scholars sensitive to the experiences and claims of religious practitioners. This immanent transcendence has the salutary effect of acting as a break against the temptation of claiming that we can discover the secret of religion or culture once and for all, whether it be the operations of society, the dialectics of class struggle, the dynamics of the psyche, the evolution and architecture of the brain, or the sequences that make up our genome. And yet, all these variables play a role in the manufacture of religion. The challenge is to understand how they afford each other, how they combine and cross-fertilize in particular situations to give rise to a multiplicity of religious phenomena as well as to enduring cross-cultural and *longue durée* patterns.

My approach to religion, thus, stands firmly within the "immanent frame," which philosopher Charles Taylor argues is the hallmark of our present secular age.[1] I operate within this frame not because I think that religion is irrelevant or that the experiences of the practitioner can be dismissed as false consciousness, ultimately explainable by "real," more material processes. Quite the contrary: immanence for me is a way to restore the full materiality of our being-in-the-world, and particularly of religion as a dimension of that being. By adopting an immanent frame, we can fully reintroduce embodiment, emplacement, and practice to the discipline of religion, which has been, at best, highly ambivalent about these existential realities. Hence, the turn to immanence is my response to Robert Orsi's challenge to develop a "materialist phenomenology of religion" that is open to lived religions' astonishing range of practices.[2] In that sense, non-reductive materialism's main "cash value" is that it allows scholars of religion to highlight phenomena that are salient in everyday life, phenomena that exercise palpable power on and through the lives of practitioners but that have been neglected by traditional religious studies approaches. More specifically, I find an immanent materialist frame most fruitful in exploring the portability of religion today, the videotaped sermons, ritual objects, traveling spirits, self-help New Age paraphernalia, architectural patterns, liturgical styles, sacred music, and missionary subjectivities that enter transnational and global networks. A frame of this sort can also help us understand how immigrants draw from their religious resources to build transnational identities and carve out spaces of livelihood. This frame brings into focus enduring and powerful religious expressions that have been dismissed as primitive, heretical, or naïvely enchanted: Pentecostals baptized by the Holy Spirit who speak in tongues, heal bodies ravaged by drugs, and wage warfare against the territorial spirits of "witchcraft"; or the Santeros who incorporate the Orichas or exchange vital energies with them through animal sacrifices; or the first-generation Hindu immigrants in the United States and Britain who try to pass on Hindu culture to their children through *rasa* or through the performance of *puja*s to divinities materialized in *murti*s, not by lecturing them on the Upanishads' metaphysics.

By immanence, I simply mean here that the study of religion can and should proceed without making any appeal to some supernatural or supra-historical force or entity such as God, the Holy, or the sacred. Whether these forces or entities exist is not a question that religious studies can answer or should spend time contemplating. For getting entangled in these intractable metaphysical questions is both a symptom and a source of Cartesian anxiety, somatophobia, and all kinds of disabling dualisms. In principle, an immanent frame is compatible with either "religious" or "secular" worldviews. For example, drawing from Spinoza, Stuart Kauffman (2008) "reinvents" the notion of the sacred to characterize the self-creativity of complex natural systems. While Kauffman forsakes any appeal to a divine creator or any supernatural beings in order to explain the complexity and irreducibility of the biosphere, he wishes to preserve the sense of awe, mystery, and transcendence that is usually attached to the concept of god. "God is our chosen name for the ceaseless creativity in the natural universe, biosphere, and human culture" (Kauffman 2008: xi).[3] As my discussion of Nietzsche, Deleuze, and Guattari shows, one can also view this creativity, intra-historical transcendence, and relatively indeterminacy in purely secular terms. What is important is that we do not come to study of religion with a closed mind, either in the direction of theism or non-theism. As anthropologist of religion Thomas Csordas (2004) tells us, it is vital that the scholar of religion remain open to be surprised by alterity and the unfamiliar, by the surplus that is constitutive of our being-in-the-world, whatever form it may take.

That religion scholars should not appeal to supernatural and supra-historical forces or beings does not mean the people we study, the religious practitioners, will not appeal to them. They, in fact, almost invariably do, demonstrating thus the real, lived desire for and power of transcendence in everyday life. To account for this desire and power, the immanent frame cannot be closed. It has to be open, meaning that transcendence must be intrinsic to it. Transcendence is an essential feature of an immanent frame that is attentive to the complexities, contradictions, paradoxes, relations of reciprocal determination, multi-causal dynamics, and, more generally, the indeterminacies in the ways in which various materialities interact to constitute us in the world.

The attempt to overcome the duality between an other-worldly transcendence and a this-worldly immanence, to propose transcendence within immanence, is what led me to dialogue with thinkers as diverse as Spinoza, Nietzsche, Merleau-Ponty, Deleuze, Guattari, Haraway, Gibson, and Barad, all of whom see matter not as a brute, inert substance standing against us, against our divine spirits. Instead, they view matter as a dynamic, protean, relatively indeterminate, and fully potent reality that is our flesh, the flesh that enables and emplaces our discursive and nondiscursive practices. Matter, like the immanent frame that discloses it to us, is open. "The universe is agential intra-activity in its becoming" (Barad 2008: 141).

My immanent frame, therefore, takes Mircea Eliade's warnings about reductionism seriously, but without resorting to a transhistorical, onto--theo-logocentric sacred. Materialism, even of the non-eliminativist sort, cannot but subscribe to naturalism when it comes to religion and culture. Yet a scholar of religion can be non-reductive and still hold firmly to the principle that religion is a natural and historical phenomenon, one whose study requires empathy, reflexive humility, and rigor. The choice is not between being a pious caretaker or an implacable critic. Such polemical dichotomies are not productive in the long term. A more productive way of formulating the task from a non-reductive materialist framework is to approach religion as any other cultural reality, as often polyvalent, contradictory, and perspectival.

It is quite possible that my materialist and immanentist critique will not satisfy those who argue that the only way to get rid of the "private-affair tradition" in the study of religion is by jettisoning the category of religion itself (Fitzgerald 2000). For these scholars, religion "as a distinct and substantive reality in the world and as a universal and autonomous domain of human experience and action is a myth, a discursive formation . . . [and] religious studies is an agency for uncritically formulating and legitimating this myth and embedding it into the warp and woof of our collective consciousness" (Fitzgerald 2007: 9–10). While I have been very critical of any attempts to disembed religion from materiality and to treat it as an autonomous and universal substance, I have used the category throughout the book. So, it would seem that, in the end, I may have not gone far enough. As McCutcheon puts it in his helpful review of this manuscript, today there is a new generation of scholars who critique past scholarship "because it did not allow them to find religion in enough places." While appearing radical, this critique, in fact, gives religious studies a new lease on life, since it opens the possibility of seeing religion everywhere, in everyday life.

The totalizing critique of the category of religion makes sense to a point, although, if pushed to the extreme, it becomes self-contradictory, since it depends on the existence of the very term it wants to eliminate for its expressions of outrage. My position here is eminently pragmatic: even if religion is an illusion or a myth inextricably connected to Western modernity, capitalism, nationalism, and colonialism, it is, as Fitzgerald (2007: 9) himself admits it, "powerful" and "widely disseminated." Thus, we need to move beyond nominalism and develop robust critical tools to assess the power, operation, and circulation of religion, not just in academia but also in everyday life. We need tools to analyze the multiple practices and processes through which people, including scholars, sacralize an enormous variety of elements in their lifeworld, oftentimes designating these elements as religious. In these situations, we are "left with no other choice than to study religion as we find it" (Strenki 2006: 340).

While scholars had and continue to have a major hand in the construction of religion, the category no longer belongs to us (if it ever did!). I agree that our primary task as scholars is to historicize, contextualize, and materialize religion. However, it is naïve to think that simply by getting rid of the category through discursive deconstruction and genealogical analysis, all epistemological and methodological problems will fade. Paradoxically, by abandoning the category of religion altogether, scholars who fashion themselves as radical critics end up placing objects, identities, practices, symbols, and institutions that are constructed and experienced as religious beyond the reach of rigorous empirically based analysis (Lincoln 2007: 168). As Foucault (1980: 133) tells us, ultimately the problem is not ideology, "changing people's consciousness . . . or what's in their heads." Rather, the task is to "detach the power of truth [or of the category of religion] from the forms of hegemony, social, economic and cultural, within which it operates at present time." Nuanced materialist approaches, which reintroduce history, practice, embodiment, and emplacement, are crucial in this process of ongoing strategic detaching.

As I stated in my introduction, I had hoped in this volume to discuss a wide range of religious materialities. However, the complexities and scope of survey of this nature forced me to focus strategically on embodiment, practice, and emplacement. Thus, much remains to be done. I have only briefly touched on a variety of topics that fall within the purview of a non-reductive materialist framework. For example, more attention should be given to the widespread circulation of religious artifacts and images through mass media and cyberspace. It would be fruitful to explore how this circulation interacts with religious visual practices to "order space and time, imagine community . . . influence thought and behavior by persuasion of magic, [and] displace rival images and ideologies" (Morgan 2005: 55).

From another angle, we could study the ways in which this circulation of religious artifacts is connected and/or stands in tension with global capitalism, particularly with the contemporary politics of consumption. Building on but going beyond Marx's notion of the fetishism of commodities, scholars such as Michael Taussig, Birgit Meyer, and Jean Comaroff have shown how global neoliberal capitalism has strong elective affinities with the ubiquity of traveling spirits, particularly with the devil. This ubiquity is both due to and a justification for the spread of "strong religions," especially Evangelical Christianity, which use global media to broadcast their message of spiritual warfare against deterritorializing and reterritorializing demonic spirits that have been detached from their local contexts. In the process of spreading their message, these religions often rely on millenarian and apocalyptic visions that are concretized in material objects, such as Christian novels and rock music, and the built environment.

I have argued elsewhere that in the rapid worldwide growth of Charismatic Christianities, we might be witnessing the rise of a highly portable polymorphus "pneumatic materialism," a new highly malleable "spirit-matter" nexus that, in blending the non-dualism of tradition and the simultaneous experience of overproduction and scarcity at the heart of late modernity, is able to bridge in multiple contexts the tension between the seen and the unseen, among the personal, the local, and the global. This pneumatic materialism can address the otherwise intractable condition of physical and spiritual insecurity faced by vast sectors of the world's population, particularly in Latin America and Africa, and among immigrants in the metropoles. If that is the case, we might need a different, materialist, postcolonial, and transnational "phenomenology of the spirit" beyond Hegel's (Vásquez 2008).

Pneumatic materialism may be a powerful creative response to the disembeddedness and disembodiment produced not only by global capitalism, but more dramatically by computer-generated communications. Electronic communications are giving rise to cyberspaces that do not depend on the metaphysics of presence, the privileging of face-to-face interaction as the most authentic form of communication. The new metaphysics of cyberspace, thus, has serious implications for the ways in which we experience our bodies and in which we sacralize space and time. Is cyberspace the fulfillment of the Cartesian dream of being everywhere and nowhere? Is the Internet divinizing humanity by extending our neural networks onto the whole world? Or does cyberspace generate its own form of materiality, its own forms of being-in-the-world, which interact with age-old practices of subjectivation and panoptical control? These are complex questions that a non-reductive materialist approach to religion should tackle.

Another important dimension of material religions that I left mostly unexplored is connected to performance. How is religion embodied and emplaced through dance and theater? What does religion add to artistic performances? What kind of embodied aesthetics accompany the processes of sacralization and desacralization? How does this aesthetics articulate the relationship between text and ritual, between specifically semiotic practices and those practices that are not purely about the production of meaning? How would our understanding of religion change if we approach it through a fully dramaturgical attitude? How does power in its various forms enter the performance of religion? Is it possible and desirable to work toward a phenomenology of religious performances, specifying differences and family resemblances in practices as diverse as praying, chanting, baptizing, incorporating spirits, exorcising spirits, sacrifice, *puja*, ingesting psychoactive substances, pilgrimage, processing, *darshan* (seeing and being seen by the deity), glossolalia, rites of passage, reenactments of the Christ passion or of the lives of great religious figures, among others? How do these performances reproduce and transform our ecologies of life? How do they express and alter our body schemas and our neurophysiology?

I only scratched the surface on a rapidly growing literature on religion and nature that ranges from the work of anthropologist Roy Rappaport to that of bioregionalists such as Wendell Berry and Wes Jackson and environmental philosophers interested in religious worldviews such as J. Baird Callicott and Holmes Rolston, as well as religious ethicists like Bron Taylor and Anna Peterson. This is a field that has great potential to cross-fertilize with materialist approaches to religion in socio-biology, evolutionary psychology, ecology, ethology, and the neurosciences. Finally, a materialist perspective also enables productive research on the roles religion plays in a myriad of other areas of everyday life, including sexuality, violence, food, agriculture, disability, architecture, landscaping, sports, and popular culture. I hope to address some of these topics in my future work, but perhaps others will build on my effort to set some flexible epistemological bases to rematerialize the study of religion.

Notes

Introduction

1. Juan Soldado is considered by many the patron saint of immigrants. He was a private in the Mexican army based in Tijuana in the 1930s who was executed, unjustly according to his devotees. He is, thus, seen as a martyr, a "man wronged by the system." His cult is "a testament to the hardships of border life and the suffering of migrants" (Watson 2001). He has many shrines across northwestern Mexico and the southwestern United States, where many immigrants come to pray, light candles, and make vows for safe passage across the border and for help with urgent health and family matters. See Vanderwood (2004).

2. See Strenski (2003).

3. In an auspicious sign, a new journal called *Material Religion* emerged a few years ago.

4. I share what philosopher of science Joseph Rouse (2002: 3) calls "the Nietzschean commitment of contemporary naturalism, in honor of perhaps its most relentless adherent." This commitment holds that human beings are "natural beings, embodied, causally intra-active, and historically and biologically evolved." I also agree with Rouse that "endorsement of this commitment need not presume an already established boundary between the 'natural' and the 'supernatural.'" These two categories are transitive, contested, and marked and relatively stabilized by the practices of scholars and the people they study.

5. Emic and etic are terms derived from linguistics that are widely used in anthropology to denote standpoints for the description of cultural phenomena. An emic analysis draws its analytical categories from those used by the people under study. In contrast, the etic perspective uses analytical categories extrinsic to the phenomenon in question. Pike saw these standpoints as potentially complementary and mutually correcting rather than dichotomous. See McCutcheon (1999).

6. See Braun (2000), J. Z. Smith (1982), Chidester (1996), and Masuzawa (2005).

7. Those familiar with debates in the philosophy of science will recognize in this position a version of Imre Lakatos's methodology of research programmes, which was an attempt to reformulate Karl Popper's naïve falsificationism in light of Thomas Kuhn's accounts of how science works. See Lakatos (1970).

8. As Feyerabend (1988) argues in response to Lakatos, we cannot assume that time will solve all forms of incommensurability. Some portions of a research programme

may not be fully translatable into competing alternatives, a fact that should caution us against assuming that scientific knowledge is always cumulative (Kuhn 2000). Furthermore, as scholars in science studies, such as Bruno Latour (1988), tell us, the process of adjudicating among competing research programmes is embedded in sociopolitical contexts and networks that condition which theories or concepts gain hegemony.

Chapter 1

1. See book 7 of Plato's *Republic*. All references to *The Republic* come from B. Jowett's translation (Plato 1991).

2. *Phaedo*, p. 392. All references to *Phaedo* are taken from B. Jowett's translation (Plato 1908).

3. *Phaedo*, p. 407.

4. *Republic*, book 6, p. 249.

5. *Republic*, book 10, p. 384.

6. *Timaeus*, p. 18. All quotations from *Timaeus* are taken from Robin Waterfield's translation (Plato 2008).

7. *Timaeus*, p. 19.

8. *Timaeus*, p. 20.

9. *Timaeus*, p. 22.

10. *Timaeus*, p. 34.

11. *On the Soul* 2.1.412a. All citations from Aristotle are taken from McKeon (1947).

12. *On the Soul* 2.4.415a.

13. On *the Soul* 2.1.412b.

14. *On the Soul* 3.4.429b.

15. *On the Soul* 3.5.430a.

16. *On the Soul* 3.5.430a.

17. *The Enneads* 6.9.9. All citations from *The Enneads* come from the MacKenna translation (Plotinus 1957).

18. *The Enneads* 1.6.9.

19. All citations from the New Testament are taken from the Revised Standard Version.

20. Kallistos Ware argues that tension in Paul is not so much between body (*soma*) and soul (*psyche*), a tension more common in Hellenistic dualisms, but between the "flesh" (*sarx*) and spirit (*pneuma*). These last two terms "indicate, not components of the person, but relationships embracing personhood in its totality. 'Flesh' is the *whole* person fallen, 'spirit' the *whole* person redeemed" (Ware 1997: 93).

21. See also John 17:15–18 and 18:36. According to Karen King (2008: 75, 76), "the letters of Paul do not offer a well-bounded homogenous entity or type of Christianity but multiformity, polyphony, and dialogical engagement with select Graeco-Roman and Jewish materials in a variety of social contexts." They offer "evidence of a variety of viewpoints among and within the churches he addressed, as well as diversity of ethnicity, gender, marital status, age, economic status, and social status. . . ."

22. Karen King (2003) argues that the category of Gnosticism has been reified as a histor-ical reality by reducing widely diverse texts to a coherent ideology that stands in stark con-trast to normative Christianity and by assuming, without adequate social and historical evidence, that this ideology bears a one-to-one relationship with the practices of particular communities. In reality, the so-called Gnostic texts "show a variety of cosmological posi-tions, not only the presence of anticosmic dualism, but also milder forms of dualism, tran-scendentalism, and most surprisingly, both radical and moderate forms of monism." (13).

23. Cullman (1962), for example, saw a clear shift in Christian eschatology from a focus among early Christians on Jesus Christ's imminent return and the radical trans-formation of the now to the search in the Middle Ages for salvation in the beyond or at the end of time.

24. McDannell might be overplaying her argument here. Griffith demonstrates that Puritans were strongly interested in "the body's potential as an instrument of salvation as well as damnation." The material world was of central concern in the articulation of morality. "Bodies and desires were . . . fundamental to Puritan under-standings of domestic and social order," making sexual pleasure and procreation within the confines of the male-dominated household totally compatible (Griffith 2004: 49).

25. See Augustine's *De Trinitate* 15.17.11.

26. See Augustine's *De Genesi ad litteram* 12.35.68.

27. Augustine had already prefigured the cogito in *City of God* in his statement "*si fallor, sum*" [If I am mistaken, I exist]. "A non-existent being cannot be mistaken; there-fore I must exist, if I am mistaken. Then since my being mistaken proves that I exist, how can I be mistaken in thinking that I exist, seeing that my mistake establishes my existence? Since therefore I must exist in order to be mistaken, then even if I am mis-taken, there can be no doubt that I am not mistaken in my knowledge that I exist. It follows that I am not mistaken that in knowing that I exist" (Augustine 2003: 460).

28. See the Sixth Meditation.

29. These questions were raised early on by Descartes's contemporaries like Gassendi and Princess Elizabeth of Bohemia. See Descartes (1970).

30. There have been efforts to show that the Cartesian mind-body dualism is not incoherent, since the interaction between heterogeneous substances is said to be non-mechanical causation. Others have argued that Descartes is more of a "trialist" than a dualist: the union of mind and body yields another substance with its own attributes. See Rozemond (1998). I take a pragmatist approach on these debates. It may be tenable to reconcile some version of interactionism with Cartesian dualism. However, the fact that this dualism generates far more problems than it solves indicates that it may be more productive to adopt an alternative epistemology.

Chapter 2

1. See Frank and Leaman (2003). In Ravven and Goodman (2002), Spinoza emerges as the proponent of a modern synthesis of Judeo-Islamic naturalism.

2. *Ethics*, Part I, Definitions 6. All Spinoza citations are taken from Spinoza (2002).

3. *Ethics*, Part I, Proposition 14.

4. Letter 43.

5. *Ethics*, Part IV, Preface.

6. *Ethics*, Part I, Proposition 17.

7. *Ethics*, Part II, Proposition 11.

8. *Ethics*, Part II, Proposition 21.

9. *Ethics*, Part II, Proposition 13.

10. *Ethics*, Part II, Proposition 23.

11. *Ethics*, Part II, Proposition 16.

12. *Ethics*, Part II, Proposition 22.

13. Ravven argues that Damasio's reading is still dualistic. Spinoza views mind and body as not just two "parallel and mutually correlated processes," but two active expressions of a single materiality. According to her, Spinoza offers a radical "psychophysical monism, a mind-body identity theory that reduces neither body to mind nor mind to body. He maintains the causal efficacy of both the mental and physical" (Ravven 2003: 258).

14. *Ethics*, Part II, Proposition 48.

15. *Ethics*, Part I, Proposition 17, Scholium.

16. *Theological-Political Treatise*, Part III, Proposition 45–6.

17. *Ethics*, Part III, Preface.

18. *Political Treatise*, Chapter 1, number [4].

19. Following the *conatus* of the mind, which is directed toward knowledge of God, is blessedness. "Blessedness is not the reward of virtue, but virtue itself. We do not enjoy blessedness because we keep our lust in check. On the contrary, it is because we enjoyed blessedness that we are able to keep our lust in check." *Ethics*, Part IV, Proposition 42.

20. *Ethics*, Part IV, Appendix 4.

21. Leibniz's notion of preestablished harmony also introduces its own version of determinism. Further, the defense of divine free will brings back the threat of dualism.

22. *Ethics*, Part III, Proposition 2, Scholium.

23. See his *Birth of the Tragedy from the Spirit of the Music*.

24. Actually, Nietzsche characterizes the struggle over Western civilization as "Rome against Judea, Judea against Rome." "Rome felt the Jew to be something like anti-nature itself, its antipodal monstrosity as it were: in Rome the Jew stood '*convicted* of hatred for the whole human race;' and rightly, provided one has a right to link salvation and future of the human race with the unconditional dominance of aristocratic values, Roman values" (1969: 52–53). By essentializing Roman and Jewish cultures and histories (and equating Christianity with Judaism), Nietzsche betrays his own call to engage in nuanced genealogical analysis. This essentialism leads him to an unjustifiable and untenable anti-Semitism. As we have seen with Spinoza, Judaism contained a strong affirmation of the body, nature, and history. Conversely, there are "life-denying" strands in Greco-Roman thought.

25. This is an arguable interpretation, perhaps more applicable to the reactive nihilist than to Nietzschean enfleshed perspectivism.

Chapter 3

1. The term phenomenology was actually used for the first time by German mathematician and physicist Johann Heinrich Lambert in a letter to Kant proposing to collaborate. See James (1985).

2. Kant confronted the problem of how to speak intelligibly of the noumena if our horizon is the phenomenal world. He attempts to resolve this problem by arguing that the noumenal functions primarily as a negative category to mark the limits of what can be known, limits which are thinkable but not knowable.

3. Ryba (2006: 100) sees two distinctive notions of pre-Husserlian phenomenology. "By one notion, phenomenology gives access to *a priori* conditions of appearance in any human experience. . . . By the other notion, phenomenology is directed to *a posteriori* classification of empirical data according to resemblances and differences." Ryba's two notions overlap to some extent with my characterization of transcendental and historicist strands in phenomenology.

4. Husserl's thought cannot be considered as evolving linearly, from psychologism to descriptive phenomenology and finally to transcendental phenomenology. According to Moran (2000: 62), Husserl was a "perpetual beginner." What we find are themes that crisscross his work, which he highlighted, reworked, and deepened at different periods of his life and in different texts.

5. Husserl saw the empirical sciences as "pre-theoretical," also operating through the natural attitude. This is the reason why he understands phenomenology not just as a descriptive and analytical method but as a meta-science, a true science of the experience of consciousness.

6. "Do not wish to go out; go back into yourself. Truth dwells in the inner man," *De vera religione*, 39, no. 72.

7. On the concept of empathy and its role in enabling monadological intersubjectivity, see especially the fifth meditation in Husserl (1973).

8. I focus here on Heidegger's early works, namely *Being and Time* (1927) and the lectures that he gave immediately after the publication of this work (*Basic Problems in Phenomenology* and *Metaphysical Foundations of Logic*, both composed in 1928) to clarify and elaborate it. These are the works in which Heidegger lays out most clearly his phenomenological hermeneutics of *Dasein* in conversation with Husserl. Although many of the themes of his early work resonate throughout his oeuvre, in his later works Heidegger increasingly turned away from the question of how *Dasein* asks about and discloses Being through its practices, an approach he felt was still trapped in a Cartesian, instrumentalist attitude, toward how Being graciously makes itself available to us despite our fallenness into the world of things.

9. For example, see Kierkegaard (1962).

10. This line of inquiry extends to symbolic interactionism and ethnomethodology, which show how the procedures that individuals use to build, maintain, and contest the cognitive infrastructure of everyday life.

11. Heidegger uses the term Ek-sistence rather than existence to highlight the uniqueness of *Dasein*, which does not merely exist like other things, but which is open to transcendence as it hears the call of Being.

12. In *Being and Time*, for example, Heidegger writes that our "'bodily nature' hides a whole problematic of its own, though we shall not treat it here" (1962: 143).

13. See, for example, Heidegger 1977b.

14. Later on in *The Visible and the Invisible*, Merleau-Ponty actually rejects the trope of layers and leaves to characterize the body as already too schematic. "If one wants metaphors, it would be better to say that the body sensed and the body sentient are as the obverse and the reverse, or again, as two segments of one circular course which goes above from left to right and below from right to left, but which is but one sole movement in its two phases" (1968: 138).

15. Flesh is a holistic way of being, a kind of non-dualistic facticity. "The flesh is not matter, is not mind, is not substance. To designate it, we would need the old term 'element,' in the sense that it was used to speak of water, air, earth, and fire, that is in the sense of a general thing, midway between the spatio-temporal individual and the idea, a sort of incarnate principle that brings a style of being wherever there is a fragment of being. The flesh is in this sense an 'element' of Being" (Merleau-Ponty 1968: 139).

16. Merleau-Ponty's move from the phenomenology of the body to the ontology of the flesh breaks with the subjectivism behind the notion of cogito. However, it does so at the cost of erasing practice, which necessarily involves the reflective activity of self upon others and itself (Shusterman 2008). The flesh is too undifferentiated a category to illuminate the non-reductive interaction between social, biological, and psychological material processes that make possible the tight intertwining of subjectivity and objectivity.

17. To illustrate this point, Lakoff and Johnson offer the famous example of color. "Color concepts are 'interactional'; they arise from the interaction of our bodies, our brains, the reflective properties of objects, and electromagnetic radiation. Colors are not objective; there is in the grass or the sky no greenness or blueness independent of retinas, color cones, neural circuitry, and brain. Nor are colors purely subjective; they are neither a figment of our imaginations nor spontaneous creations of our brain" (1999: 24–25).

18. I do not discuss Jean-Paul Sartre here because he compounds the contradictions already present in Heidegger's privileging of *Dasein*. By insisting on an utterly free subject making him/herself anew at every turn, Sartre produces a decontextualized account of praxis that fails to see how our embodiment and emplacement enable and constrain activity (see his *Being and Nothingness*, 303–59). For a comparative discussion of Sartre and Merleau-Ponty, see Stewart (1998).

19. Interestingly, Merleau-Ponty thought that Christianity, and particularly Catholicism, was right on target in stressing the mystery of the incarnation. However, he felt

that Christianity took the wrong approach to the mystery, setting a dualism between God and humanity (Moran 2000: 430).

Chapter 4

1. See Cox (2006), Ryba (1991) and Sharma (2001). These genealogies also tell us that it is a mistake to conflate phenomenology and history of religions. The relation between these two approaches has been one of tension and cross-fertilization, depending on the particular scholar under consideration.

2. McCutcheon (1997: 15) rightly points out that Rudolf Otto, Wilfred Cantwell Smith, and Mircea Eliade betray "the continuing influence of Friedrich Schleiermacher." The three of them agree that in religion "the interior, interpersonally unavailable *feeling, faith,* or *consciousness* . . . is primary and underivable." In all fairness to Schleiermacher, he stressed not only the need to "divine" the "inner life" of the author of a text but also to study the language in which s/he is embedded. Still, for Schleiermacher, the process of interpretation is primarily internalist because it takes place between two sovereign subjectivities—author and reader.

3. See King (1999).

4. Since I am citing extensively from relatively old scholarly sources, which tend to use the masculine as the universal, I will mark only the first instance of non-gender-neutral language in the chapter in order to avoid having to flag texts every time this use takes place.

5. Kristensen breaks with Tiele's evolutionary approach, seeking more explicitly to understand the essences behind religious life from the believer's perspective. As he puts, "Believers have never conceived of their own religion as a link in a chain of development. No believer considers his own faith to be somewhat primitive, and the moment we begin to think of it, we have actually lost touch with it" (Kristensen 1960: 13). Because it fails to recognize fully the distinctiveness and value of every religion, the evolutionary point of view is an "unhistorical view-point" (Kristensen 1960: 15).

6. In contrast to Otto, Kristensen is not primarily interested in how the Holy reveals itself. He focuses on the believer's ideas and feeling about the sacred. "We should not take the concept of 'holiness' as our starting point, asking, for example, how the numinous is revealed in natural phenomena. On the contrary, we should ask how the believer conceives the phenomena he calls 'the holy'" (Kristensen 1960: 17).

7. Armin Geertz (2004: 55–56) makes a similar point when he argues that Eliade's new humanism is really a new primitivism, a new expression of the "urge to help heal humanity of its lost harmony and to regenerate it through the idealizing study of archaic religion." This urge turns specific historical indigenous people into an object of the West's desire for redemption and nostalgia for origins.

8. Reacting to Kant's overly rationalistic approach to religion, Otto argues that the Holy is also "a purely a priori category," since it is not "evolved from any sort of sense-perception." In fact, the a priori of the Holy is even "deeper than 'pure reason,' at least

as this is usually understood, namely to that which mysticism has rightly named the *fundus animae*, the 'bottom' or 'ground of the soul' (*Seelengrund*). The ideas of the numinous and the feelings that correspond to them are, quite as much as rational ideas and feelings, absolutely 'pure'" (Otto 1958: 112).

9. Eliade understands ritual as the derivate reenactment of "cosmogonic myth," as a nostalgic reliving of events that took place in *illo tempore*. Since myths of origin "constitute paradigmatic models for all human activities" (Eliade 1959a: 105; see also 1967: 14–17), they precede ritual practices. To the degree that practices are foundational, it is as practices of the gods.

10. Wiebe (1999: 44) charges Eliade, van der Leeuw, and Otto with subverting the initial historical and scientific impetus behind the early phenomenologists, in effect pulling the study of religion "back into the theological domain."

11. According to W. C. Smith (1991: 51), the concept of religion in the West has become reified, "mentally making religion into a thing, gradually coming to conceive it as an objective systematic entity."

12. For a good overview of the literature on anthropology and the body, see Csordas (1999).

13. Jackson gives the example of the mother-child bond, which "is mediated by various modes of behavioral synchrony and affect attunement, including smell, touch, gaze, sympathetic laughter and tears, cradling, lulling embraces, interactive play, and the rhythmic interchanges of motherese" (1998: 11).

14. This position resonates with Owen Flanagan's "neuroexistentialism," which "conceives of our predicament in accordance with Charles Darwin plus neuroscience. The prospects for our kind of being-in-the-world are limited by our natures as smart but fully embodied short-lived animals." See Flanagan (2009: 41).

15. Csordas recognizes this problem when he admits that "alterity is hardly specific to religion." There are forms of alterity involved in racial conflict and political violence. Yet, in a move reminiscent of Eliade's claim that we are all *homo religiosus*, Csordas argues that all forms of alterity may have a "religious structure." However, Csordas acknowledges that his approach does not yet "account for how or why different religious forms and institutions are elaborated" (2004:176). In other words, the claim that "alterity itself is the object of religion" works only because he holds a very abstract concept of religion that comes at the cost of sacrificing the concreteness and contested nature of lived religious practices. Once again, temptation of transcendence gets in the way a truly materialist and historicist phenomenology.

16. See, for example, Guha (1997).

Chapter 5

1. Since I am citing extensively from relatively old scholarly sources, which tend to use the masculine as the universal, I will mark only the first instance of non-gender-neutral language in the chapter in order to avoid having to flag texts every time this use takes place.

2. The tradition of sociology of knowledge continues in the sociology of science, particularly in the work of Barry Barnes, David Bloor, Bruno Latour, and Steve Woolgar, who examine how the practices of scientists are conditioned by their embeddedness in society. See Pickering (1992). This research programme has been most recently attacked by physicist Alan Sokal, who submitted a satirical essay to *Social Text*, a leading cultural studies journal, which in essence argued that gravity is socially constructed. That the essay was accepted without rigorous vetting means for Sokal that postmodern humanities and social sciences are engaged in "a particular kind of nonsense and sloppy thinking: one that denies the existence of objective realities, or (when challenged) admits their existence but downplays their practical relevance." Against this "epistemic relativism" and "subjectivist thinking," Sokal declares that "[t]here is a real world; its properties are not merely social constructions; facts and evidence do matter" (Sokal 1996: 63).

3. Heidegger, for example, had attacked Jean-Paul Sartre's existentialism for being too dependent on an instrumentalist subjectivism in "Letter on Humanism."

4. This was, in fact, the thesis of Frankfurt School theorists Max Horkheimer and Theodor Adorno in *Dialectic of Enlightenment*.

5. The term "panoptical society" derives from Jeremy Bentham's panopticon, a circular prison he designed in the eighteenth century to maximize surveillance from a central point. See Foucault (1977b). Foucault views the panopticon as a specific technology of power designed to fulfill the Enlightenment's ambition of attainting "universal visibility." In that sense, the panopticon is also a trope for tyranny of the gaze that Foucault feels is at the heart of modernity.

6. According to Foucault, an episteme is "the total set of relations that unite, at a given period, the discursive practices that give rise to epistemological figures, sciences, and possibly formalized systems . . . it is the totality of relations that can be discovered, for a given period, between the sciences when one analyses them at the level of discursive regularities" (1972: 191).

7. Foucault refuses "analyses couched in terms of the symbolic field or the domain of signifying structures." Instead he relies on "analyses in terms of the genealogy of relations of force, strategic developments, and tactics. Here I believe one's point of reference should not be the model of language (*langue*) and signs, but that of war and battle. The history which bears and determines us has the form of a war rather than that of language: relations of power, not relations of meaning" (1980: 114). Foucault is implicitly critiquing structuralism, but the same point applies to Derrida and Geertz.

8. In fact, at one point, Foucault states that the target of his analyses is not institutions or ideologies, but "regimes of practices," "programmes of conduct which have both prescriptive effects regarding what is to be done . . . and codifying effects regarding what is to be known (1991: 75). He is interested in regimes of embodied and signifying practices.

9. The implication here is that power not a monolith that bulldozes everything in its path. Rather power is always dependent on "a multiplicity of points of resistance: these

play the role of adversary, target, support, or handle in power relations. These points of resistance are present everywhere in the power network." Conversely, resistance is never pure, "never in a position of exteriority in relation to power" (1978: 95).

10. After Jacques Lacan's "structuralist" reading of Freud, there are theorists broadly working within the psychoanalytical research programme who emphasize the unstable, symbolically mediated, differential, and non-totalizing aspects of "the self." I am thinking here of Julia Kristeva, Luce Irrigaray, and Slavoj Žižek. The question is the extent to which the semiotics or poetics of the unconscious can be reconciled with Freud's materialism. Freud may be faulted for many things, but his stress on the biological origins of the psyche, on organic drives like aggression and self-preservation, is a valuable resource to craft a moderate social constructionism.

11. This appeal to a core of distinctive feminine qualities that can stand against the patriarchal ideologies of domination is found among theorists as diverse as Luce Irigaray, Julia Kristeva, Nancy Chodorow, and Carol Gilligan. Butler argues that this appeal reproduces the hegemonic binary logic of heterosexuality, of presenting gender differences as a congealed reality.

12. Althusser argued that ideology functions by "interpellating," that is, hailing or calling forth particular kinds of subjects that not only fulfill various functions within the interlocking structures of capitalism but also misrecognize their emergence and positioning. Speech-act theorists were interested in the ways in which language operates in everyday life. Certain acts, such as christening as ship or pronouncing a couple married, are not merely descriptive. Language performs the act that it describes, bringing forth a change of status for both the subject and the object of the speech.

13. In *The Phenomenology of Mind*, arguably the pinnacle of European Idealism, Hegel had claimed that "whatever is is rational and whatever is rational is." Along the same lines, Colebrook (2000: 78) argues that "Butler's account (like Hegel's *Logic*) conflates the *being* of a thing with the mode in which that thing is known. The body is, it is true, only thought after the event of discourse. But does this render the body itself an *effect* of that event?"

Chapter 6

1. Butler (1992) argues that even in instances where violence against women appears overwhelmingly physical, as in the case of rape, there is always symbolic mediation. For example, the definition of rape has changed over time with the evolution of legal systems.

2. As with Heisenberg's uncertainty principle (roughly stated: it is impossible to know simultaneously the position and momentum of an electron, since by measuring one, the scientist affects the other), Bohr recognizes that "there is no ambiguous way to differentiate between the 'object' and the 'agencies of observation'" (Barad 1999: 3). "While, within the scope of classical physics, the interaction between object and apparatus can be neglected or, if necessary, compensated for, in quantum physics this interaction thus forms an inseparable part of the phenomenon. Accordingly, the

unambiguous account of proper quantum phenomena must, in principle, include a description of all the relevant features of the experimental arrangement" (Bohr 1963: 4).

3. Barad (2007: 411) recognizes Pickering's valuable critique of dualism and representationalism but faults him for ignoring "important discursive dimensions of scientific practices, including questions of meaning, intelligibility, significance, identity, and power, which are central to poststructuralist invocations of performativity and feminist accounts of technoscientific practices." On the discussion of social constructionism and science, see also Latour (1999) and Rouse (2002).

4. As we saw with her notion of the "abject," Judith Butler shares Lacan's "ontology of negativity" (Braidotti 2002: 56), as does Slavoj Žižek.

5. Here Deleuze and Guattari are blending Nietzsche's anti-essentialist notion of the will to power, Freud's libidinal materialism, and Marx's historical materialism (with its emphasis on labor and production). The decentered unconscious is the working class, whose productive power is alienated into the ego and super-ego, which become fetishized as the source of civilization.

6. There is no consensus on what Deleuze and Guattari meant by the body without organs. Some scholars see it as another version of Foucault understanding of the body as a tabula rasa that gets inscribed by cultural forces. I read the body without organs not as a passive substance, but as fleeting, sheer, and unsegmented generativity, very much like Nietzsche's notion of the moment, which contains all eternity. The BwO is "the full egg before the extension of the organism and the organization of the organs, before the formation of strata; as the intense egg defined by axes and vectors, gradients and thresholds, by dynamic tendencies involving energy transformation and kinematic movements involving group displacement, by migrations: all independent of accessory forms because the organs appear and function here only as pure intensities" (Deleuze and Guattari 1987: 153). The BwO is not some pristine origin before our fall into culture. "[I]t is already under way the moment the body has had enough of organs and wants to slough them off, or loses them" (Deleuze and Guattari 1987: 150).

7. The term transcendental here does not entail the search for a priori foundational structures as in Kant's transcendental idealism or Husserl's transcendental reduction. Deleuze uses the term transcendental to highlight the fact that his philosophy departs from the experience of becoming (ergo the term empiricism) and that this experience is its own ground. The transcendental empiricist is radically immanent and non-dualistic. "Absolute immanence is in itself: it is not in something, to something; it does not depend on an object or belong to a subject. In Spinoza, immanence is not immanence to substance; rather, substance and modes are in immanence" (Deleuze 2001: 26).

8. Viveiros de Castro (1998). See also Harvey (2005) on the "new animism."

9. Other boundary figures in Haraway's work include onco-mice, primates, and companion species.

10. Haraway is critical of Deleuze and Guattari's characterization of the process of becoming-woman and becoming-animal. She thinks that their overemphasis on mobility ("lines of flight") is too abstract, too removed from "the ordinariness of the

flesh" and "daily becoming-with" (Haraway 2008: 27–31, 314–15). However, Haraway clearly states that she finds the notion of assemblages very helpful.

Chapter 7

1. Still, artificial networks used experimentally are far cry from real neural networks. The latter "are much more complicated, with billions of neurons and trillions of connections. Moreover . . . [real] neurons have dozens of neurotransmitters that provide chemical links between them, so the brain must be considered in chemical as well as electrical terms. Real neurons undergo changes in synaptic and nonsynaptic properties that go beyond what is modeled in artificial neural networks" (Thagard 2005: 127).

2. See also Barkow, Cosmides, and Tooby (1992). They compare the brain to a Swiss-army knife, with multiple, independent-yet-interconnected dedicated functions. The neurophysiological evidence for massive modularity, particularly involving higher cognitive processes, is scant.

3. Varela developed the notion of autopoiesis independently, through his collaborative work with biologist Humberto Maturana. A biological model of autopoiesis is the eukaryotic cell. "A cell is a thermodynamically open system, continually exchanging matter and energy with its environments. Some molecules are imported through the membrane and participate in processes inside the cell, whereas other molecules are excreted as waste. Throughout this exchange, the cell produces a host of substances that both remain within the cell (thanks to its membrane) and participate in those very same production processes. In other words, a cell produces its own components, which in turn produce it, in an on-going circular process" (Thompson 2007: 98).

4. See Petit (2005). Geertz (1973b: 68) makes the same point when he argues that "the reciprocally creative relationship between somatic and extrasomatic phenomena seems to have been of crucial significance during the whole of the primate advance." More specifically, a dramatic cortical expansion in *Homo sapiens*'s brain accompanied the rise of culture. "Tools, hunting, family organization, and, later, art, religion, and 'science' molded man [*sic*] somatically" (Geertz 1973b: 83).

5. On epidemiological approaches to cultural evolution, see also Atran (2002).

6. Dawkins strongly disputes the idea of a religion module, arguing instead that religion is the "by-product of the misfiring" of other modules, such those dealing with kinship, reciprocal exchanges, and empathy (Dawkins 2006: 179).

7. Other research focuses on the activities of the limbic system, particularly of the amygdala and the hippocampus.

8. Peterson (2003: 18–19) distinguishes between "hostile reductions," which seek to discredit religious belief by showing that it is the effect of physical causes, and "friendly reductions," such as neurotheology and the God-gene thesis that, while reducing religion to biological processes, focus on religion's naturalness and its positive role in evolutionary adaptation. This distinction is helpful. However, the real problem is strong reductionism, whatever its valence.

9. Carol Albright criticizes the "God module" hypothesis because it assumes the "religious experience is basically unidimensional—mystical—rather than comprising a rich menu of various kinds of experience" (2000: 737). Moving beyond the view of cognition as the coordination of relatively encapsulated domains and echoing Varela's argument about brainwebs or large-scale phase synchronizations, she argues provocatively that, if anything, "the entire human brain might be described as a 'God module'" (Albright 2000: 735).

10. See the website of the Society of European Neurotheology: http://www.neurotheology.org/.

11. Postictal psychosis is a condition in which the subject experience delusions, depressive or manic psychosis, or bizarre thoughts and behavior within seven days after the epileptic seizure.

12. As Csordas (1994b: 287) puts it for the case of a Navajo informant with a similar brain injury, certain experiences are "thematized as religious not because religious experience is reducible to a neurological discharge but because it is a strategy of the self in need of a powerful idiom for orientation in the world." See chapter 4.

13. Despite stressing that evolution is a blind process, Dawkins often falls into the teleological trap, as when he quotes geneticist Richard Lewontin: "That is the one point which I think all evolutionists are agreed upon, that it is virtually impossible to do a better job than an organism is doing in its own environment" (Dawkins 2006: 164). For a critique of the reading of evolution as "reverse engineering," see Gould (1977).

14. Even E. O. Wilson (1975) accepts this proscriptive view, referring more to "genetic biases" for certain kinds of behaviors rather than to widespread genetically determined conduct. Roy Rappaport puts it well when he writes that "adaptation is not a maximizing, or even an immediately optimizing process. Adaptations need not be the best possible solutions to problems, but only 'good enough.'" He adds that maximizing and optimizing of immediate pay-offs may in fact "reduce long-term flexibility" because they would require specialization (Rappaport 1979: 64).

15. According to Grosz, Darwin's stress on both random variation and natural selection "provide[s] something of a bridge between the emphasis on determinism that is so powerful in classical science and the place of indetermination that has been so central to the contemporary postmodern forms of the humanities. Evolution is neither free nor unconstrained, nor determined and predictable in advance" (Grosz 2008: 45).

16. See McCauley and Lawson (2002).

17. To the extent that McCauley and Lawson (2002) take into account the physicality of religious rituals, it is only instrumentally, as mnemonic/motivational devices. The differential level of "sensory pageantry" shapes the way we store and transmit religion. Gavin Brown (2003) recognizes that most rituals are rule bound and tightly structured. However, building on the late work of Victor Turner, he argues that this strong formalism is a response to the ever-present threat of indeterminacy and chaos that is part and parcel of any ritual performance.

18. New mechanicists abandon the search for global accounts of cognition, which are predicated on "a straight arrow of reduction down to molecular neuroscience."

Instead, they seek "network[s] of explanations crossing levels" that account for specific localized mechanisms. "The situation in social neuroscience can probably best characterized as coevolution of theories at different levels . . . mutual adjustment of concepts and theories, and explanatory pluralism" (Looren de Jung and Schouten 2007: 317–18).

19. For McGinn, the mystery lies in the "deep connection between the mind and brain" and the "sharp distinction in the faculties through which we apprehend them." "[W]e are aware of consciousness inwardly, while we are aware of the brain outwardly. But . . . introspection cannot teach you a thing about the brain as a physical object, even though consciousness is a property of the brain, and outer perception cannot give you access to consciousness, even though consciousness is rooted in the observable brain. There must be an underlying unity in the mind-brain link, but there is an irreducible duality in the faculties through which we come to know about the mind and brain" (1999: 46, 47).

20. Wilson concedes that "the magnitude of the technical problems facing social theorists in particular is . . . extremely daunting." "Questioning the very idea of consilience from biology to culture, [some philosophers] point to the non-linearity of the viable equations, to second- and third-order interaction of factors, to stochasticity, and to all the other monsters that dwelleth in the Great Maelstrom Sea, and they sigh, *No hope, no hope*." In the face of this pessimism, Wilson can only offer humanists hope and Promethean determination. "It is better to press on as if they [the philosophers] were wrong. There is only one way to find out. The more forbidding the task, the greater the prize for those who dare to undertake it" (1998: 208–9).

21. I will discuss the concepts of obduracy and affordance in chapter 11.

Chapter 8

1. See Harris (1999).

2. The "Wiener Kries" was a group of mathematicians, physicists, and philosophers of science that came together in at the turn of the twentieth century. Among them were Rudolf Carnap, Moritz Schlick, and Otto Neurath. The Circle was dissolved in the 1930s, as many of its members who were Jewish and politically progressive fled Nazi persecution.

3. See Wittgenstein (2007).

4. See Wittgenstein (2009).

5. The late Wittgenstein influenced "ordinary language philosophers," such as Austin and Searle.

6. See Weber (1963), especially chapter 7.

7. For a similar critique of Geertz, see Howes (2006).

8. Durkheim also linked transformations in consciousness and religion to the progress of structural differentiation, as a society moves from mechanical to organic solidarity. This line of thinking led to the hypothesis that secularization follows modernization.

9. See Descombes (1980). In *Tristes Tropiques*, Lévi-Strauss rejects phenomenology and existentialism for their "sentimentality" and their "over-indulgent attitude towards the illusions of subjectivity" (1973: 58).

10. Lévi-Strauss allows some limited space for practice through the figure of the "bricoleur," who makes do "with 'whatever is at hand,' that is to say with a set of tools and material which is always finite and is also heterogeneous because what it contains bears no relation to the current project, or indeed to any particular project, but is the contingent result of all the occasions there have been to renew or enrich the stock or to maintain it with the remains of previous constructions or destructions" (Lévi-Strauss 1966: 17).

11. As we saw in chapter 3, Heidegger (1962) takes Husserl to task for relying on a Cartesian notion of subjectivity marked by a disabling mind-body duality. Heidegger instead uses the term *Dasein* to stress the self's facticity, historicity, and contingency, as well as its inextricable relation with Being-itself. Derrida is influenced by Heidegger's critique of Husserl and Western metaphysics, but he reads this critique through the lens of structuralism.

12. A similar debate takes place in postcolonial studies between scholars who decenter history as written by elites in the urban metropole by recovering the voices of the rural poor in the periphery, and Gayatri Spivak (1988), who, influenced by Derrida, questions the possibility that the subaltern can speak authoritatively in a discourse other than the oppressor's.

13. In later years, Derrida qualified his textual monism. "What I call the 'text' is not distinct from action or opposed to action. Of course, if you reduce a text to a book or to something that is written on pages, then perhaps there will be a problem with action. Although even a text in the form of a book . . . is already something like action. There is no action, even in the classical sense of the word, no political or action which could be simply dissociated from, or opposed to, discourse. There is no politics without discourse, there is no politics without the book in our culture" (Derrida 1999: 65–66). This maneuver mirrors Geertz's protestations that "interpretive anthropology is very practice oriented so texts are performed" (Panourgiá 2002: 427). Both thinkers see practices primarily through the prism of signification.

14. Bourdieu (1984: 496) makes a similar point. Because Derrida denies any textual exteriority, he elevates philosophical discourse above the necessities of ordinary life, preserving a "stock of consecrated texts from becoming dead letters, mere archival material, fit at best for the history of ideas or the sociology of knowledge." This repository of consecrated texts that must be interpreted endlessly and requires the rare competence of making constant intertextual references is the core of Derrida's symbolic power as a philosopher.

Chapter 9

1. See chapters 3–5 of book 6 of *Nichomachean Ethics*. For good treatments of praxis and phronesis in Aristotle and after, see Gadamer (1975).

2. See Lobkowicz (1983). The conflation of these categories is not altogether unproblematic. There is a whole tradition stretching from Heidegger, Gadamer, and the Frankfurt School to Hannah Arendt and Alasdair McIntyre which denounces the instrumentalization politics and the life-world under the weight of *theoria* and *techne*. Through his focus on production and his affirmation of the positive power of technology to change the world, Marx contributes to the dominance of a means-ends rationality. Thus, we should be careful not to appropriate wholesale the Marxist definition of praxis. It needs to be critiqued by other perspectives that decenter the subject, such as hermeneutics, semiotics, neurophenomenology, and evolution.

3. See Bernstein (1983).

4. See Bell (1997).

5. Since I am citing extensively from relatively old scholarly sources, which tend to use the masculine as the universal, I will mark only the first instance of non-gender-neutral language in the chapter in order to avoid having to flag texts every time this use takes place.

6. For a similar reading, see Radcliffe-Brown (1945).

7. For a related approach, see Norbert Elias's *The History of Manners*, in which he argues that "the psychogenesis of the adult makeup in civilized society cannot . . . be understood if considered independently of the sociogenesis of our 'civilization'" (1978: xiii). In the West, the concept of civilization is predicated on the regulation of people's manners, gestures, speech, clothing, and housing to move them away from nature, and particularly bodily functions, considered primitive, barbaric, and vulgar. Elias sees in the new habits "embodiments of a different mental and emotional structure" (56). Elias's work is problematic in many ways. He adopted a thesis of European exceptionalism, which counterposed a civilized West to *Naturvolk*, unburdened primitives in other parts of the world. Further, he traced the civilizing process through texts, failing to conduct any fieldwork on evolving practices. Finally, he had a one-sided view of the body as a passive surface for sociocultural inscription.

8. Turner saw pilgrimages as instances of "institutionalized" or "ordered" anti-structure. Because pilgrimages involve the travel over long distances of large amounts of people, they require a certain degree of organization. Thus, "the absolute communitas of unchanneled anarchy does not obtain. . . . What we see is a social system, founded in a system of religious beliefs, polarized between fixity and travel, secular and sacred, social structure and normative communitas" (1974: 171).

9. Dilthey uses the concept of "lived experience" (*Erlebnis*) to refer to the recreation and reliving of the historical flow of human expressions. All individuals are immersed in this "stream of time" as a precondition for understanding and for the creation of new life-expressions. Thinking, experience, and practice fuse in *Erlebnis*.

10. Because Turner tends to see anti-structural moments as primarily cathartic, that is, as public performances that ventilate social tensions on the way to reintegration, his processual approach ends up replaying the Durkheimian and structural-functionalist emphasis on order. Turner recognizes that not every conflict reaches a clear resolution and that reintegration changes the status quo. However, he tends to see change as

gradual and concentrated in the symbolic realm. He does not tell us how cultural processes are related to the political economy or to colonialism and capitalism. Praxis theorists after Turner have paid more attention to the anti-structural, open-ended, and indeterminate character of ritual (Brown 2003).

11. The other key figure in the social sciences is Anthony Giddens (1979). In philosophy, pragmatism, particularly as articulated by Charles Sanders Pierce, John Dewey, and George Herbert Mead, offers a thoroughly relational and historicized view of self and truth that shares a great deal with Marx's notion of praxis. Pragmatists also see socially constituted, semiotically mediated, and embodied habits as crucial for effective practice. See Bernstein (1983).

12. Therefore, the habitus "governs all forms of incorporation, choosing and modifying everything the body ingests and digests and assimilates, physiologically and psychologically" (Bourdieu 1984: 190).

13. Bourdieu (1987: 129) charges Weber with "succumbing to the naive representation of charisma as a mysterious quality inherent in a person or as a gift of nature. . . . even in his most rigorous writings Max Weber never proposes anything other than a psycho-social theory of charisma, a theory that regards it as the lived relation of a public to the charismatic personality."

14. Comaroff (1985: 5) makes the similar point: "For all its cogency, [Bourdieu's] formulation leads us so far into the domain of implicit meaning that the role of consciousness is almost totally eclipsed. In his effort to correct what he perceives to be a subjectivist bias in prevailing views of human practice, Bourdieu goes so far in the other direction that his actors seem doomed to reproduce their world mindlessly . . ."

15. See Bourdieu (1977: 168–69).

16. See Bourdieu (1991: 30).

17. See Weber (1963), especially chapter 4.

18. Foucault seems to offer a similar alternative when he tells us that "where there is power, there is resistance, and yet, or rather consequently, this resistance is never in a position of exteriority in relation to power" (1978: 95). So, intellectuals interested in change need to ally themselves with local insurrectional subjugated knowledges operating at the synapses where power is directly applied to bodies and, thus, where it is most vulnerable (1980: 83).

19. See Scott (1985). Also important in identifying the "arts of resistance" are Mikhail Bakhtin's notions of "heteroglossia" and the grotesque in carnival. They highlight the agonistic role that symbolic inversion, earthy humor, and jargon play for those at the margins of society. See Bakhtin (1984).

20. Comaroff (1985: 262) writes: "In my analysis of Tshidi Zionism I have attempted to show that its coded forms did not spell out a mere apolitical escapism but an attempt, under pitifully restrained circumstances, to address and redress experiential conflict. Far from being a liminal refuge, the movement was an integral part of the culture of the wider social community, drawing upon a common stock of symbols, commenting upon relations of inequality both local and more global, and communicating a message of defiance beyond its own limited confines."

21. Echoing Mauss and foreshadowing Bourdieu, and Foucault, Thompson tells us that Methodism was about "the cultivation of one's own soul." "Methodism was the desolate inner landscape of Utilitarianism in an era of transition to the work-discipline of industrial capitalism. As the 'working paroxysms' of the hand-worker are methodised and his unworkful impulses are brought under control, so his emotional and spiritual paroxysms increase" (1966: 365). But if Methodism provided disciplinary technologies and a sporadic, localized catharsis for the worker, its utopianism also inspired socialist movements such as Owenism (1966: 802–6).

22. Vásquez (2005).

23. This work, which Orsi describes as the "corporalization of the sacred," includes many of the disciplinary techniques of the body mentioned by Mauss, Asad, and Foucault. For example, "nuns were determined to instill a passionate prayer life in children and to form their limbs in the appropriate devotional posture" (Orsi 2005: 85).

24. McCutcheon sees Orsi as a "caretaker," a "modern-day instance of Mircea Eliade's well-known notion of a new humanism—in which the scholar is thought vicariously to re-experience the supposedly deep existential situations contained in the remnants and artifacts of other people's lives" (McCutcheon 2006: 726). Given Orsi's vigorous challenge to Puritan-centered readings of U.S. religious history, it is too facile to identify him with the private affair tradition. I have argued that it is possible to develop a robust and critical non-internalist and non-mentalist phenomenology of religion that takes as its point of departure the vitality and richness of the religious person's embodied practices and experiences.

25. Rather than positing a center from which all power emanates, Foucault suggests that we "conduct an ascending analysis of power, starting, that is, from its infinitesimal mechanisms, which each have their own history, their own trajectory, their own techniques and tactics, and then see how these mechanisms of power have been—and continue to be—invested, colonised, utilised, involuted, transformed, displaced, extended, etc. by ever more general mechanisms and by forms of global domination" (1980: 99).

26. For example, see Burdick (1993), Dean (1999), Ireland (1992), Levine (1992), Norget (2006), Peterson (1997), and Vásquez (1998).

Chapter 10

1. Kim Knott rightly observes that space was not of special concern to Müller, Tiele, Chantepie de la Saussaye, and other founding fathers of the academic study of religion. She credits Gerardus van der Leeuw's *Religion in Essence and Manifestation*, published in 1933, with focusing attention on sacred space and its phenomenological relation to power (Knott 2008: 1104). This is several decades before the social sciences, not counting geography of course, took spatial dynamics seriously.

2. Since I am citing extensively from relatively old scholarly sources, which tend to use the masculine as the universal, I will mark only the first instance of non-gender-neutral language in the chapter in order to avoid having to flag texts every time this use takes place.

3. Tuan, in fact, cites favorably Eliade's notions of hierophany and *axis mundi* in his treatment of sacred space (Tuan 1974: 146–48). Tuan sees the spatial role of religion as primarily establishing order rather than transcendence. "[A] humanistic approach to religion would require that we be aware of the differences in the human desire for coherence, and note how these differences are manifest in the organisation of space and time, and in attitudes to nature" (Tuan 1976: 272).

4. Eliade himself acknowledges the logocentric thrust of his work. "[I]t could be said that this 'primitive' ontology has a Platonic structure; and in that case Plato could be regarded as the outstanding philosopher of 'primitive mentality,' that is, as the thinker who succeeded in giving philosophical currency and validity to the modes of life and behavior of archaic humanity" (1954: 34).

5. The literature on religion, domestic spaces, and gender dynamics, with which these spaces are often intertwined, is vast. See Bourdieu (1977: 87–95), Campo (1991), Klassen (2001), McDannell (1986), and Tweed (2006: 103–9).

6. De Certeau's effort to highlight the multivocality of spaces resonates with the work of Henri Lefebvre. The latter refers to the historical production of three interconnected kinds of spaces: perceived space, which is embodied in the spatial practices of daily life and urban reality; conceived space, as the abstract construct of planners and technocrats; and lived space, as creatively imagined through non-verbal symbols, signs, and memories (Lefebvre 1991: 31–46).

7. See Gramsci (1971: 323).

8. See also Brown (1999) and McAlister (1998).

9. See Clifford (1997).

Chapter 11

1. Jean Baudrillard (1995), for example, argues that the social has totally imploded, leaving only the "desert of the real," an endless procession of simulacra.

2. For more on this project, see http://www.latam.ufl.edu/NewFordProjectSite/index.shtml.

3. For an interesting attempt to bring network analysis and Bourdieu's notion of social fields into dialogue, see de Nooy (2003).

4. For an excellent contemporary application of Mauss's work on the gift, see Schmidt (1997).

5. I thank James Cochrane for this valuable insight.

6. Drawing from Bourdieu (1977), I rework De Preester's and Knockaert's suggestion that we adopt a "dynamic structuralism" to understand the plasticity of neural networks. See De Preester and Knockaert (2005).

7. Hegel (1967: 79) uses this humorous expression to criticize Fichte's naïve notion that absolute knowledge is immediately given, accessible without conflict and negation. The claim that everything is flows may fall into a similar form of undifferentiated unity.

8. There are fierce debates as to whether nature exists, since human praxis has thoroughly transformed it. For a good summary see Peterson (2001).

9. Messer (2001: 13) notes that "Rappaport's 'systems' thinking . . . blocked any theoretical accommodation with those who observed and thought about the practical impact of human purpose or individual decision making on system dynamics." Rappaport never considered human agency and praxis "to be his principal areas of interest."

10. Hayles's position bears some interesting connections with debates on shamanic multinaturalism, the capacity of the shaman to assume diverse embodied perspectives, from the viewpoints of animals, humans, plants, or the ancestor spirits, because we are all part of an interconnected ensouled reality (Viveiros de Castro 1998: 317).

11. Haraway (2008: 362) refers to "naturalcultural" contact zones to stress the co-constitution of human and companion species and to transcend the "dualistic assumption that people change culturally, but animals change only biologically, since they have no culture."

12. David Morgan makes a similar point when he writes that "*the study of visual culture should attempt to balance reception with production.* To this must be added an acknowledgement of the important influence that the physical features and appearance of an image exert on its reception." Thus, according to Morgan, "vision is a complex assemblage of seeing what is there, seeing by virtue of habit what one expects to see there, what one desires to be there, and seeing what one is told to see there" (2005: 73–74, italics in the original).

By the Way of a Conclusion

1. Charles Taylor uses the term immanent frame to characterize "the different structures we live in: scientific, social, technological, and so on . . . [that] are part of a 'natural,' or 'this-wordly' order which can be understood in its own terms, without reference to the 'supernatural' or 'transcendent.' But this order of itself leaves the issue open whether, for the purposes of ultimate explanation, or spiritual transformation, or final sense-making, we might have to invoke something transcendent" (Taylor 2007: 594). I do not agree with Taylor's characterization of transcendence, which is strongly shaped by unstated theistic, Christian assumptions. Instead, I see transcendence as diverse, contextual and intra-historical material expressions of the immanent frame's openness, fecundity, and complexity. For a rich discussion of Taylor's *A Secular Age*, see http://blogs.ssrc.org/tif/author/taylor/ (particularly the contribution by William Connolly).

2. Orsi (1997: 8).

3. Gregersen (2006) identifies at least five types of theism that are commensurable with non-reductive materialism.

References

Abram, David. 1996. *The Spell of the Sensuous: Perception and Language in a More-Than-Human World*. New York: Pantheon Books.

Albright, Carol R. 2000. "The 'God Module' and the Complexifying Brain." *Zygon: Journal of Religion & Science* 35(4): 735–44.

Althusser, Louis. 1997. "The Only Materialist Tradition, Part I: Spinoza." In *The New Spinoza*, edited by Warren Montag and Ted Stolze, 3–18. Minneapolis: University of Minnesota Press.

Appadurai, Arjun, ed. 1986. *The Social Life of Things: Commodities in a Cultural Perspective*. Cambridge: Cambridge University Press.

———. 1996. *Modernity at Large: Cultural Dimensions of Globalization*. Minneapolis: University of Minnesota Press.

———. 2006. "The Thing Itself." *Public Culture* 18(1): 15–21.

Arweck, Elisabeth, and William Keenan. 2006. *Materialising Religion: Expression, Performance, and Ritual*. London: Ashgate.

Asad, Talal. 1993. *Genealogies of Religion*. Baltimore: Johns Hopkins University Press.

———. 2003. *Formations of the Secular: Christianity, Islam, Modernity*. Stanford, Calif.: Stanford University Press.

Atran, Scott. 2002. *In God We Trust*. New York: Oxford University Press.

Augustine. 1974. *The Essential Augustine*, edited by Vernon Bourke. Indianapolis, Ind.: Hackett Publishing.

———. 2001. *The Confessions of St. Augustine*. New York: Signet Classic.

———. 2003. *Concerning the City of God against the Pagans*. New York: Penguin Books.

Austin, J. L. 1971. *How to Do Things with Words: The William James Lectures Delivered at Harvard University, 1955*. Oxford: Oxford University Press.

Bakhtin, Mikhail. 1984. *Rabelais and His World*. Bloomington: Indiana University Press.

Barad, Karen. 1999. "Agential Realism: Feminist Interventions in Understanding Scientific Practices." In *The Science Studies Reader*, edited by Mario Biagioli, 1–11. New York: Routledge.

———. 2007. *Meeting the Universe Halfway: Quantum Physics and the Entanglement of Matter and Meaning*. Durham, N.C.: Duke University Press.

———. 2008. "Posthumanist Performativity: Toward an Understand of How Matter Comes to Matter." In *Material Feminisms*, edited by Stacy Alaimo and Susan Hekman, 120–54. Bloomington: Indiana University Press.

Barkow, Jerome, Leda Cosmides, and John Tooby. 1992. *The Adapted Mind: Evolutionary Psychology and the Generation of Culture*. New York: Oxford University Press.

Barrett, Justin. 2004. *Why Would Anyone Believe in God?* Walnut Creek, Calif.: AltaMira Press.

Basso, Keith. 1996. *Wisdom Sits in Places: Landscape and Language among the Western Apache*. Albuquerque: University of New Mexico Press.

Bateson, Gregory. 1972. *Steps to an Ecology of Mind*. New York: Ballantine.

Baudrillard, Jean. 1995. *Simulacra and Simulation*. Ann Arbor: University of Michigan Press.

Bauman, Zygmunt. 1998. *Globalization: The Human Consequences*. New York: Columbia University Press.

Bechtel, William. 2007. "Reducing Psychology while Maintaining its Autonomy via Mechanistic Explanations." In *The Matter of the Mind: Philosophical Essay on Psychology, Neuroscience, and Reduction*, edited by Maurice Schouten and Huib Looren de Jong, 172–98. London: Blackwell.

Begley, Sharon. 2000. "Music on the Mind." *Newsweek*, 24 July, 50–52.

Bell, Catherine. 1997. *Ritual: Perspectives and Dimensions*. New York: Oxford University Press.

———. 2008. "Extracting the Paradigm—Ouch!" *Method and Theory in the Study of Religion* 20(2): 114–24.

Benavides, Gustavo. 2003. "There Is Data for Religion." *Journal of the American Academy of Religion* 71(4): 895–903.

Berger, Peter. 1969. *The Sacred Canopy: Elements of a Theory of Religion*. New York: Anchor Books.

Berger, Peter, and Thomas Luckmann. 1966. *The Social Construction of Reality: A Treatise in Social Knowledge*. Garden City, N.Y.: Doubleday.

Bernstein, Richard. 1983. *Beyond Objectivism and Relativism: Science, Hermeneutics, and Praxis*. Philadelphia: University of Pennsylvania Press.

Berry, Wendell. 1987. *Home Economics*. New York: North Point Press.

Blackmore, Susan. 2006. *Conversations on Consciousness: What the Best Minds Think about the Brain, Free Will, and What It Means to Be Human*. New York: Oxford University Press.

Bohr, Niels. 1963. *The Philosophical Writings of Niels Bohr*. Vols. 1 and 2, *On Atomic Physics and Human Knowledge*. Woodbridge, Conn.: Ox Bow Press.

Bordo, Susan. 1987. *The Flight to Objectivity*. Albany: State University of New York Press.

———. 1993. *Unbearable Weight: Feminism, Western Culture, and the Body*. Berkeley and Los Angeles: University of California Press.

———. 1998. "Bringing Body to Theory." In *Body and Flesh: A Philosophical Reader*, edited by Donn Welton, 84–97. Oxford: Blackwell.

Bourdieu, Pierre. 1977. *Outline of a Theory of Practice*. Cambridge: Cambridge University Press.

———. 1984. *Distinction: A Social Critique of the Judgement of Taste*. Cambridge, Mass.: Harvard University Press.

———. 1987. "Legitimation and Structured Interests in Weber's Sociology of Religion." In *Max Weber: Rationality and Modernity*, edited by S. Whimster and S. Lash, 119–36. London: Allen & Unwin.

———. 1990. *The Logic of Practice*. Stanford, Calif.: Stanford University Press.

———. 1991. "Genesis and Structure of the Religious Field." *Comparative Social Research* 13: 1–44.

———. 1998. *Practical Reason: On the Theory of Action*. Stanford, Calif.: Stanford University Press.

Boyd, Monica. 1989. "Family and Personal Networks in International Migration: Recent Developments and New Agendas." *International Migration Review* 23(3): 638–70.

Boyer, Pascal. 2000. "Evolution of a Modern Mind and the Origins of Culture: Religious Concepts as a Limiting Case." *In Evolution and the Human Mind: Modularity, Language, and Meta-Cognition*, edited by Peter Carruthers and Andrew Chamberlain, 93–112. Cambridge: Cambridge University Press.

———. 2001. *Religion Explained: The Evolutionary Origins of Religious Thought*. New York: Basic Books.

Braidotti, Rosi. 2002. *Metamorphoses: Toward a Materialist Theory of Becoming*. Cambridge: Polity.

Braun, Willi. 2000. "Religion." In *Guide to the Study of Religion*, edited by Willi Braun and Russell McCutcheon. London: Cassell.

Brown, Gavin. 2003. "Theorizing Ritual as Performance: Exploration of Ritual Indeterminacy." *Journal of Ritual Studies* 17(1): 3–18.

Brown, Karen McCarthy. 1999. "Staying Grounded in a High-Rise Building: Ecological Dissonance and Ritual Accommodation in Haitian Vodou." In *Gods of the City: Religion and the American Urban Landscape*, edited by Robert Orsi, 79–102. Bloomington: Indiana University Press.

Brown, Peter. 1981. *The Cult of the Saints*. Chicago: University of Chicago Press.

———. 1988. *The Body and Society: Men, Women, and Sexual Renunciation in Early Christianity*. New York: Columbia University Press.

Bulkeley, Kelly. 2008. *Dreaming in the World's Religions: A Comparative History*. New York: New York University Press.

Burdick, John. 1993. *Looking for God in Brazil: Progressive Catholicism in Urban Brazil's Religious Arena*. Berkeley and Los Angeles: University of California Press.

Butler, Judith. 1990. *Gender Trouble: Feminism and the Subversion of Identity*. New York: Routledge.

————. 1992. "Contingent Foundations: Feminism and the Question of Postmodernism." In *Feminists Theorize the Political*, edited by Judith Butler and Joan Scott, 3–21. New York: Routledge.

————. 1993. *Bodies that Matter: On the Discursive Limits of "Sex."* New York: Routledge.

————. 1997. *The Psychic Life of Power: Theories in Subjection*. Stanford, Calif.: Stanford University Press.

————. 1999. "Foucault and the Paradox of Bodily Inscriptions." In *The Body: Classic and Contemporary Readings*, edited by Donn Welton, 307–13. Oxford: Blackwell.

Bynum, Caroline Walker. 1987. *Holy Feast and Holy Fast: The Religious Significance of Food to Medieval Women*. Berkeley and Los Angeles: University of California Press.

————. 1995. *The Resurrection of the Body in Western Christianity, 200–1336*. New York: Columbia University Press.

Callicott, J. Baird. 1994. *Earth's Insights: A Survey of Ecological Ethics from the Mediterranean Basin to the Australian Outback*. Berkeley and Los Angeles: University of California Press.

Callon, Michel. 1986. "Some Elements of a Sociology of Translation: Domestication of the Scallops and the Fishermen of St Brieuc Bay." In *Power, Action, and Belief: A New Sociology of Knowledge*, edited by John Law, 196–233. London: Routledge & Kegan Paul.

Campo, Juan. 1991. *The Other Sides of Paradise: Explorations into the Religious Meanings of Domestic Space in Islam*. Columbia: University of South Carolina Press.

Carrasco, David. 1999. *City of Sacrifice: The Aztec Empire and the Role of Violence in Civilization*. Boston: Beacon Press.

Casey, Edward. 1998. "The Ghost of Embodiment: On Bodily Habitudes and Schemata." In *Body and Flesh: A Philosophical Reader*, edited by Donn Welton, 207–25. Oxford: Blackwell.

Castells, Manuel. 1996. *The Rise of the Network Society*. Oxford: Blackwell.

Certeau, Michel de. 1984. *The Practice of Everyday Life*. Berkeley and Los Angeles: University of California Press.

Chalmers, David. 1995. "Facing up to the Problem of Consciousness." *Journal of Consciousness Studies* 2(3): 200–219.

Chantepie de la Saussaye, Pierre. 1891. *Manual of the Science of Religion*. London: Longmans, Green & Co.

Chidester, David. 1996. *Savage Systems: Colonialism and Comparative Religion in Southern Africa*. Charlottesville: University of Virginia Press.

————. 2005. *Authentic Fakes: Religion and American Popular Culture*. Berkeley and Los Angeles: University of California Press.

Chidester, David, and Edward Linenthal, eds. 1995. "Introduction." In *American Sacred Space*, edited by David Chidester and Edward Linenthal, 1–42. Bloomington: Indiana University Press.

Cho, Francisca, and Richard K. Squier. 2008. "Reductionism: Be Afraid, Be *Very* Afraid." *Journal of the American Academy of Religion* 76(2): 412–17.

Churchland, Patricia. 1986. *Neurophilosophy: Toward a Unified Science of the Mind-Brain*. Cambridge, Mass.: MIT Press.

Churchland, Paul. 1988. *Matter and Consciousness: A Contemporary Introduction to the Philosophy of Mind*. Cambridge, Mass.: MIT Press.

Clifford, James. 1997. *Routes: Travel and Translation in the Late Twentieth Century*. Cambridge, Mass.: Harvard University Press.

Colebrook, Claire. 2000. "From Radical Representations to Corporeal Becomings: The Feminist Philosophy of Lloyd, Grosz, and Gatens." *Hypatia* 15(2): 76–93.

———. 2008. "On Not Becoming Man: The Materialist Politics of Unactualized Potential." In *Material Feminisms*, edited by Stacy Alaimo and Susan Hekman, 52–84. Bloomington: Indiana University Press.

Coles, Alistair. 2008. "God, Theologian and Humble Neurologist." *Brain* 131: 1953–59.

Comaroff, Jean. 1985. *Body of Power, Spirit of Resistance: The Culture and History of a South African People*. Chicago: University of Chicago Press.

Comaroff, Jean, and John Comaroff. 2001. "Millennial Capitalism: First Thoughts on a Second Coming." In *Millennial Capitalism and the Culture of Neoliberalism*, edited by John Comaroff, 1–56. Durham, N.C.: Duke University Press.

Cooke, Miriam, and Bruce Lawrence, eds. 2005. *Muslim Networks: From Hajj to Hip Hop*. Chapel Hill: University of North Carolina Press.

Cox, James. 2006. *A Guide to the Phenomenology of Religion: Key Figures, Formative Influences, and Subsequent Debates*. London: Continuum.

Csordas, Thomas. 1990. "Embodiment as a Paradigm for Anthropology." *Ethos* 18:5–47.

———. 1994a. *The Sacred Self: A Cultural Phenomenology of Charismatic Healing*. Berkeley and Los Angeles: University of California Press.

———. 1994b. "Words from the Holy People: A Case Study in Cultural Phenomenology." In *Embodiment and Experience: The Existential Ground of Culture and Self*, edited by Thomas Csordas, 269–90. Cambridge: Cambridge University Press.

———. 1997. *Language, Charisma, and Creativity: The Ritual Life of a Religious Movement*. Berkeley and Los Angeles: University of California Press.

———. 1999. "Embodiment and Cultural Phenomenology." In *Perspectives on Embodiment: The Intersections of Nature and Culture*, edited by Gail Weiss and Honi Fern Haber, 143–62. New York: Routledge.

———. 2004. "Asymptote of the Ineffable: Embodiment, Alterity, and the Theory of Religion." *Current Anthropology* 45(2): 163–76.

Cullman, Oscar. 1962. *Christ and Time: The Primitive Christian Conception of Time and History*. London: SCM Press.

Cunningham, Hilary. 2004. "Nations Rebound? Crossing Borders in a Gated Globe." *Identities: Global Studies in Culture and Power* 11: 329–50.

Damasio, Antonio. 1994. *Descartes' Error: Emotion, Reason, and the Human Brain*. New York: Avon Books.

———. 2003. *Looking for Spinoza: Joy, Sorrow, and the Feeling Brain*. Orlando, Fla.: Harcourt Books.

Daniel, Yvonne. 2005. *Dancing Wisdom: Embodied Knowledge in Haitian Vodou, Cuban Yoruba, and Bahian Candomblé*. Urbana: University of Illinois Press.

Darwin, Charles. 1982. *The Origin of Species by Means of Natural Selection: The Preservation of Favored Races in the Struggle for Life*. New York: Penguin Books.

Davis, Paul. 2006. "The Physics of Downward Causation." In *The Re-Emergence of Emergence: The Emergentist Hypothesis from Science to Religion*, edited by Philip Clayton and Paul Davis, 35–52. New York: Oxford University Press.

Dawkins, Richard. 1989. *The Selfish Gene*. Oxford and New York: Oxford University Press.

———. 2006. *The God Delusion*. New York: Houghton Mifflin Co.

Dean, Carolyn. 1999. *Inka Bodies and the Body of Christ: Corpus Christi in Colonial Cuzco, Peru*. Durham, N.C.: Duke University Press.

Debord, Guy. 1994. *The Society of the Spectacle*. New York: Zone Books.

Deleuze, Gilles. 1983. *Nietzsche and Philosophy*. New York: Columbia University Press.

———. 1990. *Expressionism in Philosophy: Spinoza*. New York: Zone Books.

———. 1992. *The Fold: Leibniz and the Baroque*. Minneapolis: University of Minnesota Press.

———. 2001. *Immanence: A Life*. New York: Zone Books.

Deleuze, Gilles, and Felix Guattari. 1983. *Anti-Oedipus: Capitalism and Schizophrenia*. Minneapolis: University of Minnesota Press.

———. 1987. *A Thousand Plateaus: Capitalism and Schizophrenia*. Minneapolis: University of Minnesota Press.

Dennett, Daniel. 1991. *Consciousness Explained*. Boston: Little, Brown and Company.

———. 2006. *Breaking the Spell: Religion as Natural Phenomena*. New York: Viking.

De Nooy, Wouter. 2003. "Fields and Networks: Correspondence Analysis and Social Network Analysis in the Framework of Field Theory." *Poetics* 31: 305–27.

Depraz, Natalie, Francisco Varela, and Pierre Vermersch. 2003. *On Becoming Aware: A Pragmatics of Experience*. Amsterdam: John Benjamins Publishing Company.

De Preester, Helena, and Veroniek Knockaert. 2005. "Introduction." In *Body Image and Body Schema*, edited by Helena De Preester and Veroniek Knockaert, 1–18. Amsterdam: John Benjamins Publishing Company.

DeRogatis, Amy. 2003. *Moral Geographies: Maps, Missionaries, and the American Frontier*. New York: Columbia University Press.

Derrida, Jacques. 1976. *Of Grammatology*. Baltimore: Johns Hopkins University Press.

———. 1978. *Writing and Difference*. Chicago: University of Chicago Press.

———. 1981. *Positions*. Chicago: University of Chicago Press.

———. 1999. "Hospitality, Justice, and Responsibility: A Dialogue with Jacques Derrida." In *Questioning Ethics: Contemporary Debates in Philosophy*, edited by Richard Kearney and Mark Dooley, 65–83. New York: Routledge.

Descartes, Rene. 1970. *Philosophical Letters*. Oxford: Oxford University Press.

———. 1979. *Meditations on First Philosophy in Which the Existence of God and the Distinction of the Soul from the Body Are Demonstrated*. Indianapolis, Ind.: Hackett Publishing.

————. 1999. *Discourse on Method and Related Writings*. New York: Penguin Classics.

Descombes, Vincent. 1980. *Modern French Philosophy*. Cambridge: Cambridge University Press.

Dewey, John. 1922. *Human Nature and Conduct: An Introduction to Social Psychology*. New York: Henry Holt & Co.

Dicken, Peter, et al. 2001. "Chains and Networks, Territories and Scales: Towards a Relational Framework for Analysing the Global Economy." *Global Networks* 1(2): 89–112.

Dillon, John. 1995. "Rejecting the Body, Refining the Body: Some Remarks on the Development of Platonic Asceticism." In *Asceticism*, edited by Vincent Wimbush and Richard Valantasis, 80–87. New York: Oxford University Press.

Douglas, Mary. 1966. *Purity and Danger: An Analysis of Concepts of Purity and Taboo*. London: Routledge & Kegan Paul.

————. 1982. *Natural Symbols: Explorations in Cosmology*. New York: Pantheon Books.

Dubuisson, Daniel. 2003. *The Western Construction of Religion*. Baltimore: Johns Hopkins University Press.

Durkheim, Emile. 1964. *The Rules for Sociological Method*. New York: Free Press.

————. 1965. *The Elementary Forms of Religious Life*. New York: Free Press.

Dupré, Louis. 1993. *Passage to Modernity: An Essay in the Hermeneutics of Nature and Culture*. New Haven, Conn.: Yale University Press.

Dreyfus, Hubert. 1991. *Being-in-the-World: A Commentary on Heidegger's* Being and Time. Cambridge, Mass.: MIT Press.

Eagleton, Terry. 2003. *After Theory*. New York: Basic Books.

Ebaugh, Helen Rose, and Janet Chafetz, eds. 2002. *Religion across Borders: Transnational Immigrant Networks*. Walnut Creek, Calif.: AltaMira Press.

Eck, Diana. 1998. *Darsan: Seeing the Divine Image in India*. New York: Columbia University Press.

Eliade, Mircea. 1954. *The Myth of the Eternal Return or, Cosmos and History*. Princeton, N.J.: Princeton University Press.

————. 1959a. *The Sacred and the Profane: The Nature of Religion*. New York: Harcourt Brace Jovanovich.

————. 1959b. "Methodological Remarks on the Study of Religious Symbolism." In *The History of Religions: Essays in Methodology*, edited by Mircea Eliade and Joseph M. Kitagawa, 86–107. Chicago: University of Chicago Press.

————. 1961. *Images and Symbols: Studies in Religious Symbolism*. New York: Sheed & Ward.

————. 1967. *Myth, Dreams, and Mysteries*. New York: Harper & Row.

————. 1969. *The Quest: History and Meaning in Religion*. Chicago: University of Chicago Press.

————. 1982. *Ordeal by Labyrinth*. Chicago: University of Chicago Press.

————. 1996. *Patterns in Comparative Religion*. Lincoln: University of Nebraska Press.

Elias, Norbert. 1978. *The History of Manners*. Vol. 1, *The Civilizing Process*. New York: Pantheon.

Emirbayer, Mustafa, and Jeff Goodwin. 1994. "Network Analysis, Culture, and the Problems of Agency." *American Journal of Sociology* 99(6): 1411–54.

Feyerabend, Paul. 1988. *Against Method*. London: Verso.

Fitzgerald, Timothy. 2000. *The Ideology of Religious Studies*. New York: Oxford University Press.

———. 2007. *Discourse on Civility and Barbarity: A Critical History of Religion and Related Categories*. New York: Oxford University Press.

Flaccus, Gillian. 2006. "Spanish-Language Media Credited on Pro-Immigration Rallies." *Boston Globe*, 29 March.

Flanagan, Owen. 2007. *The Really Hard Problem: Meaning in a Material World*. Cambridge, Mass.: MIT Press.

———. 2009. "One Enchanted Being: Neuroexistentialism and Meaning." *Zygon* 44(1): 41–49.

Flood, Gavin. 1999. *Beyond Phenomenology: Rethinking the Study of Religion*. New York: Cassell.

Fodor, Jerry. 1983. *The Modularity of the Mind*. Cambridge, Mass.: MIT Press.

Fogelin, Lars. 2006. *The Archaeology of Early Buddhism*. Lanham, Md.: AltaMira.

Foltz, Richard. 1999. *Religions of the Silk Road: Overland Trade and Cultural Exchange from Antiquity to the Fifteenth Century*. New York: St. Martin's Press.

Forbes, Bruce David, and Jeffrey Mahan, eds. 2005. *Religion and Popular Culture in America*. Berkeley and Los Angeles: University of California Press.

Foucault, Michel. 1965. *Madness and Civilization: A History of Insanity in the Age of Reason*. New York: Random House.

———. 1972. *The Archaeology of Knowledge*. New York: Pantheon.

———. 1973. *The Order of Things: An Archeology of the Human Sciences*. New York: Vintage/Random House.

———. 1977a. *Language, Counter-Memory, Practice: Selected Essays and Interviews by Michel Foucault*. Ithaca, N.Y.: Cornell University Press.

———. 1977b. *Discipline and Punish: The Birth of the Prison*. New York: Vintage.

———. 1978. *The History of Sexuality*. Vol. 1. *An Introduction*. New York: Vintage.

———. 1980. *Power/Knowledge: Selected Interviews and Other Writings, 1972–1977*. New York: Pantheon.

———. 1982. "Afterword: The Subject and Power." In *Michel Foucault: Beyond Structuralism and Hermeneutics*, by Hubert Dreyfus and Paul Rabinow, 208–26. Chicago: University of Chicago Press.

———. 1984. *The Foucault Reader*. New York: Pantheon Books.

———. 1988. "Technologies of the Self." In *Technologies of the Self: A Seminar with Michel Foucault*, edited by Luther Martin, Huck Gutman, and Patrick Hutton, 16–49. Amherst, Mass.: University of Massachusetts Press.

———. 1991. "Questions of Method." In *The Foucault Effect: Studies in Governmentality*, edited by Graham Burchell, Collin Gordon, and Peter Miller, 73–86. Chicago: University of Chicago Press.

———. 1998. "My Body, This Paper, This Fire." In *Michel Foucault: Ethics, Method, and Epistemology*, edited by James Faubion, 393–418. New York: New Press.

———. 1999. *Religion and Culture by Michel Foucault*. Edited by Jeremy Carrette. New York: Routledge.

Frank, Daniel, and Oliver Leaman, eds. 2003. *The Cambridge Companion to Jewish Literature*. Cambridge: Cambridge University Press.

Fraser, Nancy. 1997. *Justice Interruptus: Critical Reflections on the 'Postsocialist' Condition*. New York: Routledge.

Gadamer, Hans-Georg. 1975. *Truth and Method*. London: Continuum.

Gallagher, Shaun. 2005. *How the Body Shapes the Mind*. New York: Oxford University Press.

Geertz, Armin. 2004. "Can We Move Beyond Primitivism? On Recovering the Indigenes of Indigenous Religions in the Academic Study of Religion." In *Beyond Primitivism: Indigenous Religious Traditions and Modernity*, edited by Jacob Olupona, 37–70. New York: Routledge.

Geertz, Clifford. 1973. *Interpretation of Cultures*. New York: Harper & Row.

Gibson, James. 1979. *The Ecological Approach to Visual Perception*. New York: Houghton Mifflin.

———. 1982. "Notes on Affordances." In *Reasons for Realism: Selected Essays of James J. Gibson*, edited by Edward Reed and Rebecca Jones, 401–18. Hillsdale, N.J.: Lawrence Erlbaum Associates.

Giddens, Anthony. 1979. *Central Problems in Social Theory: Action, Structure, and Contradiction in Social Analysis*. Berkeley and Los Angeles: University of California Press.

———. 1990. *The Consequences of Modernity*. Stanford, Calif.: Stanford University Press.

Gilchrist, Roberta. 1994. *Gender and Material Culture: The Archaeology of Religious Women*. London: Routledge.

Gill, Sam. 1987. *Mother Earth: An American Story*. Chicago: University of Chicago Press.

———. 1998. "Territory." In *Critical Terms for Religious Studies*, edited by Mark C. Taylor. Chicago: University of Chicago Press.

Glick-Schiller, Nina. 2005. "Transnational Social Fields and Imperialism: Bringing a Theory of Power to Transnational Studies." *Anthropological Theory* 5(4): 439–61.

Goddard, Michael. 2001. "The Scattering of Time Crystals: Deleuze, Mysticism, and Cinema." In *Deleuze and Religion*, edited by Mary Bryden, 53–64. New York: Routledge.

Goodman, Lenn. 2002. "What Does Spinoza's *Ethics* Contribute to Jewish Philosophy?" In *Jewish Themes in Spinoza's Philosophy*, edited by Heidi Ravven and Lenn Goodman, 17–89. Albany: State University of New York Press.

Gould, Stephen Jay. 1977. *Ever since Darwin: Reflections in Natural History*. New York: W. W. Norton.

Gramsci, Antonio. 1971. *Selections from the Prison Notebooks*. New York: International Publishers.

Grandin, Temple, and Catherine Johnson. 2005. *Animals in Translation*. Orlando, Fla.: Harcourt Inc.

Granovetter, Mark. 1973. "The Strength of Weak Ties." *American Journal of Sociology* 78(6): 1360–80.

Gregersen, Niels Henrik. 2006. "Emergence: What Is at Stake for Religious Reflection?" In *The Re-Emergence of Emergence: The Emergentist Hypothesis from Science to Religion*, edited by Philip Clayton and Paul Davis, 279–302. New York: Oxford University Press.

Griffith, R. Marie. 2004. *Born Again Bodies: Flesh and Spirit in American Christianity*. Berkeley and Los Angeles: University of California Press.

Gros, Claudius. 2008. *Complex and Adaptive Dynamical Systems: A Primer*. Berlin: Springer-Verlag.

Grosz, Elizabeth. 2008. "Darwin and Feminism: Preliminary Investigations for a Possible Alliance." In *Material Feminisms*, edited by Stacy Alaimo and Susan Hekman, 23–51. Bloomington: Indiana University Press.

Guha, Ranajit, ed. 1997. *A Subaltern Studies Reader, 1986–1995*. Minneapolis: University of Minnesota Press.

Guss, David. 1989. *To Weave and Sing: Art, Symbol, and Narrative in the South American Rainforest*. Berkeley and Los Angeles: University of California Press.

Guthrie, Stewart Elliot. 1993. *Faces in the Clouds: A New Theory of Religion*. New York: Oxford University Press.

Hacking, Ian. 1999. *The Social Construction of What?* Cambridge, Mass.: Harvard University Press.

Hall, David, ed. 1997. *Lived Religion in America: Toward a History of Practice*. Princeton, N.J.: Princeton University Press.

Hamer, Dean. 2005. *The God Gene: How Faith Is Hardwired into Our Genes*. New York: Anchor.

Haraway, Donna. 1988. "Situated Knowledge: The Science Question in Feminism and the Privilege of Partial Perspective." *Feminist Studies* 14(3): 575–600.

———. 1991. *Simians, Cyborgs, and Women: The Reinvention of Nature*. New York: Routledge.

———. 2000. *How Like a Leaf*. New York: Routledge.

———. 2008. *When Species Meet*. Minneapolis: University of Minnesota Press.

Hardt, Michael, and Antonio Negri. 2000. *Empire*. Cambridge, Mass.: Harvard University Press.

Harrington, Anne, and Arthur Zajonc, eds. 2003. *The Dalai Lama at MIT*. Cambridge, Mass.: Harvard University Press.

Harris, Marvin. 1999. *Theories of Culture in Postmodern Times*. Walnut Creek, Calif.: AltaMira Press.

———. 2001. *Cultural Materialism: The Struggle for the Science of Culture*. Walnut Creek, Calif.: AltaMira Press.

Harvey, David. 1989. *The Conditions of Postmodernity*. Oxford: Blackwell.

———. 2000. *Spaces of Hope*. Berkeley and Los Angeles: University of California Press.

Harvey, Graham. 2005. *Animism: Respecting the Living World.* New York: Columbia University Press.

Harvey, Susan Ashbrook. 2006. *Scenting Salvation: Ancient Christianity and the Olfactory Imagination.* Berkeley and Los Angeles: University of California Press.

Haugerud, Angelique, et al. 2000. *Commodities and Globalization: Anthropological Perspectives.* London: Rowman & Littlefield.

Hayles, Katherine. 1995. "Searching for Common Ground." In *Reinventing Nature? Responses to Postmodern Deconstruction*, edited by Michael Soulé and Gary Lease, 47–63. Washington, D.C.: Island Press.

Hegel, Georg Wilhelm. 1967. *The Phenomenology of Mind.* Translated by J. B. Baillie. New York: Harper & Row.

———. 2008. *Philosophy of Right.* New York: Cosimo.

Heidegger, Martin. 1962. *Being and Time.* New York: Harper & Row.

———. 1977a. "Letter on Humanism." In *Basic Writings*, edited by David Krell, 213–66. New York: HarperCollins.

———. 1977b. *The Question Concerning Technology and Other Essays.* New York: Harper & Row.

———. 1984. *The Metaphysical Foundations of Logic.* Bloomington: Indiana University Press.

Hekman, Susan. 2008. "Constructing the Ballast: An Ontology for Feminism." In *Material Feminisms*, edited by Stacy Alaimo and Susan Hekman, 85–119. Bloomington: Indiana University Press.

Higgins, Kathleen. 2007. "An Alchemy of Emotion: *Rasa* and Aesthetic Breakthroughs." *Journal of Aesthetics and Art Criticism* 65(1): 43–54.

Hobbes, Thomas. 1999. *Human Nature and De Corpore Politico.* New York: Oxford University Press.

Holdrege, Barbara. 2008. "Body." In *Studying Hinduism: Key Concepts and Methods*, edited by Sushil Mittal and Gene Thursby, 19–40. London: Routledge.

Horkheimer, Max and Theodor Adorno. 2002. *Dialectic of Enlightenment.* Stanford, Calif.: Stanford University Press.

Hornborg, Alf. 2001. *The Power of the Machine: Global Inequalities of Economy, Technology, and Environment.* Walnut Creek, Calif.: AltaMira Press.

Hourani, George. 1951. *Arab Seafaring in the Indian Ocean in Ancient and Early Medieval Times.* Princeton, N.J.: Princeton University Press.

Howes, David. 2006. *Sensual Relations: Engaging the Senses in Culture and Social Theory.* Ann Arbor: University of Michigan Press.

Hughes, Alex, and Suzanne Reimer. 2004. *Geographies of Commodity Chains.* New York: Routledge.

Husserl, Edmund. 1970. *The Crisis of European Sciences and Transcendental Phenomenology.* Evanston, Ill.: Northwestern University Press.

———. 1973. *Cartesian Meditations: An Introduction to Phenomenology.* The Hague: Martinus Nijhoff.

———. 1999. *The Essential Husserl: Basic Writings in Transcendental Phenomenology.* Edited by Donn Welton. Bloomington: Indiana University Press.

Ileto, Reynaldo. 1979. *Pasyon and Revolution: Popular Movements in the Philippines, 1840–1910.* Manila: Ateneo de Manila University Press.

Ingold, Tim. 2000. *The Perception of the Environment: Essays in Livelihood, Dwelling, and Skill.* London: Routledge.

———. 2001. "From the Transmission of Representations to the Education of Attention." In *The Debated Mind: Evolutionary Psychology Versus Ethnography*, edited by Harvey Whitehouse, 113–53. Oxford: Berg.

———. 2007. "Movement, Knowledge and Description." In *Holistic Anthropology: Emergence and Convergence*, edited by David Parkin and Stanley Ulijaszek, 194–211. New York: Berghahn Books

Insoll, Timothy. 2004. *Archaeology, Ritual, Religion.* London: Routledge.

Ireland, Rowan. 1992. *Kingdoms Come: Religion and Politics in Brazil.* Pittsburgh: University of Pittsburgh Press.

Isambert, François. 1982. *Le sense du sacré: Fête et religion populaire.* Paris: Minuit.

Jackson, Michael. 1989. *Paths toward a Clearing: Radical Empiricism and Ethnographic Inquiry.* Bloomington: Indiana University Press.

———, ed. 1996. *Things as They Are: New Directions in Phenomenological Anthropology.* Bloomington: Indiana University Press.

———. 1998. *Minima Ethnographica: Intersubjectivity and the Anthropological Project.* Chicago: University of Chicago Press.

Jackson, Wes. 1994. *Becoming Native to This Place.* Lexington: University Press of Kentucky.

James, George. 1985. "Phenomenology and the Study of Religion: The Archeology of an Approach." *Journal of Religion* 65(3): 311–35.

James, William. 1961. *The Varieties of Religious Experience: A Study in Human Nature.* New York: Collier.

Jameson, Fredric. 1984. "Postmodernism, or the Cultural Logic of Late Capitalism." *New Left Review* 146: 53–96.

Johnson, Paul Christopher. 2007. *Diaspora Conversions: Black Carib Religion and the Recovery of Africa.* Berkeley and Los Angeles: University of California Press.

Kauffman, Stuart. 2008. *Reinventing the Sacred: A New View of Science, Reason, and Religion.* New York: Basic Books.

Keller, Pierre. 1999. *Husserl and Heidegger on Human Experience.* Cambridge: Cambridge University Press.

Kieckhefer, Richard. 2004. *Theology in Stone: Church Architecture from Byzantium to Berkeley.* New York: Oxford University Press.

Kierkegaard, Søren. 1962. *The Present Age.* New York: Harper & Row.

Kilde, Jeanne. 2004. *When Church Became Theater: The Transformation of Evangelical Architecture and Worship in Nineteenth-Century America.* New York: Oxford University Press.

———. 2008. *Sacred Power, Sacred Space: An Introduction to Christian Architecture and Worship*. New York: Oxford University Press.

Kim, Jaegwon. 2006. "Emergence: Core Ideas and Issues." *Synthese: An International Journal for Epistemology, Methodology and Philosophy of Science* 151(3): 547–59.

King, Barbara. 2007. *Evolving God: A Provocative View of the Origins of Religion*. New York: Doubleday.

King, Karen. 2003. *What Is Gnosticism?* Cambridge, Mass.: Harvard University Press.

———. 2008. "Which Early Christianity?" In *The Oxford Handbook of Early Christian Studies*, edited by Susan Ashbrook Harvey and David Hunter, 66–84. New York: Oxford University Press.

King, Richard. 1999. *Orientalism and Religion: Post-Colonial Theory, India, and the Mystic East*. London: Routledge.

Kirby, Vicki. 2008. "Natural Convers(at)ion: Or What If Culture Was Really Nature All Along?" In *Material Feminisms*, edited by Stacy Alaimo and Susan Hekman, 214–35. Bloomington: Indiana University Press.

Klassen, Pamela. 2001. *Blessed Events: Religion and Home Birth in America*. Princeton, N.J.: Princeton University Press.

Klein, Herbert. 1999. *The Atlantic Slave Trade*. Cambridge: Cambridge University Press.

Klima, Alan. 2002. *Funeral Casino: Meditation, Massacre, and Exchange with the Dead in Thailand*. Princeton, N.J.: Princeton University Press.

Knott, Kim. 2008. "Spatial Theory and the Study of Religion." *Religion Compass* 2(6): 1102–16.

Kristensen, W. Brede. 1960. *The Meaning of Religion: Lectures in the Phenomenology of Religion*. The Hague: Martinus Nijhoff.

Kuhn, Thomas. 2000. *The Road since Structure: Philosophical Essays, 1970–1993*. Chicago: University of Chicago Press.

Kurtzman, Charles. 2005. "The Network Metaphor and the Mosque Network in Iran, 1978–1979." In *Muslim Networks: From Hajj to Hip Hop*, edited by Miriam Cooke and Bruce Lawrence, 69–83. Chapel Hill, N.C.: University of North Carolina Press.

Lacan, Jacques. 2002. *Ecrits: The First Complete English Translation*. New York: W. W. Norton.

Laderman, Gary. 1999. *Sacred Remains: American Attitudes Toward Death*. New Haven, Conn.: Yale University Press.

Lakatos, Imre. 1970. "Falsificationism and the Methodology of Scientific Research Programmes." In *Criticism and the Growth of Knowledge*, edited by Imre Lakatos and Alan Musgrave, 91–196. Cambridge: Cambridge University Press.

Lakoff, George, and Mark Johnson. 1999. *Philosophy in the Flesh: The Embodied Mind and Its Challenge to Western Thought*. New York: Basic Books.

Lane, Belden. 2001. *Landscapes of the Sacred: Geography and Narrative in American Spirituality*. Baltimore: Johns Hopkins University Press.

Latour, Bruno. 1988. *Science in Action: How to Follow Scientists and Engineers through Society*. Cambridge, Mass.: Harvard University Press.

————. 1999. *Pandora's Hope: Essays on the Reality of Science Studies*. Cambridge, Mass.: Harvard University Press.

————. 2005. *Reassembling the Social: An Introduction to Actor-Network Theory*. New York: Oxford University Press.

Laughlin, Charles, and Jason Throop. 2006. "Cultural Neurophenomenology: Integrating Experience, Culture, and Reality through Fisher Information." *Culture & Psychology* 12(3): 305–37.

Law, John. 2003. "Notes on the Theory of Actor Network: Ordering, Strategy, and Heterogeneity." www.lancs.ac.uk/fass/sociology/papers/law-notes-on-ant.pdf. Accessed last on 7 March 2009.

Lee, Jo, and Tim Ingold. 2006. "Fieldwork on Foot: Perceiving, Routing, Socializing." In *Locating the Field: Space, Place and Context in Anthropology*, edited by Simon Coleman and Peter Collins, 67–85. Oxford: Berg.

Lefebvre, Henri. 1991. *The Production of Space*. Oxford: Blackwell.

Levine, Daniel. 1992. *Popular Voices in Latin American Catholicism*. Princeton, N.J.: Princeton University Press.

Levine, Joseph. 1983. "Materialism and Qualia: The Explanatory Gap." *Pacific Philosophical Quarterly* 64: 354–61.

Lévi-Strauss, Claude. 1969. *The Raw and the Cooked*. New York: Harper & Row.

————. 1973. *Triste Tropiques*. Toronto: The Murray Printing Company.

Levitt, Peggy. 2001. "Transnational Migration: Taking Stock and Future Directions." *Global Networks* 1(3): 195–216.

Levitt, Peggy, and Nina Glick-Schiller. 2004. "Conceptualizing Simultaneity: A Transnational Social Field Perspective on Society." *International Migration Review* 38(4): 1002–39.

Lincoln, Bruce. 1996. "Theses on Method." *Method and Theory in the Study of Religion* 8(3): 225–27.

————. 2007. "Concessions, Confessions, Clarifications, Ripostes: By Way of Response to Tim Fitzgerald." *Method and Theory in the Study of Religion* 19 (1–2): 163–68.

Lingis, Alphonso. 1985. "The Will to Power." In *The New Nietzsche*, edited by David Allison, 5–36. Cambridge, Mass.: MIT Press.

Lobkowicz, Nikolaus. 1983. *Theory and Practice: History of a Concept from Aristotle to Marx*. Lanham, Md.: University Press of America.

Looren de Jong, Huib. 2006. "Explicating Pluralism: Where the Mind to Molecule Pathway Gets Off the Track—Reply to Bickle." *Synthese: An International Journal for Epistemology, Methodology and Philosophy of Science* 151(3): 435–43.

Looren de Jong, Huib, and Maurice Schouten. 2007. "Mind Reading and Mirror Neurons: Exploring Reduction." In *The Matter of the Mind: Philosophical Essay on Psychology, Neuroscience, and Reduction*, edited by Maurice Schouten and Huib Looren de Jong, 298–322. London: Blackwell.

Lovato, Roberto. 2008. "Juan Crow in Georgia." *The Nation*, 26 May, 20–24.

Low, Setha, and Denise Lawrence-Zuñiga, eds. 2003. *The Anthropology of Space and Place: Locating Culture*. Oxford: Blackwell.

Luther, Martin. 2008. *Collected Works of Martin Luther.* BiblioBazaar. www.bibliobazaar. com/.

Lutz, Antoine, John Dunne, and Richard Davidson. 2007. "Meditation and the Neuro-science of Consciousness: An Introduction." In *The Cambridge Handbook of Consciousness,* edited by Philip Zelazo, Morris Moscovitch, and Evan Thompson, 499–551. Cambridge: Cambridge University Press.

Machamer, Peter, Lindley Darden, and Carl Craver. 2000. "Thinking about Mechanisms." *Philosophy of Science* 67(1): 1–25.

Macheray, Pierre. 1998. *In a Materialist Way: Selected Essays by Pierre Macherey.* Edited by Warren Montag. London: Verso.

Mann, Michael. 1986. *The Sources of Social Power.* Vol. 1. Cambridge: Cambridge University Press.

Mannheim, Karl. 1936. *Ideology and Utopia: An Introduction to the Sociology of Knowledge.* New York: Harcourt, Brace & World.

Margolis, Joseph. 2001. *Selves and Other Texts: The Case for Cultural Realism.* University Park: Pennsylvania State University Press.

Marx, Karl. 1978a. *Capital, Volume One.* In *The Marx-Engels Reader,* edited by Robert Tucker, 294–438. New York: W. W. Norton.

———. 1978b. *The Eighteenth Brumaire of Louis Bonaparte.* In *The Marx-Engels Reader,* edited by Robert Tucker, 594–617. New York: W. W. Norton.

———. 1978c. *The German Ideology: Part I.* In *The Marx-Engels Reader,* edited by Robert Tucker, 146–202. New York: W. W. Norton.

———. 1978d. *The Manifesto of the Communist Party.* In *The Marx-Engels Reader,* edited by Robert Tucker, 469–500. New York: W. W. Norton.

———. 1978e. "Theses on Feuerbach." In *The Marx-Engels Reader,* edited by Robert Tucker, 143–45. New York: W. W. Norton.

Massey, Doreen. 1994. *Space, Place, and Gender.* Minneapolis: University of Minnesota Press.

Masuzawa, Tomoko. 2005. *The Invention of World Religions, Or, How European Universalism Was Preserved in the Language of Pluralism.* Chicago: University of Chicago Press.

Mauss, Marcel. 1979. "Body Techniques." In *Sociology and Psychology: Essays.* Edited and translated by B. Brewster, 95–123. London: Routledge & Kegan Paul.

———. 1990. *The Gift: The Form and Reason for Exchange in Archaic Societies.* New York: W. W. Norton.

McAlister, Elizabeth. 1998. "The Madonna of 115th Street Revisited: Vodou and Haitian Catholicism in the Age of Transnationalism." In *Gatherings in Diaspora: Religious Communities and the New Immigration,* edited by Stephen Warner and Judith Wittner, 123–60. Philadelphia: Temple University Press.

———. 2002. *Rara! Vodou, Power and Performance in Haiti and Its Diaspora.* Berkeley and Los Angeles: University of California Press.

McCauley, Robert. 1995. "Overcoming Barriers to a Cognitive Psychology of Religion." In *Perspectives on Method and Theory in the Study of Religion,* edited by Armin Geertz and Russell McCutcheon, 141–61. Leiden: Brill.

McCauley, Robert, and William Bechtel. 2001. "Explanatory Pluralism and the Heuristic Identity Theory." *Theory and Psychology* 11: 736–60.

McCauley, Robert, and E. Thomas Lawson. 2002. *Bringing Ritual to Mind: Psychological Foundations of Cultural Forms.* Cambridge: Cambridge University Press.

McCutcheon, Russell. 1997. *Manufacturing Religion: The Discourse on Sui Generis Religion and the Politics of Nostalgia.* New York: Oxford University Press.

———, ed. 1999. *The Insider/Outsider Problem in the Study of Religion: A Reader.* London: Cassell.

———. 2001. *Critics Not Caretakers: Redescribing the Public Study of Religion.* Albany: State University of New York Press.

———. 2003. *The Discipline of Religion: Structure, Meaning, Rhetoric.* London: Routledge.

———. 2006. "'It's a Lie. There's No Truth in It! It's a Sin!': On the Limits of the Humanistic Study of Religion and the Costs of Saving Others from Themselves." *Journal of the American Academy of Religion* 74(3): 720–50.

McDannell, Colleen. 1986. *The Christian Home in Victorian America, 1840–1900.* Bloomington: Indiana University Press.

———. 1995a. *Material Christianity: Religion and Popular Culture in America.* New Haven, Conn.: Yale University Press.

———. 1995b. "Creating the Christian Home: Home Schooling in America." In *American Sacred Space*, edited by David Chidester and Edward Linenthal, 187–219. Bloomington: Indiana University Press.

McEwan, Gordon. 2006. *The Incas: New Perspectives.* New York: W. W. Norton.

McGinn, Colin. 1999. *The Mysterious Flame: Conscious Minds in a Material World.* New York: Basic Books.

McKeon, Richard, ed. 1947. *Introduction to Aristotle.* New York: Random House.

McLuhan, Marshall. 1964. *Understanding the Media: The Extensions of Man.* New York: Signet.

Mellor, Philip A., and Chris Shilling. 1997. *Re-Forming the Body: Religion, Community and Modernity.* London: Sage.

Menjívar, Cecilia. 2000. *Fragmented Ties: Salvadoran Immigrant Networks in America.* Berkeley and Los Angeles: University of California Press.

Menn, Stephen. 1998. *Descartes and Augustine.* Cambridge: Cambridge University Press.

Merchant, Carolyn. 1983. *The Death of Nature: Women, Ecology, and the Scientific Revolution.* New York: HarperCollins.

Merleau-Ponty, Maurice. 1964. *The Primacy of Perception: And Other Essays on Phenomenological Psychology, the Philosophy of Art, History, and Politics.* Evanston, Ill.: Northwestern University Press.

———. 1968. *The Visible and the Invisible.* Evanston, Ill.: Northwestern University Press.

———. 2002. *The Phenomenology of Perception: An Introduction.* New York: Routledge.

Messer, Ellen. 2001. "Thinking and Engaging the Whole: The Anthropology of Roy Rappaport." In *Ecology and the Sacred: Engaging the Anthropology of Roy A.*

Rappaport, edited by Ellen Messer and Michael Lambek, 1–38. Ann Arbor: University of Michigan Press.

Meyer, Birgit. 2002. "Commodities and the Power of Prayer: Pentecostalist Attitudes toward Consumption in Contemporary Ghana." In *The Anthropology of Globalization: A Reader*, edited by Jonathan Inda and Renato Rosaldo, 247–69. Oxford: Blackwell.

Meyer, Birgit, and Peter Geschiere. 1999. *Globalization and Identity: Dialectics of Flow and Closure*. London: Blackwell.

Meyer, Jeffrey. 2001. *Myth in Stone: Religious Dimensions of Washington, D.C.* Berkeley and Los Angeles: University of California Press.

Mitchell, J. Clyde. 1969. *Social Networks in Urban Situations*. Manchester: Manchester University Press.

Mohanty, J. N. 1995. "The Development of Husserl's Thought." In *The Cambridge Companion to Husserl*, edited by Barry Smith and David Woodruff Smith, 45–77. Cambridge: Cambridge University Press.

Moran, Dermot. 2000. *Introduction to Phenomenology*. New York: Routledge.

Morgan, David. 2005. *The Sacred Gaze: Religious Visual Culture in Theory and Practice*. Berkeley and Los Angeles: University of California Press.

Muir, Edward. 1997. *Ritual in Early Modern Europe*. Cambridge: Cambridge University Press.

Müller, Max. 2002. *The Essential Max Müller: Language, Mythology, and Religion*. Edited by Jon Stone. New York: Palgrave Macmillan.

Murphy, Tim. 2001. "Eliade, Subjectivity, and Hermeneutics." In *Changing Religious Worlds: The Meaning and End of Mircea Eliade*, edited by Bryan Rennie, 35–48. Albany: State University of New York Press.

Nadeau, Jean-Guy. 2002. "Dichotomy or Union of Soul and Body? The Origins of the Ambivalence of Christianity to the Body." In *The Body and Religion*, ed. Regina Ammicht-Quinn and Elsa Tamez, 57–65. London: SCM Press.

Narayanan, Vasudha. 2003. "Embodied Cosmologies: Sights of Piety, Sights of Power." *Journal of the American Academy of Religion* 71(3): 495–520.

Newberg, A. B., Eugene d'Aquili, and Vince Rouse. 2001. *Why God Won't Go Away: Brain Science and the Biology of Belief*. New York: Ballantine.

Nietzsche, Friedrich. 1954. *The Portable Nietzsche*. New York: Penguin Books.

———. 1967. *The Will to Power*. New York: Vintage Books.

———. 1969. *On the Genealogy of Morals and Ecce Homo*. New York: Vintage Books.

Norget, Kristin. 2006. *Days of Death, Days of Life: Ritual in the Popular Culture of Oaxaca*. New York: Columbia University Press.

Ong, Aihwa. 2003. *Buddha Is Hiding: Refugees, Citizenship, the New America*. Berkeley and Los Angeles: University of California Press.

Orsi, Robert. 1997. "Everyday Miracles: The Study of Lived Religion." In *Lived Religion in America: Toward a History of Practice*, edited by David Hall, 3–21. Princeton, N.J.: Princeton University Press.

———, ed. 1999. *Gods of the City: Religion and the American Urban Landscape*. Bloomington: Indiana University Press.

————. 2005. *Between Heaven and Earth: The Religious Worlds People Make and the Scholars Who Study Them*. Princeton, N.J.: Princeton University Press.

————. 2008. "The 'So-Called History' of the Study of Religion." *Method and Theory in the Study of Religion* 20(2): 134–38.

Ortner, Sherry. 2005. "Subjectivity and Cultural Critique." *Anthropological Theory* 5(1): 31–52.

Otto, Rudolf. 1958. *The Idea of the Holy*. Oxford: Oxford University Press.

Panourgiá, Neni. 2002. "Interview with Clifford Geertz." *Anthropological Theory* 2(4): 421–31.

Peña, Elaine. Forthcoming. *Performing Piety: Building, Walking, and Conquering in Central México and the Midwest*. Berkeley and Los Angeles: University of California Press.

Persinger, Michael. 1987. *The Neuropsychological Bases of God Beliefs*. New York: Praeger.

Peterson, Anna. 1997. *Martyrdom and the Politics of Religion: Progressive Catholicism in El Salvador's Civil War*. Albany: State University of New York Press.

————. 2001. *Being Human: Ethics, Environment, and our Place in the World*. Berkeley and Los Angeles: University of California Press.

Peterson, Gregory. 2003. *Minding God: Theology and the Cognitive Sciences*. Minneapolis: Fortress Press.

Petit, Jean-Luc. 2005. "A Functional Neurodynamics for the Constitution of the Own Body." In *Body Image and Body Schema*, edited by Helena De Preester and Veroniek Knockaert, 189–209. Amsterdam: John Benjamins Publishing Company.

Pettazzoni, Raffaele. 1967. "History and Phenomenology in the Science of Religion." In *Essays on the History of Religions*, 215–19. Leiden: Brill.

Pickering, Andrew, ed. 1992. *Science as Practice and Culture*. Chicago: University of Chicago Press.

————. 1995. *The Mangle of Practice: Time, Agency, and Science*. Chicago: University of Chicago Press.

Plato. 1908. The *Dialogues of Plato*. Translated with analyses and introductions by B. Jowett. New York: Charles Scribner's Sons.

————. 1991. *The Republic*. Translated by B. Jowett. New York: Vintage.

————. 2008. *Timaeus and Critias*. Translated by Robin Waterfield. Oxford: Oxford University Press.

Plotinus. 1957. *The Enneads*. Translated by Stephen MacKenna. New York: Pantheon.

Poceski, Mario. 2009. *Introducing Chinese Religions*. New York: Routledge.

Porterfield, Amanda. 2005. *Healing in the History of Christianity*. New York: Oxford University Press.

Portes, Alejandro, ed. 1995. *The Economic Sociology of Immigration*. New York: Russell Sage Foundation.

Potter, David, S. 1999. "Odor and Power in the Roman Empire." In *Constructions of the Classical Body*, edited by James I. Potter, 169–89. Ann Arbor: University of Michigan Press.

Potter, James, I., 1999. "Introduction." In *Constructions of the Classical Body*, edited by James I. Potter, 1–18. Ann Arbor: University of Michigan Press.

Poxon, Judith. 2001. "Embodied Anti-Theology: The Body without Organs and the Judgment of God." In *Deleuze and Religion*, edited by Mary Bryden, 42–50. New York: Routledge.

Pyysiäinen, Ilkka. 2001. *How Religion Works: Towards a New Cognitive Science of Religion*. Leiden: Brill.

———. 2002. "Introduction: Cognition and Culture in the Construction of Religion." In *Current Approaches in the Cognitive Science of Religion*, edited by Ilkka Pyysiainen and Veikko Anttonen, 1–13. London: Continuum.

———. 2004. *Magic, Miracles, and Religion: A Scientist's Perspective*. Walnut Creek, Calif.: AltaMira Press.

Radcliffe-Brown, Alfred. 1945. "Religion and Society." *The Journal of the Royal Anthropological Institute of Great Britain and Ireland* 75(1/2): 33–43.

Ram, Kalpana. 2000. "Dancing the Past into Life: The *Rasa*, *Nrtta* and *Raga* of Immigrant Existence." *The Australian Journal of Anthropology* 11(3): 261–73.

Ramachandran, V. S., and Sandra Blakeslee. 1998. *Phantoms in the Brain: Probing the Mysteries of the Human Mind*. New York: HarperCollins.

Rappaport, Roy. 1979. *Ecology, Meaning, and Religion*. Berkeley, Calif.: North Atlantic Books.

———. 1999. *Ritual and Religion in the Making of Humanity*. Cambridge: Cambridge University Press.

Ravven, Heidi. 2003. "Spinoza's Anticipation of Contemporary Affective Neuroscience." *Consciousness & Emotion* 4(2): 257–90.

Ravven, Heidi, and Lenn Goodman, eds. 2002. *Jewish Themes in Spinoza's Philosophy*. Albany: State University of New York Press.

Ray, Himanshu. 1994. *Winds of Change: Buddhism and the Maritime Links of Early South Asia*. Oxford: Oxford University Press.

Read, Kay. 1998. *Time and Sacrifice in the Aztec Cosmos*. Bloomington: Indiana University Press.

Ricoeur, Paul. 1974. *Conflict of Interpretations: Essays in Hermeneutics*. Evanston, Ill.: Northwestern University Press.

———. 1979. "The Model of the Text: Meaningful Action Considered as a Text." In *Interpretive Social Science: A Reader*, edited by Paul Rabinow and William M. Sullivan, 73–101. Berkeley and Los Angeles: University of California Press.

Risso, Patricia. 1995. *Merchants and Faith: Muslim Culture and Commerce in the Indian Ocean*. Boulder: Westview.

Robertson Smith, William. 1973. "The Study of the Religion of the Semites." In *Classical Approaches to the Study of Religion: Aims, Methods and Theories of Research*, edited by Jacques Waardenburg, 151–59. The Hague: Mouton.

Robinson, Mary. 2004. "Political Science and Human Rights: Tackling Global Inequalities." Speech to the 100th Annual Meeting of the American Political Sciences Association. Chicago, 4 September.

Rolston, Holmes. 1999. *Genes, Genesis, and God: Values and Their Origins in Natural and Human History*. Cambridge: Cambridge University Press.

Rorty, Richard. 1979. *Philosophy and the Mirror of Nature*. Princeton, N.J.: Princeton University Press.

Roseberry, William. 1989. "Balinese Cockfights and the Seduction of Anthropology." In *Anthropologies and Histories: Essays in Culture, History, and Political Economy*, 17–29. New Brunswick, N.J.: Rutgers University Press.

Rouse, Joseph. 2002. *How Scientific Practices Matter: Reclaiming Philosophical Naturalism*. Chicago: University of Chicago Press.

Rouse, Roger. 1991. "Mexican Migration and the Social Space of Postmodernism." *Diaspora* 1(1): 8–23.

Rozemond, Marleen. 1998. *Descartes's Dualism*. Cambridge, Mass.: Harvard University Press.

Ryba, Thomas. 1991. *Essence of Phenomenology and Its Meaning for the Scientific Study of Religion*. Berne: Peter Lang Publishers.

———. 2006. "Phenomenology of Religion." In *The Blackwell Companion to the Study of Religion*, edited by Robert Segal, 91–122. Oxford: Blackwell.

Scaperlanda, Michael A. 2008. "Immigration and the Bishops." *First Things: The Journal of Religion, Culture and Public Life*. www.firstthings.com/article.php3?id_article=6139. Accessed last on 19 May 2008.

Schatzki, Theodore, Karen Knorr Cetina, and Eike von Savigny, eds. 2001. *The Practice Turn in Contemporary Theory*. London: Routledge.

Schechner, Richard. 2003. *Performance Theory*. London: Routledge.

Schleiermacher, Fredrich. 1988. *On Religion: Speeches to Its Cultured Despisers*. Cambridge: Cambridge University Press.

Schmidt, Leigh. 1995. *Consumer Rites: The Buying and Selling of American Holidays*. Princeton, N.J.: Princeton University Press.

———. 1997. "Practices of Exchange: From Market Culture to Gift Economy in the Interpretation of American Religion." In *Lived Religion in America: Toward a History of Practice*, edited by David Hall, 69–91. Princeton, N.J.: Princeton University Press.

———. 2000. *Hearing Things: Religion, Illusion, and the American Enlightenment*. Cambridge, Mass.: Harvard University Press.

———. 2005. *Restless Souls: The Making of American Spirituality from Emerson to Oprah*. New York: HarperCollins.

Schutz, Alfred, and Thomas Luckmann. 1973. *The Structures of the Life-World*. Evanston, Ill.: Northwestern University Press.

Schwartz, Susan. 2004. *Rasa: Performing the Divine in India*. New York: Columbia University Press.

Scott, James. 1985. *Weapons of the Weak: Everyday Forms of Peasant Resistance*. New Haven, Conn.: Yale University Press.

Searle, John. 1969. *Speech Acts: An Essay in the Philosophy of Language*. Cambridge: Cambridge University Press.

———. 1997. *The Mystery of Consciousness*. New York: New York Review of Books.

Sewell, William H. 1999. "Geertz, Cultural Systems, and History: From Synchrony to Transformation." In *The Fate of "Culture": Geertz and Beyond*, edited by Sherry Ortner, 35–55. Berkeley and Los Angeles: University of California Press.

Shamir, Ronen. 2005. "Without Borders? Notes on Globalization as a Mobility Regime." *Sociological Theory* 23(2): 197–217.

Sharma, Arvind. 2001. *To the Things Themselves: Essays on the Discourse and Practice of the Phenomenology of Religion*. Berlin: Walter de Gruyter.

Shildrick, Margrit, and Janet Price. 1999. "Openings on the Body: A Critical Introduction." In *Feminist Theory and the Body*, edited by Janet Price and Margrit Shildrick, 1–13. London: Routledge.

Shusterman, Richard. 2008. *Body Consciousness: A Philosophy of Mindfulness and Somatoaesthetics*. Cambridge: Cambridge University Press.

Simmel, Georg. 1950. *The Sociology of Georg Simmel*. Translated, edited, and with an introduction by Kurt Wolff. New York: The Free Press.

Slingerland, Edward. 2008a. *What Science Offers the Humanities: Integrating Body and Culture*. Cambridge: Cambridge University Press.

———. 2008b. "Who's Afraid of Reductionism? The Study of Religion in the Age of Cognitive Science." *Journal of the American Academy of Religion* 76(2): 375–411.

Smart, Ninian. 1973. *The Phenomenon of Religion*. New York: Herder and Herder.

———. 1983. *Worldviews: Crosscultural Explorations of Human Beliefs*. New York: Scribner.

———. 1996. *Dimensions of the Sacred: An Anatomy of the World's Beliefs*. Berkeley and Los Angeles: University of California Press.

Smilde, David. 2004. "Popular Publics: Street Protest and Plaza Preachers in Caracas." *International Review of Social History* 49:179–95.

———. 2005. "A Qualitative Comparative Analysis of Conversion to Venezuelan Evangelicalism: How Networks Matter." *American Journal of Sociology* 111(3): 757–96.

Smith, A. D. 2003. *Routledge Philosophy Guidebook to Husserl and the Cartesian Mediations*. New York: Routledge.

Smith, Jonathan Z. 1978. *Map Is Not Territory: Studies in the History of Religions*. Chicago: University of Chicago Press.

———. 1982. *Imagining Religion: From Babylon to Jonestown*. Chicago: University of Chicago Press.

———. 1987. *To Take Place: Toward a Theory in Ritual*. Chicago: University of Chicago Press.

———. 2004. *Relating Religion: Essays in the Study of Religion*. Chicago: University of Chicago Press.

Smith, Wilfred Cantwell. 1991. *The Meaning and End of Religion*. Minneapolis: Fortress Press.

Soja, Edward. 1989. *Postmodern Geographies: The Reassertion of Space in Critical Social Theory*. London: Verso.

———. 1996. *Thirdspace: Journeys to Los Angeles and Other Real-and-Imagined Places*. Oxford: Blackwell.

Sokal, Alan. 1996. "A Physicist Experiments with Cultural Studies." *Lingua Franca* (May/June): 62–64.

Solé, Ricard, and Jordi Bascompte. 2006. *Self-Organization in Complex Ecosystems.* Princeton, N.J.: Princeton University Press.

Sperber, Dan. 1996. *Explaining Culture: A Naturalistic Approach.* London: Blackwell.

———. 2001. "Mental Modularity and Cultural Diversity." In *The Debated Mind: Evolutionary Psychology Versus Ethnography*, edited by Harvey Whitehouse, 23–56. Oxford: Berg.

Spinoza, Benedictus de. 2002. *Complete Works.* Translated by Samuel Shirley. Indianapolis, Ind.: Hackett Publishing.

Spivak, Gayatri. 1988. "Can the Subaltern Speak?" In *Marxism and the Interpretation of Culture*, edited by Cary Nelson and Lawrence Grossberg, 271–313. Urbana: University of Illinois Press.

Stark, Rodney, and Roger Finke. 2000. *Acts of Religion: Explaining the Human Side of Religion.* Berkeley and Los Angeles: University of California Press.

Stewart, Jon, ed. 1998. *The Debate between Sartre and Merleau-Ponty.* Evanston, Ill.: Northwestern University Press.

Stoller, Paul. 1997. *Sensuous Scholarship.* Philadelphia: University of Pennsylvania Press.

Strenski, Ivan. 2003. "Material Culture and the Varieties of Religious Imagination." www.shrines.ucr.edu/article.html. Accessed last on 28 February 2009.

———. 2006. *Thinking about Religion: A Historical Introduction to Theories of Religion.* Oxford: Blackwell.

Taussig, Michael. 1997. *The Magic of the State.* New York: Routledge.

Taves, Ann. 1999. *Fits, Trances, and Visions; Experiencing Religion and Explaining Experience from Wesley to James.* Princeton, N.J.: Princeton University Press.

———. 2009. "Bridging Science and Religion: 'The More' and 'the Less' in William James and Owen Flanagan." *Zygon* 44(1): 9–17.

Taylor, Bron. 2010. *Dark Green Religion: Nature Spirituality and the Planetary Future.* Berkeley and Los Angeles: University of California Press.

Taylor, Charles. 2007. *A Secular Age.* Cambridge, Mass. Harvard University Press.

Taylor, Mark C. 2001. *The Moment of Complexity: Emerging Network Culture.* Chicago: University of Chicago Press.

———. 2007. *After God.* Chicago: University of Chicago Press.

Thagard, Paul. 2005. *Mind: Introduction to Cognitive Science.* Cambridge, Mass: MIT Press.

Thompson, E. P. 1966. *The Making of the English Working Class.* New York: Verso.

Thompson, Evan. 2007. *Mind in Life: Biology, Phenomenology, and the Sciences of the Mind.* Cambridge, Mass.: Harvard University Press.

Thompson, Evan, and Francisco Varela. 2001. "Radical Embodiment: Neural Dynamics and Consciousness." *Trends in Cognitive Science* 5: 418–25.

Tiele, C. P. 1979. *Elements of the Science of Religion: Part I. Morphological.* Edinburgh: William Blackwood and Sons.

Tillich, Paul. 1948. "Nature and Sacrament." In *The Protestant Era*, 94–112. Chicago: University of Chicago Press.

Trimble, Michael. 2007. *The Soul in the Brain: The Cerebral Basis of Language, Art, and Belief.* Baltimore: Johns Hopkins University Press.

Trimble, Michael, and Anthony Freeman. 2006. "An Investigation of Religiosity and the Gastaut-Geschwind Syndrome in Patients with Temporal Lobe Epilepsy." *Epilepsy & Behavior* 9(3): 407–14.

Tsing, Anna. 2005. *Friction: An Ethnography of Global Connection.* Princeton, N.J.: Princeton University Press.

Tuan, Yi-Fu. 1974. *Topophilia: A Study of Environmental Perception, Attitudes, and Values.* New York: Columbia University Press.

———. 1976. "Humanistic Geography." *Annals of the Association of American Geographers* 66(2): 266–76.

———. 1977. *Space and Place: The Perspective of Experience.* Minneapolis: University of Minnesota Press.

Turner, Victor. 1968. *The Drums of Affliction: A Study of Religious Processes among the Ndembu of Zambia.* Oxford: Clarendon.

———. 1969. *The Ritual Process: Structure and Anti-Structure.* Ithaca, N.Y.: Cornell University Press.

———. 1974. *Dramas, Fields, and Metaphors: Symbolic Action in Human Society.* Ithaca, N.Y.: Cornell University Press.

———. 1982. *From Ritual to Theatre: The Human Seriousness of Play.* New York: Performing Arts Journal Publications.

Tweed, Thomas. 1997. *Our Lady of the Exile: Diasporic Religion at a Catholic Shrine in Miami.* New York: Oxford University Press.

———. 1999. "Diasporic Nationalism and Urban Landscape: Cuban Immigrants at a Catholic Shrine in Miami." In *Gods of the City: Religion and the American Urban Landscape*, edited by Robert Orsi, 131–54. Bloomington: Indiana University Press.

———. 2006. *Crossing and Dwelling: A Theory of Religion.* Cambridge, Mass.: Harvard University Press.

Valantasis, Richard. 1995. "A Theory of the Social Function of Asceticism." In *Asceticism*, edited by Vincent Wimbush and Richard Valantasis, 544–52. New York: Oxford University Press.

Van der Leeuw, Gerardus. 1963. *Religion in Essence and Manifestation.* Vols 1 and 2. New York: Harper & Row.

———. 1973. "Some Recent Achievements of Psychological Research and the Application to History, in Particular the History of Religion." In *Classical Approaches to the Study of Religion: Aims, Methods, and Theories of Research. Introduction and Anthology*, edited by Jacques Waardenburg, 399–406. The Hague: Mouton.

Van Gennep, Arnold. 1960. *The Rites of Passage.* Chicago: University of Chicago Press.

Vanderwood, Paul. 2004. *Juan Soldado: Rapist, Murderer, Martyr, Saint.* Durham, N.C.: Duke University Press.

Varela, Francisco. 1996. "Neurophenomenology: A Methodological Remedy for the Hard Problem." *Journal of Consciousness Studies* 3: 330–50.

Varela, Francisco, Humberto Maturana, and R. Uribe. 1974. "Autopoiesis: The Organization of Living Systems, Its Characterization and a Model." *Biosystems* 5: 187–96.

Varela, Francisco, Evan Thompson, and Eleanor Rosch. 1991. *The Embodied Mind: Cognitive Science and Human Experience.* Cambridge, Mass.: MIT Press.

Varela, Francisco, et al. 2001. "The Brainweb: Phase Synchronization and Large-Scale Integration." *Neuroscience* 2:229–39.

Vásquez, Manuel A. 1998. *The Brazilian Popular Church and the Crisis of Modernity.* Cambridge: Cambridge University Press.

———. 2005. "Historicizing and Materializing the Study of Religion: The Contributions of Migration Studies." In *Immigrant Faiths: Transforming Religious Life in America,* edited by Karen Leonard, Alex Stepick, Manuel Vásquez, and Jennifer Holdaway, 219–42. Walnut Creek, Calif.: AltaMira.

———. 2008. "The Global Portability of Pneumatic Christianity: Comparing and Contrasting African and Latin American Pentecostalisms." *African Studies* 68(2): 273–86.

Vásquez, Manuel A., and Marie Friedmann Marquardt. 2003. *Globalizing the Sacred: Religion across the Americas.* New Brunswick, N.J.: Rutgers University Press.

Vertovec, Steven. 2003. "Migration and Other Modes of Transnationalism: Towards Conceptual Cross-Fertilization." *International Migration Review* 37(3): 641–65.

Viveiros de Castro, Eduardo. 1998. "Cosmological Deixis and Ameridian Perspectivism." *Journal of the Royal Anthropological Institute* 4(3): 469–88.

Von Staden, Heinrich. 2000. "Body, Soul, Nerves: Epicurus, Herophilus, Erasistratus, the Stoics, and Galen." In *Psyche and Soma: Physicians and Metaphysicians on the Mind-Body Problem from Antiquity to Enlightenment,* edited by John P. Wright and Paul Potter, 79–116. Oxford: Oxford University Press.

Waardenburg, Jacques. 1978. *Reflections on the Study of Religion.* The Hague: Mouton.

Waghorne, Joanne Punzo. 2004. *Diaspora of the Gods: Modern Hindu Temples in an Urban Middle-Class World.* Oxford: Oxford University Press.

Ware, Kallistos. 1997. "'My Helper and My Enemy': The Body in Greek Christianity." In *Religion and the Body,* edited by Sarah Coakley, 90–110. Cambridge: Cambridge University Press.

Watson, Julie. 2001. "Believers Flock to Underdog Icons of the People." *Los Angeles Times.* http://articles.latimes.com/2001/dec/23/local/me-17425. Accessed last 6 March 2009.

Weber, Max. 1958. *The Protestant Ethic and the Spirit of Capitalism.* New York: Scribner.

———. 1963. *The Sociology of Religion.* Boston: Beacon.

Wellman, Barry, and S. D. Berkowitz. 1988. "Introduction: Studying Social Structures." In *Social Structures: A Network Approach,* edited by Barry Wellman and S. D. Berkowitz, 1–18. Cambridge: Cambridge University Press.

White, Harrison. 1992. *Identity and Control.* Princeton, N.J.: Princeton University Press.

Whitehouse, Harvey. 2001. "Introduction." In *The Debated Mind: Evolutionary Psychology Versus Ethnography,* edited by Harvey Whitehouse, 1–20. Oxford: Berg.

———. 2004. *Modes of Religiosity: A Cognitive Theory of Religious Transmission.* Walnut Creek, Calif.: AltaMira Press.

Wiebe, Donald. 1999. *The Politics of Religious Studies.* London: Macmillan.

Williams, Raymond. 1977. *Marxism and Literature.* Oxford and New York: Oxford University Press.

———. 1981. *Problems in Materialism and Culture.* London: Verso.

Wilson, Edward O. 1975. *Sociobiology: The New Synthesis.* Cambridge, Mass.: Harvard University Press.

———. 1998. *Consilience: The Unity of Knowledge.* New York: Alfred A. Knopf.

Wimmer, Andreas, and Nina Glick-Schiller. 2003. "Methodological Nationalism, the Social Sciences, and the Study of Migration: An Essay in Historical Epistemology." *International Migration Review* 37(3): 576–610.

Witgenstein, Ludwig. 2007. *Tractatus Logico-Philosophicus.* New York: Cosimo.

———. 2009. *Philosophical Investigations.* Malden, Mass.: Blackwell.

World Bank. 2001. *World Development Report 2000/2001: Attacking Poverty.* Oxford: Oxford University Press.

Worster, Donald. 1994. *Nature's Economy: A History of Ecological Ideas.* 2nd ed. Cambridge: Cambridge University Press.

Zarrilli, Phillip. 1990. "What Does It Mean to 'Become the Character': Power, Presence, and Transcendence in Asian In-Body Disciplines of Practice." In *By Means of Performance,* edited by Richard Schechner and Willa Appel, 131–48. Cambridge: Cambridge University Press.

Zimmerman, Michael. 1997. *Contesting Earth's Future: Radical Ecology and Postmodernity.* Berkeley and Los Angeles: University of California Press.

Index